Power Shift

Power Shift

China and Asia's New Dynamics

EDITED BY

David Shambaugh

UNIVERSITY OF CALIFORNIA PRESS

Berkeley   Los Angeles   London

University of California Press
Berkeley and Los Angeles, California

University of California Press, Ltd.
London, England

Library of Congress Cataloging-in-Publication Data

Power shift : China and Asia's new dynamics / edited by David
Shambaugh.
   p. cm.
  Proceedings from the conference "China and Asia: Towards a New
Regional Order," convened in December 2003 at The George
Washington University — Acknowledgments
   ISBN-13 978-0-520-24570-9 (pbk. : alk. paper)
   ISBN-10 0-520-24570-9 (pbk. : alk. paper)
   1. Asia—Relations—China—Congresses. 2. China—Relations—
Asia—Congresses. I. Title: China and Asia's new dynamics. II.
Shambaugh, David L.
DS33.4.C5P68 2006
327.5051'09051—dc22

                                 2005011747

Manufactured in the United States of America

14   13   12   11   10   09   08   07
10   9   8   7   6   5   4

Printed on Ecobook 50 containing a minimum 50% post-consumer
waste, processed chlorine free. The balance contains virgin pulp,
including 25% Forest Stewardship Council Certified for no old
growth tree cutting, processed either TCF or ECF. The sheet is acid-
free and meets the minimum requirements of ANSI/NISO
Z39.48–1992 (R 1997) (Permanence of Paper).

This volume is admiringly dedicated to
Professor Wang Gungwu
for all of his contributions to Chinese studies

CONTENTS

ILLUSTRATIONS

ACKNOWLEDGMENTS

This volume is truly a collaborative effort. All of the authors not only contributed their expertise in their respective areas, but also assisted with conceptualizing the subject. During two intensive days of discussion at the conference "China and Asia: Towards a New Regional Order," convened in December 2003 at The George Washington University, all of the contributors (together with a number of leading experts from the Washington, D.C., policy community) brainstormed over the parameters and implications of China's emergence as a major power in Asia. We went into the conference to explore the hypothesis that China was becoming *the* major power in Asia and that the regional system was again becoming Sinocentric, as it was centuries ago. We collectively concluded, however, that this is decidedly not the case—at least not yet. Coming to this conclusion required intensive examination of numerous variables, as well as extensive debate. The conference and its end product, this volume, reflect the best of intellectual interchange and cooperation, and I am very grateful to all who participated in this project for their contributions.

No project of this nature could be completed without strong institutional, financial, and staff support. Institutionally, the project was sponsored by the China Policy Program of the Elliott School of International Affairs at The George Washington University. Since 1998 the China Policy Program has been engaged in a variety of scholarly and policy-related activities intended to broaden understanding of contemporary China in the United States, and has collaborated with institutions in Europe, China, and throughout the Asian region to this end. In the case of this project, I would particularly like to thank Mr. Christopher Fussner, an alumnus of the Elliott School and President of Transtechnologies Ltd. in Singapore, without whose support this project would not have been realized. I also wish to thank Professor Mike

Mochizuki, former Director of the Sigur Center of Asian Studies in the Elliott School, as well as Deborah Toy and Ikuko Turner, for all of their logistical help in bringing the conference and project to fruition. To all I am most grateful.

David Shambaugh
Washington, D.C.
January 2005

CONTRIBUTORS

Robert F. Ash is Professor of Economics at the School of Oriental and African Studies (SOAS) in the University of London and Director of the SOAS Taiwan Studies Program. Between 1986 and 1995, he was Director of the SOAS Contemporary China Institute, and from 1997 to 2001, Coordinator of the EU-China Academic Network (ECAN). A specialist of China and Taiwan's economies, Professor Ash has authored or edited twelve books and has published more than a hundred book chapters, journal articles, and reports on various aspects of China's economic development. His most recent publication (with Christopher Howe and Y. Y. Kueh) is *China's Economic Reform: A Study with Documents* (Routledge Curzon, 2003). His current work focuses on agricultural development in China and Taiwan, and demographic and labor issues in China—the latter in his capacity as a consultant with the International Labor Organization (Geneva).

Richard Bush is a Senior Fellow in the Foreign Policy Studies Program and Director of its Center for Northeast Asian Policy Studies (CNAPS) at the Brookings Institution in Washington, D.C. He came to Brookings after serving five years as the Chairman and Managing Director of the American Institute in Taiwan, the mechanism through which the United States government conducts substantive relations with Taiwan in the absence of diplomatic relations. He previously served with the China Council of the Asia Society and the House of Representatives Foreign Affairs Committee's Subcommittee on East Asian and Pacific Affairs, and was the National Intelligence Officer for East Asia at the U.S. National Intelligence Council. He received his undergraduate education at Lawrence University in Appleton, Wisconsin. He did his graduate work in political science at Columbia University, receiving an M.A. in 1973 and his Ph.D. in 1978.

Jae-ho Chung is Professor of International Relations and Director of the Center for International Studies at Seoul National University, Republic of Korea. Professor Chung is a policy advisor for the National Security Council, consultant for the Federation of Korean Industries (FKI), and nonresident fellow at the Korean Institute for Defense Analysis (KIDA). Before joining Seoul National University, he taught at the Hong Kong University of Science and Technology (HKUST) during 1993–96 and was a CNAPS Fellow at the Brookings Institution during 2002–2003. Professor Chung is the author or editor of seven books, including *Central Control and Local Discretion in China* (Oxford University Press, 2000) and *Provincial Strategies of Economic Reform in Post-Mao China* (M. E. Sharpe, 1998). He has also published more than forty articles in various journals, such as *China Quarterly, China Journal, Asian Survey, Studies in Comparative Communism,* and *Pacific Affairs.* He also serves on the editorial committees of *China: An International Journal, China Perspectives,* and *Provincial China.*

John W. Garver is Professor in the Sam Nunn School of International Affairs at the Georgia Institute of Technology. He is a member of the editorial boards of the journals *China Quarterly, Journal of Contemporary China,* and the *Journal of American–East Asian Relations,* and he is a member of the National Committee on U.S.-China Relations. He is the author of seven books and more than sixty articles dealing with China's foreign relations. His books include *The Protracted Contest: China-Indian Rivalry in the Twentieth Century* and *Face Off: China, the United States, and Taiwan's Democratization* (University of Washington Press, 2000 and 1997, respectively); *The Sino-American Alliance: Nationalist China and U.S. Cold War Strategy in Asia* (M. E. Sharpe, 1997); *The Foreign Relations of the People's Republic of China* (Prentice Hall, 1993), one of the most widely used textbooks on PRC foreign relations; *Chinese-Soviet Relations, 1937–1945: The Diplomacy of Chinese Nationalism* (Oxford University Press, 1988); and *China's Decision for Rapprochement with the United States* (Westview, 1982).

Bates Gill holds the Freeman Chair in China Studies at the Center for Strategic and International Studies (CSIS) in Washington, D.C. He recently coauthored a study on China's reemergence in Central Asia, and is completing a book manuscript on China's evolving foreign policy and its implications for the United States. Among his professional affiliations, Dr. Gill serves on the board of directors of the National Committee on United States–China Relations, the U.S.-China Policy Foundation, the American Association for Chinese Studies, the Feris Foundation of America, and he is on the editorial board of the *Journal of Contemporary China* and the *Washington Journal of Modern China.* He is also a member of the Council on Foreign Relations and the International Institute of Strategic Studies.

David M. Lampton is George and Sadie Hyman Professor and Director of China Studies at the Johns Hopkins University School of Advanced International Studies and Director of China Studies at the Nixon Center. Before assuming the position at SAIS in December 1997, for the previous ten years he was President of the National Committee on United States–China Relations in New York City. Prior to 1988, Dr. Lampton was Director of the China Policy Program at the American Enterprise Institute in Washington, D.C., and Associate Professor of Political Science at Ohio State University. Professor Lampton is the author of numerous books and articles on Chinese domestic and foreign affairs, with articles appearing in *Foreign Affairs, Foreign Policy, China Quarterly, National Interest, Asian Survey, American Political Science Review, Time Magazine (Asia)*, the *New York Times*, the *International Herald Tribune*, the *Christian Science Monitor*, and other publications. Professor Lampton received his Ph.D. and undergraduate degrees from Stanford University. He has an honorary doctorate from the Russian Academy of Sciences, Institute of Far Eastern Studies. His most recent books and monographs are *Same Bed, Different Dreams: Managing U.S.-China Relations, 1989–2000* (University of California Press, 2001), which was updated and published in Chinese by Chinese University of Hong Kong Press in 2003; *The Making of Chinese Foreign and Security Policy in the Era of Reform* (editor, Stanford University Press, 2001); and, with Richard Daniel Ewing, *U.S.-China Relations in a Post–September 11th World* (Nixon Center, 2002). He is consultant to the Aspen Institute's Congressional Program, the Kettering Foundation, and various corporations and government agencies.

Mike M. Mochizuki holds the Japan-U.S. Relations Chair in Memory of Gaston Sigur in the Elliott School of International Affairs, and was director of the Sigur Center for Asian Studies at The George Washington University (2001–2005). He received his Ph.D. in political science from Harvard University in 1982. Prior to his faculty appointment at The George Washington University in 1999, Professor Mochizuki was a Senior Fellow in the Foreign Policy Studies Program at the Brookings Institution in Washington, D.C. (1995–99). Before Brookings, he held the following positions: Co-Director of the Center for Asia-Pacific Policy at the RAND Corporation, Associate Professor of International Relations at the University of Southern California in Los Angeles, and Assistant Professor of Political Science at Yale University. Professor Mochizuki is a specialist of Japanese politics and foreign policy, U.S.-Japan relations, and East Asian security affairs. His recent books include an edited volume entitled *Toward a True Alliance: Restructuring U.S.-Japan Security Relations* (Brookings Institution Press, 1997) and *Crisis on the Korean Peninsula: How to Deal with a Nuclear North Korea* (coauthored with Michael O'Hanlon, McGraw-Hill, 2003). His next book project is *The New Strategic Triangle: the U.S.-Japan Alliance and the Rise of China*.

Hideo Ohashi received his B.A. in journalism from Sophia University and completed his M.A. and Ph.D. in international relations from the University of Tsukuba. He is currently Professor in the Department of Economics at Senshu University. He was a Research Fellow at the Mitsubishi Research Institute during 1984–92, the Consulate-General of Japan in Hong Kong during 1989–91, and the Japan Institute of International Affairs during 1992–2001. He was also a visiting scholar at the Sigur Center for Asian Studies, The George Washington University, in 1995–96, and a visiting scholar at the Graduate School of International Relations and Pacific Studies, University of California, San Diego, in 2001–2002. His publications focus on economic development and political economy in East Asia, and include *U.S.-China Trade Friction* (in Japanese) (Keiso Shobo, 1998) and *Globalization of China's Economy* (in Japanese) (Nagoya Daigaku Shuppankai, 2003).

Jonathan D. Pollack is Professor of Asian and Pacific Studies, Chairman of the Strategic Research Department, and Chair of the Asia-Pacific Studies Group at the U.S. Naval War College in Newport, Rhode Island. A specialist on East Asian political and strategic affairs (especially China), Dr. Pollack was previously affiliated with the Rand Corporation in various research and senior management capacities. He received his M.A. and Ph.D. from the University of Michigan, and was a Postdoctoral Fellow at Harvard University. He has taught at Brandeis University, UCLA, the Rand Graduate School of Policy Studies, and the Naval War College. He is a member of the Council on Foreign Relations, the International Institute for Strategic Studies, the Committee on International Security and Arms Control of the National Academy of Sciences, and the National Committee on U.S.-China Relations. Professor Pollack has published widely on China's political and strategic roles; the international politics of Northeast Asia; U.S. policy in Asia and the Pacific; and Chinese technological and military development. His publications include numerous studies and articles in professional journals and symposia on U.S.-Asian relations, China's military modernization, China's policy toward Taiwan, Korean politics and foreign policy, Russian policy in Asia, and the international politics of East Asia.

David Shambaugh is Professor of Political Science and International Affairs and Director of the China Policy Program in the Elliott School of International Affairs at The George Washington University. He is also a Non-Resident Senior Fellow in the Foreign Policy Studies Program at the Brookings Institution and was a 2002–2003 Fellow at the Woodrow Wilson International Center for Scholars. Before joining the faculty at The George Washington University in 1996, he was Lecturer, Senior Lecturer, and Reader in Chinese politics in the University of London's School of Oriental and African Studies (1988–96). He specializes in China's domestic politics, foreign relations, and military affairs, the international politics and security in the Asian region, and U.S. policy towards Asia. He is a widely published author of numerous books, articles, book chapters, and newspaper editorials. Professor Shambaugh has authored or edited seventeen volumes, including the recently published *Modernizing China's Military* (University of California Press, 2003), *Making China Policy* (with Ramon Myers and Michel Oksenberg, Rowman and Littlefield, 2001), and *The Odyssey of China's Imperial Art Treasures* (with Jeannette Shambaugh Elliott, University of Washington Press, 2005). His articles have appeared in journals such as *International Security, Survival, China Quarterly, Asian Survey, Washington Quarterly, Current History,* and *Annals of the American Academy of Political and Social Science.* The former editor of *China Quarterly,* he previously served in the Department of State and National Security Council, directed the Asia Program at the Woodrow Wilson International Center for Scholars, and is consultant to foundations, corporations, and the U.S. government. He is a member of the Council on Foreign Relations, World Economic Forum, International Institute of Strategic Studies, National Committee on U.S.-China Relations, Pacific Council on International Affairs, and other organizations. He received his B.A. in East Asian Studies from The George Washington University, his M.A. in International Affairs from Johns Hopkins University School of Advanced International Studies, and his Ph.D. in Political Science from the University of Michigan.

Robert Sutter has been a Visiting Professor in the School of Foreign Service at Georgetown University since 2001. Professor Sutter specialized in Asian and Pacific Affairs and U.S. foreign policy during a U.S. government career of thirty years. He held a variety of analytical and supervisory positions with the Library of Congress for more than twenty years, and he also worked with the Central Intelligence Agency, the Department of State, and the Senate Foreign Relations Committee. After leaving the Library of Congress, where he for many years the Senior Specialist in International Politics for the Congressional Research Service, Professor Sutter served as the National Intelligence Officer for East Asia and the Pacific at the National Intelligence Council. He received a Ph.D. in History and East Asian Languages from Harvard University. He has held adjunct faculty positions at The George Washington University, Johns Hopkins University, and the University of Virginia. He has published fourteen books, numerous articles, and several hundred government reports dealing with contemporary East Asian and Pacific countries and their relations with the United States. His most recent book is *China's Rise in Asia: Promises and Perils* (Rowman and Littlefield, 2005).

Michael D. Swaine is Senior Associate and Co-Director of the China Program at the Carnegie Endowment for International Peace. He came to the Carnegie Endowment after twelve years at the Rand Corporation. He specializes in Chinese security and foreign policy, U.S.-China relations, and East Asian international relations. One of the most prominent U.S. analysts in Chinese security studies, he is the author of more than ten monographs on security policy in the region. At Rand, he was a Senior Political Scientist in international studies, and he was also Research Director of the Rand Center for Asia-Pacific Policy. Prior to joining Rand, he was a consultant with a private-sector firm, a Postdoctoral Fellow at the Center for Chinese Studies, University of California, Berkeley, and a Research Associate at Harvard University. He attended the Taipei and Tokyo Inter-University Centers for Language Study Administered by Stanford University, for training in Mandarin Chinese and Japanese. He received his B.A. in East Asian Studies from The George Washington University, and his M.A. and Ph.D. in Government from Harvard University.

Tang Shiping is Associate Research Fellow and Deputy Director at the Center for Regional Security Studies, Institute of Asia-Pacific Studies, Chinese Academy of Social Sciences. He is also Co-director of the Sino-American Security Dialogue. He has a B.A. in Paleontology from China University of Geosciences (1985), an M.A. in molecular biology from University of Science and Technology of China (1988), a Ph.D. in molecular biology and genetics from Wayne State University School of Medicine (1995), and an M.A. in international studies from University of California at Berkeley (1999). His research falls into two general areas: the psychological dimension of international politics (reputation, credibility, leadership, images, and beliefs), the systemic nature of the security environment, and grand strategy. He has published articles in Chinese journals such as *China Social Science, Strategy and Management, International Economic Review,* and *World Economics and Politics,* and in English-language journals such as *Asian Survey, Global Economic Review,* and *Journal of East Asian Affairs.* His commentaries have appeared in *Asia Times, China Daily, China Economic Times,* the *Christian Science Monitor, Lianhe Zaobao, Korea Herald,* and *Strait Times.* His most recent book (in Chinese) is *Grand Strategy: Constructing China's Ideal Security Environment* (China Social Science Press, 2004).

Wang Gungwu is Director of the East Asian Institute and Faculty Professor in the Faculty of Arts and Social Sciences, National University of Singapore; Chairman of the Board, Institute of Southeast Asian Studies; and Emeritus Professor of the Australian National University, Canberra. His first degrees were from the University of Malaya, Singapore, and he received his Ph.D. from the School of Oriental and African Studies, University of London. He has taught at the University of Malaya in Singapore and in Kuala Lumpur. At Australian National University, Canberra, he was Professor of Far Eastern History and also Director of the Research School of Pacific Studies. He then served as Vice-Chancellor of the University of Hong Kong. Among his recent books are *The Chinese Overseas: From Earthbound China to the Quest for Autonomy* (Harvard University Press, 2002), *Don't Leave Home: Migration and the Chinese* (International Specialized Book Services, 2001), *Bind Us in Time: Nation and Civilization in Asia* (International Specialized Book Services 2003), and *Anglo-Chinese Encounters Since 1800: War, Trade, Science and Governance* (Cambridge University Press, 2003). He also edited *The Chinese Diaspora* (with Wang Ling-chi, Eastern Universities Press, 1998), *Reform, Legitimacy and Dilemmas: China's Politics and Society* (with Zheng Yongnian, Singapore University Press, 2001), and *Damage Control: The CCP in the Era of Jiang Zemin* (with Zheng Yongnian, Eastern Universities Press, 2003).

Michael Yahuda is Professor Emeritus of International Relations at the London School of Economics and Political Science. He is currently a Visiting Scholar at the Sigur Center for Asian Studies in the Elliott School of International Affairs at The George Washington University. He is also a Research Affiliate of the Fairbank Center for East Asian Studies at Harvard University. He is the author of five books and numerous scholarly articles and book chapters. He has recently completed a revised version of his book *The International Politics of the Asia-Pacific* (Routledge, 2005).

Yu Bin is an Associate Professor in the Political Science Department of Wittenberg University and Advisor/Senior Research Associate at the Shanghai Association of American Studies. He earned his Ph.D. from Stanford University and his M.A. from the Chinese Academy of Social Sciences. He is also Faculty Associate of the Mershon Center at Ohio State University, and was a Visiting Fellow at the Center for Asia/Pacific Research Center of Stanford University (1998), the East-West Center (1994–95), and a MacArthur Fellow at the Center for International Security and Arms Control of Stanford University (1985–89). He was the President of the Association of Chinese Scholars of Political Science and International Studies (1992–94). Yu is the coauthor and editor of several books, including, most recently, *Mao's Generals Remember Korea* (University of Kansas Press, 2001). He has published many articles in journals including *World Politics, Strategic Review, Comparative Connections, Asian Survey, International Journal of Korean Studies, Harvard International Review, Asian Thought and Society*. He also frequently contributes to many English- and Chinese-language media outlets.

Zhang Yunling is Professor of International Economics, Director of the Institute of Asia-Pacific Studies (IAPS), and Director of APEC Policy Research Center (APRC) at the Chinese Academy of Social Sciences (CASS) in Beijing. He previously served as Director of the Institute of European Studies at CASS, and has held numerous visiting research appointments abroad. His research focuses on international economics and Asian security and economic integration.

Introduction

The Rise of China and Asia's New Dynamics

David Shambaugh

Asia is changing, and China is a principal cause. The structure of power and parameters of interactions that have characterized international relations in the Asian region over the last half century are being fundamentally affected by, among other factors, China's growing economic and military power, rising political influence, distinctive diplomatic voice, and increasing involvement in regional multilateral institutions. This volume offers an in-depth and careful assessment of China's new behavior and linkages with the region. The study further examines the impact that China's rise, in all of its dimensions, is having on the international relations of Asia, and the implications for the United States.

China has always been a significant presence looming over Asia, even before the People's Republic was established in 1949, but its impact on the dynamics of the region was usually felt much less than that of other major powers, despite its nearer proximity. Beijing's relative lack of regional influence sometimes caused it to recoil into an autarkic cocoon or necessitated alignment with external powers (the United States and Soviet Union) to augment its security. At other times China exerted a negative influence in the region by attempting to subvert neighboring noncommunist governments or as a result of its own domestic dislocations. When the PRC behaved in these ways, as a non–status quo power, it only became more marginalized from the principal actors and central dynamics of the region. Deng Xiaoping clearly recognized this and, after gaining power in 1978, made it one of his highest priorities to try and reintegrate China into the Asian region. Much was accomplished in ameliorating long-standing tensions and building ties during Deng's tenure, but even more substantial progress was made during the 1990s. Much credit is due China's former foreign minister and foreign policy czar Qian Qichen for mapping out and implementing the PRC's new approach to the region.[1]

The contributions to this volume are testimony to the fact that China's behavior has changed a great deal—and, with it, the dynamics of Asia as well. China is no longer out of the mainstream, but is repositioning itself both as a (and some believe *the*) central actor in the region and as a responsible power seeking to enhance the stability and security of the area. This new posture is relatively recent. Although China abandoned its subversive regional foreign policy in the early 1980s, until the late 1990s its regional posture remained somewhat aloof and less than fully engaged. Since 1997–98, however, Beijing has demonstrated a new confidence in its external posture, and its ties with neighbors and regional organizations have exhibited a number of new features.

ORGANIZATION OF THE VOLUME

The following chapters elucidate the various aspects and potential consequences of China's new posture. The volume is organized into six principal sections.

The volume opens with two overarching chapters that lay out the parameters of China's new engagement with the Asian region. My own introductory chapter sets the scene by elaborating the various manifestations of China's new regional posture, identifying some of the factors that catalyzed the new posture, discussing some historical parallels for it, and offering some cautionary views. It describes China's dramatically improved relationships with three former adversaries—Vietnam, South Korea, and India—as well as Beijing's recent proactive diplomacy and embrace of regional multilateral organizations. I conclude that the centrality of China in Asian regional affairs depends very much on the functional sphere: China is most central in the economic realm, increasingly so in the political/diplomatic realm, and least so in the security realm (although it is growing more so). To be sure, China's diplomatic influence and its military posture are increasingly being felt throughout the region, but not yet as demonstrably as its economic importance.

I also observe that while China's hard power is growing quickly, its soft power is increasingly more slowly. Despite a growing convergence between China and ASEAN about security norms and interstate behavior, China seems to have little in the realm of soft power—for example, philosophies or ideologies, popular or high culture, sports, fashion, or role models—to "export" to the rest of the region. Joseph Nye's classic study of soft power also finds China lacking in many of these elements of soft power attraction, especially when contrasted with Japan or Western nations.[2]

The next chapter is authored by two of China's leading experts on the Asian region, Tang Shiping and Zhang Yunling. Their chapter offers a unique and candid description of China's grand strategy and regional strategy and how the two strategies interact and reinforce each other. Their assessment is a sophisticated and subtle consideration of the economic, political, and security components in China's strategic thinking and external behavior. They also show how bilateral and multilateral approaches supplement each other in Chinese diplomacy. Finally, they assess the role of the United States in China's regional strategy, and they offer some scenarios for the future interaction of the two powers.

The second section of the book examines the economic dimension of China's place in the Asian region. It is in this dimension that China's regional impact is felt most strongly, and it is in this realm that there is some cause to conclude that China is becoming the principal actor in the region. The two subsequent chapters explore China's economic impact on Asia, and vice versa. There is a great deal of rich new empirical data and detail contained in these two chapters. Both identify and elaborate the complex and rapidly forming linkages and interdependence among the Chinese and neighboring economies.

The first, by Hideo Ohashi, describes China's regional trade and investment profile. Although it is not widely known, more than half of China's total trade volume is now within the East Asian region. Ohashi also observes that China has positioned itself at the center of the economic division of labor in East Asia. He argues that China imports a large number of intermediate goods (parts and components) from neighbors, assembles them into final-demand goods, and has thus positioned itself as the principal export platform of final-demand goods to North American and European markets. By being the main creator of demand for intermediate goods China has become a locomotive of intraregional trade in East Asia. Ohashi thinks that ultimately, as the national economy and domestic consumer demand develop, China itself will become the recipient of final-demand produced goods and services. Fueling much of this phenomenon is the unprecedented amount of foreign direct investment (FDI) flowing into China, the majority of it originating in East Asia. China is also becoming an increasing source of outbound direct investment (ODI) back into the region, thus creating even thicker interdependent linkages. Ohashi also notes that China has also become a major proponent and initiator of regional free trade liberalization initiatives, most notably its stunning proposal to create a Free Trade Area (FTA) with the ten nations of the Association of Southeast Asian Nations (ASEAN). By doing so, the PRC has opted for integration and positive-sum benefits over narrow zero-sum mercantilism. Ohashi concludes that all of these phenomena are reorienting the East Asian economic system in an increasingly Sinocentric direction.

The next chapter, by Robert Ash, looks at China's regional economic linkages even more closely by examining a heretofore unexplored subject: the increased economic interactions of China's macroregions with neighboring countries and their cross-border linkages. Robert Scalapino once termed this phenomenon "natural economic territories" (NETs), while economists have long written about comparable "growth triangles." But, until this study by Professor Ash, no economist had attempted such a systematic analysis of the linkages of China's internal regional economies with their adjacent external regional economies. He finds considerable evidence of such linkages being forged in recent years—particularly between the Yangzi Delta region and Taiwan; the Pearl River Delta region and Hong Kong, but also increasingly Indochina and Southeast Asia; southwest China and South Asia; northwest China and Central Asia; and northeast China and Northeast Asia. This is not necessarily surprising, but Ash provides the hard data to sustain the proposition. He also shows domestic regional linkages further afield, with Europe and North America. In many cases, by showing these broader linkages Ash has elucidated the very way that globalization—at least in the investment and manufacturing sectors—works in today's world.

The third section of the book examines China's political and diplomatic ties with its neighbors. In some cases (Japan, Korea, Russia, and Taiwan) these are analyzed by contributors bilaterally, while in other cases (Southeast, South, and Central Asia) it is done subregionally. Mike Mochizuki opens the section by examining what is probably China's most problematic relationship in Asia, that with Japan. He describes the "friendship diplomacy" framework that guided Sino-Japanese relations for more than two decades, institutionalizing the relationship and managing to establish a foundation and set parameters for bilateral ties. But Mochizuki and other observers note that this framework eroded over time and fully broke down during the latter part of the 1990s. While he argues that a new framework for relations has yet to fully fill the void, he presents some alternatives. One is an emerging rivalry for regional leadership. Another is a steady deterioration in ties that would destabilize the region. Mochizuki believes that neither of these models accurately describes the present or future of the Sino-Japanese relationship. Rather, he elaborates the view that the relationship is in a healthy period of readjustment, during which candor is replacing both wishful thinking and excessive pessimism, and both countries are fully realizing the importance of the relationship. However, even with more prudent and pragmatic approaches on both sides, Sino-Japanese relations must still cope with the lingering residue of the past as well as several thorny contemporary problems.

In China, this reevaluation has even resulted in the recent emergence of a school of "new thinking on Japan," with certain Chinese journalists and scholars, (e.g., Ma Licheng, Shi Yinhong, and Feng Zhaokui) calling for the PRC to "get over" its "Japan problem," relegate the past to the past, and realize what is at stake for China.[3] Further, according to such "new thinking,"

Japan is a critically important nation for China (Shi Yinhong even went so far as to argue that Japan may be strategically useful in China's struggle against American hegemony), and their relationship is critical to regional stability. While such bold thinking is refreshing, it is by no means predominant in China. In fact, after articles on this subject were published in 2003, there was an extreme domestic backlash against the authors, who were accused of all sorts of traitorous intent. Much of the backlash came in the form of what Peter Gries terms China's new "internet nationalism."[4] A series of other unfortunate events in late 2003 and early 2004 continued to sour Sino-Japanese relations.

Professor Mochizuki argues that, despite these strains, a readjusted relationship between Beijing and Tokyo is taking shape, a relationship that is more realistic than the previous framework, and therefore he is "cautiously optimistic" that there is emerging a "new equilibrium" in which there will be frictions, but manageable ones that will be dealt with in mature ways. He believes that the competitive elements in the relationship can be contained. He also sees an increasing number of coinciding interests and policies between the two governments (which his chapter elaborates in some detail) that further auger for stability and expanded cooperation between China and Japan.

In the next chapter, Jae-Ho Chung traces the evolution of China's approach and policies toward North and South Korea. He reveals the remarkable development in Sino–South Korean ties over the past decade. There is no other bilateral relationship in all of Asia that has developed as quickly and cooperatively over the last decade as that between Beijing and Seoul. This progress has had a major positive impact on the stability and security of Northeast Asia. It has also served as an important buffer against instability or aggression caused by North Korea. Yet it is also evident that the closeness of the Seoul-Beijing relationship has limited the capacity of the United States to pursue a muscular strategy toward North Korea.

Chung also shows how Beijing's thinking, tactics, and policies toward the North Korean regime have evolved considerably. He offers a careful case study in this regard with respect to the second North Korean nuclear crisis that began in 2002. Finally, he considers the impact of China's dramatically improved relations with South Korea on its allied relationship with the United States. While the Republic of Korea's (ROK) ties with China have deepened and grown closer, its alliance with the United States has concomitantly grown more strained. Seoul's challenge is to balance its relationship with the two countries, and Chung argues that both serve as a hedge against the ROK's dependency on the other.

Next, Richard Bush examines the most nettlesome regional relationship for China, its relationship with Taiwan. Bush's chapter is a refined distillation of an enormously complex relationship, which contains centripetal as well centrifugal forces. He describes the increasing interdependent links across the Taiwan Strait in trade, investment, education, tourism, and other areas. He also notes how the two governments quietly cooperate to combat terrorism, smuggling, organized crime, hijacking, piracy, and other nontraditional security challenges. While these exchanges help to stabilize the cross-strait situation, Bush also notes the concerns that some on Taiwan have about their effects, especially the way in which they foster Taiwan's dependency on the mainland rather than the two areas' interdependency. But, as Bush succinctly states, "Like it or not, Taiwan has been pulled into the PRC's economic orbit, and its companies have long since accepted the centrality of the mainland for their future." He also elaborates the "security dilemma" that has emerged between China and Taiwan, which has triggered something of an arms race between the two sides. The political dimension of cross-strait relations is, of course, inextricably bound up in issues of sovereignty, history, and identity. It is also bound up in the murkiness of domestic politics on the island, all of which he also spells out with clarity. Finally, he offers a series of potential scenarios for the evolution of China-Taiwan relations, but concludes that Taiwan must undertake a number of actions to "fortify" itself—economically, militarily, politically, legally, and internationally—if it is to avoid having its future determined by an increasingly powerful China.

Moving down to Southeast Asia, Wang Gungwu describes the long and ambivalent history that China has shared with Southeast Asia (and vice versa). This history, he argues, continues to cast a long shadow over the evolving relationship—although it is evident that China and ASEAN (the amalgam organization of states in place since 1967) have established an unprecedented relationship today. Not only is the relationship politically warm and functional (no small achievement given the past), it is also evident that China and ASEAN have discovered complementarities of normative perspectives and economic interests. The Chinese have embraced many aspects of the "ASEAN Way," a set of normative principles that have been the bedrock of interstate relations within the organization for forty years. To be sure, these principles derive, to no small extent, from the Five Principles of Peaceful Coexistence first put forward by Premier Zhou Enlai at the 1955 Bandung Summit of the Afro-Asian People's Solidarity Organization (AAPSO). Thereafter, these principles germinated in the region and bloomed in the context of ASEAN. More recently, China has discovered that its own "new security concept," first enunciated in Singapore in 1997, dovetails almost identically with ASEAN's guiding principles.

This intersection of normative perspectives has helped to defuse latent fears and misperceptions between the two sides, has done much to forge a new strategic partnership between them, and has driven Beijing to more fully embrace regional multilateralism. Moreover, in 2003 China acceded to ASEAN's Treaty of Amity and Cooperation, making the PRC the first foreign nation to do so. The Chinese government also stunned the region with its proposal to create a Free Trade Area with ASEAN over the course of a decade. This has done much to alleviate the angst in Southeast Asia over China's increasing share of East Asia's exports to Western markets.

Despite all of this progress in China–Southeast Asian relations in recent years, Wang offers some cautionary perspectives on the limits to further development. First, he notes some of the intrinsic differences within ASEAN, which make it difficult for the member states to act with solidarity of purpose on all issues at all times. Second, he reminds us of the memories and continuing legacies of China's past behavior in the region—during the premodern, modern, and contemporary periods—that leave many Southeast Asians wary of Chinese designs and influence. Nonetheless, despite these cautionary notes, Wang sees a corner being turned in China's relations with the region, which offers good potential for growth, mutual benefit, and continued regional stability.

Pivoting further around the arc of Asia, John Garver's chapter addresses China's relations with the nations of South and Central Asia. Garver's analysis centers on the instruments of Chinese presence in these vast and distinct regions, and he weighs Chinese influence vis-à-vis that of other intra- and extraregional powers. In a unique approach, he evaluates China's initiatives to build infrastructural links—primarily a network of roads, rail lines, and pipelines—tying southwest, west, and northwest China to their cross-border neighbors. These linkages are helping to facilitate the growing economic linkages described earlier in Robert Ash's chapter. In addition to these infrastructure linkages, Garver notes the nascent détente between China and India, the long-standing ties with Pakistan (China's "all-weather friend"), and the central role the PRC has played in the Shanghai Cooperation Organization (SCO).

Despite these developments, Garver is guarded about the prospects for growth in China's influence in each case. Indeed, he concludes that Beijing possesses relatively little influence in these areas. South Asia very much remains dominated by Indian power and geographic centrality. He notes that in Central Asia Russia and China compete for influence, and Moscow has hardly ceded its interests in the area to Beijing. Moreover, Garver draws our attention to the dramatic increase in American interests and presence in Central and Southwest Asia since 2001. In his view, it is the long shadow of American power and influence—rather than China's—that defines these regions today.

The final chapter in this section concerns relations between China and Russia. Yu Bin reminds us that this relationship, similar to virtually all other relationships around China's extensive periphery, also carries with it much historical baggage. Yet, as is the case with Southeast Asia, today China and

Russia find themselves in a period of peace and cooperation that is probably unparalleled. Yu Bin elaborates the reasons and the path that brought this strategic partnership into being, but he is quite cautious about its persistence. Yu identifies a number of factors, primarily on the Russian side, that could cause the current concord to unravel. He thus finds something of a disconnect in the relationship, which is characterized by high-level harmony but underlying frictions and suspicions.

Taken together, the chapters in this section evince an ambivalence about China's relations with its neighbors. On the one hand, the chapters clearly reveal the extent to which Beijing has succeeded in normalizing diplomatic relations and consolidating political ties, settling many nagging border disputes, building up extensive trade links and other exchanges, and projecting the image of being a cooperative neighbor. On the other hand, all the chapters reveal lingering misgivings about China. Many of these arise from historical experiences, but they also reflect concerns about China's future ambitions. Clearly, Beijing still has much work to do to assure and assuage its neighbors of China's intentions and the use to which the nation's growing military and economic capabilities will be put, but it is equally clear that China has made a good effort in recent years, and this has begun to win Beijing a level of trust and a depth of ties not seen before in the modern era.

The fourth section of the volume shifts from politics and diplomacy to examine China's regional security strategy and military posture. Bates Gill's chapter argues that China's regional security strategy has pursued three main goals in recent years: (1) maintain a pacific periphery so as to be able to concentrate on internal reforms and growth (the "peace and development" strategy); (2) manage its growing wealth and power in ways that reassure, rather than threaten, neighbors; and (3) cope with preponderant American power around its periphery without confronting the United States directly. Gill describes various instruments China has used and methods that China has undertaken to achieve these three goals. They include the elaboration of the "new security concept," the publication of defense white papers and marginally improved military transparency, more proactive policies to diffuse simmering regional problems and "hot spots," building a series of strategic partnerships with nations near and far, increased involvement in regional cooperative security regimes, deeper involvement in addressing nontraditional security threats, increased willingness to participate in military exercises with foreign nations, and other forms of regional cooperation.

This is an impressive range of new initiatives undertaken by China in recent years, and they have won new respect for Beijing. Yet regional security challenges—Gill identifies those related to North Korea and Taiwan, in particular—remain that will challenge Beijing. He also notes that the nature of the U.S.-China relationship will largely determine Beijing's approach to regional security problems. He concludes, however, that China's increased involvement in regional security affairs is not a passing moment, but is going to be a permanent feature of the Asian security landscape and architecture.

Michael Swaine examines the "hard" dimension of China's regional security stance, its military posture. His analysis is sobering. He concludes that "China is in the process of acquiring new military capabilities and undertaking new force deployments that will fundamentally alter security perceptions in the region and stimulate a more widespread military response among the major powers. Although this dynamic is not fated to produce conflict—even in the case of Taiwan—it will likely increase the chances of regional tension and instability, thus requiring more deliberate and coordinated political, diplomatic, and military efforts to control. The United States will, by necessity, play the most decisive role in this effort." In his chapter Swaine elaborates the various developments in the modernization program of the People's Liberation Army (PLA) that led to his predictions. To do so he not only inventories the hardware in China's land, air, and sea arsenals, at present and in the medium-term future (to 2020), but he also takes account of China's regional defense policy objectives and evolving military doctrine.

Swaine's analysis and prognosis is a realist one. In his thinking hard power is primary, and it trumps other forces and factors at work. This line of analysis differs from China's increased integration into the Asian region or the normative efforts of Chinese diplomacy described in several other chapters. Yet hard military power is an important part of the evolving equation in Asia. The PLA's rapidly improving capabilities will, as Swaine correctly argues, have a major impact on the overall strategic balance in the region. The outstanding question is whether it will create, as he predicts, an increasing "security dilemma" confronted by China and its neighbors, causing the latter to adopt balancing tactics and countervailing actions against the former.

The fifth section of the book examines the potential impact that China's rise and increased centrality in Asia will have on U.S.-China relations and the role and interests of the United States in the region. Interestingly, the two chapters in this section lead the contributing authors to (1) different assessments of China's goals in the region vis-à-vis the United States, and (2) different conclusions about the potential influence on American national interests in the region.

Robert Sutter views China's primary goal in Asia to be *regional preeminence* in all respects. This overriding aspiration, Sutter argues, is fundamentally at odds with the United States—both American priorities and the existing American preeminence in the region. It is, in essence, both a zero-sum view and a structural assessment. Sutter sees China maneuvering steadily but subtly in the region to counter and undercut the U.S. position and influence.

Yet Sutter also acknowledges that Chinese officials and experts uniformly recognize both that American dominance will likely continue for the foreseeable future, and that it is not in China's interests to confront the United States directly. This means, in his analysis, that China's long-term strategy runs counter to U.S. interests, but that the near- and middle-term reality of predominant U.S. power dictates that China's tactics accommodate American interests. Sutter's policy prescription, therefore, is for the United States to maintain its confidence and strength in the Asian theater so as "to hold in check long-standing Chinese tendencies to assertively challenge U.S. interests and perceived adverse Asian developments." He concludes his chapter by raising the specter of a conscious U.S. decision *not* to maintain regional dominance ad infinitum, thus "set[ting] the stage for a different kind of Sino-American accommodation where the United States pulls back strategically from Asia as China rises to regional leadership."

Mike Lampton offers a different assessment of China's aspirations and goals in Asia, which leads him to different conclusions about the impact and policy implications for the United States. While he agrees with Sutter that "constraining the unbridled exercise of American power" is a priority for Beijing, he sees it as one among many goals and not the central motive of Chinese strategic policy. Lampton notes that reassurance of China's neighbors and peacefully securing China's economic lifelines and energy resources are additional priorities. He continues in his chapter to disaggregate the different components of the Chinese "power mix" by dividing it into coercive, normative, and remunerative categories (following the typology of sociologist Amitai Etzioni). He argues that China's remunerative power has grown the most and provides Beijing with considerable regional influence. China's normative power and influence, as described in earlier chapters, is rising more modestly, but it is also intersecting with the perspectives of a growing number of Asian states, particularly as they become increasingly disenchanted with America's overreliance on coercive power. Finally, Lampton, in contrast to Swaine, argues that China's coercive power is growing steadily, but at a measured pace. He observes that the speed of China's military modernization will in part be governed by developments in U.S. and Japanese military power. Above all, Lampton emphasizes the profound impact that the forces of globalization are having on China, its strategic choices, and therefore its external behavior—all of which leads Beijing toward increased interdependence with its neighbors and more status quo behavior.[5]

The implications for the United States, Lampton concludes, need not be negative. He sees "the principal directions in which Chinese policy has moved . . . to be consistent with fundamental U.S. interests." China's rise will necessarily cause the United States to make adjustments along the way, but the basic tendency of increased interdependence and integration is, he argues, very much in American national interests. This does not inevitably mean that China's rise will ultimately prove to be fully in U.S. interests, but to date, the two powers have managed to coexist and cooperate quite fruitfully.

The final section of this study focuses on the broader implications of China's rise for the regional order. Jonathan Pollack and Michael Yahuda tackle the impact on regional security and the political/diplomatic order, respectively. Pollack delineates the increasingly complex and multilayered security agenda and architecture that is emerging in the Asian theater. While he detects that "an unmistakable recalibration of power and influence is underway," owing to China's ascendance and the "dilution" of American primacy, Pollack observes that a truly integrated regional security system has yet to emerge: "Any characterization of an 'Asian security order' (or, even less, a presumptive Sinocentric order) is a major oversimplification." Notwithstanding some of the nontraditional security challenges of terrorism, HIV and AIDS, nuclear proliferation, human smuggling, and other pan-regional challenges, Pollack notes that regional security is still primarily oriented toward "hard security" issues in four distinct subregions, Northeast, Southeast, South, and Central Asia. He also points out that China has become the only regional actor to have a meaningful security involvement in all four subregions, and his chapter chronicles this growing involvement on China's part. At the same time that China is increasing its regional security involvement, it is also pursuing strategies to forestall a hostile American posture. As Pollack puts it, "China is attempting to limit its exposure in America's strategic headlights." Becoming more involved in sub- and pan-regional security affairs is precisely part of Beijing's strategy to dilute U.S. influence and "forestall or discourage coordinated regional responses to its enhanced economic power, military capabilities, and political influence," Pollack argues.

Pollack's chapter also contains an interesting comparison of the internal strategic discourses in China and the United States about the other. He finds some interesting parallels between these two communities. At the end of the day, Pollack believes that the nature of Sino-American relations will determine the shape of the regional security order, and he describes four alternative strategic futures in this regard:

- · A convergent, more diversified security order largely acceptable to the United States and China;
- · A mixed security order simultaneously entailing elements of Sino-American competition and collaboration;
- · An overt Sino-American political-military competition;
- · A Sino-American regional security condominium.

He explores the possibilities for each alternative but does not predict the realization of any single one. Pollack concludes that the evolving and emerging regional security order is very fluid, and that its nature remains to be determined, but that, one way or the other, China and the U.S.-China relationship will be central to the outcome.

The final chapter in the volume, by Michael Yahuda, focuses on the evolving regional political/diplomatic order. Like Pollack, Yahuda describes a multilayered and complex mosaic that comprises the Asian political "system" today. He also finds that, as in the economic and, to a lesser extent, security realms, China's political integration in the region has been pronounced in recent years. Yahuda also discusses the emergence of regional institutionalism in Asia and finds that, while it does not have the institutional character of Europe, multilateral institutionalism is nonetheless firmly becoming a part of the regional landscape. He explains how China has not only come to accept such regional institutionalism, but has also grown to become an active and constructive participant in the process. Like Pollack, Yahuda also finds China more proactively engaged in all four subregions of Asia, and he shows how Beijing mixes bilateral and multilateral instruments and involvement in each area. Yet, also like Pollack, Yahuda finds that each subregion continues to have its own intrinsic dynamics—and, hence, a truly regional "order" has yet to emerge.

THE ASIAN SYSTEM: EVOLVING TO WHAT MODEL?

Given the various elements noted in the chapters in this volume, and especially the last two, what might China's growing power and influence mean for the evolving Asian system? What is the nature of the emerging regional order? In my own contribution to this discussion, let me offer seven possibilities.

A Hegemonic System

A number of observers, particularly in the United States, Japan, and India, remain skeptical about China's motivations and the sustainability of its new cooperative posture. These skeptics see China's "new face" as a tactical ploy to lull the region into a false sense of complacency, until China builds up its comprehensive strength in anticipation of the day when it can dominate and dictate to the region. Such a strategy is captured in Deng Xiaoping's admonition *taoguang, yanghui* (bide one's time while building up capability).

A China-dominant system would be a *hegemonic system*—either coercive *(badao)* or benign *(wangdao)*. Under such a system, other nations would either be subsumed by a domineering China or would choose, in a looser hegemonic system, to "bandwagon" with Beijing as the best means to protect themselves and their equities. Another variation of this model would be a *hierarchical* model, with China as the major power at the apex of the regional hierarchical pyramid—reconstituting, in essence, a twenty-first-century version of the ancient "tribute system."[6]

Such a system not only assumes China's desire for such dominance, but it would also certainly require the complete diminution of American power and influence and its withdrawal from the region. Neither condition seems likely.[7] It also presumes, as in balance-of-power systems, that China would be a (singular) pole to which all other regional nations would be attracted, like a magnet. Such poles, such as the United States and the Soviet Union during the Cold War, usually attract others via a combination of an appealing ideology, extensive economic assistance, extended deterrence and military protection, international diplomatic support, and other means. China today, and likely into the future, offers few of these advantages to its neighbors. As a result, the essential requirements for a hegemonic system to take shape in Asia have not been fulfilled: neither does China have significant potential to become a pole, nor do incentives for others to bandwagon exist.

Major Power Rivalry

Other skeptics anticipate an inevitable clash between the existing dominant power (the United States) and the rising power (China), owing to the asymmetric structural properties of the regional system. The classic statement of this view is offered by Aaron Friedberg.[8] They argue that, historically, rising powers inevitably challenge dominant powers, and that this zero-sum competition for dominance is a virtual law of international relations, at least for the realist school. For this school, the period of "power transition" is particularly unstable and conflict-prone.[9] A variant of this is the traditional bipolar balance-of-power model (presumably with the United States and China as the two poles), in which two major competitive powers possess roughly equal distribution of power, thus offsetting each other and maintaining the balance.

For this situation to obtain, China's comprehensive national strength, particularly in the military realm, would have to match that of the United States. Again, this is difficult to envision in the near and medium term. It would also require that the United States and China experience conflicting interests and policies over a wide range of regional and global issues—a dysfunctional relationship quite different from the currently cooperative state of Sino-American relations.[10]

The "Hub and Spokes" Model

A third conceptual model is the American-centric "hub and spokes" alliance system that has existed since the dissolution of SEATO in the early 1970s. This is a system of bilateral military allies (the United States with Japan,

South Korea, the Philippines, Thailand, and Australia). In such a conceptualization the United States is thought to be the hub of a wheel, with each of the bilateral alliances the spokes of the wheel.

This system has served the allies and the region well for three decades. It has been central to the maintenance of strategic stability and economic development throughout the East Asian region, has deterred a hostile North Korea, was significant in rolling back Vietnamese aggression in Cambodia, has played a role in maintaining peace in the Taiwan Strait, has kept open the sea lanes of communication (SLOCs), and has provided for the national security of the allied states. In addition, while not full allies, a number of other East Asian states (e.g., Singapore) have been full security partners in this system. China too has benefited from this system, for all of these reasons.

Although this system has stabilized the region well and has the potential to continue to do so in the future, the structure is not sufficient to constitute a true regional system. A large number of countries—and this includes China—remain unallied or unaffiliated with the system and have no compelling reasons to join. Thus, although the structure goes a long way toward integrating a number of key nations in the region in a common security network, it is highly unlikely that the "hub and spokes" system will enlarge to become a full regional system in the future. Indeed, if the Korean peninsula were to be unified, two key legs of the system, U.S. alliances with South Korea and Japan, would potentially be undermined. Thus by itself, the U.S.-led alliance system is insufficient to constitute a full regional security structure.

A Concert of Powers

A fourth potential model of the evolving Asian system is a concert of powers, in which rivalry is not inherent, but rather the maintenance of stability is shared among several major nations or alliances of nations. The best example of this type of system is, of course, the Concert of Europe, which functioned for almost half a century in the wake of the Congress of Vienna of 1815. It was a system that kept the peace and maintained a balance among the main powers of the era (Britain, Russia, Austria, Prussia, France, Italy, and Turkey). It functioned well because no nation possessed disproportionate power and influence, and because all agreed to regular consultations via a series of diplomatic conferences. It was, in effect, the world's first de facto regional security regime.

For such a system to evolve in Asia would require a more equal distribution of hard power. It would certainly require that American power decline substantially and relatively, while the individual power distribution of China, Japan, India, and Southeast Asia would grow to be roughly equal. It would also require that each member of the concert enjoy generally harmonious and nonconflictual relations among themselves. Although the latter condition may be possible (notwithstanding deep-rooted Sino-Japanese antagonism), and the relative power of the four noted above could generally equalize over time, it remains difficult to envision such a diminution of U.S. power or its presence in the region.

A Condominium of Power

A fifth possibility is a condominium of power by the two dominant powers in the region, the United States and China. Although this possibility seems remote these days, given continuing tensions over Taiwan and latent strategy rivalry, it is not out of the realm of possibility that such a condominium could emerge.

For such a scenario to materialize would require a number of developments, none of which seems likely. First, the dispute over Taiwan would have to be resolved. Second, China would have to fully accommodate itself to the U.S. alliance system in East Asia, budding defense ties with India, and the growing military presence in Central Asia. Third, both countries' remaining suspicions of the other as a strategic competitor or security threat would have to be resolved. Indeed, condominiums usually require that the two dominant powers be either allied or mutually trusting. Although the United States and China are enjoying their best relationship in many years, including at the strategic level, it is difficult to imagine the two forging a condominium of power in Asia for the foregoing reasons. Not insignificantly, it would also require other major nations in the region to accept and accommodate such a Sino-American condominium—again, a very unlikely prospect. Finally, the emergence of such a condominium would necessitate the substantial and qualitative decline of Japan as a regional and global actor, which is a highly unlikely development.

A Normative Community

A sixth possibility entails the emergence of a region-wide community of nations that shares a series of normative rules and goals and agrees to abide by them for the larger collective interest. Such is the case among the Association of Southeast Asian Nations (ASEAN). Such a normative regional order could either be heavily codified and institutionalized or could operate more loosely based on shared goals and interactions. Among others, Amitav Acharya and Muthiah Alagappa have been the primary exponents of this model.[11]

Obviously, for such an order to emerge requires consensual agreement among participants as to the norms, goals, and rules to govern interstate and other behavior. While ASEAN and the ASEAN Regional Forum (ARF) have been able to achieve this to a certain extent, and the Shanghai Cooperation Organization to a lesser extent, and China's "new security concept" dovetails to a large extent with both, the region as a whole remains a very long way from forging such a consensus, much less institutionalizing it. Nonetheless, China's growing embrace of the ARF and a potential "regional security community" is a positive sign and may move the region gradually in the direction of further institutionalization.[12]

Complex Interdependence

The final potential model for the evolving and future Asian system is oriented not around security affairs, but rather around the dense web of economic, technological, and other ties between nations in the era of accelerating globalization. The core actor in this model is not the nation-state, but a plethora of nonstate actors and processes—many of which are difficult to measure with any precision—that operate at the societal level. These multiple threads bind societies together in complex and interdependent ways. Indeed, they point to another significant way that the Asian region is changing, which is that the traditional geographic subcomponents of the region—Northeast Asia, Southeast Asia, South Asia, and Central Asia—are no longer useful intellectual constructs for dividing or distinguishing the macro-processes occurring throughout the region. In the twenty-first century, these four subregions are all interconnected and interdependent at numerous levels.

There is considerable evidence that complex interdependence has taken hold throughout the Asian region—and it will only accelerate in speed and scope over time. There is no escaping the dynamic, which is a powerful deterrent to conflict and is conducive to peace and stability, as all nations and people become tied together in one large interdependent web.

Yet as profound as this process is, and as deeply rooted as it is becoming in Asia, complex interdependence is by itself insufficient to establish a dominant regional system, precisely because it does not operate at the nation-state level and does not intrinsically entail security arrangements. Any truly regional system must involve both.

A Mosaic of Models

If these seven models for an evolving regional system in Asia individually fail to fully describe the future toward which the region is moving, where does this leave us analytically? Surely, one size does not, and cannot, fit all in a region as diffuse and diverse as Asia.

What is emerging in the Asian region—stretching from Afghanistan in the southwest to Russia in the north to Japan in the northeast to Australia in the southeast—is a multitextured and multilayered hybrid system that shares elements of three of the aforementioned models: "hub and spokes," normative community, and complex interdependence. There is also an element of the balance-of-power system looming in the background, although it is dormant and would require considerable adjustments among regional states for it to fully emerge. One reason it will likely never emerge is because having to choose between Beijing and Washington as a primary benefactor is the nightmare scenario for the vast majority of Asian states. It is for this same reason that Asian states "bandwagoning" with a rising China will also not likely emerge on a full regional basis (although it might in certain bilateral cases, as some may seek to balance against China). It is not an exaggeration that all Asian states seek to have sound, extensive, and cooperative relations with *both* the United States and China, and thus will do much to avoid being put into a bipolar dilemma. Some states in fact play a kind of balancing role between the two regional powers—tilting first toward Washington and then toward Beijing—so as to hedge their bets, protect their interests, and keep both engaged.

Clearly, the U.S.-led alliance system remains the predominant regional security architecture. It has been the bedrock of regional stability since the end of the Vietnam War, has served the region well, and is unlikely to be cast aside by the participants in the "hub and spokes" system (including the non-allied partners and beneficiaries of the system). China tried to challenge this system, at least rhetorically, in the 1997–98 period, and it was roundly rebuffed by its neighbors throughout the region. Arguably, only North Korea seeks the dissolution of this system.

This system relies on hard power, and the threat of it. At the same time, we are witnessing the emergence of a "soft power" architecture in the region, based on a series of increasingly shared norms about interstate relations, security, and the emergence of state and nonstate institutions to advance these norms. ASEAN and the ASEAN Regional Forum (ARF), backstopped by the nongovernmental Committee on Security Cooperation in the Asia-Pacific (CSCAP), is the cornerstone of this emerging regional community, but the Shanghai Cooperation Organization and the South Asia Association for Regional Security (SAARC) are also important components. These organizations are forms of cooperative, rather than collective, security, and they augment the more formal "hub and spokes" alliance-based system.

Finally, the Asian region has been witnessing the growth of intraregional linkages of all varieties—including economic, cultural, technological, educational, and ideational—at a dizzying speed. Asia, long known for its diver-

sity and disconnectedness, is rapidly becoming a seamless web of intercon-
nections and interdependencies.

One key dimension of this interdependence not often considered by
analysts is the impact of China's own internal stability on regional stability.
That is, if China's domestic reforms were to stall, or if there were significant
social upheaval internally,[13] it would have major—and decidedly negative—
implications for the region.

Looking ahead over the next two decades it is evident that China has
entered a new phase in its development in which the principal challenge will
be to provide a range of public goods to the populace in order to improve
the nation's quality of life. Much of China has now become a newly industrialized country (NIC) where public demands are no longer focused on basic
consumer durables or disposable income, but increasingly on a range of
quality of life issues such as full access to education at all levels, universal and
quality health care, environmental protection, workplace and public safety,
efficient transportation and communications, high-quality construction,
accountability and transparency in government, lack of corruption in government and business, decreasing social stratification and alleviating
absolute poverty, effective and fair enforcement of law, and a combination
of social welfare financing (including unemployment insurance, retirement
annuities, and workplace injury compensation). The public in China is
increasingly and appropriately demanding these public goods, just as they
have done previously in other NICs throughout East Asia, Latin America,
and Europe. Providing and delivering them is a challenge of governance,
with the responsibility falling primarily on a combination of central, intermediate, and local governments in China, although private sector nongovernmental organizations and the marketplace can provide for some
(such as pension schemes). There is the view that provision of public goods
by China's government has declined dramatically over the course of the last
twenty years of economic expansion and reforms, and that the country faces
a "governance crisis."[14] There is a degree of truth in this assessment, as the
SARS crisis of 2002–2003 exposed in the public health arena. One finds similar chronic shortcomings in most of the other areas noted above as well.
There is no doubt that compared to the prereform era, when China's socialist government provided many of these public goods, state capacity in this
area has declined. Yet this declining capacity should not be overstated either;
for example, when compared with Indonesia, North Korea, Myanmar,
Bangladesh, India, and Pakistan, the Chinese government still provides
more of these basic public goods for the majority of its 1.3 billion people.

Thus, improving state capacity to provide these public goods and meet
governance responsibilities is *the* principal challenge for the Chinese government at all levels over the next couple of decades. The current Chinese
government, under the leadership of President Hu Jintao and Premier Wen

Jiabao, seems to be acutely attuned to meeting these challenges and is beginning to devote increased attention and resources accordingly.[15]

China's governance challenges will also increasingly become the responsibility of China's neighbors, as well as other nations and international organizations. That is, given the interdependence described above, China's neighbors now have a much increased stake in assisting China to meet these governance challenges and provide the public goods noted above, because if China is not successful in these tasks, then the resulting domestic dislocations inside China will spill over its borders and become destabilizing factors affecting the regional order. In other words, the rest of the region, and even the world beyond, has a greater stake in China's domestic development and reforms than it ever has before. It is very much in the national interests of other Asian countries for China to succeed in meeting these internal challenges and to strengthen its state capacity in critical areas such as public health, environmental protection, rule of law, civil society, government transparency, poverty alleviation, and nonproliferation. The European Union and Japan have long established such policy priorities and have contributed a great deal of tangible assistance and resources to these ends (China is the largest single recipient of overseas development assistance from each).[16] It can therefore be anticipated (and recommended) that rising levels of aid and development assistance as well as investment in these areas will be increasingly forthcoming from other Asian governments and private sector agencies. It is very much in the interests of the other governments to provide such assistance, as it will be an investment in their own futures and regional stability. Such is the nature of interdependence in Asia today and into the future.

The following chapters elaborate and elucidate the many ways in which the Asian region and system are changing as a result of China's growing power and influence. While there has been much written about the impact of China's rise on the global system, there has been considerably less speculation devoted to the regional context. This volume attempts to offer such analysis, in a judicious and balanced manner, by some of the world's leading scholars in the field of China's foreign relations.

NOTES

I am grateful to all of the contributors to this volume, but particularly Mike Lampton and Jonathan Pollack, for their comments and shaping my thinking on specific parts of this chapter. Parts of this and the next chapter previously appeared in David Shambaugh, "China Engages Asia: Reshaping the Regional Order," *International Security* 29, no. 3 (Winter 2004/2005): 64–99. Reprint permission granted by MIT Press.

1. Qian's memoirs are a good chronicle of his personal role. See Qian Qichen, *Waijiao Shiji* [Ten stories of diplomacy] (Beijing: Shijie Zhishi chubanshe, 2003), particularly chapter 5.

2. Joseph S. Nye Jr., *Soft Power: The Means to Success in World Politics* (New York: Public Affairs, 2004), 88.

3. Ma Licheng, "Dui Ri guanxi xinsiwei: Zhong-Ri minjian zhihou" [New thinking in policies toward Japan: Concerns for the Chinese and Japanese peoples], *Zhanlue yu Guanli* [Strategy and management] 6 (December 2002); Shi Yinhong, "Zhong-Ri jiejin yu 'waijiao geming'" [Closer Sino-Japanese relations and diplomatic revolution], *Zhanlue yu Guanli* [Strategy and management] 2 (April 2003).

4. Peter Hayes Gries, "China's 'New Thinking' on Japan," unpublished paper.

5. For this line of argument, also see Alastair I. Johnston, "Is China a Status-Quo Power?" *International Security* 27, no. 4 (Spring 2003): 5–56.

6. This model has been put forward by David C. Kang in "Getting Asia Wrong: The Need for New Analytic Frameworks," *International Security* 27, no. 4 (Summer 2003): 57–85.

7. For further elaboration of this and other scenarios, see my "Chinese Hegemony over Asia by 2015?" *Korean Journal of Defense Analysis* 9, no. 1 (Summer 1997): 7–28.

8. Aaron Friedberg, "Ripe for Rivalry: Prospects for Peace in a Multipolar Asia," *International Security* 18, no. 3 (Winter 1993/1994): 5–33.

9. See, for example, Ronald L. Tammen et al., *Power Transitions: Strategies for the 21ˢᵗ Century* (London: Chatham House, 2000).

10. See the discussion in my "China Engages Asia: Reshaping the Regional Order," *International Security* 29, no. 3 (Winter 2004/2005): 89–94.

11. See Muthiah Alagappa, ed., *Asian Security Order: Instrumental and Normative Features* (Stanford, CA: Stanford University Press, 2003), especially chapter 2 by Alagappa and chapter 6 by Amitav Acharya. More recently, see Acharya's "Will Asia's Past Be Its Future?" *International Security* 28, no. 3 (Winter 2003/2004): 149–64.

12. See the excellent and path-breaking study of China and the ARF by Alastair I. Johnston, "Socialization in International Relations: The ASEAN Way and International Relations Theory," in *International Relations Theory and the Asia-Pacific*, ed. G. John Ikenberry and Michael Mastanduno (New York: Columbia University Press, 2003).

13. See David Shambaugh, *Is China Unstable?* (Armonk, NY: M. E. Sharpe, 2000); Murray Scot Tanner, "Cracks in the Wall: China's Eroding Coercive State," *Current History* (September 2001): 243–49; and "China Rethinks Unrest," *Washington Quarterly* (Spring 2004).

14. Minxin Pei, "China's Governance Crisis," *Foreign Affairs* 81, no. 5 (2002): 96–109.

15. See Wen Jiabao, Premier of the State Council of the People's Republic of China, "Report on the Work of the Government," delivered to the Second Session of the Tenth National People's Congress, March 16, 2004, available at http://neews.xinhuanet.com/english/2004-03/16/content_1368830.htm.

16. See, for example, Marie Söderberg, "Japan's ODA Policy in Northeast Asia," in *New Northeast Asian Initiatives: Cooperation for Regional Development and Security*, ed. Masako Ikegami (Stockholm: Stockholm University Center for Pacific Asia Studies, 2003); European Commission, *A Maturing Partnership—Shared Interests and Challenges in EU-China Relations* (Brussels: European Commission, 2003).

PART ONE

China and the Changing Asian Landscape

1

Return to the Middle Kingdom?

China and Asia in the Early Twenty-First Century

David Shambaugh

The tectonic plates of power that have characterized Asia for half a century are shifting, and China may be returning to its traditional role as the central actor in Asia. As China has continued to accrue the traditional attributes of power, its influence in the region has also steadily increased. China's neighbors are increasingly looking to Beijing for regional leadership, or, at a minimum, they are taking account of China's interests and concerns. China's own diplomacy has grown more confident, omnidirectional, and proactive; its economy is now a major engine of regional growth; its military is steadily modernizing; and its regional security posture is increasingly seen as benign. China has also coupled these developments with an assertive propaganda campaign during 2003–2004 championing its "peaceful rise," a campaign that was aimed at regional and other foreign audiences and was intended to rebut the twin "China threat" and "China collapse" theories.[1]

As a result of China's regional rise, countries all around China's periphery are adjusting their relations with Beijing, as well as with each other. Consequently, a new regional order is taking shape. While the North Korea and Taiwan situations could always erupt in conflict and puncture the peace, the predominant trend in the region is the creation of an extensive web of mutual interdependence among states and nonstate actors, with China increasingly at the center of the web. This phenomenon has begun to draw increased attention from leading media[2] and academic specialists alike.[3]

Despite the significance of China's regional rise, it is tempting to conclude that the Asian regional system is becoming "China-dominant," but such a conclusion is premature. This is decidedly not the case. China shares the regional stage with the United States, Japan, ASEAN, and, increasingly, India as well. The United States remains the region's most powerful actor, although its power and influence are neither unconstrained nor uncontested. Japan's economic weight and ASEAN's normative influence are also significant, and regional multilateral organizations are becoming more firmly rooted. The Asian regional order at the outset of the twenty-first century is an increasingly complex mosaic of actors and factors. To be sure, China is one of the principal ones, and its influence is being increasingly felt, but it is far too early to conclude that the regional order has become Sinocentric. Nonetheless, China's growing strength and authority are altering regional dynamics and giving shape to a new Asian order.

Not only is China's power and influence increasing, but Beijing is also exerting its new prowess in ways that seek to stabilize the region and alleviate latent fears about China's intentions. The growing perception that China is a status quo power is especially remarkable when one recalls the earlier era of the 1950s and 1960s, when China sought to destabilize regional governments by supporting armed insurgencies and exporting Maoism, and had border disputes or conflicts with virtually every contiguous country. Today, virtually all the territorial disputes have been negotiated and resolved successfully, resulting in treaties that delimit 20,222 kilometers of land boundaries,[4] and there is new impetus to resolve the final outstanding dispute between China and India.[5] China is now the exporter of goodwill and consumer durables instead of weapons and revolution. Consider also that merely a decade or so ago China did not even enjoy full diplomatic relations with South Korea, Indonesia, or Singapore; ties with Vietnam and India were very strained and their borders militarized; and China was ostracized in the world because of the events of 1989. At the same time, with the collapse of the Soviet Union and East European party-states, China's leadership was very insecure and insular. Today ties with these countries are robust, and, domestically, a thorough generational transfer of power has brought new leaders to power who brim with confidence and competence. They face daunting challenges at home, but they are coming to grips with them. Abroad, China's relations with the major powers, including the United States, Russia, and the European Union, have rarely been better, which has only served to further strengthen Beijing's confidence and regional hand.

ENGAGING THE PERIPHERY

China's new regional posture is reflected in virtually all policy spheres. Overcoming its earlier hesitancy, China is now an involved actor in the vast majority of regional issues, and has become a proactive partner in helping to alleviate or resolve many of them. Beijing's diplomacy has been remarkably adept and nuanced, earning it praise around the region. Concomitantly, fears voiced throughout the region just a few years ago about a Chinese hegemon seeking to impose itself and dominate regional affairs have now become muted. Today, China is increasingly seen as a good neighbor, con-

structive partner, and careful listener. Importantly, it is also increasingly multilateral in its diplomacy.[6] China also seems to be shedding its traditional twin
identities of historical victim and object of great power manipulation.

China's new posture has resulted in a blizzard of meetings and exchanges
among Chinese officials and their neighboring counterparts, both civilian
and military.[7] The sheer volume of diplomacy and discourse is staggering.
China now participates in annual heads-of-state summits with virtually all of
its neighbors, and there is a constant series of ministerial and subminister-
ial exchanges. China is now posting some of its most seasoned and sophisticated diplomats in key regional embassies, and they are becoming proactive and well known in their local communities. China's new embrace of
regional multilateralism was highlighted by its hosting of the 2001 APEC
meeting in Shanghai and the attention given President Hu Jintao at the
2003 APEC meeting in Bangkok, although Chinese diplomats are also now
deeply engaged in a variety of other regional organizations.

China's growing regional influence derives not only from its hard
power—its growing economic weight and military power—but its influence
is also growing in ways associated with soft power. While Beijing is certainly
not trying to export an ideology today as it did in the past (indeed, the Chinese Communist Party today does not seem even to possess an ideology to
export, even if it were inclined to do so), Beijing does seem to exert some
influence in at least two areas.

The first is in the normative realm, where Beijing's enunciation of the
"new security concept," "strategic partnerships," and other initiatives to
fashion a new set of norms to govern interstate relations and prevent conflict resonates positively among many Asian nations. This is particularly the
case in ASEAN, where China's initiatives dovetail very closely with ASEAN's
own norms articulated over many years.

The second area of potential Chinese soft power lies in the realm of
higher education. Training future generations of intellectuals, technicians,
and political elites from other nations is a subtle but very important form of
soft power. This was the role of Great Britain at its imperial zenith and of the
United States ever since the 1950s, and now China increasingly fills this
role. During the 2003 academic year, there were 77,628 foreign students
studying for advanced degrees in China's universities, approximately 80
percent of which came from other Asian countries. South Korea sent by far
the largest number of these students (35,363), while Japan sent 12,765,
Vietnam 3,487, Indonesia 2,563, Thailand 1,554, and Nepal 1,199.[8] During that same year there were 3,693 students from the United States. The
precise influence that this training will have on future generations of Asian
elites is difficult to predict, but these individuals will certainly be sensitized
to Chinese viewpoints and interests, and they will have a knowledge of the
Chinese language, society, culture, history, and politics. Although this form

of influence is important, one does not yet find evidence of other traditional forms of soft power—such as Chinese media and popular culture—
spreading around the Asian region; if anything, China is increasingly
absorbing popular culture, managerial methods, forms of governance, and
information from around the region.

To be sure, not all on China's periphery are persuaded by China's "charm
offensive."[9] One still occasionally encounters concerns about a looming
"China threat" among regional security specialists—notably in Tokyo,
Taipei, Hanoi, and New Delhi—but this view is held by a progressively
smaller number, even in these capitals. In the economic sphere, China has
been able, through a variety of efforts—ranging from responsible management of its currency during the Asian financial crisis, to timely grants of aid
and loans, to increased trade, to growing outbound direct investment
(ODI), to its stunning proposal to establish a Free Trade Area (FTA) with
ASEAN—to similarly assuage angst among Southeast Asian countries about
the Chinese trade behemoth.

PERCEIVING THE PERIPHERY

How did China come around to its new engagement with Asia? Six sets of
events in the early and late 1990s appear, in retrospect, to have been important in laying the perceptual groundwork for the policy changes that would
emerge around the turn of the millennium.

The first important event occurred in the wake of the June 4, 1989, incident, when many Asian countries did not join the rest of the world in condemning, sanctioning, and ostracizing the PRC government for the Chinese military's killing of civilians in Beijing.[10] Only Japan explicitly
condemned the use of force. The South Korean government used mild language, claiming that the "incident was regrettable," while Southeast Asian
states said nothing at all or, in the case of Thailand and Malaysia, simply
stated that it was an "internal affair" of China.[11] Even Japan was reticent to
sustain the sanctions and ostracism, and it began to opt out of the sanctions
the following year.[12] Thereafter, the ASEAN states lead a diplomatic campaign to "engage," rather than isolate, China.[13] Although more critical of
Beijing's actions than other Southeast Asian states, Singapore and its prime
minister Lee Kuan Yew were the notable conceptualizers and movers
behind the engagement strategy.[14] ASEAN's policy thus apparently left an
impression on the Chinese leadership. While the rest of the world was doing
its best to isolate China, ASEAN reached out to Beijing.

This PRC perception of ASEAN was a factor during the second apparent
turning point in 1997–98, inspired by the sudden Asian financial crisis. The
Chinese government was deeply shaken by the depth and breadth of the
currency crisis in the region, but it acted in a responsible and stabilizing way

by not devaluing its currency and offering packages of aid and low-interest loans to several Southeast Asian countries. These actions were not only appreciated in the region, thus puncturing the image of China as either aloof or hegemonic, but they also served to arrest the crisis to some extent. For Beijing, the success of its actions apparently provided a greater sense of diplomatic confidence among its leaders.

The third turning point was more of a gradual process than a single event. Although it is difficult to pinpoint with precision, between roughly 1997 and 2001 the Chinese government underwent a fundamental evolution in its views of regional multilateral organizations, particularly security-related institutions.[15] During this period, China evolved from being suspicious of, to uncertain about, to supportive of such organizations. At first, these organizations were viewed as potential tools of the United States to be used in the containment of China. After China had sent observers to the meetings of the ASEAN Regional Forum (ARF) and the Council on Security Cooperation in the Asia-Pacific (CSCAP) as well as to other "Track II" meetings for a year or two, its view changed. Chinese observers became more agnostic and more open to learning about these organizations as it soon became clear to them that the United States did not drive these organizations; to the contrary, Washington tended to dismiss or ignore them.[16] They further discovered that the cooperative security approach that lay at the heart of these organizations, as pushed by ASEAN states, was quite compatible with China's own "new security concept," which was unveiled by Beijing in 1996–97. By 1999–2000 Beijing's greater receptivity had given way to full-blown involvement and participation in regional multilateral organizations, paralleling a more general embrace globally. As the director general of Asian affairs in China's Ministry of Foreign Affairs put it, "It was a gradual learning process for us, as we needed to become more familiar with how these organizations worked and to learn how to play the game."[17] This evolution and China's "learning" have done much to shift China's regional stance from passivity to proactivity.

The fourth experience for China came in 1997, when its diplomatic and military officials toured the region calling for the abrogation of all alliances worldwide as an unnecessary vestige of the Cold War. China's reasoning was that since these alliances were formed against a specific enemy during the Cold War era, they were no longer necessary now that the Soviet Union had ceased to exist and the Cold War had ended. China's logic rested upon a zero-sum understanding of alliances, that is, that alliances need to be against another state, rather than upon a positive-sum view that alliances have utility for the maintenance of security and stability. According to China's logic, this argument applied not only to bilateral alliances (such as the five among the United States, Japan, South Korea, the Philippines, Thailand, and Australia), but also to multilateral alliances like NATO. It is difficult to tell how seriously China took its own official rhetoric at the time, but in any event Beijing's call fell on deaf ears throughout the region and the world. In fact, a number of Asian governments privately told Beijing that such calls were unwelcome and that they had no intention of severing their alliances with the United States.[18] The reaction caught Chinese officials off guard, as they apparently had not expected other nations to defend their security ties with the United States. After eight months or so Beijing cooled its rhetoric.

The fifth experience that helps to explain the new cast of Chinese diplomacy toward Asia, particularly its proactivity, was the result of a heated internal debate in the wake of the bombing of the Chinese embassy in Belgrade during the 1999 war in Kosovo. In the wake of this war and attack, international relations experts and officials in China began to question Deng Xiaoping's 1985 pronouncement that the principal characteristics of international relations during the current era were "peace and development" *(heping yu fazhan)*. Not only did Deng deem "peace and development" to be the trend of the times, but he also claimed that China needed a peaceful environment in order to pursue its economic development. Deng's definitive assessment *(tifa)* had been *the* guiding analytical paradigm and diplomatic blueprint for China for the previous fourteen years (although the 1991 Gulf War and the series of global ethnic conflicts during the mid-1990s had also called it into question). An important corollary to Deng's thesis was that the leading hegemonic power, the United States, had entered a period of gradual relative decline. Yet, by 1999, neither the core thesis nor the corollary appeared to be valid in the eyes of many Chinese analysts. After several months of heated internal debate,[19] it was concluded that, although there had been some notable "contradictions" in world affairs in recent years, and the United States did not appear to be in decline (in fact, just the opposite), the general thesis was still valid. However, it was concluded that, in order to have a peaceful environment conducive to domestic development, China needed to be more proactive in shaping its regional environment.[20] Chinese analysts concluded that China could not just sit by and idly absorb whatever events took place on its periphery, but Beijing needed to be more active in shaping that environment. A further corollary of this conclusion was that China needed to stabilize and improve its relationship with the United States.[21] Thus, not only the proactive diplomacy that China is currently demonstrating, but also the FTA initiative with ASEAN, derives to some degree from the outcome of the 1999 "peace and development" debate.

Finally, despite the volatile nature of world affairs in the wake of 9/11 and the war and occupation in Iraq, Chinese analysts tend to view their regional security environment *(zhoubian anquan diqu)* as generally benign and non-threatening to China. This is evident in recent annual assessments published by the Ministry of Foreign Affairs, the prestigious PLA Academy of Military

Sciences, the China Institute of Contemporary International Relations (China's leading civilian intelligence institution), and the Institute of Asia-Pacific Studies of the Chinese Academy of Social Sciences.[22] While Chinese analysts do note the instability caused by global terrorism, North Korea's pursuit of nuclear weapons, and the Kashmir dispute, on the whole they are remarkably relaxed in their overall assessments of regional security and China's national security.[23] Although this is the predominant view, not all Chinese analyses are as sanguine.[24] One 2003 assessment of China's relations with neighboring countries argued that China was now effectively encircled by the five U.S. bilateral alliances in East Asia, U.S. military forces in Central Asia and Southwest Asia, increased U.S. deployments in Southeast Asia and the southwest Pacific, and increased cooperation between the U.S. military and the Indian, Pakistani, and Mongolian militaries.[25] Still, despite this observation, the overall sense of the study was that there is a peaceful periphery conducive to China's national security and development.[26]

Taken together, these six factors help to explain how China perceives its regional environment, and they go some distance toward explaining Beijing's new proactive diplomacy around its periphery. How have these perceptions been translated into practice?

MEASURING CHINA'S NEW REGIONAL POSTURE

The breadth and depth of China's new regional posture is explored in the following chapters. It will suffice here to note some of the key dimensions of these growing ties. At least four overarching characteristics are evident when one surveys China's recent interaction around its periphery: (1) the effort to build strategic partnerships and work with regional organizations; (2) the effort to deepen bilateral political and economic interaction; (3) the effort to expand economic ties; and (4) the effort to remove distrust and anxiety in the security sphere. Let us examine each of these briefly in turn.

Engaging Regional Organizations

With the exception of ASEAN, the growth in regional organizations and multilateralism is a rather recent development. Many analysts have long argued that Asia, with its diversity of nations, societies, political systems, and security interests, is not ripe for regionalism and pan-regional cooperation, but this earlier prognosis seems to have been premature. Although cooperation in Asia is still nascent and a long way from the level of regional cooperation to be found in Europe or North or South America, a number of subregional organizations and dialogue groupings have nonetheless sprouted in Asia in recent years, including ASEAN Plus One (ASEAN and China), ASEAN

Plus Three (ASEAN, China, Japan, and South Korea), the ASEAN Regional Forum, the ASEAN Vision Group, the ASEAN Senior Officials Meeting (SOM), the Shanghai Cooperation Organization (SCO), the Pacific Basin Economic Council (PBEC), and others. Although limited to East Asian and Pacific Rim nations, APEC (the Asia-Pacific Economic Cooperation group) is the only true regional intergovernmental organization, while ASEM (the Asia-Europe Meeting) has emerged as something of a counterpart linking Asia and Europe together, while the East Asia–Latin American Cooperation Forum, established in 1999, does the same for these two continents. In late 2003 China also proposed that an annual Security Policy Conference be held within the ARF framework at the vice-ministerial or ARF senior official level.[27] There are also a host of nongovernmental "Track II" groups and dialogues active in the region, most notably the Council on Security Cooperation in the Asia-Pacific (CSCAP), the Northeast Asia Security Cooperation Dialogue (NEASCD), and the Shangri-la Dialogue (convened in Singapore).

China is active in all of these, and has even launched its own regional dialogue mechanism, the Boao Forum, which meets annually at a large convention site on Hainan Island.[28] The 2003 and 2004 sessions were attended by numerous heads of government and more than one thousand delegates from around the region. As noted above, China's involvement in these organizations and forums has grown progressively more comfortable and active since the late 1990s.[29] This increased level of involvement reflects many factors, particularly the fact that these are not intrinsically hostile groups aimed at containing or constraining China. Quite to the contrary, China has begun to realize that these groupings are amenable to China's perspectives and influence, and may also have some utility in constraining American dominance in the region.[30]

Of these regional organizations, China has become most deeply involved with ASEAN and the SCO. As the former director general of the Department of Asian Affairs in China's Ministry of Foreign Affairs noted, "Taking the East Asian 10 + 3 cooperation and SCO as two focal points, China will make pioneering efforts to set up regional cooperation and push for the establishment of a regional cooperation framework conforming to the characteristic of regional diversity."[31]

The SCO was formally established in June 2001 and grew out of the so-called "Shanghai Five" grouping created by China in 1994. Today the SCO is comprised of China, Russia, Tajikistan, Kazakhstan, Kyrgyzstan, and Uzbekistan. Reflecting China's instrumental role and influence, a permanent secretariat headquarters, largely paid for by China, is being established in Beijing.[32] The organization has an office, located in Biskek, Uzbekistan, to coordinate counterterrorism efforts.

From its inception, the SCO and its predecessor have focused primarily on nontraditional security threats in the Central Asian region, particularly counterterrorism. The SCO also did much in the mid-1990s to institute a range of confidence-building and security measures (CBSMs) among the member states, particularly in their mutual border regions. Two landmark treaties were signed by member states: the Agreement on Confidence Building in the Military Field along the Border Areas (1996) and the Agreement on the Mutual Reduction of Military Forces in the Border Areas (1997). The signatories agreed to force reductions limiting each to a maximum of 130,400 troops, 3,900 tanks, and 4,500 armored vehicles within one hundred kilometers of each mutual border. In addition, the agreements prohibited military exercises exceeding 40,000 personnel; required that prior notification be given before exercises involving more than 35,000 personnel, and that observers from other member states must be invited to monitor them; and limited exercises involving 25,000 personnel or more to one a year. Since the treaties were signed, the members have begun to engage in cross-border military and counterterrorism exercises. When China participated in these in 2002, it was the first time in the history of the People's Liberation Army (PLA) that it had engaged in a joint military exercise. Although it is highly unusual—even unprecedented—for China to participate in organizations whose primary purpose is security cooperation, Beijing saw an important opportunity to engage Russia and the Central Asian states in the post-Soviet period in an effort to stabilize its northern periphery, from whence China's security threats have traditionally come.

More recently, the SCO has begun to evolve into a broader and more comprehensive organization, reflecting Beijing's goal of building "comprehensive strategic partnerships." At its 2003 annual meeting, the SCO broadened its focus to include economic cooperation. At the meeting Chinese premier Wen Jiabao proposed setting up a free trade zone among members, and Wen set forth series of proposals to reduce nontariff barriers in a variety of areas. The political interaction among SCO members is also extensive. In addition to the annual summit and frequent bilateral state visits, SCO ministerial-level officials meet and consult on a regular basis, and a large number of joint working groups have been established at the functional working level. China and Russia alone have established thirty-five such working groups.[33]

China's engagement with ASEAN (and vice versa) is equally impressive, if not more so. Over the last few years China and ASEAN have jointly undertaken a series of important steps to build their relationship. Several of these steps are of considerable significance for the international relations of the entire Asian region.

At their landmark summit in November 2002 China and ASEAN signed four key agreements: the Declaration on Conduct of Parties in the South China Sea,[34] the Declaration on Cooperation in the Field of Non-Traditional Security Issues,[35] the Framework Agreement on Comprehensive Economic

Cooperation,[36] and the Memorandum of Understanding on Agricultural Cooperation.[37] Of further importance, at their October 2003 summit China formally acceded to ASEAN's Treaty of Amity and Cooperation,[38] becoming the first non-ASEAN nation to do so (India subsequently followed suit). This unprecedented accession commits China to the core elements of ASEAN's 1967 charter. Having also signed the Declaration of Conduct on the South China Sea, China has now formally committed itself to nonaggression, non-interference, and a variety of other conflict resolution mechanisms. At the same Bali summit, the ASEAN and China signed the Joint Declaration on Strategic Partnership for Peace and Prosperity,[39] which sets out wide-ranging areas of cooperation in the political, social, economic, and security fields. Separate protocols have also been concluded in the areas of human resource development, public health, information and communication technology, transportation, development assistance, the environment, cultural and academic exchanges, and codevelopment of the Mekong River Basin. These agreements are all of considerable significance, but perhaps the most significant was the Framework Agreement on Economic Cooperation and Establishment of an ASEAN-China Free Trade Area (FTA), agreed upon at the 2001 ASEAN-China Summit and amended at the 2002 Summit.[40] This agreement has done much to address Southeast Asian concerns about the potential for their economies to be eclipsed and displaced by China.[41] With total ASEAN-China trade growing rapidly ($78.2 billion in 2003),[42] Chinese premier Wen Jiabao set $100 billion as a target to be achieved by 2005.[43] Premier Wen further opined that by 2010, when the FTA comes fully into effect, the member states will likely have a combined population of two billion and collective GDP of $3 trillion.[44] There is little doubt that there are tremendous economic complementarities as well as redundancies between China and ASEAN, and that two-way trade and investment can be expected to grow healthily in coming years.[45]

There are further indications of China's increased involvement in Southeast Asia. First, Beijing once offered to mediate between the government of Myanmar (Burma), ASEAN, the United Nations, and Western countries to try to break the deadlock over the status of Nobel laureate Aung San Suu Kyi and the Burmese junta's international isolation.[46] Second, China's relationship with Vietnam, with which it fought a border war in 1979, has markedly improved in recent years (see below).

All in all, China and ASEAN are forging a productive and lasting relationship that erases the memories and tensions of the past.[47] It is more than merely a "charm offensive," as Beijing has committed itself to some fundamental compromises that enmesh China in multilateral frameworks and regional interdependencies.[48] Neither have the Southeast Asian states entered into these arrangements with their eyes closed. As former *Far Eastern Economic Review* editor Michael Vatikiotis aptly notes, "Steeped in a long historical experience of dealing with a more powerful imperial China, the region is well equipped for the emergence of China as a superpower in the 21st century."[49]

China also seems quite realistic about the not-always-positive history of its relations with Southeast Asian countries. For example, a major study of post–Cold War ASEAN policy toward China compiled by many of China's leading Southeast Asia experts is quite candid and reflective about China's past interventions in the region and the lingering distrust they bred.[50] It cites the attempts to export "leftism" during the Cultural Revolution, support for regional armed insurgencies, manipulation of overseas Chinese *(huaqiao),* and historical memories of the Chinese empire as legacies that China needs to understand and overcome. In the contemporary, post–Cold War period, it notes the ill will bred by China's "uncompromising" stance on the South China Sea and Taiwan issues, China's military modernization, and the economic challenge that a "South China Economic Circle" (composed of Southern China, Hong Kong, and Taiwan) poses to ASEAN economies. The study also correctly notes that ASEAN seeks to maintain close ties to the United States, so as not to be drawn into a Chinese sphere of influence, and that most ASEAN states believe that "U.S. predominance is conducive to the regional balance and stability."[51]

Taken together, China's expanded engagement with ASEAN and the SCO, as well as with other East Asian organizations, reveals one key element of the PRC's enhanced regional profile that can also be seen in China's bilateral ties.

IMPROVING BILATERAL TIES

This is not the place to chronicle China's ties all around its periphery, as this is done in considerable detail elsewhere in this volume. It is instructive, however, to consider the dramatic improvement in China's relations with three nations with which it had minimal interaction, or even hostile relations, just a decade ago: South Korea, Vietnam, and India.

China and South Korea. China's relations with South Korea have been dramatically transformed over the past decade.[52] Government-to-government ties are intensive. The prime ministers of the two countries have held reciprocal summits each year, ministerial-level officials interact regularly, and even the two militaries engage in increasingly regular and deep exchanges. Today, China is the ROK's largest trading partner, while South Korea ranks number three in China's trade profile. Trade between the two nations totaled $63.2 billion in 2003.[53] The ROK is the fifth largest foreign direct investor in China. More than one million South Koreans visited China in 2002, while approximately half that many (490,000) Chinese visited South

Korea. There are currently 60,000 long-term South Korean residents in China. Of these, approximately 36,000 are students. In the most recent academic year (2002–2003), China had a total of approximately 78,000 foreign students studying in Chinese universities, and nearly half were from South Korea.[54] Approximately 10,000 South Korean companies operate in China, many having representative offices in addition to production facilities. Each week seven hundred air flights shuttle back and forth between the two countries. South Korean businessmen regularly fly over for a day's business and return by evening. Shipping links are also numerous.

China's strategy for building ties with South Korea is born not only of economic motive, but also strategic calculus. Since the rapprochement more than a decade ago, Beijing realized that it would have little leverage is shaping the eventual outcome of the divided Korean peninsula if it didn't enjoy strong ties with the south. Such ties would also serve to offset any potential threat from the U.S.-ROK alliance and U.S. forces on the peninsula. They would also serve to undercut or offset Japanese attempts to gain a stronger foothold on the peninsula. Beijing's strategy has been a net success, and it has benefited both China and South Korea. Ties between the two countries have also become a central leg in the new dynamics of power in Northeast Asia.

China and Vietnam.   China's relations with Vietnam have similarly transformed, albeit not as dramatically. Since China and Vietnam renormalized diplomatic relations in 1991, progress has been made in broadening state-to-state, party-to-party, and military ties.[55] There are now annual meetings between the heads of state and about one hundred working visits at the ministerial or vice-ministerial level every year. In February 1999 the two governments signed the Agreement on Friendship, Good Neighborliness, and Longstanding Stability. During a state visit by former Chinese president Jiang Zemin in February 2002, a four-point "framework to develop ties" was agreed upon. It entailed:

- Political exchanges at a variety of levels;
- The exchange of experiences about economic development;
- Youth exchanges (China created a 120,000 RMB fund for this purpose);
- The strengthening of cooperation in international and regional forums.

Sino-Vietnamese economic ties are also improving, although the volume of trade remains low. Bilateral trade tripled from $1.1 billion in 1996 to $3 billion in 2001, and reached $4.6 billion in 2003. Vietnam mainly exports marine products and oil and gas to China, while importing from China machinery, fertilizers, and consumer durables. China also provides low-interest loans (101 million RMB since 1991) to upgrade factories, mainly iron and steel plants, previously built by China. Altogether, China has invested $330 million in 320 joint venture projects in Vietnam. With respect to territorial issues, the two countries signed a treaty on the land border in December 1999, and another on the sea boundary in the Gulf of Tonkin in December 2000. They have also established a forum for discussion of unresolved conflicts related to the disputed Paracel and Spratly Islands, and both are signatories to the Code of Conduct between China and ASEAN.

Relations between the Chinese and Vietnamese Communist Parties were also normalized in 1991, and now every year the party leaders meet (although in China's case the state president and the party general secretary are one and the same). Hu Jintao has visited Vietnam twice, most recently as the head of a CCP delegation to the VCP's Ninth Congress in 2001. There are also numerous exchanges between the VCP's External Relations Department and the CCP's International Department. In addition, the two central party schools have exchanges of faculty and joint conferences.

Finally, there are irregular exchanges between the ministers of defense, as well as between individual departments and services. In addition, the Chinese People's Liberation Army (PLA) Chengdu and Guangzhou Military Region (MR) commanders meet their counterparts (First, Second, and Third MRs in Vietnam) annually, as well as military district commanders. There are exchanges of military staff colleges, too. In 2001 a Chinese naval ship made its first port call to Vietnam. The two militaries are involved in joint search-and-rescue missions at sea, and participate in cross-border anti-smuggling operations. There are no agreements about prior notification of exercises in the border region, but each side tries to provide it in advance.

China and India.   Perhaps one of the most important, yet least recognized, international events of 2003 was the state visit to China paid by Indian prime minister Atal Bihari Vajpayee. The capstone of a decade-long gradual rapprochement, punctuated by the political fallout from India's nuclear tests in 1998, the visit symbolized one of the most critical developments in Asian affairs.

Indian prime minister Vajpayee and Chinese premier Wen Jiabao signed the overarching Declaration on Cooperation and a total of nine separate protocols for different spheres of bilateral cooperation—thus fully normalizing relations and pledging that their countries would work together for regional stability and peace.[56] Progress was even made on their long-standing and difficult mutual boundary dispute as they codified the Agreement on the Actual Line of Control and agreed to exchange high-level emissaries to negotiate a final settlement of the thirty-four-year dispute. Once the 4,500-kilometer border is fully demarcated and delimited, China will have resolved all of its border disputes. India also reiterated its acknowledgment that Tibet is part of China and promised not to support any "splittist" activities undertaken by Tibetan exiles in India. Trade between the two countries, although only $7.6 billion in 2003, is expected to grow quickly (between 2002 and 2003 bilateral trade jumped 53.6 percent).[57]

All in all, the Sino-Indian Summit represented the final piece in the puzzle of China's blitz in peripheral diplomacy in recent years. China has now turned all of its former adversarial relationships—with Russia, South Korea, Vietnam, and India—into positive partnerships. This not only benefits the countries concerned, but also removes key sources of tension from the region.

ECONOMIC TIES

Perhaps the most noteworthy dimension of China's new engagement with the Asian region is in the economic domain. According to official Chinese customs statistics, in 2003 trade between China and the rest of Asia topped $495 billion, up 36.5 percent from 2002.[58] This growth was stimulated particularly by sharp rises in China's imports from around the region, which jumped 42.4 percent in 2003 to $272.9 billion.[59] China's imports from other East Asian countries more than doubled from 1995 to 2002, rising from $72 billion to $161 billion.[60] In 2003 alone China's imports from Japan leapt by 38.7 percent, from South Korea 51 percent, from ASEAN 51.7 percent, and from India 87 percent.[61] Today nearly half of China's total trade volume is intraregional, and it is relatively balanced (unlike China's trade with the West).

Despite this rapid and impressive growth in China's intraregional trade, China is a very long way from dominating East Asian trade patterns. According to 2002 data, total regional imports from China are estimated to amount to only 9 percent, while imports from Japan amounted to 17 percent and imports from the United States 18 percent.[62] Although China's trade with some Asian countries is quite developed and growing quickly, with others it remains quite underdeveloped, as is evident in table 1.

Not only is China increasingly trading with its neighbors and receiving foreign direct investment (FDI) from them (an estimated 70 percent of China's inbound FDI originates in Asia), but Chinese companies are also investing in the region. China's outbound direct investment (ODI) to other East Asian countries totaled approximately $1.2 billion in 2001,[63] out of a total of an estimated $7.1 billion globally.[64] Some estimate that it reached the $3–4 billion range in 2003. Another estimate, based on a careful analysis of Chinese government statistics, indicates that China's ODI to the entire Asian region, including India but excluding Russia and Central Asia, totaled $1.57 billion in 2001, representing 39 percent of China's global ODI.[65] In ASEAN countries alone, by the end of 2001 China had invested

TABLE 1. China's Trade with Neighboring Countries, 2003

	Total trade volume (U.S.$)
Afghanistan ·	27 million
Australia	13.56 billion
Bangladesh	1.36 billion
Dem. Republic of North Korea	1.02 billion
India	7.59 billion
Indonesia	10.2 billion
Japan	133.57 billion
Kazakhstan	3.28 billion
Laos	109.4 million
Malaysia	20.12 billion
Mongolia	439.8 million
Myanmar	1.07 billion
Nepal	127.3 million
New Zealand	1.82 billion
Pakistan	2.42 billion
Philippines	9.4 billion
Republic of Korea	63.23 billion
Russia	15.7 billion
Singapore	19.3 billion
Sri Lanka	524.2 million
Tajikistan	38.8 million
Thailand	12.65 billion
Vietnam	4.63 billion

SOURCE: China's General Administration of Customs, published in Ministry of Foreign Affairs of the People's Republic of China, *China's Foreign Affairs 2004* (Beijing: World Affairs Press, 2004).

in 740 projects, with a total accumulated investment of $1.091 billion, of which $655 million is direct Chinese investment.[66] China has also recently begun to increase its aid and development assistance to other Asian nations, allocating loans of $150 million for Vietnam, $400 million for Indonesia, $200 million for Afghanistan, and $200 million for Myanmar (Burma) in 2002.[67]

Taken together, China's inbound and outbound trade and FDI are quickly becoming the engine of regional economic growth in Asia, and China now supplements Japan as the "lead goose" in a new model of regional development.[68] This gives Asian countries a huge stake in China's continued economic growth and stability, although some have continuing reservations that China's comparative economic advantages of labor and capital combined with the business acumen of Chinese companies and government negotiators will never permit a level playing field on which smaller Asian countries can effectively compete with China. While Premier Wen Jiabao describes China as a "friendly elephant" only interested in win-win commercial ties with its neighbors, other Asian nations worry that an elephant, no matter how friendly, will leave trampled grass in its wake.[69]

CHINA AND REGIONAL SECURITY

The final area in which China's new approach to Asia is evident is security, both conventional (military) and nonconventional. These issues are more fully explored elsewhere in this volume, but here I will note several distinct aspects of China's emerging regional security posture, which can be divided into three categories: unilateral, bilateral, and multilateral activities.

First, China's regional security posture is evident in its own military modernization program, which is being undertaken unilaterally, without great concern for the interests or concerns of China's neighbors. There are two primary "drivers" for this military modernization program: (1) the desire to build and deploy a comprehensively modern military commensurate with China's status as a major power; and (2) the desire to build certain capabilities with various Taiwan military scenarios in mind. In my view, *both* considerations drive China's military modernization program, while the demands of each determine certain choices in the allocation of resources, weapons procurement, training, and organization of the PLA.

To be sure, China's military modernization program is a large and complex undertaking with many different dimensions.[70] Of key importance to China's neighbors is, first, the development of power-projection capabilities and the doctrine that would underlie it, and, second, the potential for the use of force against Taiwan. The potential for China, having acceded to the Code of Conduct on the South China Sea and the Treaty of Amity and Cooperation with ASEAN, to use force in the South China Sea now seems considerably dissipated, but the development of power projection and the possible use of force over Taiwan are still real concerns for China's neighbors.

With respect to power-projection capabilities, there does not seem to be much progress being made by the PLA in this area, nor does it seem to be much of a priority. No aircraft carrier battle groups are being built, few new and truly "blue water" surface combatants have been built and deployed in recent years, no long-range bombers are being built or deployed, no airborne command-and-control aircraft have been procured (although this is under negotiation with Russia), no military bases are being acquired abroad, very little training over water or far from China's shores is occurring, nor is there any apparent doctrine that would guide such a forward force projection capability. Nor is it clear that the PLA Air Force (PLAAF) has mastered the in-flight refueling of its fighters, a necessary capability for projecting sustained air power. It is true that the PLA Navy (PLAN) has procured a number of Kilo-class conventional attack submarines from Russia and is building its own new 093 and 094 classes of SSN and SSBN subs, and it is also true that the PLAN has now deployed three marine brigades on Hainan Island, but these capabilities must be seen in the light of potential Taiwan scenarios. Thus, in my view, the PLA has not yet developed (or even placed a priority on developing) a power-projection capability.

What the PLA *has* done, and what *is* of concern to China's neighbors, is to build up various military capabilities for potential use, in a number of different contingencies, against Taiwan. The PLA's actions are well known:

·   Deploying approximately seven hundred short-range ballistic missiles (SRBMs) opposite Taiwan (it is also modernizing its intermediate and intercontinental range missile force);
·   Deploying large numbers of attack fighters opposite Taiwan;
·   Building up surface and submarine deployments within range of Taiwan;
·   Conducting frequent, often large-scale exercises around Taiwan;
·   Refusing to foreswear the possible use of force against Taiwan.

Although this buildup is clearly directed at Taiwan, China's other neighbors are also watching these developments closely, and they rightly worry about the very negative impact on regional security and stability that would result should China decide to use force or coercion against the island.

These unilateral developments in China's military are simultaneously cause for relief and concern among China neighbors (although they are certainly cause for concern on Taiwan). Although China's overall regional military posture does not seem to demonstrate a drive for power projection, and this is reassuring, China nonetheless possesses a navy and air force that numerically exceeds that of any other country in the region—and its entire force structure is becoming more modern and professional by the day.

Yet, thus far, China has been able to offset these unilateral moves, some of which provoke concern in the region, with a series of bilateral and multilateral confidence-building measures. In the bilateral and multilateral realms, China has engaged in five principal types of security activities in the region.

The first is the establishment of bilateral governmental "security dialogues" with some neighboring countries. To date, these have been initiated with Australia, Thailand, Vietnam, Mongolia, Japan, South Korea, Pakistan, India, Kazakhstan, and Kyrgyzstan. They occur once per year, in alternating capitals, with participation of both civilian (Foreign Ministry) and military (PLA) personnel. China also participates in a number of unofficial "Track II" security dialogues, usually undertaken on the Chinese side by the China Institute of International Strategic Studies (CIISS) or the China Foundation for International Strategic Studies (FISS), which are both affiliated with the PLA General Staff's Second Department (Intelligence).

The second type is official military-military exchanges. In recent years, China has stepped up its regional exchanges of delegations,[71] and China's navy has stepped up exchanges of port calls with other regional navies. China has also demonstrated a recent willingness to engage, for the first time since 1949, in bilateral military exercises with other nations. During 2003 joint exercises were undertaken with Kazakhstan, Pakistan, and India. In the latter two cases, the respective navies undertook joint naval search-and-rescue exercises off China's coast; in the case of Kazakhstan, the joint exercises were cross-border counterterrorism drills.

A third form has been China's increased willingness to participate actively in the ASEAN Regional Forum (ARF). China has become much more proactive in the ARF since 2001 and sees it as a potential basis for establishing a regional cooperative security community. At the 2004 Boao Forum China's president Hu Jintao asserted that China "will give full play to existing multilateral security mechanisms. China is ready to set up a security dialogue mechanism with other Asian countries and actively promote confidence-building cooperation in the military field."[72] This statement reflects China's overall embrace of multilateral cooperative security mechanisms. At the November 2003 ARF Inter-Sessional Group (ISG) meeting, China startled other members by tabling a wide-ranging set of proposals for increased regional military exchanges and establishing an annual Security Policy Conference (SPC), in which China is prepared to discuss a range of issues it was previously unwilling to entertain in such a regional forum, such as future challenges to regional security, military strategies and doctrines of member states, the Revolution in Military Affairs (RMA) and defense modernization in the region, the role of regional militaries in nontraditional security, defense conversion, civil-military relations, and other unspecified issues.[73] ASEAN quickly realized the importance of China's proposal and moved promptly to consolidate the initiative.[74] This paper was adopted by the ARF at its July 2004 meeting, and the first SPC convened in November of the same year. Chinese security specialists have also floated the idea of forming an East Asian Security Community (EASC), built upon the ARF, which would better institutionalize security dialogue and cooperation throughout East Asia.[75] Another recent idea, gaining some currency in Beijing, is to convert the Six-Party Talks (concerned with the North Korean nuclear program) into some kind of permanent entity in Northeast Asia.

Fourth, China has gradually increased its military transparency, as indicated through the publication of defense white papers in recent years. This has come about in part because of consistent urging by ASEAN, Australia, Japan, and South Korea, as well as by Western governments. Discussions with PLA and Foreign Ministry personnel suggest that it was ASEAN's encouragement and pressure that particularly prompted China to issue these documents and gradually improve its military transparency.[76]

In all of these ways, Beijing's confidence and level of involvement in regional security affairs have grown considerably in the last few years.[77] This does not mean that regional concerns about China's rise have melted away,[78] but they have apparently dissipated considerably as a result of China's new engagement in the aforementioned security realms. China's promulgation of its "new security concept" (NSC) after 1998 has also enhanced its image in the region, particularly insofar as it thematically dovetails with ASEAN's own normative approaches to cooperative security and conflict management. The NSC is premised on the principles of mutual trust, mutual benefit, equality, cooperation, and the resolution of differences in a peaceful manner. In his 2004 Boao Forum speech, China's president Hu Jintao supplemented these guiding principles by asserting that China "hopes to establish a security relationship and cooperation featuring non-alignment, non-confrontation, and non-targeting at any third party."[79]

CONCLUSION

In all of the ways discussed in this chapter, China's new regional posture is evident. The development of this new posture is still a very fluid and ongoing process, and China remains a long way from achieving preeminence or dominance in the region, but its power and influence are growing steadily.

Although China's posture of late has been largely reassuring to the region, its past behavior has not always been so. Long memories, residual concerns, and irredentist issues remain. Then, of course, there are more traditional, realist, balance-of-power concerns about a rising power, and as a consequence several regional states appear to be practicing various types of "hedging" strategies. Finally, no Asian states (except perhaps North Korea) wish to see the American presence and role in Asia diminished. None wish to be put in the position of having to choose between Beijing and Washington, and all wish to see the United States remain fully engaged, and militarily deployed, in the Asia-Pacific region.

At the end of the day, the future of international politics in the Asian region will rest on the relationship between the United States and China. Asia is certainly big enough for both powers to exercise their influence and power. And although some neoconservative observers in the United States believe that there is an inherent and inevitable structural conflict between the United States and China in the region, and even globally, this is not necessarily the case. On balance, the United States and China find themselves on the same side of many of the key issues affecting the future of the Asian region. This augurs well for opportunities for tangible cooperation between the two governments. If the two powers have a positive and cooperative bilateral relationship, manage their difficulties well, and keep the Taiwan issue in check, this will only strengthen the stability, security, and development of the region. Conversely, China's integration into the region will condition Sino-American relations and lend powerful forces for stability in that relationship. In short, the relationship between China, the United States, and other states of the Asian region is a positive-sum development.

All nations in the region, including the United States, must adjust to the various and complex realities presented by China's ascent. It is not intrinsically something to be feared or opposed, although many may wish to hedge against potentially disruptive consequences. Moreover, China's own preferences may well coincide with those of its neighbors and the United States, which provides ample opportunities for mutual and regional collaboration to resolve problems and challenges. Integrating China into the regional order has been a longstanding goal of ASEAN, China, and the United States. Now that it is coming to pass, the United States should welcome China's place at the regional table and the constructive role that Beijing is increasingly playing in addressing regional challenges. If anything, it is the United States, with its strong preference for bilateralism and alliances, that is increasingly not taking a seat at the regional table and is seen to be myopically pursuing its singular war on terrorism to the exclusion of most other regional and global challenges. If America's influence in regional problem solving declines and China's rises, it will have as much to do with Washington "opting out" as with Beijing "opting in."

NOTES

1. The "peaceful rise theory" was first put forward by Zheng Bijian at the 2003 Boao Forum; see http://www.boaoforum.org. See also Xu Jian, "A Peaceful Rise: China's Strategic Option," *International Studies* (March 2004): 1–20.

2. See Jane Perlez, "The Charm from Beijing: China Strives to Keep Its Backyard Tranquil," *New York Times*, October 8, 2003; Jane Perlez, "Asian Leaders Find China a More Cordial Neighbor: Beijing's Soaring Economy Weakens U.S. Sway," *New York Times*, October 18, 2003; Editorial, "China's More Nuanced Diplomacy," *New York Times*, October 14, 2003; Philip Pan, "China's Improving Image Challenges U.S. in Asia," *Washington Post*, November 15, 2003; Michael Vatikiotis and Murray Hiebert, "How China Is Building an Empire," *Far Eastern Economic Review*, November 20, 2003.

3. Morton Abramowitz and Stephen Bosworth, "Adjusting to the New Asia," *Foreign Affairs* 82, no. 4 (July–August 2003): 119–31; David C. Kang, "Getting Asia

Wrong: The Need for New Analytical Frameworks," *International Security* 27, no. 4 (Spring 2003): 57–85.

4. Fu Ying, "China and Asia in the New Period," *Foreign Affairs Journal* 69 (September 2003): 1. A similar version of this article was published as "China and Asia in a New Era," *China: An International Journal* 1, no. 2 (September 2003): 304–12.

5. S. N. M. Abdi, "China, India to Resume Border Talks Next Week," *South China Morning Post,* January 6, 2004. Also see Srikanth Kondapalli, "India-China Border Issues and Confidence Building Measures: An Assessment," paper presented at the Shanghai Institute of International Studies, November 12, 2003.

6. Among others who make this argument, see Evan Medeiros and M. Taylor Fravel, "China's New Diplomacy," *Foreign Affairs* 82, no. 6 (November–December 2003): 22–35.

7. The volume of official exchanges is far surpassed by a wide range of nonofficial business, tourist, and student exchanges.

8. Data derived from "Table of Overseas Students Accepted by China from Countries Having Diplomatic Ties with China (2003)," Ministry of Foreign Affairs, *China's Foreign Affairs 2004* (Beijing: World Affairs Press, 2004), 577–80.

9. See Asia-Pacific Center for Security Studies, *Asia's China Debate: A Special Assessment* (Honolulu: Asia-Pacific Center for Security Studies, 2003).

10. Conversation with Chinese policy analyst, October 19, 2003, Beijing.

11. For an excellent survey of the period and different regional reactions, see Seiichiro Takagi, "The Asia-Pacific Nations: Searching for Leverage," in *Making China Policy,* ed. Ramon H. Myers, Michel C. Oksenberg, and David Shambaugh (Lanham, MD: Rowman and Littlefield, 2001), 241–68.

12. Ibid. See also Seiichiro Takagi, "Human Rights in Japanese Foreign Policy: Japan's Policy Towards China After Tiananmen," in *Human Rights and International Relations in the Asia-Pacific Region,* ed. James T. H. Tang (London: Pinter, 1995).

13. This is well chronicled in Alastair Iain Johnston and Robert S. Ross, eds., *Engaging China: The Management of an Emerging Power* (London: Routledge, 1999).

14. See Lee Kuan Yew, *From Third World to First: The Singapore Story, 1965–2000* (Singapore: Straits Times Press, 2000), chapters 39–40.

15. For excellent analyses of Chinese thinking about such organizations, see Alastair I. Johnston and Paul Evans, "China's Engagement with Multilateral Security Institutions," in *Engaging China: The Management of an Emerging Power,* chapter 10; Jing-dong Yuan, "Regional Institutions and Cooperative Security: Chinese Approaches and Policies," *Korean Journal of Defense Analysis* 13, no. 1 (Autumn 2001): 263–94.

16. Conversation with Foreign Ministry official deeply involved in the ARF and CSCAP processes, November 6, 2003.

17. Interview with Cui Tiankai, June 11, 2004, Beijing.

18. This response was conveyed at high official levels as well as at regional forums. For example, at the 1999 Meeting of the East Asia Vision Group, ASEAN representatives informed their Chinese counterparts that relations between China and ASEAN could develop well if Beijing met two conditions: (1) it did not push ASEAN governments to break their alliances or security arrangements with the United States; and (2) it did not mobilize overseas Chinese *(huaqiao)* politically. Interview with Chinese representative, October 18, 2003, Beijing.

19. For an excellent analysis of this debate, see David Finkelstein, *China Reconsiders Its National Security: The Great Peace and Development Debate of 1999 (Alexandria, VA: CNA Corporation, 2000).*

20. Interviews with various Chinese international relations analysts, 2000–2003.

21. See my "New Stability in the U.S.-China Relations: Causes and Consequences," in *U.S.-China Relations in the Mid-Term: Scenarios and Implications,* ed. Jonathan D. Pollack (Newport, RI: U.S. Naval War College, 2004).

22. Department of Policy Planning, Ministry of Foreign Affairs, *China's Foreign Affairs, 2003* (Beijing: World Affairs Press, 2003), 12–41; Ba Zongtan, ed., *Zhongguo Guojia Anquan Zhanlue Wenti Yanjiu* [Research on issues in China's national security strategy] (Beijing: Junshi Kexueyuan Chubanshe, 2003), chapters 2, 3, and 5; China Institute of Contemporary International Relations, *Ya-Tai Zhanluechang* [The strategic arena in the Asia-Pacific] (Beijing: Shishi Chubanshe, 2002); China Institute of Contemporary International Relations, *Guoji Zhanlue yu Anquan Xingshi Pinggu* [Review of the international strategic and security situation] (Beijing: Shishi Chubanshe, 2004), chapter 7; Zhang Yunling and Sun Shihai, eds., *Ya-Tai Lanpishu: Ya-Tai Diqu Fazhan Baogao* [Blue Book on the Asia-Pacific: The Asia-Pacific Region Development Report, 2001] (Beijing: Shehui Kexue Wenzhai Chubanshe, 2002).

23. China Institute of Contemporary International Relations, *Guoji Zhanlue yu Anquan Xingxhi Nianjian Pinggu* (Beijing: Shishi Chubanshe, 2004).

24. See, for example, my "China's Military Views the World," *International Security* (Winter 1999–2000): 52–79

25. Tang Xizhong, Liu Shaohua, and Chen Benhong, *Zhongguo yu Zhoubian Guojia Guanxi* [China and relations with neighboring countries] (Beijing: Zhongguo Shehui Kexue Chubanshe, 2003).

26. The study distinguishes four different dimensions of China's national security: political, economic, cultural, and military. The authors found China to be secure and stable in all but the latter category.

27. "ARF Security Policy Conference—A Concept Paper for Discussion," paper presented by China to the ARF Inter-Sessional Group (ISG), November 20–22, 2003, Beijing.

28. See http://www.boaoforum/org.

29. See Xiao Chengfeng, "Cong Xin Diquzhuyi Shijiao Zhongguo Duobian Waijiao Zhanlue" [New regionalism and China's multilateral policy strategy], *Guoji Wenti Luntan* 34 (2004): 80–89.

30. For a useful discussion of China's growing involvement in regional multilateral organizations, see "Statement of Susan Shirk" before the U.S.-China Economic and Security Review Commission, February 12–13, 2004, available at http://www.uscc.gov.

31. Fu, "China and Asia in the New Period."

32. Louisa Lim, "China and Central Asia Boost Ties," September 24, 2003, available at http://news.bbc.co.uk/1/hi/world/asia-pacific/3130852.stm.

33. Interview with U.S. diplomat, October 20, 2003, Beijing.

34. "Declaration on the Conduct of Parties in the South China Sea," available at http://www.aseansec.org/13163.htm.

35. "Joint Declaration of ASEAN and China on Cooperation in the Field of Non-Traditional Security Issues," available at http://www.aseansec.org/13185.htm.

36. "Framework Agreement on Comprehensive Economic Cooperation Between the Association of Southeast Asian Nations and the People's Republic of China," available at http://www.aseansec.org/13196.htm.

37. "Memorandum of Understanding Between the ASEAN Secretariat and Ministry of Agriculture of the People's Republic of China," available at http://www.aseansec.org/13214.htm.

38. "Instrument of Accession to the Treaty of Amity and Cooperation in Southeast Asia," available at http://www.aseansec.org/15271.htm.

39. "Joint Declaration of the Heads of State/Government of ASEAN and the People's Republic of China on Strategic Partnership for Peace and Prosperity," available at http://www.aseansec.org/15265.htm.

40. "Framework Agreement on Comprehensive Economic Cooperation Between the Association of Southeast Asian Nations and the People's Republic of China," available at http://www.aseansec.org/13196.htm.

41. See John Wong and Sarah Chan, "China-ASEAN Free Trade Agreement: Shaping Future Economic Relations," *Asian Survey* (May–June 2003): 507–26.

42. Ministry of Foreign Affairs, *China's Foreign Affairs 2004*, 41.

43. Sun Shangwu, "Asia to Benefit as Ties Improve," *China Daily*, October 9, 2003.

44. John McBeth, "Taking the Helm," *Far Eastern Economic Review*, October 16, 2003.

45. See Michael Vatikiotis and Murray Hiebert, "China's Tight Embrace," *Far Eastern Economic Review*, July 17, 2003.

46. "China Offers to Mediate Deadlock in Myanmar," *International Herald Tribune*, October 22, 2003.

47. See Alice D. Ba, "China and ASEAN: Reinvigorating Relations for the 21st Century," *Asian Survey* (July–August 2003): 622–47.

48. See Amitav Acharya, "China, ASEAN, and the Asian Security Order," CSIS Freeman Chair in China Studies Report, August 2003, available at http://www.csis.org/china/index.htm; and Amitav Acharya, "China's Charm Offensive in Southeast Asia," *International Herald Tribune*, November 8–9, 2003.

49. See Michael R. J. Vatikiotis, "Catching the Dragon's Tail: China and Southeast Asia in the 21st Century," *Contemporary Southeast Asia* 25, no. 1 (April 2003): 77.

50. Chen Qiaozhi, ed., *Leng Zhan Hou Dongmeng Guojia dui Hua Zhengce Yanjiu* [Post–Cold War ASEAN policy towards China] (Beijing: Zhongguo shehui kexue chubanshe, 2001), chapter 1.

51. Ibid., 44.

52. The following figures were largely derived from a visit to Seoul in July 2003. Also see my "China and the Korean Peninsula: Playing for the Long Term," *Washington Quarterly* (Spring 2003): 43–56.

53. Ministry of Foreign Affairs, *China's Foreign Affairs 2004* (Beijing: Shijie Zhishi chubanshe, 2004), 575.

54. Chinese students in South Korean universities comprise a slightly higher percentage. For example, during the 2003–2004 academic year, 780 of the 1,200 foreign students at Seoul National University came from China. I am grateful to Kyoong-soo Loh for this information.

55. The following derives from a series of meetings in Hanoi during December 2002, with the Ministry of Foreign Affairs, Ministry of Defense, Vietnamese Com-

munist Party External Relations Department, Institute of International Relations, and Institute of Chinese Studies at the National Center for Social Sciences and Humanities.

56. "China, India Sign Nine Documents in Beijing," available at http://english .eastday.com/epublish/gb/paper1/class000100004/hwz143868.htm.

57. Ministry of Foreign Affairs, *China's Foreign Affairs 2004*, 41.

58. Ibid.

59. Ibid.

60. Ben Dolven and David Murphy, "Riding Out a Storm," *Far Eastern Economic Review*, October 9, 2003, 40.

61. Ministry of Foreign Affairs, *China's Foreign Affairs 2004*, 41.

62. Statement of Edward J. Lincoln, "East Asia and China," to the U.S.-China Economic and Security Review Commission, December 4, 2003, 83, available at http://www.uscc.gov.

63. Ministry of Foreign Trade and Economic Cooperation (MOFTEC), *Almanac of China's Foreign Relations and Trade 2002*, as quoted in *Japan Economic and Trade Research Organization (JETRO)*, China data File 2002/2003. I am indebted to Naoko Munakata for these data.

64. Michael Vatikiotis and David Murphy, "Birth of a Trading Empire," *Far Eastern Economic Review*, March 20, 2003, 28.

65. John Wong and Sarah Chan, "China's Outward Direct Investment: Expanding Worldwide," *China: An International Journal* 1, no. 2 (September 2003): 287.

66. Fu, "China and Asia in the New Period," 4

67. Joseph Kahn, "China at Korea Talks: Taking Diplomacy Upstage," *New York Times*, August 30, 2003; Raymond Bonner, "No Progress on Burmese Democracy," *International Herald Tribune*, September 15, 2003.

68. See Trish Saywell, "Powering Asia's Growth," *Far Eastern Economic Review*, August 2, 2001; "Why Europe Was the Past, the U.S. Is the Present, and a China-Dominated Asia Is the Future of the Global Economy," *Financial Times*, September 22, 2003.

69. Michael Vatikiotis, "A Too Friendly Embrace," *Far Eastern Economic Review*, June 17, 2004.

70. See my *Modernizing China's Military: Progress, Problems & Prospects* (Berkeley: University of California Press, 2002).

71. See, for example, "Chief of Staff Wraps Up Tour of Three Asian Countries," available at http://news.xinhuanet.com/mil/2003-09/20/con.

72. Hu Jintao, "China's Development Is an Opportunity for Asia," speech at the opening ceremony of the Boao Forum for Asia 2004 Annual Conference, April 24, 2004, available at www.chinaview.cn.

73. "ARF Security Policy Conference: A Concept Paper for Discussion (Draft)," paper presented by China to the ARF Inter-Sessional Group (ISG), November 20–22, 2003, Beijing.

74. Discussion with Indonesian security expert Jusuf Wanandi, July 2, 2004, Barcelona, Spain. Wanandi has been very involved in the ARF process for many years.

75. See Yan Xuetong and Liu Jiangyong, "Solidifying East Asian Security," *China Daily*, April 14, 2004.

76. Interviews, June 2004, Beijing.

77. See Yuan, "China's Engagement with Multilateral Security Institutions." Also see Wu Xinbo, *Prospect of Multilateral Security in the Asia-Pacific: A Chinese Perspective* (Washington, DC: Sasakawa Peace Foundation, 2000). For a broader assessment of China's participation in international organizations, see Wang Yizhou, ed., *Construction Within Contradiction* (Beijing: China Development Publishing House, 2003).

78. See Carolyn W. Pumphrey, ed., *The Rise of China in Asia: Security Implications* (Carlisle Barracks, PA: U.S. Army War College, 2002).

79. Hu, "China's Development is an Opportunity for Asia."

2

China's Regional Strategy

Zhang Yunling and Tang Shiping

In the past few years, both Chinese and foreign analysts have begun to reach the conclusion that China has developed a fairly consistent and coherent grand strategy in the past decade, even though they may disagree somewhat on the nature and content of that grand strategy.[1] Assuming that China's regional strategy reflects and supports China's grand strategy, this chapter will offer an assessment of China's regional strategy. Because China is a regional power with very limited global interests, we also presume that China's regional strategy largely corresponds to its grand strategy.

This chapter will first briefly describe China's grand strategy by elaborating its core ideas and practices. Second, it will offer an assessment of China's regional strategy, highlighting its goals, strategic thinking, and outcomes. Finally, it will draw some implications for the future of the region and U.S.-China relations.

ASSESSING CHINA'S GRAND STRATEGY

Because economic development is considered the only way to tackle all the pressing challenges that China is facing and will face, China's grand strategy must serve the central purpose of development.[2] Therefore, the central objective of China's grand strategy in the past two decades—a strategy that may well last to 2050—can be captured in just one phrase: to secure and shape a security, economic, and political environment that is conducive to China concentrating on its economic, social, and political development.

Conceptualizing China's Grand Strategy

Four core concepts underpin China's current grand strategy. The first can be traced back to Sun Yat-sen, the father of modern China. Chinese leaders since Sun's time have always believed that China rightly belongs to the "great power" *(da guo)* club by virtue of its size, population, civilization, history, and, more recently, its growing wealth. Even if China was not a great power during the past two centuries, China's current goal is to make China a great power again.

Secondly, Deng Xiaoping realized early on that China needs a stable and peaceful international environment for its "Four Modernizations" program to succeed. However, when he toured several Southeast Asian countries in 1978, Deng was surprised to find that not many of China's neighbors trusted China; China's communist political system, earlier policies of exporting revolution, and the sensitive issue of overseas Chinese in Southeast Asia had made many countries in the region suspicious of China's intentions. This made Deng realize that China's security conundrum in the 1960–70s had not been the work of external forces alone, but rather the product of the interaction between China's behavior and the outside world. Deng's realization was a momentous shift: in essence, he grasped the existence of the security dilemma.[3] Since then, this realization has exerted a profound influence on China's strategic thinking and behavior.[4]

The third concept is self-restraint, embodied in Deng's famous doctrine *buyao dangtou* (do not seek leadership).[5] In his numerous speeches between 1990 and 1992, Deng repeatedly warned his successors against actively seeking leadership in global or regional affairs and shouldering responsibilities that China cannot bear. In essence, Deng was preaching a doctrine of self-restraint.

The fourth concept began to take shape under Deng, but it developed more fully under Jiang Zemin, especially after the 1997 Asian financial crisis. Living in an increasingly interdependent world, many Chinese analysts and policy makers gradually came to realize that both China's economic welfare and its security depend heavily on its interaction with the outside world; therefore, China has to participate in world affairs more actively.[6] Yet joining the world not only affords China the opportunity for gain, but it also requires that China shoulder certain burdens and responsibilities. China thus has to behave as a "responsible great power" *(fuzeren de daguo)*.[7] Recognizing the existence of the security dilemma and exercising self-restraint are hallmarks of "defensive realism,"[8] while accepting interdependence as a fact of life and behaving responsibly are trademarks of neoliberalism.[9]

The Practice of China's Grand Strategy

Four features distinguish China's current practice of grand strategy. First, in accordance with its self-image as a great power, China has maintained an active "great power diplomacy" *(daguo waijiao)*. Its goal is to maintain a workable relationship with all major great powers and project an image of China as a great power both abroad and at home.[10] In particular, recognizing that the United States is the world's sole superpower and one of China's key providers of capital, technology, and market, China can ill afford to have an irreparable rupture in the Sino-U.S. relationship. Accordingly, China's great power diplomacy is very much oriented toward the United States. Chinese policy makers have worked hard to maintain a workable relationship with Washington, despite strong domestic opposition against being too accommodating of the United States, especially after incidents like the 1995–96 crisis in the Taiwan Strait, the 1999 bombing of the Chinese embassy in Belgrade, and the 2001 EP-3 spy plane incident.

Second, related to its recognition of the security dilemma and its understanding that the Sino-U.S. relationship will always have its ups and downs, China has pursued a strategy of maintaining amicable relationships with its neighbors *(mulin youhao, wending zhoubian)* to hedge against downturns in Sino-U.S. relations. Deng Xiaoping and his successors understand clearly that, with more than fifteen countries bordering China, an aggressive posture is simply not in China's interest, no matter how powerful China becomes, because aggression would lead to a counterbalancing alliance of China's neighbors and a distant power (the United States). If, however, China adopts a defensive realist approach, most regional countries would be reluctant to adopt a policy of hard containment, and thus China would likely enjoy a benign regional security environment. To this end, China has made strenuous efforts to improve its relationships with its neighboring countries, sometimes by making significant concessions despite strong domestic opposition.[11]

Third, since the early 1990s China has begun to take a more active stand in regional and global multilateral institutions and initiatives, even though China's embrace of multilateralism has been gradual and incomplete (every state is a limited multilateralist).[12] Moreover, understanding the difference between cooperation in economic and security arenas,[13] China has been more active in multilateral economic institutions than in security institutions. Therefore, while China has taken the lead in pushing forward some regional multilateral economic cooperation initiatives,[14] it has been less enthusiastic about moving from consultations and confidence-building measures (CBMs) to more codified and institutionalized security arrangements.[15] With China's "new security concept" *(xin anquan guandian)* emphasizing security cooperation measures such as CBMs rather than multilateral security institutions,[16] this reluctance is apparent.

Fourth, while China has gradually become more willing to shoulder certain responsibilities as required by the international community, it has been highly selective in choosing the sorts of responsibilities it is willing to accept. Ascribing to a traditional definition of sovereignty, China has consistently opposed international interventions unless a state requested such intervention and the intervention has the authorization of the United Nations.[17]

Because China is a regional power with limited global interests, China's regional strategy is, to a large extent, the core of its grand strategy, and both the ideas and practices of its regional strategy reflect the imperatives of its grand strategy.[18] Asia is the only region in which all aspects of China's national interest—security, economic, and political—are present. Therefore, the way that China pursues the objectives of its regional strategy—an integrated approach that simultaneously pursues security, economic, and political interests—cannot be easily applied to any other region (say, Africa or Europe).

The Security-Economic-Political Axis

China realizes that, in the security sphere, Asia is the region with the world's highest concentration of major power interaction. Accordingly, the number one goal of China's regional security strategy is to maintain at least a workable relationship with all the major powers in the region (the United States, Russia, Japan, and India) so that China will never again become isolated and encircled by great powers. Because China views the region as a shield from pressure exerted by other great powers, the second security goal of China's regional strategy is to maintain a cordial relationship with regional states in order to prevent a containment coalition led by any combination of the external great powers from emerging.

China understands that it is already a regional economic power, and its weight will continue to increase if its economy continues to grow. The challenge confronting China is how to make China's economic growth an opportunity for the region rather than a threat, so that regional states will not coalesce to thwart China's economic growth. Because of the prevalent perceptions that foreign direct investment (FDI) formerly going to ASEAN countries is now being sucked into China, and that China is gaining competitive advantages over ASEAN countries in many sectors,[19] China has to alleviate the fears of ASEAN and other countries in the region that China will pose undue economic challenges, which in turn could generate a more general fear of China. Increasingly, assuming neoliberalism's core belief that economic interdependence creates common interest and lessens the probability of conflict, China has decided that the best strategy is eventually to make China a locomotive for regional growth by serving as a market for regional states and a provider of investment and technology for the region.[20]

China understands that, politically, it will have only limited global influence for many decades to come,[21] and thus in the near term the main theater for China to exert its political influence will be the Asian region. Recognizing that it cannot expect to have a global voice if it cannot even be a regional political heavyweight, as part of its regional strategy, China seeks to establish the country as indispensable for addressing regional issues. Since political influence can only be effective when other states respect not only a nation's power but also its opinion, China reasons that the best way to achieve regional political influence is through cultivating an image as a responsible (regional) great power that is constructively involved in addressing and alleviating various regional issues.

Strategic Thinking and the Practice of China's Regional Strategy

Like its grand strategy, China's regional strategy is also underpinned by several important ideas. The first idea underpinning China's regional strategy is the desirability of seeking comprehensive cooperation and partnership relationships with all regional states. For instance, China's initial interaction with ASEAN came via the ARF, which remains quite security-oriented; lately, however, China has elevated its relationship with ASEAN to a strategic partnership by further developing its economic and political relationships through the ASEAN-China Free Trade Area (ACFTA) and the Treaty of Amity and Cooperation in Southeast Asia (TAC-SEA).[22] Likewise, China's relationship with Russia and Central Asian states used to be heavily security-oriented, but China has similarly been actively pursuing closer economic integration with Russia and Central Asian states under the framework of the Shanghai Cooperation Organization (SCO).[23] In contrast, China's relationship with South Korea was mostly commercial at the beginning, yet China has now developed a rather close, if not cordial, relationship with South Korea in the security and political arenas, too.[24] Similarly, participation in regional or subregional initiatives—such as the Kunming Initiative and the Greater Mekong Program—also aims to improve China's security and political relationships with regional countries like India and Vietnam.

The second idea is that the most effective way for China to show that it is a responsible power is to shoulder responsibilities placed upon it and to demonstrate its benign intentions by exercising self-restraint and displaying willingness to be restrained.[25] This idea has led directly to actions such as not devaluing the renminbi during the 1997 Asian financial crisis, joining the TAC-SEA, and largely letting ASEAN states dictate the norms regarding the South China Sea dispute.[26]

The third idea is that as long as the United States does not threaten China's core interests, China can live with a "hegemonic power" (although not with "hegemonic behavior").[27] Therefore, there is no need for China to counter the United States simply because the latter is powerful. Instead, China merely needs to work with others to restrain U.S. hegemonic behavior when America acts against international norms.[28] Following this logic, many experts in China have argued that as long as Washington acts like a responsible power and obeys international law and norms, it is in China's interest to integrate into the international system rather than remain an outsider. If China rises inside the system, rather than aiming for fundamental transformation of the system, not only will it have more influence on reshaping the future of the system, but it will also be more likely that China's rise is a peaceful one.[29] Chinese leaders and foreign policy experts have undertaken a careful survey of other rising powers in history in order to draw appropriate lessons and not repeat mistakes made by other great powers. Fundamentally, China wants a "peaceful rise" *(heping jueqi)*, and most Chinese elites believe that only an intrasystem rise can be a peaceful one.[30]

More importantly, China realizes that the U.S. presence in the region is useful to some extent, and that the U.S. security umbrella makes regional states more comfortable in dealing with China.[31] The result is that China has now publicly acknowledged and accepted the utility of the American presence in the region, as indicated by Chinese officials' repeated assurances to U.S. officials that "China does not wish to push the U.S. out of the region."

The fourth idea concerns China's regional economic development strategy. As China's economy expanded, Beijing had to choose between two alternative approaches for becoming more integrated with the rest of the region: China could follow the approach taken by Japan, investing in the region but keeping its domestic market largely closed, or the approach taken by the United States, opening its domestic market and creating interdependence. China decided that the U.S. approach was more appropriate and effective. By opening up its own market and letting regional states establish a commercial presence in China, Beijing also hopes that regional states will be more receptive to China's economic growth and consider it a greater opportunity than a threat.[32]

The fifth idea is embracing regional multilateralism. China's increased involvement in regional institutions demonstrates China's benign intentions and its willingness to have its power constrained; this is increasingly appreciated throughout Asia, and regional multilateralism is now accepted as one of the keys for China and regional states to comanage the rise of China and to shape the evolving regional order.[33] China's experience in the ARF and SCO also gave China more confidence in playing a more active role in regional multilateral platforms.[34] By embracing regional multilateral initiatives and channeling its growing power into a more institutionalized setting, China also hopes to make its closer relationship with regional states less alarming to the United States.

Finally, because of China's growing confidence in its ability to shape the regional environment, China is becoming more active on the global stage, including in multilateral institutions and the security arena.[35] With a new "fourth generation" of leadership in power in Beijing, the early indication is that this new activism will continue, and likely even increase.[36]

Practices and Outcomes

China's practice of regional strategy—which can be summarized as "participate actively, demonstrate restraint, offer reassurance, open markets, foster interdependence, create common interests, and reduce conflict"—is far more active, flexible, and comprehensive than ever before.[37] Clearly, among Chinese leaders and the policy elite there is general satisfaction with China's regional strategy and its largely positive outcomes to date.[38] This general satisfaction is also reflected in the writings of international affairs experts: most analysts agree that China's security environment is improving rather than deteriorating.[39]

In Southeast Asia, the interactions between ASEAN countries and China have led to a mitigation rather than an exacerbation of the security dilemma between them.[40] All ASEAN countries have explicitly rejected a containment approach toward China,[41] and emphasize that the ARF is not intended to contain China but merely to socialize China.[42] China, on the other hand, while aware of ASEAN's intention of constraining China through socialization, has actually come to recognize the utility of this approach because it can serve as a credible signal of reassurance to ASEAN states.

Of real importance, by signing the TAC-SEA and Declaration of Conduct in the South China Sea with ASEAN, China has renounced the option of force for settling disputes. And if ASEAN is indeed evolving toward a regional security community,[43] China has signaled that it may be interested in being part of that security community, too. By initiating a Free Trade Area (FTA) with ASEAN countries, China has indicated that it desires a more integrated regional economy. The result is that ASEAN countries and China are engaged in constructive cooperation and coexistence rather than confrontation.[44]

In Northeast Asia, China has dramatically improved its relationships with Russia, South Korea, and Mongolia and has managed to largely repair its estranged relationship with North Korea. Even with respect to the more difficult Sino-Japanese relationship, China has consistently pursued an accommodating relationship with Japan despite strong domestic opposition. The hotly contested domestic debate about China's policy toward Japan,[45] the continuing interest in a China–Japan–South Korea FTA,[46] and the call for letting ASEAN and South Korea bring China and Japan together under

"10 + 3"[47] all underscore that China understands that the future of the region depends upon a constructive relationship between China and Japan.[48] Therefore, while Japan and China are far from reaching a complete reconciliation for the time being, and their uneasy relationship remains a critical source of the uncertainty for the region, the probability of conflict between the two countries remains slim.[49]

China is adopting an approach toward Russia and Central Asia that is similar to the one it has adopted toward East Asia by developing a comprehensive relationship with regional states. By working closely with Russia and Central Asian states, China has successfully brought SCO through the storm of 9/11 in much better shape than most would have predicted. With economic integration now operating as its second leg, the SCO is becoming an anchor for stability in the Eurasian heartland. By pushing for economic integration in Central Asia, China again signaled its willingness to let Central Asian states share the opportunity associated with China's development, especially with its "Western Development" policy.

In South Asia, China has also achieved a breakthrough in its difficult relationship with India, although India continues to view China warily. There are three main dimensions to the improved Sino-Indian relationship. First of all, the geographic presence of the Himalayas renders the security dilemma between India and China less severe. Second, while China still treasures its close ties with Pakistan, China has not allowed Sino-Indian ties to be held hostage to Sino-Pakistan ties. Third, India, and especially those in its military, now recognize that China's challenge to India is more about economics than about security.[50] With trade between India and China increasing rapidly in recent years, it is possible to imagine that the two countries will find their shared interests to be substantial enough to warrant more effort toward reaching an accommodation on their border dispute in the next couple of years.

On the central question of U.S.-China relations, after the rocky period when the administration of George W. Bush took power, the relationship is now back on track, partly thanks to 9/11.[51] Although it is difficult to argue that there has been a qualitative shift in the relationship, a qualified optimism about the near-term prospects of the relationship exists in both capitals. With the United States deeply engaged in its war against terrorism, and China taking some of the responsibility for managing the North Korean crisis, both governments seem ready to let events play out for a little while so that they can gain a better understanding of the other side's intentions. The danger with this arrangement is, of course, that while they are cooperating well on regional and global issues, the Taiwan situation has worsened and contains significant dangers for derailing the otherwise positive relationship.

Overall, most Chinese policy elites agree that China's regional strategy, despite its imperfections, has proven very successful in recent years. Hence, one would expect the current strategy to continue, unless something dramatic alters its course.

THE FUTURE OF CHINA'S REGIONAL STRATEGY AND ITS IMPLICATIONS

What could change the current course of China's regional strategy? Two external factors, dynamically linked with the debate on "peace and development" inside China, will shape China's regional strategy in the future.[52]

U.S. Perceptions and U.S.-China Interactions

Because the United States remains at the center of China's strategic calculus, the first external factor that is going to influence the future of China's regional strategy is U.S. long-term strategic intentions toward China and how Washington views China's interaction with regional countries. What the United States is doing, plans to do, or even is rumored to do will influence China's behavior.[53]

In dealing with the United States, however, China faces a conundrum that cannot be easily overcome. Because there will always be voices inside the United States arguing that China will become an inevitable foe, and some, looking through the zero-sum prism, will continue to view any perceived or real increase of Chinese influence in the region as at least potentially detrimental to U.S. interests, China faces a difficult balancing act in dealing with regional states but reassuring Washington. If China actively participates in regional affairs and norms, some in the United States will take it as a sign that China is aiming to challenge U.S. dominance. At the same time, international politics is becoming more regional,[54] and this again puts China in a difficult situation.

There are three possible scenarios for how the U.S.-China relationship may evolve in a regional context. The first scenario is that even though many regional initiatives (for instance, the ARF and ASEAN Plus Three, or APT) were not originally China's idea, China has begun to actively participate in them for fear of being left out. As China increases its involvement in these bodies, the United States may deem that China and other Asian states are trying to exclude the United States from the region. Second, there are some regional programs that did evolve from China's initiatives, but these initiatives were actually designed to assure regional states of China's benign intentions (e.g., ASEAN-China FTA, and the recent ARF Security Policy Conference).[55] Nonetheless, because these initiatives originated with China, they arouse U.S. suspicions. Finally, there are initiatives (e.g., SCO) that are designed to limit U.S. influence.[56] The problem is that the United States will pay attention only to its exclusion, even though the SCO is a stabilizing force.[57]

On the other hand, over the years China has come to recognize that regional states are more qualified to comment on the "China threat" because of their geographical proximity and relatively smaller size (thus they are more vulnerable and sensitive), yet it is exactly in these countries that the China threat theory is losing its audience.[58] On the contrary, the global hegemon, the United States, tends to exaggerate other countries' capabilities and hostility, as it did in the case of the Soviet Union and Japan. Accordingly, China should pay less attention to rhetoric about the China threat coming out from the United States. This, in turn, causes many Chinese analysts to argue that China should pay more attention to working with regional states and putting the region in good order rather than appeasing the "Blue Team" in the United States. The rationale is that as long as regional states do not consider China a clear and present danger, and China and regional states can manage the region well, the United States will be hard pressed to forge a containment coalition. This means that regional states are becoming more important to China, and the weight of the United States in China's strategic calculus may face a reevaluation.[59]

With the United States taking active measures to hedge against or even contain China's rise, and China becoming less attentive to U.S. concerns when it believes it is acting together with regional states, both situations have potential to increase the mutual suspicion between the two countries, resulting in a classic security dilemma. This security dilemma will add yet another dimension of uncertainty to bilateral relations.

China's current grand and regional strategies do not rely upon pushing the United States out of Asia, not only because China lacks the capacity to do so, but also because China does not deem this to be in its own best interests or those of the region.[60] Chinese leaders now appreciate that the United States plays some indispensable constructive roles in the region. This recognition has led China to repeatedly reassure the United States that China does not want to expel the United States from China and welcomes their constructive presence in the region.[61]

Yet the picture from Washington is less clear. Despite the recent warming of the U.S.-China relationship and a few U.S. signals of assurance, especially on Taiwan, China is concerned about the possibility that those measures designed to contain China (outlined in the Pentagon's *Quadrennial Defense Review*, but put on hold because of September 11) will be resurrected when Washington finishes its business in Afghanistan and Iraq.

If the United States is serious about its engagement policy with China, then it must be ready to assure China that a certain increase in China's influence in the region need not be threatening, but could actually be desirable for long-term U.S. interests, as long as China plays according to international and regional norms and its influence is channeled through and within regional multilateral institutions. Indeed, as China becomes more integrated into the region, it becomes a pillar for long-term regional stability, and serves long-term U.S. interests far better than a China that remains a regional outcast.[62] Moreover, this recognition could actually gain the United States more respect, and thus more influence, in the region, because although Asian states do want the United States to stay engaged in the region, they do not want an unwarranted confrontation between the United States and China because of an active containment policy pursued by Washington.[63]

Such a recognition by Washington will demand a few fundamental changes in the American mentality and will require abandoning several self-propagated myths: (1) that because the United States is the "indispensable nation," it has to lead all global and regional initiatives all the time; (2) that China seeks to push the United States out of the region and reestablish the "Middle Kingdom order" in East Asia; and (3) that a divided East Asia is in the interests of the United States.[64]

CHINA AND REGIONAL STATES: FROM UNEASY COEXISTENCE TO SECURITY COMMUNITY?

When the Chinese economy entered a new boom phase in the mid-1990s, the China threat theory, popularized by prominent Western commentators such as Charles Krauthammer and the late Gerald Segal,[65] began to resonate in the Asian region. With a decade behind us, however, the possibility that China is going to march down the South China Sea because of its insatiable demand for oil has yet to become reality, and it in fact may never come to pass.[66] While one can argue that it is the U.S. forward military presence and other restraining forces that prevented China from taking any expansionist action, another explanation should also be seriously considered: China may harbor no such evil design on its neighbors after all.

One can expect that after all that China has done in the past twenty years to improve its relations with its neighbors, the China threat theory would have lost some of its audience in the region.[67] That is indeed the case, and in some areas the transformation of attitudes has been remarkable. Because assurance cannot be absolute among states, and it is always difficult to gauge regional states' confidence in China's benign intentions, the question is how many regional states have come to appreciate that China can also be a benign power, and how much do these states trust China's benign intentions?[68]

In Southeast Asia, although ASEAN states are not ready to completely relax their vigilance against China yet, as indicated by their various security arrangements with the United States,[69] neither do they expect that China will conquer Southeast Asia in the future. More tellingly, they refuse to adopt the hard containment approach against China advocated by some in the Bush administration.[70] There have been remarkable changes in the ASEAN states' perceptions of China's intentions: most ASEAN states have come to recognize that China does not pose a real security threat for them, and the principal challenge they face is commercial. The result is that ASEAN's perception of China has improved more significantly than most would have predicted just a few years ago.[71] Likewise, China's relationship with Russia and Central Asian states is evolving in the same direction. Despite lingering suspicion, Russia's perception of China has greatly improved.[72]

Nonetheless, distrust of China persists in Asia.[73] Whether this persistent distrust is due to deep-seated historical factors or exists because it is profitable to keep China off balance is not the question. The crucial point is that this persisting doubt about Chinese intentions undercuts support for China's current benign strategy toward the region.

Some foreign policy specialists in China believe that most regional states have been so intoxicated by the China threat myth that it is hopeless to convince them of its fallacy, and that China should thus not try to appease them. These Chinese analysts argue that no matter what China does, Asian states will never come to trust China. This persistent distrust of China is creating a new kind of "victim syndrome" and playing into the hands of pessimists inside China. If regional states continue to view China skeptically, despite China's persistent effort to appease its neighbors, the Chinese leadership may eventually reach the same conclusion as the pessimists. The rest of the world must try to understand that too much distrust of China's benign intentions may produce the opposite effect. This disastrous scenario is something that China and regional countries must work together to prevent.

CONCLUSION AND OUTLOOK

Until the late 1990s, many observers would have agreed that China was still searching for a coherent national identity and was not sure of its proper role in the Asian region.[74] Today, we can perhaps argue that China has largely completed its painful search for a national identity, thus becoming more confident of its relationships and its position in the region. Today, China no longer sees itself as a country facing imminent external danger or on the verge of internal implosion. Instead, it sees itself as a country with resources for managing its grand transformation and a growing ability to shape its environment.[75] One would expect that as long as China's optimistic assessment of its external environment and its self-identify as a responsible great power continue to hold,[76] China's current grand and regional strategies will also continue. If this is so, the world and the region can take a more relaxed posture toward this "fourth rise of China" and behave accordingly,[77] and this will in turn reinforce the domestic support for China's current grand

and regional strategies.[78] In the end, the future of the Asia-Pacific region depends not only upon China's choice of strategy, but also upon the strategies of other countries in the region, including the United States.

NOTES

1. Thomas W. Robinson and David Shambaugh, eds., *Chinese Foreign Policy: Theory and Practice* (Oxford: Clarendon Press, 1997); Jonathan Pollack and Richard Yang, eds., *In China's Shadow: Regional Perspectives on Chinese Foreign Policy and Military Development* (Santa Monica, CA: Rand, 1998); Wu Xinbo, "China: Security Practice of a Modernizing and Ascending Power," in *Asian Security Practice*, ed. Muthiah Alagappa (Stanford, CA: Stanford University Press, 1998); Chu Shulong, "Development of China's Security Thinking in the Post–Cold War Era," *Shijie Jingji yu Zhengzhi* [World economics and politics] 9 (1999): 11–15; Michael Swaine and Ashley Tellis, *Interpreting China's Grand Strategy: Past, Present, and Future* (Santa Monica, CA: Rand, 2000); Avery Goldstein, "The Diplomatic Face of China's Grand Strategy: A Rising Power's Emerging Choice," *China Quarterly* 168 (December 2001): 835–64; Tang Shiping, "Understanding China's Security Strategy," *Guoji Zhengzhi Yanjiu* [Studies of international politics] 3 (2002): 128–35; Tang Shiping and Peter Hayes Gries, "China's Security Strategy: From Offensive to Defensive Realism and Beyond," EAI Working Paper No. 97 (October 2002), East Asian Institute, National University of Singapore; Evan Medeiros and Taylor Fravel, "China's New Diplomacy," *Foreign Affairs* 82, no. 6 (November–December 2003): 22–35.

2. This section of the chapter draws heavily from Tang Shiping and Peter Gries, "China's Security Strategy."

3. For more on the security dilemma, see John Herz, "Idealist Internationalism and the Security Dilemma," *World Politics* 2 (January 1950): 157–80; Robert Jervis, "Cooperation under the Security Dilemma," *World Politics* 30 (January 1978): 189–214; Charles Glaser, "Political Consequences of Military Strategy: Expanding and Refining the Spiral and Deterrence Models," *World Politics* 44 (July 1992): 497–538; Charles L. Glaser, "The Security Dilemma Revisited," *World Politics* 50 (October 1997): 171–201.

4. Former prime minister of Singapore Lee Kuan Yew might have played a pivotal role in transforming Deng's understanding. See Lee Kuan Yew, *From Third World to First: The Singapore Story 1965–2000* (Singapore: Straits Times Press and Times Media, 2001), 663–68.

5. Deng Xiaoping, *Deng Xiaoping Wenxuan* [Selected works of Deng Xiaoping] (Beijing: Renmin Chubanshe, 1993) 3: 321. Needless to say, Deng's doctrine is quite a departure from Mao's desire to be a leader in the socialist camp and the third world.

6. In academia, Zhang Yunling's 1998 article on interdependence can serve as the harbinger. Zhang Yunling, "Interdependence in World Economy," *Ouzhou Yanjiu* [European studies] 4 (1988): 1–10.

7. Wang Yizhou, "Three Tasks: Development, Sovereignty, and Responsibility," *Shijie Zhishi* 5 (2001): 8–10. "Responsible great power" began to appear frequently in official Chinese pronouncements following the Asian financial crisis.

8. For more on defensive realism, see Jeffery W. Talioferro, "Security Seeking under Anarchy," *International Security* 25, no. 3 (Winter 2000/2001): 128–61.

9. For more on neoliberalism, see Robert O. Keohane and Joseph S. Nye, *Power and Interdependence*, 2d ed. (Glenview, IL: Scott Foresman and Co., 1989).

10. Ye Zicheng, "The Inevitability of China's Great Power Diplomacy," *Shijie Jingji yu Zhengzhi* [World economics and politics] 1 (2001): 10.

11. China has demonstrated remarkable restraint, for example, in dealing with Japan on the Diaoyu Island dispute and in dealing with ASEAN countries over the South China Sea dispute. For this point, see James Miles, "Chinese Nationalism, U.S. Policy and Asian Security," *Survival* 42, no. 4 (Winter 2000/2001): 51–72; S. D. Muni, "China's Strategic Engagement with the New ASEAN," IDSS Monograph No. 2 (Singapore: Institute of Defense and Strategic Studies, 2002). Also noteworthy is that in resolving border disputes with other countries, it has been China that often makes the most concessions (Taylor Fravel, personal communication).

12. For China's engagement in multilateral economic and security institutions, see Margaret M. Pearson, "The Major Multilateral Economic Institutions Engage China" and Alastair Iain Johnston and Paul Evans, "China's Engagement with Multilateral Security Institutions," both in *Engaging China: The Management of an Emerging Power*, ed. Alastair Iain Johnston and Robert S. Ross (London: Routledge, 1999), 207–34 and 235–72.

13. Charles Lipson, "International Cooperation in Security and Economic Affairs," *World Politics* 37 (October 1984): 1–23.

14. These initiatives include China's Free Trade Area with ASEAN, the Kunming Initiative, and the Greater Mekong Program. For more on the China-ASEAN Free Trade Area, see Mark Wang, "Why China Speeded up Plans for FTA with ASEAN," *Straits Times,* November 14, 2001. For the Kunming Initiative, which covers India, Myanmar, Bangladesh, and southwestern China, see P. V. Indiresan, "The Kunming Initiative," *Frontline* (New Delhi) 17, no. 7 (April 14, 2000): 98–102; Ramtanu Maitra, "Prospects Brighten for Kunming Initiative," *Asia Times,* February 12, 2003, available at http://www.atimes.com/atimes/south_asia/EB12Df04.html; Zhang Guangping, "Framework Proposal for Sub-regional Economic Cooperation between Bengal Gulf States and China's Southwest," *Yazhou Luntan* [Asia forum] 1 (1999): 47–50. For the Greater Mekong Program, which covers southwest China, Laos, Myanmar, Thailand, Cambodia, and Vietnam, see "Multinational Greater Mekong Program Gears Up," available at http://www.china.org.cn/english/2002/Jun/35761.htm.

15. The most notable case is China's reluctance to move from supporting CBMs to preventive diplomacy (PD) within the ASEAN Regional Forum (ARF). See Pan Zhenqiang, "A Chinese Perspective," in *The Future of the ARF,* ed. Khoo How San, 49–57 (Singapore: Institute of Defense and Strategic Studies, 1999); Ding Kuisong, "ARF and Security Cooperation in Asia-Pacific," *Xiandai Guoji Guanxi* [Contemporary international relations] 7 (1998): 6–12; Liang Yunxiang and Zhao Tian, "ARF: Understanding its Function and Role," *Shijie Jingji yu Zhengzhi* [World economics and politics] 1 (2001): 41–45. Whether this attitude is changing is not clear.

16. For a similar assessment, see Chu Shulong, "Development of China's Security Thinking in the post–Cold War Era," *Shijie Jingji yu Zhengzhi* [World economics and politics] 10 (1999): 11–15; Wu Peng, "China's View Toward Security in Asia

Pacific and Its Development," *Shijie Jingji yu Zhengzhi* [World economics and politics] 5 (1999): 12–16.

17. Tang Yongshen, "The Evolution of U.N. Peacekeeping and Trends," *Shijie Jingji yu Zhengzhi* [World economics and politics] 5 (2001): 65–70. For an overview of China's attitude toward international intervention, see Bates Gill and James Reilly, "Sovereignty, Intervention, and Peacekeeping: The View from Beijing," *Survival* 42, no. 3 (Autumn 2000): 41–59. So far, China has participated in international peacekeeping missions in Cambodia, East Timor, former Yugoslavia, and Africa.

18. Here "Asia" means the broad Asian continent.

19. Whether China is siphoning off FDI that was previously destined for ASEAN countries is a debatable. See "Economic Survey of Singapore, Foreign Direct Investments to China and ASEAN: Has ASEAN Been Losing Out?" third quarter, 2002, available at http://www.mti.gov.sg/public/PDF/CMT/NWS_2002Q3_FDI1.pdf?sid =92&cid = 1418.

20. Since 2000 China's imports from ASEAN countries have been increasing at an annual rate of 30 to 40 percent. More importantly, in contrast to conventional wisdom, major exports from ASEAN countries to China have not been primarily raw material, but mostly electronics components. For a detailed discussion, see Chen Wen, "China-ASEAN Bilateral Trade," *Dangdai Yatai* [Contemporary Asia] 8 (2003): 42–49; Kwei-bo Huang, "The China-ASEAN Free Trade Area: Background, Framework, and Political Implications," available at http://www.dsis.org.tw/peaceforum/papers/2002–02/APE0202001e.htm.

21. For an explicit argument that China will never become a global power (and, therefore, that China should be satisfied with being a regional power), see Chu Shulong, "China's National Interest, Power, and Strategy," *Zhanlue yu Guanli* [Strategy and management] 4 (1999): 13–18; Tang Shiping, "Once Again on China's Grand Strategy," *Zhanlue yu Guanli* [Strategy and management] 4 (2001): 29–37.

22. "China-ASEAN Strategic Partnership," press release from ASEAN Secretariat, available at http://www.aseansec.org/15286.htm.

23. "Declaration of the Heads of Government of the Member States of the Shanghai Cooperation Organization, 2002," available at http://www.mfa.kz/english/sco/140901.htm. For early ideas regarding pushing economic integration in the SCO, see Tang Shiping, "Central Asia Economic Integration in the Shadow of Sino-Russia Strategic Partnership," *Dangdai Yatai* [Contemporary Asia] 7 (2000): 27–33, and "Regional Economic Integration in Central Asia: The Sino-Russia Relationship," *Asian Survey* 40, no. 2 (March–April 2000): 360–76.

24. Jae-ho Chung, "South Korea Between Eagle and Dragon: Perceptual Ambivalence and Strategic Dilemma," *Asian Survey* 41, no. 4 (September–October 2001): 777–96.

25. For the theoretical foundation of this argument, see Tang Shiping, "A Systemic Theory of Security Environment," *Journal of Strategic Studies,* forthcoming. For its shorter Chinese version, see Tang Shiping, "A Systemic Theory of Security Environment," *Shijie Jingji yu Zhengzhi* [World economics and politics] 8 (2001): 16–22. For similar arguments intended for other countries (mostly the United States), see G. John Ikenberry, *After Victory: Institutions, Strategic Restraint, and the Rebuilding of*

Order after Major Wars (Princeton, NJ: Princeton University Press, 2001); Chong Guan Kwa and See Seng Tan, "The Keystone of World Order," *Washington Quarterly* 24, no. 3 (Fall 2001): 95–103.

26. As Medeiros and Fravel have noted, the Joint Declaration on the Code of Conduct over the South China Sea between ASEAN and China contained mostly language chosen by ASEAN and few words sought by the Chinese side. See Medeiros and Fravel, "China's New Diplomacy," 26. For the joint declaration, see "ASEAN and China Sign Declaration on the Code of Conduct in the South China Sea," November 4, 2002, available at http://www.aseansec.org.

27. Wang Jisi, "How U.S. Hegemonic Thinking Was Born," *Huanqiu Shibao* [Global times], September 19, 2003; "The Logic of American Hegemony," *Meiguo Yanjiu* [American studies] 3 (2003): 7–30. Wang's idea basically reflects the logic of "balance-of-threat" theory, developed by Stephen Walt in *The Origin of Alliances* (Ithaca, NY: Cornell University Press, 1987).

28. For the idea of forming an "axis of restraining," see Tang Shiping, "Washington: Bully in a China Shop," *Straits Times*, March 31, 2003.

29. Tang Shiping, "Once Again on China's Grand Strategy," 29–37; Zhang Baijia, "Change Oneself, Change the World," *Zhongguo Shehui Kexue* [China social science] 1 (2002): 4–19.

30. For *"heping jueqi,"* see Yoichi Funabashi, "China Is Preparing a 'Peaceful Ascendancy,'" *International Herald Tribune*, December 30, 2003; Zheng Bijian, "China's Peaceful Rise and the Future of Asia," speech delivered to the Boao Asia Forum, available at http://www.china.org.cn/chinese/OP-c/448115.htm.

31. For instance, the United States can maintain security arrangements with Singapore, Malaysia, and Indonesia and still manage to limit the security dilemma between these countries. It is difficult to imagine that China could achieve the same feat.

32. China's FTA initiative with ASEAN is a clear manifestation of this intention to let regional states share the growth opportunity associated with China's economic transformation. See Zhang Yunling, "Why Push East Asian Regional Cooperation," *Guoji Jingji Pinglun* [International economy review] 5 (2003): 48–50; Chen Hong, "Sharing Growth: East Asian Regional Economic Cooperation," in ibid, 51–55.

33. Men Honghua, "International Regimes and China's Strategic Choice," *Zhongguo Shehui Kexue* [China social science] 2 (2001): 178–87; Pan Zhongying, "China's Asia Strategy: Flexible Multilateralism," *Shijie Jingji yu Zhengzhi* [World economics and politics] 10 (2001): 30–35; Wang Yizhou, "China in the New Century and Multilateralism Diplomacy," *Taipingyang Xuebao* [Asia-Pacific studies] 4 (2001): 4–12.

34. For argument that China's ARF experience has been transformational, see Rosemary Foot, "China in the ASEAN Regional Forum: Organization Process and Domestic Models of Thought," *Asian Survey* 38, no. 5 (May 1998): 425–40.

35. Cheng-chwee Kuik, "Multilateralism in China's ASEAN policy," SAIS Working Paper Series, WP-05–03, available at http://www.sais-jhu.edu/workingpapers/WP-05–03b.pdf; Philip Burdon, "China's Changing Role in the Asia-Pacific Region," speech delivered at the New Zealand China Friendship Society, available at http://www.nzchinasociety.org.nz/conferencespeeches.html#philip.

36. For Chinese readings of the style of diplomacy of the new leadership, see Zhuang Liwei, "Hu Jintao: Critical Trip," *Nanfang Zhuang* [Southern circle] 239 (June 2003): 12–14.

37. This is our own description and is not in the official Chinese diplomatic lexicon.

38. Jiang Zemin's speech to the 16th Party Congress still emphasized that "peace and development remain the two major trends of our time," thus temporarily foreclosing the debate that followed the U.S. bombing of the Chinese embassy in Belgrade.

39. For a comprehensive and generally optimistic assessment of China's future security environment, see Zhang Yunling, ed., *China's International Environment in Asia-Pacific 2010–2015* (Beijing: China Social Sciences Press, 2003). For a less optimistic assessment of China's future security environment, see Yan Xuetong, "Assessing and Pondering China's Security Environment," *Shijie Jingji yu Zhengzhi* [World economics and politics] 2 (2000): 5–10; Zhang Ruizhuang, "Reassessing China's International Environment: Peace and Development Is Not the Trend of Our Time," *Zhanlue yu Guanli* [Strategy and management] 1 (2001): 20–30.

40. Alan Collins, *The Security Dilemmas of Southeast Asia* (London: Macmillan, 2000), chapter 5.

41. Amitav Acharya argued that ASEAN countries are generally adopting a mixed strategy called "counter-dominance" toward external great powers, including China. Amitav Acharya, "Engagement, Containment, or Counter-Dominance: Malaysia's Response to the Rise of China," in *Engaging China,* ed. Johnston and Ross, 129–51; see also David Shambaugh, "Containment or Engagement of China: Calculating Beijing's Response," *International Security* 21, no. 2 (Fall 1996): 180–209, at p. 186.

42. Jusuf Wanandi, "ASEAN's China Strategy: Towards Deeper Engagement," *Survival* 38, no. 3 (Autumn 1996): 117–28; Amitav Acharya, "Seeking Security in the Dragon's Shadow: China and Southeast Asia in the Emerging Asia Order," Institute of Defense and Strategic Studies (IDSS) Working Paper No. 44 (2003), available at http://www.idss.edu.sg/WorkingPapers/WP44.pdf.

43. Amitav Acharya, *Constructing a Security Community in Southeast Asia* (London: Routledge, 2001).

44. Acharya, "Seeking Security in the Dragon's Shadow"; Alice D. Ba, "China and ASEAN: Renavigating Relations for a 21st Century Asia," *Asian Survey* 43, no. 4 (July–August 2003): 622–47.

45. Ma Lichen, "New Thinking toward Japan: Anxiety among Chinese and Japanese Public," *Zhanlue yu Guanli* [Strategy and management] 6 (2002): 41–47; Shi Yinhong, "Sino-Japan Rapprochement and China's Diplomatic Revolution," *Zhanlue yu Guanli* [Strategy and management] 2 (2003): 71–75.

46. Chi Yuanjie and Tian Zhongjing, "Building a China–Japan–South Korea Economic Cooperation Entity," *Shijie Jingji yu Zhengzhi* [World economics and politics] 10 (2001): 33–37.

47. Tang Shiping and Zhou Xiaobing, "ASEAN, China, Japan and the Future of East Asia," *Guoji Jingji Pinglun* [International economy review] 6 (2001): 19–24.

48. Tang Shiping, "Last Chance for East Asian Economic Integration," *Straits Times,* November 19, 2002; "Japan's Choice and the Future of East Asia," *Zhongguo*

Jingji Shibao [China economic times], July 20, 2001; Zhang, "Why Push East Asian Regional Cooperation."

49. For similar arguments, see David Lampton and Gregory C. May, *A Big Power Agenda for East Asia: America, China, and Japan,* Nixon Center Monograph, pp. 49–59, available at http://www.nixoncenter.org/publications/monographs/mis-silemono.pdf; Michael A. McDevitt, "History and Geostrategy in East Asia," PacNet Newsletter, August 10, 2001.

50. The recent China-India joint naval maneuver is an indication that the two countries do not see each other as an imminent threat. See "China Holds Maneuvers with India," *Associated Press,* November 14, 2003.

51. For an upbeat statement from the former secretary of state, see Colin Powell, "Remarks at Conference on China-U.S. Relations," available at http://www.state.gov/secretary/rm/2003/25950.htm. Also see David Shambaugh, "The New Stability in US-China Relations: Causes and Consequences," in *Strategic Surprise: U.S.-China Relations in the Early 21st Century,* ed. Jonathan Pollack (Newport, RI: Naval War College Press, 2004); Thomas J. Christensen, "PRC Security Relations with the United States: Why Things Are Going So Well," available at http://www.chinaleadershipmonitor.org/20034/tc.pdf.

52. The debate on "peace and development" reignited after the 1999 U.S. bombing of the Chinese embassy in Belgrade. Two questions are crucial in this debate: (1) Is the outside world (mostly the United States and regional states) generally friendly or fundamentally hostile to China? (2) Has human history really entered into an era of "peace and development," or was this assessment simply a Chinese dream? The journal *Shijie Zhishi* [World affairs] devoted two special issues to this debate. See *Shijie Zhishi* nos. 15 and 16 (April 2000). Also see Zhang, "Reassessing China's International Environment"; Shi Yinhong, "Correctly Assess World Order and Its Trend," *Zhanlue yu Guanli* [Strategy and management] 4 (1999): 103–5.

53. As Jervis puts it, "Countries like the United States which are large, powerful, and speak out on most issues with enormous volume, if not with enormous clarity, can influence others' definition of reality" (Robert Jervis, *The Symbolic Nature of Nuclear Politics* [Urbana, IL: University of Illinois Press, 1987], 4).

54. See Amitav Acharya, "Regionalism and the Coming World Order," unpublished paper; David A. Lake and Patrick Morgan, eds., *Regional Order: Building Security in a New World* (College Park, PA: Pennsylvania State University Press, 1997); S. Neil MacFarlane and Thomas G. Weiss, "Regional Organizations and Regional Security," *Security Studies* 2, no. 3 (Fall 1992): 6–37. For Chinese analysts' writing on this issue, see Wang Xueyu, "Regionalization of International Security: An Analytical Framework," *Shijie Jingji yu Zhengzhi* [World economics and politics] 3 (2003): 17–22; Su Hao, "Regionalism and the Making of Regional Cooperation Framework in East Asia," *Waijiao Xueyuan Xuebao* [Journal of Foreign Affairs College] 1 (2003): 1–8.

55. For instance, it was reported that former premier Zhu Rongji made the decision to table the ASEAN-China FTA proposal (which was originally put forward by an expert group of which Zhang Yunling is a member) because he had just experienced (during the 2000 ASEAN-China Summit) a full day of ASEAN complaining that China was going to squeeze them to death economically. Likewise, China's pro-

posal for an East Asian military dialogue was an initiative to dispel regional states' perception that China is not interested in multilateral military-to-military dialogue. For the story behind ASEAN-China FTA, see Lee Siew Hua, "Shocking Proposition: How an Uncertain ASEAN Came to Accept China's Free-Trade Idea," *Straits Times,* March 15, 2002.

56. SCO came to exist largely because China, Russia, and the three Central Asian states did not want to squander the goodwill generated from the successful demarcation of their borders.

57. Admittedly, states (and people) generally pay more attention to bad news than to good, whether it is real or perceived. Of course, if one state is already convinced of another state's malign intention, it is extremely difficult to change that perception. See Robert Jervis, *Perception and Misperceptions in International Politics* (Princeton, NJ: Princeton University Press, 1976), 372, 310–15.

58. For surveys of regional states' perception of the "China threat," see Herbert Yee and Ian Storey, eds., *The China Threat: Perceptions, Myths and Reality* (London: Routledge Curzon, 2002).

59. Tang Shiping, "China's Security Environment in 2010–2015: Critical Factors and Trends," *Zhanlue yu Guanli* [Strategy and management] 5 (October 2002): 34–45, at 42–43.

60. Goldstein, "Diplomatic Face of China's Grand Strategy," 854; Medeiros and Fravel, "China's New Diplomacy"; Tang Shiping and Cao Xiaoyang, "China, U.S., and Japan: Searching for the Foundation of Mutual Security," *Zhanlue yu Guanli* [Strategy and management] 1 (2002): 99–109.

61. Some may argue that such public assurance is not credible because China does not have the capability to expel the United States from the region anyway. But according to the theory of "costly signaling," this rhetoric, which is not domestically popular, is credible because it is also costly. Likewise, if the U.S. administration were to make a statement that was domestically costly, it would be a credible signal to China. For the theory of "costly signaling," see James D. Morrow, "Capability, Uncertainty, and Resolve: A Limited Information Model of Crisis Bargaining," *American Journal of Political Science* 33, no. 4 (November 1989): 941–72; James D. Fearon, "Signaling Foreign Policy Interest: Typing Hands versus Sinking Cost," *Journal of Conflict Resolution* 41, no. 1 (February 1997): 68–90.

62. Charles A. Kupchan, "After Pax Americana: Benign Power, Regional Integration, and the Sources of a Stable Multipolarity," *International Security* 23, no. 2 (Fall 1998): 40–79, at 62–63.

63. Roger Mitton, "Living with Elephants," *Asiaweek*, August 31, 2001, 31–32.

64. For prominent commentators voicing concern about the U.S. divide-and-rule approach toward East Asia, see Han Sung-Joo, quoted in Tim Shorrock, "East Asian Community Remains Elusive," *Asia Times*, February 5, 2002; Wang Gungwu, "Divided Asia Plays into Hands of West," *Straits Times*, February 7, 2003.

65. See Joe Barnes, "Slaying the China Dragon: The New China Threat School," Baker Institute Working Paper (April 1999), available at http://www.rice.edu/projects/baker/Pubs/workingpapers/efac/barnes.html. For samples of the China threat argument, see Denny Roy, "Hegemon on the Horizon? China's Threat to East

Asian Security," *International Security* 19, no. 1 (Summer 1994): 149–68; Charles Krauthammer, "Why We Must Contain China" *Time*, July 31, 1995, 72; Gerald Segal, "East Asia and the 'Constrainment' of China," *International Security* 20, no. 4 (Spring 1996): 107–35.

66. Michael Gallagher, "China's Illusory Threat to the South China Sea," *International Security* 19, no. 1 (Summer 1994): 169–94; Robert A. Manning, "The Asian Energy Predicament," *Survival* 42, no. 3 (Autumn 2000): 73–88; Evan A. Feigenbaum, "China's Military Posture and the New Economics Geopolitics," *Survival* 41, no. 2 (Summer 1999): 71–88.

67. For surveys of regional states' perceptions of China's intention, see Yee and Storey, eds., *The China Threat;* Leonard C. Sebastian, "Southeast Asian Perceptions of China: The Challenge of Achieving a New Strategic Accommodation," in *Southeast Asia Perspectives on Security,* ed. Derek da Cunha, 158–81 (Singapore: Institute of Southeast Asian Studies, 2000).

68. As many have argued before, China has been historically and can become again a benign hegemon. See Wang Gungwu, "China's Place in the Region: The Search for Allies and Friends," *Indonesia Quarterly* 25, no. 4 (Winter 1997): 421; Collins, *The Security Dilemmas of Southeast Asia,* 139–44; Mohammed Mahathir, quoted in "Southeast Asia and China: Threat and Opportunities," *Asia Times,* August 2, 2003.

69. ASEAN states are thus not bandwagoning with China (because bandwagoning is primarily about security), at least not at the moment. For the argument that ASEAN states are, in fact, bandwagoning with China, see David Kang, "Getting Asia Wrong," *International Security* 27, no. 4 (Spring 2003): 57–85. The best description for ASEAN's China policy may be a combination of genuine trust and opportunism: ASEAN is taking advantage of China's economic growth but still hedging against the possibility that China will become aggressive in the future. Also see Acharya, "Seeking Security in the Dragon's Shadow."

70. For a detailed discussion, see Gaye Christoffersen, "The Role of East Asia in Sino-American Relations," *Asian Survey* 42, no. 3 (May–June 2002): 369–96. Also see Mitton, "Living with Elephants."

71. Ba, "China and ASEAN."

72. Alexander Lukin, "Russia's Image of China and Russian-Chinese Relations," Brookings Institution Center for Northeast Asia Policy Studies (CNAPS) Working Paper Series, May 2001, available at http://www.brookingsinstitution.org/dybdocroot/fp/cnaps/papers/lukinwp_01.pdf.

73. One indicator is that it took ASEAN countries quite some time to accept China's offer for a FTA with ASEAN. See Lee Siew Hua, "Shocking Proposition."

74. Robert A. Scalapino, "China's Multiple Identities in East Asia: China as a Regional Force," in *China's Quest for National Identity,* ed. Lowell Dittmer and Samuel S. Kim, 215–36 (Ithaca, NY: Cornell University Press, 1993).

75. For discussion of how China's new self-image influences its diplomacy, see Zhang Yunling and Tang Shiping, "A More Self-Confident China Will Be a Responsible Power," *Straits Times,* October 2, 2002; Xiao Huangrong, "China's Great Power Responsibility and Regionalism Strategy," *Shijie Jingji yu Zhengzhi* [World economics and politics] 1 (2003): 46–51; Medeiros and Fravel, "China's New Diplomacy."

76. Jiang Zemin's 16th Party Congress speech indicates that optimists are still carrying the day.

77. Wang Gungwu, "The Fourth Rise of China," unpublished lecture notes, December 5, 2003.

78. Early signs indicate that the new Chinese leadership will largely stick to the current strategic assessment and strategy.

PART TWO

The Economic Dimension

3

China's Regional Trade and Investment Profile

Hideo Ohashi

China's rise at the turn of the century marks a new stage in East Asian economics. China's economy grew at an average annual rate of more than 9 percent for almost a quarter of a century after an about-face in development strategy in the late 1970s, making China the world's sixth largest economy in 2002. Sharing an outward-looking development strategy with neighboring economies in East Asia contributed greatly to China's economic success. By becoming engaged with the world economy, China's economy became more efficient and market-oriented. In 2002, China ranked fifth in exports[1] and practically first in attracting foreign direct investment (FDI).[2] During this period of economic development, an FDI trade nexus emerged whereby FDI accelerates economic growth in China and enlarges exports, which in turn attracts another influx of FDI. This virtuous cycle between FDI and trade has been boosting economic growth in China since the early 1990s and resulted in China becoming the "factory of the world" and the world's largest supplier of sixty-six products in ten manufacturing industries in 2001.[3]

This economic rise of China raises the following questions: Is China changing the trade and FDI flows in East Asia? And is the regional economic system becoming increasingly Sinocentric?

The regional economic system in postwar East Asia has been described using the "flying geese" model.[4] According to this model, Japan, as an early industrialized economy in the region, has been the lead goose in the flock, followed by the newly industrialized economies (NIEs), ASEAN countries, and China. However, the FDI-trade nexus increasingly affects the regional structure of comparative advantage because it effectively transfers new technology and factors to the next "geese." China's rise, accelerated by the FDI-trade nexus, might have a serious impact on the flying wild geese model and the regional economic system in East Asia.

In this chapter, I briefly outline China's regional trade and investment profile of the past decade, and consider whether or not China's rise might lead to a Sinocentric regional economic system in East Asia.

TRADE STRUCTURE

The direction of trade in East Asia changed dramatically in the past decade, as shown in table 2. World trade increased by 177 percent during 1991–2001, while intraregional trade in East Asia swelled by 304 percent during the same period, even though most East Asian economies suffered serious damage from the financial crisis in 1997–98.

This growth in intraregional trade in East Asia is explained primarily by the rise of China. Although the surge in bilateral trade between China and the NIEs seems to have made the regional economic system more Sinocentric, it is equally important to note that China's exports to the United States have also grown more rapidly than bilateral trade between any other two countries during the past decade. China's huge trade surplus with the United States has shifted the focus of trade friction from between the United States and Japan and the NIEs to between the United States and China.

Additionally, the two economic giants, Japan and the United States, developed closer economic relations with East Asian economies in the 1990s. Japan's share of world trade declined because of its prolonged economic slump, and it became more dependent on East Asian nations. The United States did not increase exports to East Asia, but its imports from these countries expanded considerably. In an unprecedented economic boom lasting ten years from March 1991 to March 2001, the United States revived its position as a dynamic absorber of East Asian manufactured products, which were a main source of economic growth in export-oriented East Asian countries.

The 1990s also witnessed the rise of the U.S. dollar and the fall of the Japanese yen. This currency realignment changed the shape of the regional economic system in East Asia. Revaluation of the yen after the Plaza Accord in September 1985 and the rise of Taiwanese and Korean currencies in the late 1980s encouraged firms in these countries to invest abroad to cut production costs and maintain competitiveness. In search of cheap industrial labor and real estate, Japanese and NIEs firms shifted their manufacturing plants to the rest of East Asia, and their investments enlarged intraregional trade. Nevertheless, the bursting of the asset price bubble in Japan and the financial crisis eventually changed the direction of trade in East Asia in the 1990s.

East Asian economies as a whole achieved high economic growth by exporting manufactured goods to the United States from the 1970s to the

TABLE 2. Direction of Trade in East Asia, 1991 and 2001

(US$ billion, %)

Exports to	Imports from	World	East Asia[a]	(1)/(2)	NIEs	(1)/(2)	ASEAN 4	(1)/(2)	China	(1)/(2)	USA	(1)/(2)	Japan	(1)/(2)
World	(1) 2001	6,178.3	962.8	177	528.3	215	204.2	182	230.2	372	1,112.5	225	326.3	155
	(2) 1991	3,500.1	448.8		290.2		96.8		61.8		494.9		210.3	
East Asia[a]	(1) 2001	1141.3	437.1	238	227.7	304	87.5	212	104.9	356	244.1	263	138.1	298
	(2) 1991	479.0	143.8		73.1		41.2		29.5		92.9		46.3	
NIEs	(1) 2001	569.8	251.6	186	81.9	261	58.4	196	94.3	330	114.5	153	48.3	151
	(2) 1991	305.9	96.3		41.8		25.9		28.6		75.0		32.0	
ASEAN 4	(1) 2001	254.9	91.1	252	62.1	296	18.3	267	10.7	486	51.0	276	42.3	182
	(2) 1991	101.2	30.8		23.3		5.3		2.2		18.5		23.3	
China	(1) 2001	316.6	94.4	440	83.7	935	10.7	1,046	—	—	78.6	1,268	47.5	516
	(2) 1991	71.9	10.1		8.0		2.1		—		6.2		9.2	
USA	(1) 2001	730.9	117.0	173	72.2	183	25.5	214	19.2	305	—	—	57.6	120
	(2) 1991	421.7	63.8		45.6		11.9		6.3		—		48.1	
Japan	(1) 2001	404.9	158.6	129	88.7	167	38.3	195	31.7	369	122.6	133	—	—
	(2) 1991	314.8	95.1		66.9		19.6		8.6		92.2		—	

[a]East Asia comprises Asian NIEs (Korea, Taiwan, Hong Kong, and Singapore), ASEAN 4 (Thailand, Malaysia, Indonesia, and the Philippines), and China.

NOTE: The trade matrix is compiled on the basis of export statistics of the countries and areas concerned. The figures of exports to Taiwan are taken from the import statistics of Taiwan. The figures of Singapore's exports to Indonesia are derived from the import statistics of Indonesia.

SOURCES: International Monetary Fund (IMF), Direction of Trade Statistics Yearbook *1992* and *2002*, and Department of Statistics, Ministry of Finance, Monthly Statistics of Exports and Imports, Taiwan Area, December 1991 and 2001.

TABLE 3. Exports by Commodity by Destination in East Asia, 1995 and 2000

(%)

From NIEs to		U.S.	Japan	East Asia[a]	NIEs	ASEAN 4	China
Natural	2000	0.4	2.1	1.1	0.9	1.0	1.9
resources	1995	0.4	2.4	1.8	1.5	1.8	3.3
Nondurable	2000	13.8	22.5	9.5	8.0	7.1	18.3
consumer goods	1995	13.9	25.0	5.5	4.8	4.1	11.7
Intermediate	2000	42.6	43.1	68.0	67.6	70.9	63.5
goods	1995	43.8	40.9	66.5	67.6	67.0	61.2
Final demand	2000	43.3	32.3	21.4	23.5	21.0	16.3
goods	1995	42.0	31.7	26.2	26.1	27.2	23.8

From ASEAN 4 to		U.S.	Japan	East Asia[a]	NIEs	ASEAN 4	China
Natural	2000	4.4	15.1	11.9	9.6	15.7	22.4
resources	1995	7.3	25.4	18.9	16.0	25.1	32.8
Nondurable	2000	23.3	31.9	17.4	16.7	14.2	29.6
Consumer goods	1995	20.4	30.3	20.8	20.2	18.2	32.2
Intermediate	2000	40.2	30.0	55.4	57.2	55.5	40.4
goods	1995	33.4	23.2	43.7	45.7	43.0	26.7
Final demand	2000	32.2	23.0	15.3	16.4	14.5	7.5
goods	1995	38.9	21.0	16.7	18.2	13.7	8.4

mid-1980s. In the process of recovering from the financial crisis in the late 1990s, they depended on the U.S. market even more heavily than before. With the worldwide boom in information technology (IT), the leading U.S. manufacturers of IT products set up plants in East Asia and exported their products back to their home market. With a strong dollar the United States attracted money from all over the world, which later overflowed into East Asia and ultimately contributed to the financial crisis in the late 1990s. The financial crisis, at least temporarily, shrank regional demand, significantly decreased intraregional trade, and shifted exports to the United States. Without the benefit of a booming U.S. economy in the 1990s, East Asian economies could not have achieved such a short-term economic recovery.

TABLE 3 (*continued*)

(%)

From China to		U.S.	Japan	East Asia	NIEs	ASEAN 4	China
Natural	2000	1.4	8.9	5.8	4.7	14.3	—
resources	1995	3.8	13.8	7.0	6.6	9.8	—
Nondurable	2000	16.8	46.5	23.4	25.6	7.6	—
consumer goods	1995	22.8	47.0	25.0	26.2	14.8	—
Intermediate	2000	19.2	24.6	43.2	41.9	52.8	—
goods	1995	17.6	21.2	42.3	41.7	46.7	—
Final demand	2000	62.7	20.1	27.6	27.9	25.4	—
goods	1995	55.8	18.0	25.8	25.5	28.7	—

[a]East Asia comprises Asian NIEs (Korea, Taiwan, Hong Kong, and Singapore), ASEAN 4 (Thailand, Malaysia, Indonesia, and the Philippines), and China.

NOTE: The trade matrix is compiled on the basis of export statistics of the countries and areas concerned. The figures of exports to Taiwan are taken from the import statistics of Taiwan. The figures of Singapore's exports to Indonesia are derived from the import statistics of Indonesia. Each commodity group is the sum of 3-digit SITC (standard international trade classification) for SITC 0-6 and 5-digit SITC for SITC 7-8. The detailed list of commodity classification is omitted because of limited space. The commodity groups of this table are as follows: (1) natural resources for primary goods, (2) nondurable consumer goods for processed primary products, (3) intermediate goods for textile, chemical, steel, durable consumer goods, and capital goods, and (4) final demand goods for chemical, steel, durable consumer goods, and capital goods.

SOURCES: International Trade Centre UNCTAD/United Nations Statistics Division, PC/TAS *1993–1997* and *1996–2000*.

Trade Commodities

The four main groups of export commodities in 1995 and 2000, grouped by destination—NIEs, ASEAN 4 countries, and China—are indicated in table 3. These export commodities vary considerably according to their destination. First, the NIEs in general exported intermediate goods to other East Asian economies and final demand goods to the United States and Japan. Over the period 1995 to 2000 they also tended to increase their exports of nondurable consumer goods and decreased those of final demand goods to the four most developed ASEAN countries (Thailand, Malaysia, Indonesia, and the Philippines) and China. Second, the ASEAN 4 countries also exported intermediate goods to neighboring economies in East Asia. ASEAN countries are endowed with natural resources and are the leading exporters of these commodities in the region, although natural resources comprised a decreasing proportion of their exports. Third, China exported different commodities by destination, exporting final demand goods to the United States, nondurable consumer goods to Japan, and intermediate goods to neighboring economies in East Asia.

In short, East Asian economies export final demand goods to the United States and intermediate goods to their neighboring economies, including Japan. A variety of intermediate goods dominate intraregional trade, although the exports of nondurable consumer goods (processed primary products) and some final demand goods (textile final products) are gradually increasing among them. Changing trade patterns are reflected in the international division of labor in East Asia. In the 1970s and early 1980s, East Asian economies, and NIEs in particular, endeavored to promote industrialization by importing capital goods from Japan, processing and assembling intermediate goods also imported from Japan, and exporting final goods to the United States. After the mid-1980s, however, manufacturers in Hong Kong, followed by those in Taiwan and Korea, shifted their plants to China and increased the export of their products to the United States. In the 1990s, Japanese and U.S. manufacturers set up many plants in China to produce goods explicitly for export back to their home markets. With this shift, the FDI-trade nexus centering on China notably changed regional trade patterns and the international division of labor in East Asia.

China also plays a key role in intraregional trade in East Asia. Japan, as well as other East Asian economies, increased its exports of intermediate goods to China. Final products made in China with imported intermediate goods from neighboring countries are ultimately exported to the U.S. market. China's clothing exports increasingly entail the import of textile materials from Korea and Taiwan. China's exports of electronic products and electrical appliances also require a sizable number of parts and components imported from Japan, Taiwan, Korea, and Malaysia. This shift in manufacturing has placed China among the world's largest importers of intermediate goods. In 2002, China ranked first in importing synthetic fibers and fabrics and semiconductors; second in IT-related parts and devices, other electronics parts and components, plastic, and rubber; third in steel imports; and fourth in machinery.[5]

Supply and Demand

The changing direction of trade and export commodities is also reflected in the structure of supply and demand in East Asia, which can be systematically observed by using the Asian International Input-Output (I-O) Table compiled by the Institute of Developing Economies of the Japan External Trade Organization (IDE-JETRO).[6] Since the compilation of I-O tables usually requires a considerable amount of time (ordinarily several years), it is often pointed out that even the latest I-O table cannot wholly illustrate the current economic and industrial structure. In spite of such criticism, however, economic and industrial structures do not undergo fundamental changes within only a few years. It seems reasonable, therefore, to deduce the current structure from the latest I-O table.

Table 4 indicates the dependence of East Asian economies on final demands at home and abroad in 1995, and illustrates the impact of foreign demands on production at home and that of domestic demands on production abroad. The table clearly suggests the following points: First, as originally described by Simon Kuznets, trade dependence is in inverse proportion to the size of a country's economy.[7] The larger the economy, the lower the trade dependence ratio (trade/GDP). Singapore and Malaysia are more dependent on foreign demands than any other economies in the region. In other words, they are extremely sensitive or vulnerable to fluctuations in the world economy. China and other large economies, including the United States, Japan, and Indonesia, depend on domestic demand more than smaller economies in the region. Second, as one column of figures in table 4 shows, East Asian economies are more dependent on the United States and Japan than on any other economy in the region. The United States and Japan are regarded as the main absorbers of products manufactured in the region. Third, table 2 indicates that, excluding the United States and Japan, China is the largest creator of demand in the region. In 1995 dependent ratios on China in light industries were 3.2 percent for Malaysia and 2.3 percent for Korea, and those in heavy industries were 3.0 percent for Singapore, 2.6 percent for Taiwan, and 2.3 percent for Korea.[8]

Table 4 simply summarizes the regional economic and industrial links in East Asia as of 1995. By the late 1990s, Japan's economic slump, the United States' booming economy, and the rise of China were all apparent. Taking these factors into account, it seems reasonable to deduce from the I-O table of 1995 that East Asian economies, including China, depend mostly on the U.S. market, and that China additionally creates regional demands and increasingly absorbs manufactured products in East Asia.

China is basically a large, domestic, demand-led economy. As China becomes a major exporter and the largest recipient of FDI in the world, however, China's industries become more dependent on foreign demands and inputs in manufacturing products. Table 5 indicates the production demand and input structure of China's leading industries, which recorded among the highest growth rates in 1985–95.

On the demand side, domestic demand ratios for all the industries shown in table 5 decreased in 1985–95. In particular, clothing, nonferrous metal, plastic, and electrical machinery were more dependent on foreign demand than other industries and became export-oriented industries. Foreign demand originated mostly in Japan, the United States, and Hong Kong, China's gateway to the world. Korea and Taiwan became China's

TABLE 4. Dependence on Final Demands in East Asia, 1995

(%)

	ID	MY	PH	SG	TH	CN	W	KR	JP	US
Indonesia (ID)	80.5	0.6	0.1	1.2	0.3	0.2	0.5	0.4	0.2	0.1
Malaysia (MY)	0.3	40.4	0.4	3.6	0.6	0.1	0.7	0.4	0.3	0.1
Philippines (PH)	0.2	0.6	72.9	0.5	0.2	0.1	0.5	0.2	0.1	0.0
Singapore (SG)	0.5	2.3	0.2	35.0	0.8	0.2	0.4	0.3	0.2	0.1
Thailand (TH)	0.2	1.6	0.3	1.7	67.8	0.2	0.7	0.4	0.4	0.1
China (CN)	0.6	1.7	0.3	1.7	0.7	79.2	1.5	1.4	0.5	0.2
Taiwan (TW)	0.4	1.3	0.5	1.2	0.5	0.2	61.6	0.5	0.4	0.2
Korea (KR)	0.8	1.4	0.5	1.1	0.3	0.6	0.6	74.7	0.5	0.3
Japan (JP)	4.3	6.9	3.0	4.4	4.0	3.7	3.8	2.8	89.6	1.0
USA (US)	2.8	13.2	8.0	12.1	5.2	3.2	7.3	4.2	2.7	89.4
Others[a]	9.4	29.9	13.7	37.5	19.5	12.4	22.4	14.8	5.1	8.5
Total	100.0	100.0	100.0	100.0	100.0	100.0	100.0	100.0	100.0	100.0
$ billion[b]	442	205	142	223	356	1,875	566	1,058	9,746	13,456

[a]Includes induced intermediate as well as final demands.
[b]Induced production value.

SOURCE: Yoko Uchida, "Ajia Shokoku no Izondo" [Dependence on final demands of Asian countries], in *Kokusai Sangyo Renkanhyo no Sakusei to Riyo XII* [Compilation and utilization of international input-output table XII), ed. Jun Nakamura, Kazuya Tozuka, and Yoko Uchida (Chiba: IDE-JETRO, 2001), 29.

important markets by the mid-1990s, when Korea normalized diplomatic relations with China, and Taiwan successively lifted bans on economic relations with China. Demands of ASEAN 4 members rose notably by the mid-1990s, and their markets grew as large as that of one of the NIEs.

Table 5 also illustrates that China increased exports through the outward processing of Hong Kong's manufacturers in the late 1980s and early 1990s. The products manufactured in China were exported back to Hong Kong and reexported to the United States and Japan after final processing or packaging in Hong Kong. By the mid-1990s, China had begun to increase its *direct* exports to Japan and the United States, an increase that was largely attributed to the investments of the latter two countries in China. Japanese and U.S. manufacturers set up plants in China and exported their products back home.[9] China also successfully increased its exports of nondurable consumer goods to Japan, as Japanese consumers, faced with economic difficulties after the economic bubble burst, tended to prefer cost-effective consumer goods. Fundamentally, China is a domestic, demand-led, large economy, but most of the leading industries are increasingly dependent on foreign demands rather than on other domestic-oriented industries.

On the input side, export-oriented industries increased imports of intermediate goods in 1985–95. Among them, however, import ratios of clothing and plastic industries showed a downward trend, suggesting that a certain quantity of intermediate goods were supplied domestically. Japan and Hong Kong, an entrepôt for transporting Japanese commodities to China, played key roles in supplying intermediate goods to China. By the mid-1990s, Korea and Taiwan emerged as new suppliers of intermediate goods to China. Electronics parts and components were also supplied by Malaysia, which had established clusters of electronics industries in the 1980s by attracting a large amount of FDI. Increasing intraregional trade of intermediate goods has fully integrated China into the international division of labor in East Asia.

INVESTMENT STRUCTURE

A massive influx of FDI in China transformed the regional trade structure in East Asia in the 1990s. China created for foreign investors a number of favorable conditions to attract FDI. For example, China now allows export-oriented foreign invested enterprises (FIEs) to import production facilities, as well as parts and components, fully exempt from customs duties. Manufacturers who export their products are also eligible for a rebate of domestic value-added taxes. These policy measures have encouraged a number of export-oriented manufacturers to invest in China, resulting in China becoming one of the leading exporters in the world.

TABLE 5. Production Demand and Input Structure of China's Leading Industries

(%)

Demand	Clothing			Steel			Nonferrous Metal		
	1985	1990	1995	1985	1990	1995	1985	1990	1995
Domestic	72.1	48.1	53.3	94.4	82.7	75.6	87.9	71.2	63.0
Foreign	27.9	51.9	46.7	5.6	17.3	24.4	12.1	28.8	37.0
Japan	4.5	12.6	14.7	0.7	3.0	4.3	3.6	5.3	8.2
U.S.	9.7	3.1	4.0	0.9	2.4	3.6	2.2	5.5	6.7
Hong Kong	9.7	25.0	13.0	1.2	6.0	3.8	3.2	13.7	9.2
Korea	—	—	0.8	—	—	2.7	—	—	1.9
Taiwan	—	—	0.1	—	—	1.6	—	—	1.8
Singapore	0.2	0.2	0.2	0.3	0.5	0.4	0.3	0.5	0.8
ASEAN 4	0.1	0.4	0.6	0.1	1.9	2.2	0.5	0.8	1.5

Input	Clothing			Steel			Nonferrous Metal		
	1985	1990	1995	1985	1990	1995	1985	1990	1995
Intermediate input	68.0	72.0	65.6	64.3	67.7	67.8	75.0	80.5	81.2
Domestic	65.0	53.7	51.7	52.4	64.6	63.0	62.3	76.0	68.4
Imports	3.1	18.3	13.8	11.9	3.1	4.8	12.7	4.5	12.8
Japan	0.6	1.4	2.6	3.1	0.1	0.1	1.3	0.2	1.0
U.S.	0.3	0.1	0.1	0.3	0.1	0.1	0.7	0.7	1.3
Hong Kong	0.5	13.9	5.4	0.1	—	—	0.5	0.2	0.4
Korea	—	0.5	2.7	—	—	0.3	—	—	0.3
Taiwan	—	1.5	0.6	0.1	—	—	—	—	0.9
Singapore	—	—	—	—	—	0.1	—	—	—
ASEAN 4	—	—	0.3	—	—	—	0.4	0.2	—
Value-added	32.0	28.0	34.4	35.7	32.3	32.2	25.0	19.5	18.8

Taking advantage of these policy measures, FIEs are almost entirely engaged in processing trade under free trade conditions. In 2002, China's processing trade accounted for 55.3 percent of exports and 47.6 percent of imports, while ordinary trade represented 41.8 percent and 43.7 percent, respectively.[10] As major traders, FIEs accounted for more than half of China's overall trade—51.7 percent of exports and 54.0 percent of imports, respectively, in the same year. The largest exporting firm in China in 2002

General Machinery			Electric Machinery			Automobile			Plastic		
1985	1990	1995	1985	1990	1995	1985	1990	1995	1985	1990	1995
93.1	88.1	84.6	93.8	75.9	66.2	96.6	91.5	85.6	90.6	72.5	64.3
6.9	11.9	15.4	6.2	24.1	33.8	3.4	8.5	14.4	9.4	27.5	35.7
0.5	1.6	2.3	0.6	2.4	5.6	0.5	1.4	2.0	1.6	3.0	5.6
0.5	2.1	2.8	0.7	6.7	6.9	0.3	—	2.3	1.6	6.4	7.0
0.6	3.8	2.7	2.6	16.2	9.1	—	2.6	2.1	3.2	13.7	7.4
—	—	0.6	—	—	1.0	—	—	0.4	—	—	0.8
—	—	0.4	—	—	0.5	—	—	0.2	—	—	0.5
0.2	0.3	0.2	0.2	0.4	0.9	0.1	0.2	0.2	0.2	0.4	0.4
0.1	0.6	0.9	0.3	0.6	1.3	0.1	0.4	0.5	0.4	0.6	0.8

General Machinery			Electric Machinery			Automobile			Plastic		
1985	1990	1995	1985	1990	1995	1985	1990	1995	1985	1990	1995
64.4	70.9	72.3	69.8	74.6	74.9	68.8	71.2	72.4	71.2	76.2	76.6
57.9	66.0	63.2	58.6	62.8	59.1	65.0	61.4	61.1	53.6	63.4	66.0
6.5	4.9	9.2	11.2	11.8	15.8	3.8	9.7	11.3	17.5	12.8	10.6
2.9	1.2	2.5	5.2	2.8	5.9	1.7	3.2	2.7	4.9	2.1	2.0
0.3	0.6	1.0	0.7	0.4	0.9	0.1	0.6	1.0	3.6	2.2	1.2
0.3	1.1	0.6	1.5	6.6	3.3	0.1	0.4	0.3	0.5	3.1	1.5
—	0.1	0.4	—	0.4	1.2	—	—	0.3	—	0.2	1.4
—	0.1	0.5	0.1	0.5	0.4	—	0.1	0.4	0.8	1.4	0.2
—	—	0.1	0.1	0.1	0.4	—	—	—	0.5	0.7	0.4
—	—	—	—	—	0.5	—	—	0.1	0.2	0.6	0.1
35.6	29.1	27.7	30.2	25.4	25.1	31.2	28.8	27.6	28.8	23.8	23.4

SOURCE: Shuichiro Nishioka, "Chugoku" [China], in *Shin Sangyo Kozo Bunseki heno Tokeiteki Apurochi: Ajia Sangyo Renkanhyo no Oyo [A statistical approach to new industrial structure analysis: Application of Asian international I-O table]*, ed. Chiharu Tamamura and Takao Sano (Chiba: IDE-JETRO, 2001), 127–33.

was Hongfujin Precision Industry, a subsidiary of Honhai Precision Industry, Taiwan's top manufacturer in sales. That same year, nine of China's top twenty exporting firms and eighty-seven of the top two hundred exporting firms were FIEs.[11] Other leading exporting firms were mostly traditional state-owned foreign trade corporations and their successors. Most specialize in exports or imports of specific commodities. Foreign trade corporations dealing in light industry products are one of the main sources of foreign

TABLE 6. China's FIE Trade Ratio by Country/Area

(%)

	Exports			Imports		
	1999	2000	2001	1999	2000	2001
World	45.5	47.9	50.1	51.8	52.1	51.7
Japan	54.6	56.0	58.7	63.5	68.5	67.5
Hong Kong	48.9	55.7	61.2	60.2	60.3	60.3
Taiwan	50.3	49.6	51.2	65.3	64.8	65.4
Korea	44.3	45.1	49.1	57.9	59.1	59.7
ASEAN	40.5	43.2	44.8	52.2	53.5	53.8
U.S.	53.8	55.3	55.0	42.7	44.5	44.2
EU	41.9	45.3	47.1	49.1	53.9	52.0

SOURCE: Japan External Trade Organization (JETRO), *Boeki Toshi Hakusho 2003* [White paper on trade and investment 2003] (Tokyo: JETRO, 2003), 12.

exchange in China, while those dealing in machinery and natural resources inevitably have a large trade deficit. FIEs in general keep trade in general balance, which also suggests that FIEs are mostly engaged in processing trade.

Table 6 shows the ratio of FIEs to China's overall trade (the FIE trade ratio) by country or area. The FIE trade ratio is particularly high for imports from neighboring economies, which supply intermediate goods to China. It is also high for exports to Japan, the United States, and Hong Kong. FIE trade mostly takes the form of intraindustry trade.[12] Both processing trade and FIE trade ratios are even higher for Sino-Japanese trade than the overall figures mentioned above. In 2002, the processing trade ratio was 58.2 percent for exports and 56.2 percent for imports, and the FIE trade ratios were 61.8 percent and 66.9 percent, respectively.[13]

During an investment boom in China, who are the leading investors? Table 7 indicates the top ten foreign investors in China. Hong Kong and Macau were previously the top investors, but their share was reduced by half during the past decade. This decreasing share of Hong Kong and Macau indicates a diversification of foreign investors in China, with other neighboring economies emerging as lead investors in the 1990s. Although the Tiananmen Square incident in 1989 considerably decreased FDI inflows from advanced countries, China's diplomatic efforts to normalize relations with Indonesia, Singapore, and Korea paved the way for new investments in China in the early 1990s. Moreover, once indirect investment was author-

TABLE 7. Top Ten Foreign Investors in China, 1992, 1997, and 2002

(%)

	1992		1997		2002	
	Hong Kong / Macau	70.0	Hong Kong / Macau	46.5	Hong Kong / Macau	34.8
	Taiwan	9.6	Japan	9.6	Virgin Islands	11.6
	Japan	6.8	Taiwan	7.3	U.S.	10.3
	U.S.	4.7	U.S.	7.2	Japan	7.9
	Singapore	1.1	Singapore	5.8	Taiwan	7.5
	Korea	1.1	Korea	4.7	Korea	5.2
	Germany	0.8	UK	4.1	Singapore	4.4
	Thailand	0.8	Virgin Islands	3.3	Cayman Islands	2.2
	Canada	0.5	Germany	2.2	Germany	1.8
	France	0.4	France	1.0	UK	1.7
East Asian 5[a]	88.6		73.9		59.8	
FDI + Tax Havens[b]	88.6		77.2		73.6	
Total FDI ($ billion)	11.0		45.3		52.7	

[a]East Asian 5 are NIEs, Macau, and Japan.
[b]Actually used FDI. Tax havens are Virgin Islands and Cayman Islands.

SOURCES: Zhongguo Duiwai Jingji Maoyi Nianjian [Almanac of China's foreign economic relations and trade], 1993–94, 1998–99, and Shangwubu [Ministry of Commerce], "2002 Nian Bufen Guojia/Diqu Duihua Zhijietouzi Qingkuang" [2002 FDI in China by country/area], September 9, 2003, available at http://www.mofcom.gov.cn/article/200309/20030900124459_1.xml.

ized, Taiwan's manufacturers immediately shifted their plants to China. Their investments were on a huge scale that was large enough to compensate for a drop in FDI inflows from advanced countries that imposed sanctions against China after the Tiananmen incident.

Interestingly, the Virgin Islands, the Cayman Islands, and other tax havens also expanded their investments in China in the 1990s. Before the return of Hong Kong to China in 1997, Taiwanese investors rushed into Hong Kong to set up shell companies with which to make indirect investments in China. After 1997, however, they tried to register a number of investment companies in tax havens for the same purpose. Central America has also been a favored destination for Taiwan's outward investment since 1990. With investment originating in the British Virgin Islands, Xunda Computer and Dafeng Computer, for example, are both known as leading exporting firms in China, but they are also subsidiaries of Mitac Computer and Quanta Computer in Taiwan. Compared with these tax havens, Hong Kong and Macau have remarkably decreased in the relative weight of their FDI in China.

In the 1980s, a number of Japanese, U.S., and European firms invested in China through their subsidiaries in Hong Kong. Many foreign firms preferred to invest in China via Hong Kong because of diplomatic and other constraints, which was another reason why Hong Kong and Macau dominated FDI in China in the 1980s. Increase in *direct* investment and a decrease in *indirect* investment in China reduced the relative weight of Hong Kong and Macau's FDI in the 1990s. Considering these factors, then, there may not have been any major changes on the list of foreign investors in China.

Global FDI flows fell in 2001–2002, and prospects remained dim for 2003,[14] but FDI in China is still on the rise mainly due to China's accession to the World Trade Organization (WTO) at the end of 2001. NIEs and Japan, the main investors in East Asia, were faced with economic difficulties caused by the financial crisis and the prolonged recession in the late 1990s. Since then, U.S. and European firms have increasingly invested in East Asia primarily to merge and acquire excellent local companies in financial difficulty. Mergers and acquisitions (M&A) are another factor behind increased investment in China. In late 2002, as a part of its enterprise reform, China allowed foreign firms to acquire the listed shares of state-owned enterprises, and it allowed qualified foreign institutional investors (QFII) to buy and trade A shares in renminbi (RMB).[15] East Asian firms regard China as the "factory of the world," and U.S. and European firms have a strong interest in China's huge domestic market. Their contrasting expectations are reflected in the differences in industrial structure. Since U.S. and European firms generally maintain competitiveness in service areas rather than in manufacturing industries, it is quite natural for them to invest in China in search of newly opened service markets.

Since the 1980s, manufacturing industries have represented more than half of all FDI in China. Real estate projects account for another quarter of FDI, and service sectors have just opened up. FDI contributions in these areas to China's economic growth consist not only of direct effects, including an increase in capital formation, industrial production, foreign trade, employment, and tax revenue, but also of indirect effects, including technology transfer, spillover, and human development.[16] Manufacturing investments in China directly accelerate economic growth and increase exports, which in turn attracts another influx of FDI. Both trade and FDI flows in East Asia seem to be increasingly Sinocentric because FDI necessarily increases trade and vice versa. As China attracts a large amount of FDI from the rest of the world, FDI diversion can be clearly seen moving from ASEAN countries to China. A large majority of foreign investors are currently interested in China, but with the goal of risk management, they cautiously refrain from investing all their resources in China. The outbreak of severe acute respiratory syndrome (SARS) in 2003 reminded investors of the risks of undiversified investment.

New Trends in FDI in East Asia

Increasing FDI has created new trade flows centering on China that traditional trade theories cannot adequately explain. FDI is transferring new technology to manufacturing plants located in China. An influx of FDI also influences factor endowment in China. These trade flows are created not by the difference in production technology identified by the Ricardian model and in factor endowment specified by the Heckscher-Ohlin model, but instead by the economies of scale represented by increasing intraindustry trade in East Asia. The FDI-trade nexus significantly affects the international division of labor in East Asia in the following ways.

First, the product architecture revolution made positive contributions to rapid industrialization in China in the 1990s. China's FIEs in general specialize in manufacturing and exporting modular products. In modular architecture, each functional element of a product is implemented by exactly one physical component, and there are a few well-defined interactions between the components.[17] Since the interface is essentially standardized, parts and components of modular products can be widely outsourced in open markets (for lower prices) and easily assembled by unskilled workers. Modular products can enhance their performance to a certain level with less time and fewer resources. A preference for modular products has enabled China to swiftly catch up to advanced countries in some industries, such as IT products.

Modular architecture has drastically changed the assembly business. It has considerably lowered technological barriers to entry, enabling a number of new manufacturers to participate in the assembly business. As a result of intense competition among manufacturers, the earning rate in the assembly business has markedly decreased. This is one reason why a number of modular products manufacturers are increasing their investments in China, where they can take advantage of abundant cheap labor[18] and procure low-priced parts and components in unusually competitive markets. In this context, a new type of business called an electronics manufacturing service (EMS) flourishes in the electronics industry. A number of EMS firms are in operation in China, where manufacturers assemble high-tech parts and components into labor-intensive final products on a massive scale.

Second, fragmentation of integrated manufacturing processes into smaller production blocks increases FDI and intraindustry trade in East Asia.[19] A large production plant sometimes contains both technology- and labor-intensive processes along with both upstream and downstream processes. This system is far from an effective way to allocate resources. With modular products, few parts and components are usually manufactured in an assembly plant. Well-standardized interfaces enable manufacturers to produce parts apart from assembly lines. In the quest to design cost-effective operations, manufacturers have begun to reconsider an integrated manufacturing process that goes from raw material to final product, and to establish a number of production blocks in the most suitable places for each manufacturing process. Innovation in telecommunications and logistics has dramatically reduced the service link costs between production blocks. Fragmentation of integrated manufacturing processes into production blocks builds up the multilayered export production networks that are now covering East Asia. A number of manufacturers tend to place China in the center of these export production networks.

Third, agglomeration of industries attracts FDI in China. Agglomeration of industries demonstrates the superiority of investment environments and the continuity in government policies on FDI. Once industries are agglomerated, the industrial cluster attracts another influx of FDI, which further enriches the area in turn. The Pearl River Delta (PRD) in Guangdong is a good example of an IT industrial cluster that includes the manufacture of copy machines, telecom equipment, computers, and peripherals. All parts and components indispensable to the manufacture of these products can be outsourced to locations within an hour's drive. Another cluster is located in the greater Shanghai area (GSA). Agglomeration of parts and components suppliers tends to attract FDI for assemblers, and vice versa. In addition to enabling the quick procurement and delivery of parts and components, an industrial cluster provides manufacturers with the ability to share information, reduce transaction costs, and enhance the industry's political voice. In addition to abundant cheap labor, a huge domestic market, and preferential policy measures, agglomeration of industries has become another major determinant of investment in China.[20] This is why FDI in the PRD and the GSA is still increasing in spite of the relatively high costs of industrial labor and real estate. The establishment of research and development (R&D) facilities is often another outcome of agglomeration. By mid-2003, more than four hundred foreign firms had invested $3 billion into R&D centers in China.[21]

The FDI-trade nexus urges us to modify our perception of the existing economic system in East Asia, represented by the flying wild geese model and based on comparative advantage. The rise of China is changing the formation of the flying geese. Formerly regarded as a big goose flying at the rear of the formation, China has now passed the other wild geese, or East Asian economies, in a number of industries. Japanese electronics manufacturers, for example, used to transfer their technologies for manufacturing new products to their counterparts in NIEs because these products had saturated Japan's domestic market. Japanese electronics manufacturers have recently started producing in China a new generation of televisions with large, flat plasma display panel monitors or liquid crystal displays. With Japanese manufacturers' FDI, China has now exceeded the NIEs and ASEAN 4 countries in manufacturing such products.

Outward Investment from China

According to the Ministry of Commerce (MOFCOM), China's outward direct investment (ODI) included 6,960 projects, and the total contract value reached $13.8 billion at the end of 2002.[22] In the first half of 2003, another 219 firms invested abroad, the number rising by 48 percent over the same period the previous year.[23] Compared to the huge amount of inward investment, COI is still limited in scale, although it is rapidly increasing.

Taking the following points into account, however, ODI should actually be more than MOFCOM has claimed. First, China is currently one of the leading investors in the world. According to FDI statistics from recipient countries, ODI amounted to a total of $35.5 billion at the end of 2002.[24] Neighboring recipient countries also demonstrate that China has emerged as a leading investor in their economies.[25] Second, China's balance of payments statistics indicate that ODI reached an annual average of at least $2 billion in 1985–2002.[26] Third, from a macroeconomic viewpoint, China has basically maintained an account surplus since the early 1990s; in other words, savings exceed investments. This is strong evidence that, in an increase of net external assets, a portion of the country's savings flowed out of China in the 1990s and the first few years of the twenty-first century. China's flow of funds also demonstrates that China supplied a part of its savings to foreign sectors short of funds in the same period.[27]

China is among the largest exporters of capital to developing countries. Although China strictly regulates its capital outflows, it recorded a huge debit balance in the "net error and omission" item on the balance of payments statistics for twelve consecutive years from 1990 to 2001. This figure is regarded as an index of capital flight from China. Some of these funds might finance "round-tripping" investments, or FDI from China's domestic firms exported out of the country and then back into China, so as to be eligible for favorable treatment given solely to FIEs and to avoid exchange rates and other risks.[28] "Net error and omission" of the balance of payments statistics turned positive in 2002, suggesting capital inflows in anticipation of the revaluation of the RMB. In spite of strict controls on capital flows, there are actually large-scale capital flows in and out of China. Since these capital flows can be regarded as "hot money," our argument should focus on the COI based on the MOFCOM statistics in the context of China's regional trade and investment.

As shown in table 8, Hong Kong and Macau accounted for nearly half of ODI, but if ODI in trade business is excluded, the United States becomes the top destination. As of September 2001, 49.7 percent of ODI was engaged in trade business, 22.2 percent in production, and 18.1 percent in natural resource development and other developments, including agriculture, transportation, construction, consulting services, and tourism.[29] On the whole, Chinese firms invest in the service sector in advanced economies, including Hong Kong, natural resource development in the Americas and Australia, and manufacturing industries in Asia and Africa. COI in Africa is often included in China's aid program.

The main purposes of ODI are to develop foreign markets, secure natural resources, and avoid trade friction. In addition to these purposes, the following are currently emphasized. First, China embarked on restructuring domestic industries through ODI. Since the late 1990s, the Chinese government has made efforts to adjust the excessive supply capacity that resulted from overinvestment in production facilities in the first half of the 1990s. In particular, since the financial crisis, ODI has been played up as an effective means to adjust industry structure and increase exports as China faces a stagnant domestic economy. In February 1998, Jiang Zemin issued his *zou chuqu* (going abroad) strategy to promote the restructuring of domestic industries as well as to promote natural resource development abroad.[30] In this context, the Chinese government revised related laws and simplified procedures to encourage *dailiao jiagong* (processing abroad with materials imported from China). This has resulted in, for example, leading manufacturers such as Konka, Changhong, and TCL taking advantage of these preferential measures and having already set up operations in ASEAN countries to produce televisions, a typical overstocked product in China.

TABLE 8. China's Outward Investment by Region/Country

(1) Geographical distribution including trade business as of June 2001			*(2) Top ten destinations excluding trade business as of the end of 2001*		
	No.	US$ million		No.	US$ million
Hong Kong/Macau	2,184	3,683	United States	329	559
North America	774	1,074	Hong Kong	262	473
Asia	1,271	798	Canada	95	392
Africa	524	713	Australia	118	351
Latin America	307	592	Peru	13	200
Oceania	277	486	Thailand	154	194
Europe	1,102	436	Mexico	36	143
Total	6,439	7,782	Zambia	17	134
			Russia	297	130
			Cambodia	54	120
			Others	1,716	1,737
			Total	3,091	4,433

SOURCES: (1) Zhongguo WTO Niandu Baogao Bianji Weiyuanhui [China WTO Annual Report Editing Committee], ed., *Zhongguo WTO Baogao 2003* [China WTO report 2003] (Beijing: Jingji Ribao Chubanshe, 2003), 189. (2) *Zhoungguo Duiwai Jingji Maoyi Nianjian 2002* [Almanac of China's foreign economic relations and trade 2002], 1151–55.

Second, Chinese manufacturers are eager to acquire production technology, famous brands, and sales outlets in the United States. Some leading Chinese manufacturers of electronics and electrical products, such as Haier, have set up R&D centers. Others successfully achieved all three goals at the same time through M&A. Wanxiang Corporation became the largest stockholder of UAI, a major auto-parts manufacturer in the United States, and Huali purchased a mobile telecom section from Philips Electronics.

Since the *zou chuqu* strategy was set forth, China's ODI has been greatest in manufacturing industries in ASEAN countries. Processing trade represented by *dailiao jiagong* necessarily increases China's exports to other countries and has an incremental impact on the regional economic system in East Asia. ODI in the United States contributes to improvements in productivity and increased profitability for Chinese manufacturing industries. Because of the "rule of origin" of the North America Free Trade Agreement (NAFTA), however, China has not increased any processing trade with the United States. For the present, ODI in the United States has little impact on regional trade and investment in East Asia.

Finally, the Chinese government has also encouraged ODI to maintain a balance of payments and to stabilize the exchange rate since China faced mounting pressure to revalue the RMB in late 2002.[31]

CONCLUSION

By the late 1990s, the dynamic FDI-trade nexus built up multilayered export production networks and placed China at the center of the international division of labor in East Asia. It also enabled China to attract a wide range of production facilities and technologies from neighboring countries. As a result, regional trade and FDI flows are gradually becoming more Sinocentric and the FDI-trade nexus is steadily breaking the formation of the flying geese model in East Asia. Nevertheless, it is still too early to conclude that the regional economic system is becoming wholly Sinocentric.

East Asian economies, including that of China, are principally dependent on U.S. final demand. Without growing final demand in the United States, China could not create sufficient intermediate demand to maintain regional economic growth. Consequently, the regional economic system in East Asia is considerably sustained by U.S. final demand. In the postwar period, export-oriented industrialization led to the world's highest economic growth in East Asia. But as East Asian economies became heavily dependent on the U.S. market, they simultaneously became exceptionally vulnerable to the fluctuations and setbacks of the U.S. economy, and also encountered a number of trade disputes and conflicts with the United States. Since East Asian economies—the smaller economies in particular—could not easily change the course of their export-oriented growth, it was vitally important to create additional final demands within the region.

In this context, China is expected to play a key role. First, China is seen as a driving force in regional economic growth in the foreseeable future. Rising income is a prerequisite for developing regional final demands and expanding the final goods trade in East Asia. Rich consumers are likely to purchase more final goods and tend to seek differentiated products, which usually lead to an increase in final goods trade. China's remarkable economic growth is contributing to an additional increase of regional final demands.

Second, China is taking regional initiatives in trade liberalization, which is indispensable for increasing final goods trade in East Asia. In this region, the WTO, the Asia-Pacific Economic Cooperation (APEC) organization, and the ASEAN-China Free Trade Area (ACFTA) lowered tariff rates and removed a number of trade barriers over the past decade. However, many countries still continue to pursue partial import-substitution policies to protect specific domestic industries and employment. These trade policies are acting as barriers to final goods trade in the region. Currently, the booming free trade agreement could be instrumental in reforming ineffective sectors, adopting outward-looking policies, and enlarging final goods trade. China's engagement in the FTA with neighboring economies may have positive effects on trade liberalization in East Asia.

Third, China's absorptive capacity provides a number of opportunities for export-oriented economies in East Asia. China has huge potential domestic demand. The policy to develop the western part of China would entail innumerable projects, and social security reform would also require immense expenditure. Judging from macroeconomic indicators, as observed above, China has excess savings. The Chinese government has a propensity to prefer savings to consumption and has repeatedly failed to utilize the huge savings efficiently. Accumulating foreign exchange reserves, the Chinese government did not adequately relax strict restrictions on imports of consumer goods until China's accession to the WTO in 2001. China's excess savings have mainly been achieved by suppressing consumption. By increasing consumption, the Chinese people would actually realize the growth of an affluent society. Even more importantly, increasing consumption would adjust the exchange rate and would help China to avoid trade frictions.

The rise of China is also attributed to FDI and technology transfers from neighboring economies. Insofar as these economies, Japan and NIEs in particular, are technologically superior to China, it would take a long time for China to become an architect of the regional economic system in East Asia. Many of China's manufacturers are keenly aware of the importance of technology in production. Some are earnestly oriented toward high-tech and knowledge-based industries. Because of the huge labor surplus, however, China as a whole will not use a large portion of its resources for these industries, and it will unavoidably continue to concentrate on labor-intensive industries in the foreseeable future. Japan and, to some extent, the NIEs continue to be essential suppliers of capital and technology in the regional economic development in East Asia. As these countries age, their current account surplus will inevitably shrink, but as matured creditors, they will live on the remittance from their subsidiaries overseas and royalty payments from licensees abroad. China has the potential to become a main actor in visible trade while Japan and the NIEs become the key players in invisible trade in the region.

As China becomes a domestic demand-led economy, the regional trade and FDI flows will become more Sinocentric, but, taking the crucial roles of Japan and NIEs into account, the prospective regional economic system in East Asia will be more multilayered and less orderly than the preexisting system, which is represented by the flying geese model.

NOTES

1. World Trade Organization (WTO), "World Merchandise Exports by Region and Selected Economy," available at http://www.wto.org/english/res_e/statis_e/webpub_e.xls.

2. Technically, Luxembourg was reported to be the world's largest FDI recipient in 2002, but this can be explained by a series of cross-border mergers and acquisitions (M&A) that took place to establish the steel group Arcelor. This could also reflect a transfer of funds between affiliates within the same group located in different countries, or a channeling of funds to acquire companies in different countries through a holding company established in Luxembourg to take advantage of favorable intrafirm financing conditions. Consequently, it cannot be assumed that Luxembourg was the world's largest FDI recipient in 2002. See the United Nations Conference on Trade and Development (UNCTAD), *World Investment Report 2003* (Geneva: UNCTAD, 2003), 69.

3. *Chugoku Keizai* Henshubu [editor of *Chugoku Keizai*], "Chugoku ni okeru Seisanryo Sekai Daiichii no Seihin Risuto" [The list of the products made in China the largest in the world], *Chugoku Keizai* [Chinese economy] 446 (2003): 159–64.

4. The flying geese model was originally proposed by Kaname Akamatsu to describe the changing production and trade patterns that the leading industry in a country, after achieving import-substitution, had on other industries. Today, however, the model is widely used to illustrate the international or regional restructuring of industries according to the changing comparative advantage. See Kaname Akamatsu, "A Historical Pattern of Economic Growth in Developing Countries," *The Developing Economies,* Preliminary Issue, no. 1 (1962): 3–25; and Ippei Yamazawa et al., "Dynamic Interdependence among the Asia-Pacific Economies," *Keizai Bunseki* [Economic analysis] 129 (1993).

5. Japan External Trade Organization (JETRO), *Boeki Toshi Hakusho 2003* [White paper on trade and investment 2003] (Tokyo: JETRO, 2003), 11–12.

6. IDE-JETRO has compiled the Asian International I-O Tables of 1975, 1985, 1990, and 1995. These tables cover not only East Asian economies (NIEs, ASEAN 4 countries, and China), but also those of Japan and the United States. After these countries and regions publish their own I-O tables, IDE-JETRO commences analyzing their trade sectors. Consequently, it takes at least five years to compile the final table. The latest IDE-JETRO Asian International I-O Table is that of 1995, published in 2001. The 2000 table is to be published in March 2006. Chiharu Tamamura, Yoko Uchida, Nobuhiro Okamoto, "Ajia Shokoku no Seisan/Juyo Kozo to Boeki Jiyuka: Ajia Kokusai Sangyo Renkan Bunseki" [Production/demand structure and trade liberalization in Asian countries: Asian International Input-Output Analysis], *Ajia Keizai* [Asian economy] 44, nos. 5–6 (2003): 141.

7. Simon Kuznets, *Modern Economic Growth: Rate, Structure, and Spread* (New Haven, CT: Yale University Press, 1966), 300–321.

8. Yoko Uchida, "Ajia Shokoku no Izondo" [Dependence on final demands of Asian countries], in *Kokusai Sangyo Renkanhyo no Sakusei to Riyo XII* [Compilation and utilization of International Input-Output Table XII], ed. Jun Nakamura, Kazuya Tozuka, and Yoko Uchida (Chiba: IDE-JETRO, 2001), 28.

9. Intrafirm trade reached 18.1 percent of U.S. imports from China in 2000. The U.S. retailer Wal-Mart alone imported more than $10 billion worth of Chinese

goods in 2001, equivalent to around 10 percent of the total U.S. goods imported from China for that year. See U.S.-China Security Review Commission, "The National Security Implications of the Economic Relationship Between the United States and China," July 2002, available at http://www.uscc.gov/anr02.htm; and Richard MacGregor, "Beans Are on the Beijing Menu as Bush Prepares to Talk Trade," *Financial Times*, February 21, 2002. Subsidiaries of Japanese manufacturers in China exported $7.8 billion of manufactured goods to Japan, accounting for 12.6 percent of Japan's total imports from China in the fiscal year (April to March) of 2001. See Keizai Sangyosho (Ministry of Economy, Trade, and Industry), "Dai 32 Kai Heisei 14 Nen Kaigai Jigyo Katsudo Kihon Chousa" [The 32nd 2002 Basic Survey on Overseas Business Activities], June 2003, available at http://www.meti.go.jp/statistics/downloadfiles/h2c403ej.pdf. The ratio seems to be lower than expected, although it is steadily rising. Since Japanese manufacturers of nondurable consumer goods are mostly engaged in processing with Chinese counterparts, machinery takes the leading part in this survey.

10. Processing trade takes the following forms: compensation trade, processing and assembling *(lailiao jiagong)*, processing with imported materials *(jinliao jiagong)*, and warehousing and bonded trade in exports. In addition to these, two items of equipment for processing trade and equipment/materials investment by FIE are included in processing trade in imports. General Administration of Customs of the People's Republic of China, *China's Customs Statistics (Monthly Imports and Exports)*, no. 160 (December 2002), 14–15.

11. Shangwubu (Ministry of Commerce), "Quanguo Chukou 200 Qiang Qiye" [Top 200 exporting firms in China], available at http://query.fdi.cn/fdifind/Find/CNExpTop200.asp.

12. Intraindustry trade takes the following forms: (1) Trade of manufactured goods at different production stages in the same industry group. Japan exports a number of semifinished semiconductors to Malaysia. Manufacturing plants in Malaysia process and assemble them into finished goods and export them back to Japan. If a manufacturing plant located in Malaysia is a subsidiary of a Japanese manufacturer, this is an intrafirm trade. (2) Trade of manufactured goods produced using different technologies in the same industry group. Japan exports thin steel boards and seamless steel pipes to China and imports rod steel and gauge steel from China. (3) Trade of differentiated merchandize in the same industry group. Japan exports economical compact cars to Europe and imports large luxury cars from Europe.

13. *Kokusai Boeki* [International trade] no. 1580 (February 18, 2003): 2 and no. 1582 (March 4, 2003): 2.

14. "Overview," in UNCTAD, *World Investment Report 2003*, 1–11.

15. "Jinshen Kaifang Zhengquan Touzi" [Liberalize securities investment with caution], *Jingji Ribao* [Economic daily], November 14, 2002, 1.

16. See the following studies for details of FDI and economic growth in China: Zhao Jinping, ed., *Liyong Waizi yu Zhongguo Jingji Zengzhang* [Utilization of foreign capital and economic growth in China] (Beijing: Renmin Chubanshe, 2001); Jiang Xiaojuan, *Zhongguo de Waizi Jingji* [China's FDI economy] (Beijing: Zhongguo Renmin Daxue Chubanshe, 2002); Hideo Ohashi, *Keizai no Kokusaika* [Globalization of China's economy] (Nagoya: Nagoya Daigaku Shuppankai, 2003).

17. Karl T. Ulrich and Steven D. Eppinger, *Product Design and Development* (New York: McGraw-Hill, 2000), 183–84.

18. Arthur W. Lewis, "Economic Development with Unlimited Supplies of Labor," *Manchester School of Economic and Social Studies* 22 (May 1954): 139–91.

19. Fukunari Kimura, "Kokusai Boeki Riron no Aratana Choryu to Higashi Asia" [New trends in international trade theory and East Asia], *Kaihatsu Kinyu Kenkyu Shohou* [Japan Bank for International Cooperation Institute review] 14 (2003): 106–16.

20. During the initial stages of FDI in China, cultural and historical affinity was a major determinant of investment, as seen in the cases of Hong Kong's investment in Guangdong, Taiwan's in Fujian, Korea's in Yanbian Korean Autonomous Region, and Japan's in Dalian.

21. "Waiqi Yanfa Zhongxin Qinglai Zhongguo" [Foreign firms' R&D centers favor China], *Guoji Shangbao* [International business], September 10, 2003, 2.

22. "Zhengfu Ruhe Wei Qiye 'Zouchuqu' Chuangzao Tiaojian" [How the government creates the conditions for the firms to 'go abroad'], *Zhongguo Jingji Shibao* [China economic times], October 7, 2003, available at http://www.cet.com.cn/20031007/SPECIAL/200310072htm.

23. "Chugoku Kigyo Sekai he: TCL no Shogeki" [Chinese firms going abroad: The impact of TCL], *Nihon Keizai Shimbun* [Nikkei daily], November 8, 2003, 9.

24. UNCTAD, "Country Fact Sheet: China," available at http://www.unctad.org/Sections/dite_dir/docs/wir03_fs.cn.en.pdf; and "Lianheguo Tongji Muqian Zhongguo Duiwai Touzi Cunliang Da 360 Yi Meiyuan" [UN statistics say Chinese outward investment has reached $36 billion], *Zhongguo Jingji Xinxi Wang* [China economic information network], November 13, 2003, available at http://www1.cei.gov.cn/dailynews/doc/YBQHI/200311130059.htm.

25. In 2001, China was the fourth largest investor in Cambodia, the eleventh in Indonesia, the fourth in Laos, the third in Malaysia, the sixth in Myanmar, the tenth in the Philippines, and the seventh in Thailand. See ASEAN-Japan Centre, "Foreign Direct Investment in ASEAN (ASEAN Statistics)," available at http://www.asean.or.jp/general/ statistics/Statistics percent2002/inv09(02).html.

26. UNCTAD's *World Investment Report* is based on the balance of payments statistics.

27. Tables indicating China's flow of funds appear in *Zhongguo Jinrong Nianjian* [Almanac of China's finance and banking], *Zhongguo Tongji Nianjian* [China statistical yearbook], and *Zhongguo Renmin Yinhang Tongji Jibao* [Quarterly statistics of the People's Bank of China].

28. Hong Kong Bank estimated that round-tripping investment accounted for more than 25 percent of annual FDI flows in China in the mid-1990s. See World Bank, *Managing Capital Flows in East Asia* (Washington, DC: World Bank, 1996), 30. Round-tripping investment is on the decrease, however, as China relaxes the restrictions for capital flows and the preferential policies for FIE become less attractive.

29. Xu Dansong, "'Zouchuqu': Xianzhuang, Wenti ji Duice" ['Going abroad': Present state, problems, and measures], *Guoji Jingji Hezuo* [International economic cooperation] 196 (April 2002): 12.

30. These purposes of *zouchuqu* strategy are specified in the Tenth Five-Year Plan. See "Zhongguo Renmin Gongheguo Guomin Jingji he Shehui Fazhan Dishige Wun-

ian Jihua Gangyao" [Outline of the Tenth Five-Year Plan for national economic and social development, People's Republic of China], in *Zhongguo Jingji Nianjian 2001* [Almanac of China's economy 2001] (Beijing: China Statistics Press), 20.

31. Zhou Xiaochuan, governor of the People's Bank of China, proposed capital exports as well as the expansion of imports to maintain balance of payments and stabilize the exchange rates when U.S. Treasury secretary Snow visited China to call for a more flexible exchange rate system in September 2003. "Zhongguo Shizhong Zai Shixing Fudong Huilu Zhidu" [China's floating exchange rate system in operation all the time], *Jingji Cankaobao* [Economic information daily], September 4, 2003, 2.

4

China's Regional Economies and the Asian Region

Building Interdependent Linkages

Robert F. Ash

The spectacular impact of more than two decades of economic reform in China is not in doubt. Not the least dramatic aspect of such reforms has been the transformation of China's foreign economic relations through the implementation of a radical open-door strategy.[1] This development has introduced a new and major force shaping regional economic trajectories, even if the suggestion that Asia has already become Sinocentric remains premature.

This chapter addresses China's foreign trade and FDI from an internal regional perspective. A major underlying theme is the extent to which distinctive regional patterns of foreign economic relations are emerging within China. Following introductory remarks, which briefly consider some perspectives from which economic regionalization may be viewed, I present a statistical overview of relevant aspects of China's provincial and regional economies. This is followed by the two core sections of the chapter: The first is an examination of regional dimensions of China's foreign trade in 2002,[2] in which I focus on the nature and rationale of economic axes that have recently emerged across China's land borders—an aspect of its foreign economic relations that remains underresearched. The second investigates inflows of foreign direct investment (FDI), although here lack of data shifts the focus back toward China's coastal regions (especially the FDI axis between Taiwan and the Yangzi Delta). A short final section offers preliminary conclusions.[3]

CHINA'S ECONOMIC REGIONALIZATION

Since 1980 the relative contributions of primary and manufactured products to China's foreign trade have changed radically. The share of manufactured goods in total exports has risen from 50 percent to over 90 percent, while that of primary products has contracted to less than 9 percent.[4] Meanwhile, alongside burgeoning FDI, the number of foreign-funded enterprises (FFEs) has grown rapidly, their contribution to China's total export earnings having reached over 52 percent in 2002.[5]

A noteworthy feature of China's emerging trade pattern is the success with which the benefits associated with a comparative advantage in producing labor-intensive manufactures have been achieved alongside the simultaneous vigorous promotion of high-tech, knowledge-intensive industries.[6] This dichotomy is one of the factors reflected in the emergence of regional economies with distinctive characteristics, whether in terms of their output mix, technological coefficients of production, or strength of outward orientation. To cite an east-west divide within China as the exemplar of economic regionalization is misleading, although even such a simple vertical division does highlight the disproportionate impact of reform on coastal provinces and suggest the faster pace of foreign trade–oriented growth and modernization in these areas. For the purposes of my analysis here, what merits attention are the different geographical and functional elements inherent in the growing regional economic heterogeneity of post-1978 China and their potential implications for the emergence of cross-border linkages.

Even in a closed economy, where economic exchange is uniquely defined by intranational transactions, growth areas or development zones may fulfill a role analogous to that of supranational groupings in promoting efficient resource use. Before 1979, by deliberately excluding overseas capital, especially FDI, the Chinese government deprived itself of major growth benefits that had meanwhile accrued to neighboring first-echelon, newly industrializing Asian countries.[7] From this perspective, the abandonment of the previous emphasis on self-reliance in favor of embracing the principle of comparative advantage[8] as the basis for a new international orientation represented a fundamental shift in China's economic strategy. Since the early 1980s, economic exchange, whether it has involved goods, services, capital, labor, or technology, has increasingly embraced transnational as well as intranational dimensions in order to capture both the static and dynamic benefits of closer international (including cross-border) interactions. Efforts to capture such benefits are central to the emergence of transnational identities, such as "Greater China."

There are many variants of what economists often refer to as "growth triangles."[9] Their creation has often been shaped by economic imperatives, which have given a dominant role to nonstate economic actors.[10] In the context of East Asia, the notion of a "natural economic territory" (NET), as proposed by Robert Scalapino,[11] seeks to show how the diversity of a cross-border region can be accommodated to the mutual benefit of its constituent elements. Neither as an economic concept nor as an empirical device, however, does the notion of a NET significantly extend the existing framework of economic regionalization. In any case, the huge diversity of economic conditions in China—a country continental in its scope—counsels caution in using any epithet that seeks to capture the supposed universality of aspects of its development (in this case, its pursuit of foreign economic relations and associated patterns of economic regionalization). No doubt one could identify characteristics common to many forms of China's internationalization, including the economic nexus embracing South Korea (Japan, too) and parts of Northeast and North China, the economic symbiosis between Hong Kong and the Pearl River Delta, and increasing economic integration between Taiwan and the Yangzi River Delta. But the distinctiveness of each is arguably even more significant. And what of newly emerging groupings such as the Greater Mekong Subregion (GMS) or the Tumen River Area Development Programme (TRADP)?[12] Can their economic motivations and activities really be embraced within a single framework that indicates much more than the fact that they are all foci for regional growth? It seems more likely that no unambiguous economic typology of transnational groupings could be found beyond that which, unexceptionally, highlights their shared goal of realizing the benefits of economic complementarities inherent in differentiated factor endowments (including natural, energy, and mineral resources; labor; capital; technology; managerial skills; entrepreneurship; and other forms of human capital). Accordingly, the analysis given here follows an empirically driven approach rather than one dictated by a specific conceptual framework.

A REGIONAL ECONOMIC PROFILE OF CHINA

Table 9 presents a statistical profile of China's provinces and regions through estimates of their population, GDP, and foreign trade in 2002. The table highlights the diversity of economic conditions in China, whether measured in terms of structure or performance. It offers clear evidence of widening differentials, associated with the disproportionate impact of post-1978 reforms on coastal provinces.[13] The eastern seaboard region has displayed an increasingly strong outward orientation, reflected in its contribution to China's total trade and in its high trade-GDP ratio. Elsewhere, the more insignificant role and impact of foreign trade capture the essentially maritime thrust of China's foreign trade. It is, for example, instructive that the landlocked Central-Interior region has the lowest trade-GDP ratio in China, even if its share of national merchandise trade is higher than for both Northwest and Southwest China. Such perspectives are important in any attempt to assess the implications, both domestic and international, of China's various transnational economic axes.

Regional Dimensions of China's Foreign Trade

Detailed estimates of the value and direction of provincial and regional export and import trade in 2002 are set out in tables reproduced in Appendix I and II.[14] Although they are taken from the most authoritative official source of information on provincial foreign trade,[15] the figures are not wholly internally consistent and must allow for a significant margin of error.[16] The evidence they offer of changes in export and import behavior does, however, contain persuasive internal logic and coherence.

On the basis of these data, I have tried to investigate the extent and direction of foreign trade dependence in each region of China. Tables 10, 11, and 12, which are derived from the data in the appendices, provide quantitative indicators that facilitate the analysis. The estimates in these tables support the hypothesis that regional trade patterns in China reflect the emergence of transnational economic axes. Far from such cross-border linkages coming to dominate its foreign trade, however, international axes with countries and regions beyond its immediate borders point to China's wider engagement in the *global* economy.[17] Sino-U.S. economic relations are the most striking manifestation of this dimension. The United States is an important export destination for every region of China—and, according to the evidence of table 10, it is the single most important destination for four regions.[18] In addition, every region makes significant import purchases from the United States. Contrariwise, such is the higher degree of foreign trade orientation in coastal provinces that interregional differences in the absolute value of exports and imports remain wide (see tables 11 and 12).

Differences in the *level* of these regions' foreign trade are implicit in the continued dominance of "Greater China" in China's foreign economic relations.[19] It is a salutary reminder of the symbiosis that now characterizes economic ties between Hong Kong and the Pearl River Delta (PRD) to discover that more than a third of exports from Guangdong are still destined for Hong Kong.[20] Restrictions imposed by the government in Taipei have hitherto limited China's ability to ship exports on a significant scale to Taiwan.[21] But table 12 suggests that concealed within the 14 percent of all Chinese imports that originated in Taiwan in 2002,[22] the corresponding figure for the southeast was a remarkable 63 percent—and for central-eastern China, 33 percent.[23] Analysis of cross-strait economic relations frequently dwells on the threat posed to Taiwan by its rising export dependence on the mainland.[24] Without disputing such potential dangers, it deserves stating that the consequences for the two most important growth hubs in China of an interruption of their trade relations with Taiwan would also be serious.

The estimates presented above are broadly consistent with the notion that since the 1980s China's open door strategy has generated the emergence of a "Greater China" economic region.[25] But the activities of Hong Kong and Taiwanese investors have not been restricted to this single

TABLE 9. Population, GDP, and Foreign Trade in 2002: Provincial and Regional Perspectives

	Provincial [regional] population (millions)	Provincial [regional] population as share of China's total population (%)	Provincial [regional] GDP (US$ m.)	Provincial [regional] GDP as share of national GDP (%)	Value of total provincial [regional] foreign merchandise trade (US$ m.)	Average rate of growth of foreign trade, 1990–2002 (% per year)	Provincial [regional] foreign trade as share of provincial [regional] GDP (%)	Provincial [regional] foreign trade as share of China's total trade (%)
North	124.59	9.77	161,942.0	11.36	59,978.8	19.2	37.04	9.67
Beijing	14.23	1.12	38,814.9	2.72	26,702.1	21.5	68.79	4.30
Tianjin	10.07	0.79	24,781.4	1.74	22,850.2	21.5	92.21	3.68
Hebei	67.35	5.28	73,970.4	5.19	6,829.1	11.0	9.23	1.10
Shanxi	32.94	2.58	24,375.3	1.71	3,597.4	17.5	14.76	0.58
Northwest	116.52	9.14	86,992.6	6.10	10,298.7	15.5	11.84	1.66
Inner Mongolia	23.79	1.87	20,953.4	1.47	2,665.4	15.3	12.72	0.43
Shaanxi	36.74	2.88	24,597.8	1.73	2,784.1	14.0	11.32	0.45
Gansu	25.93	2.03	14,032.0	0.98	1,038.3	14.6	7.40	0.17
Qinghai	5.29	0.41	4,121.2	0.29	234.4	10.6	5.69	0.04
Ningxia	5.72	0.45	3,978.3	0.28	494.2	15.8	12.42	0.08
Xinjiang	19.05	1.49	19,309.9	1.35	3,082.3	18.3	15.96	0.50
Northeast	107.15	8.40	139,984.3	9.82	32,188.3	11.3	22.99	5.19
Liaoning	42.03	3.30	65,944.4	4.62	23,426.3	11.5	35.52	3.78
Jilin	26.99	2.12	27,136.9	1.90	4,074.3	11.5	15.01	0.66
Heilongjiang	38.13	2.99	46,903.0	3.29	4,687.7	10.0	9.99	0.76
Central Interior	327.90	25.71	259,814.9	18.22	17,280.4	11.9	6.65	2.79
Henan	96.13	7.54	74,528.6	5.23	3,730.4	11.6	5.01	0.60
Anhui	63.38	4.97	43,120.7	3.02	4,204.7	15.6	9.11	0.68
Jiangxi	42.22	3.31	29,605.9	2.08	1,996.8	10.1	9.75	0.32
Hubei	59.88	4.70	60,113.9	4.22	4,532.1	11.8	7.54	0.73
Hunan	66.29	5.20	52,445.8	3.68	3,273.4	19.3	6.24	0.53

Central-East	227.35	17.83	415,471.4	29.14	230,464.5	23.5	55.47	37.15
Shandong	90.82	7.12	127,486.5	8.94	37,369.5	20.0	29.31	6.02
Shanghai	16.25	1.27	65,346.9	4.58	72,251.3	20.9	110.57	11.65
Jiangsu	73.81	5.79	128,449.3	9.01	74,488.9	27.2	58.00	12.01
Zhejiang	46.47	3.64	94,188.7	6.61	46,354.8	27.3	49.21	7.47
Southeast	121.28	9.51	206,063.4	14.45	257,573.7	15.2	125.00	41.52
Fujian	34.66	2.72	56,566.5	3.97	30,329.2	17.6	53.62	4.89
Guangdong	78.59	6.16	142,198.0	9.97	225,451.4	15.1	158.55	36.35
Hainan	8.03	0.63	7,298.9	0.51	1,793.1	5.6	24.57	0.29
Southwest	250.39	19.64	155,618.8	10.91	12,524.6	13.5	8.05	2.02
Guangxi	48.22	3.78	29,664.9	2.08	2,606.9	9.3	8.79	0.42
Chongqing	31.07	2.44	23,816.6	1.67	2,023.1	—	8.49	0.33
Sichuan	86.73	6.80	58,899.6	4.13	4,461.5	18.6[a]	7.57	0.72
Guizhou	38.37	3.01	14,317.3	1.00	980.3	13.3	6.85	0.16
Yunnan	43.33	3.40	26,970.2	1.89	2,327.6	9.9	8.63	0.38
Tibet	2.67	0.21	1,950.2	0.14	125.2	12.6	6.42	0.02
Total (sum of provincial estimates)	1,275.18	100.00	1,425,887.4	100.00	620,309.0	17.4	43.50	100.00
Total (NBS, TJN, 2003)	1,284.53	—	1,266,045.7	—	620,766.1	—	49.03	—

[a]Growth for Sichuan, including Chongqing.

NOTE: GDP figures obtained by adjusting original yuan estimates on the basis of the official average US$-RMB exchange rate in 2002 (US$1 = 8.277 RMB).

SOURCES: Zhongguo Tongji Nianjian [China Statistical Yearbook] (Beijing: China Statistics Press, 2003), 66g; National Bureau of Statistics, *Xin Zhongguo wushi nian tongji ziliao huibian* [Compilation of statistical materials for fifty years of new China] (Beijing: Zhongguo tongji chubanshe, 1999) 159, 184, 209, 234, 259, 284, 309, 335, 359, 384, 409, 434, 459, 484, 509, 534, 559, 584, 609, 634, 659, 672, 693, 717, 742, 762, 786, 811, 836, 860, and 885.

TABLE 10. Value and Direction of Foreign Trade in Each Region of China, 2002

	Value (US$ million) and share (%) of each Chinese region's exports to, and imports from, the following countries [regions]:					
	U.S.		Hong Kong		Japan	
	Exports	*Imports*	*Exports*	*Imports*	*Exports*	*Imports*
China	69,151.9	23,399.24	56,958.1	2,403.5	47,949.0	51,332.8
	(21.7)	*(8.9)*	*(17.9)*	*(0.9)*	*(15.0)*	*(19.6)*
North	5,378.2	2,642.2	1,696.6	—	3,681.0	4,896.1
	(21.3)	*(12.0)*	*(7.1)*		*(14.6)*	*(22.2)*
Northwest	407.0	272.9	314.3	—	493.6	248.9
	(9.0)	*(8.7)*	*(7.0)*		*(10.9)*	*(7.9)*
Northeast	1,981.7	803.8	—	—	5,118.8	3,693.3
	(12.3)	*(5.9)*			*(31.8)*	*(27.0)*
Central-Interior	1,475.4	640.3	1,276.9	—	1,088.0	1,022.3
	(15.5)	*(10.0)*	*(13.4)*		*(11.4)*	*(16.0)*
Central-East	24,949.0	10,224.3	8,273.6	3,117.9	23,980	21,383.8
	(20.6)	*(10.5)*	*(6.9)*	*(3.2)*	*(19.8)*	*(21.9)*
Southeast	33,748.9	8,118.1	44,524.9	—	13,008.9	19,106.8
	(24.7)	*(7.1)*	*(32.6)*		*(9.5)*	*(16.7)*
Southwest	1,211.7	563.6	871.8	—	578.7	971.6
	(16.7)	*(12.6)*	*(12.0)*		*(8.0)*	*(21.7)*

region.[26] Nor have they monopolized it. For example, more than half of South Korean exports to China were shipped to central-eastern provinces, while almost 80 percent of its imports derived from the Central-East and Southeast (see tables 11 and 12).

What of China's land-based border regions? Here, far from maritime trading routes,[27] we would expect to find evidence of the development of truly cross-border trading links.[28] Inland border trade between the PRC and its neighbors has a long history: as early as 1950, advocacy of such trade as a means of improving local living standards was enshrined in official regulations, although it often took the form of barter.[29] By 1970, however, the Cultural Revolution had disrupted such exchanges, which did not resume until after 1980.[30] Thereafter, policy initiatives had a major impact on the expansion of cross-border trade,[31] which, as table 13 shows, underwent rapid growth until it was interrupted by a combination of factors in the late 1990s. Implied in these figures is an average annual rate of growth of 61

Value (US$ million) and share (%) of each Chinese region's exports to,
and imports from, the following countries [regions]:

EU		ROK		Taiwan		ASEAN	
Exports	Imports	Exports	Imports	Exports	Imports	Exports	Imports
34,745.0 (10.9)	34,479.5 (13.1)	14,814.2 (4.6)	27,447.2 (10.5)	—	36,149.2 (13.8)	9,090.1 (2.9)	15,122.7 (5.8)
2,360.7 (11.1)	2,063.0 (9.3)	2,469.0 (9.8)	3,464.3 (15.7)	—	1,458.0 (6.6)	—	—
—	617.8 (19.6)	445.0 (9.8)	—	—	—	—	—
—	1,777.6 (13.0)	2,042.2 (12.7)	1,812.2 (13.3)	—	—	986.8 (6.1)	—
734.7 (7.7)	1,818.8 (28.4)	607.7 (6.4)	563.6 (8.8)	—	147.4 (2.3)	—	—
13,393.3 (11.1)	10,786.2 (11.0)	7,306.0 (6.0)	12,262.1 (12.5)	—	12,025.5 (12.3)	—	—
17,987.2 (13.2)	16,922.3 (14.8)	1,776.9 (1.3)	9,087.2 (3.5)	—	22,814.2 (19.9)	7,119.7 (5.2)	15,122.7 (13.2)
—	493.8 (11.0)	—	257.8 (5.8)	—	250.1 (5.6)	983.6 (13.5)	—

SOURCES: Appendices I and II.

percent during 1988–92, although during the next six years this was transformed into negative growth of –10.6 percent. A variety of factors seems to have been responsible for this downturn, including the effect of the 1997 Asian financial crisis, major reductions and instability in the value of some border countries' currencies (e.g., Burma and Russia), and declining competitiveness in some of China's border trade enterprises.[32] In any case, recovery was swift, and border trade recorded annual growth averaging 34.9 percent between 1998 and 2002 to reach a new peak of almost $6.7 billion.[33] The more rapid expansion of exports during this period left China with a deficit of some $1.6 billion in its border trade in 2002.[34]

Overall, the evidence presented and cited in this section lends support to the claim that the emergence of transnational trade has been a significant force in China's external economic relations since the early 1980s. It is telling that estimates derived from table 10 indicate that the share of merchandise trade originating in, or destined for, countries and regions other

TABLE 11. Relative Importance of Each Chinese Region as a
Source of Exports to Major Trading Partners, 2002

| | *Contribution of each Chinese region to total Chinese export sales to the following countries [regions] (%)* | | | | | |
	U.S.	Hong Kong	Japan	EU	ROK	ASEAN
North	7.8	3.0	7.7	7.6	18.9	—
Northwest	0.6	0.6	1.0	—	3.4	1.8
Northeast	2.9	—	10.7	—	15.7	10.5
Central-Interior	2.1	2.2	2.3	2.1	4.7	1.8
Central-East	36.1	14.5	50.0	38.5	56.0	—
Southeast	48.8	78.2	27.1	51.8	—	75.5
Southwest	1.8	1.5	1.2	—	1.3	10.4

SOURCE: Appendix I.

TABLE 12. Relative Importance of Each Chinese Region as a
Destination for Imports from Major Trading Partners, 2002

| | *Share of each Chinese region in total Chinese import purchases from the following countries [regions] (%)* | | | | |
	Japan	Taiwan	EU	ROK	U.S.
North	9.5	2.5	6.0	12.6	11.3
Northwest	0.5	—	1.8	—	1.5
Northeast	7.2	—	5.2	6.6	3.4
Central-Interior	2.0	0.4	5.3	2.1	2.7
Central-East	41.7	33.3	31.3	44.7	43.7
Southeast	37.2	63.1	49.1	33.1	34.7
Southwest	1.9	0.7	1.4	0.9	2.6

SOURCE: Appendix II.

than those constituting China's main trading partners[35] was highest in the Northwest and Southwest.[36] The inference is that a major share of this balance was shipped westward to Russia and Central Asia, and perhaps to South Asia, too.[37] My estimates of the "residual" suggest that almost half of both exports from, and imports to, the Southwest were associated with trading partners other than the United States, EU member states, Hong Kong, South Korea, and Taiwan.[38]

TABLE 13. Post-1978 Expansion of China's Border Trade

	Value of all border trade (US$ million)	Value of China's border exports (US$ million)	Value of China's border imports (US$ million)
1980	13.0	9.0	4.0
1983	26.0	—	—
1988	650.0	—	—
1989	1,060.0	—	—
1991	1,900.0[a]	—	—
1992	3,950.0	—	—
1998	2,018.0	805.0	1,213.0
2002[b]	6,687.2	2,541.3	4,145.9

[a]Specified as trade between China's border provinces (regions) and countries of the former USSR, Mongolian Republic, North Korea, Pakistan, Nepal, Myanmar, Thailand, and Vietnam.
[b]Preliminary estimates.

SOURCES: Su-cheng Chao, *Zhongguo dalu xinan shengqu duiwai maoyi fazhan moshi* [The pattern of foreign trade in Southwest China] (Taipei: Yinke Publishing Company, 2002), 179–80 (1980–98); Ministry of Commerce, *Zhongguo duiwai jingji maoyi nianjian* [Yearbook of China's foreign economic relations and trade] (Beijing: Zhongguo duiwai jingji maoyi chubanshe, 2003).

China's border regions are often described as being rich in natural resources and having a comparative advantage in primary production (here taken to embrace mining as well as farming). From this perspective, it is noteworthy that the structure of border exports has shifted markedly toward industrial manufactures. In the Southwest, for example, the share of such goods in total exports in 2002 was 84, 81.3, and 91.7 percent, respectively, in Guangxi, Yunnan, and Tibet. This compared with corresponding figures of 55.6, 58.5, and 8.1 percent in 1990.[39]

It is important to keep such findings in perspective by pointing out that in 2002 the Southwest and Northwest together accounted for less than 4 percent of the value of all Chinese exports (and under 3 percent of its imports). There is evidence, too, that the share of border trade in China's border regions' total exports and imports has been in decline in recent years.[40]

Reference was made above to the sizable trade deficit experienced by China's border regions in their cross-border trade. Table 14 offers a counterpoint to that finding by showing the trade balance of each Chinese region with China's four major trading partners. The estimates require little comment. They reveal that in its bilateral merchandise trade with the United

TABLE 14. China's Regional Merchandise Trade Balances vis-à-vis
China's Four Major Trading Partners, 2002 (in US$ million)

	U.S.	Japan	EU	South Korea
China	+45,754.5	−3,383.8	+ 265.5	−12,633
North	+ 2,736	−1,215.1	+297.7	−995.3
Northwest	+134.1	+244.7	−617.8	+445.0
Northeast	+1,177.9	+1,425.5	−1,777.6	+230.0
Central-Interior	+835.1	+65.7	−1,081.1	+44.1
Central-East	+14,724.7	+2,596.2	+3,480.2	−4,956.1
Southeast	+25,630.8	−6,097.9	+1,064.9	−7,310.3
Southwest	+648.1	−392.9	−493.8	−257.8

SOURCES: Appendices I and II.

States, every region of China was in surplus. Elsewhere, however, regional surpluses and deficits counteracted each other. Most notable in this respect is the case of Japan, whose surplus with China would have been much greater were it not for the significant deficits it generated in its trade with the Northeast and Central-East. The balance in trade between China and the EU also reflected varying fortunes in terms of regional trade relations: large Chinese surpluses in central-eastern and southeastern regions contrasted with significant deficits in central-inland and northeastern provinces.

Regional Dimensions of China's Foreign Direct Investment

Comprehensive estimates for FDI flows to every Chinese province in 2002 are set out in Appendix III,[41] from which table 15 is derived. From this table, two profiles of FDI, one by destination and one by origin, can be derived (see tables 16 and 17).

As Appendix III confirms, the principal source of FDI to China is the "Greater Chinese Diaspora" (Hong Kong, Macau, Taiwan, and Singapore) and developed countries such as the United States, EU member states, and, to a lesser extent, Japan.[42] Multilateral organizations, such as the World Bank and the Asian Development Bank, have also been important donors.[43] Except for Singapore, the scope for significant FDI involvement in China from Russia and countries in central, southeastern, and south Asia has been constrained by the limited level of development achieved so far in these regions. Such factors do not, however, invalidate an attempt to identify transnational FDI links, although a hypothesis that deserves consideration is that there has been greater FDI involvement by Chinese investors in the

TABLE 15. Origins of Regional FDI, 2002

Value and origin of FDI flows to each region, 2002
(US$ million) (%)

Region (province)	FDI (US$ million)	Hong Kong	Japan	Taiwan	U.S.	EU[a]	ROK	Singapore	ASEAN	British Virgin Islands	Cayman Islands	Other
North	6,421.5	1,603.3 (25.0)	431.0 (6.7)	144.6 (2.3)	693.7 (10.8)	472.2 (7.4)	546.2 (8.5)	[206.3] (3.2)	313.2 (4.9)	1,016.8 (15.8)	165.4 (2.6)	821.0 (12.8)
Northwest	1,660.7	766.6 (46.2)	51.8 (3.1)	64.9 (3.9)	251.2 (15.1)	52.9 (3.2)	26.0 (1.6)	[1.4] ([0.1])	26.6 (1.6)	150.7 (9.1)	47.1 (2.8)	222.9 (13.4)
Northeast	8,781.1	2,468.9 (28.1)	796.8 (9.1)	359.8 (4.1)	1,336.5 (15.2)	289.0 (3.3)	1,148.4 (13.1)	[11.0] ([0.1])	11.0 (0.1)			2,470.7 (28.1)
Central	5,131.1[b]	2,289.5 (44.60)	49.8 (1.0)	466.9 (9.1)	348.8 (6.8)	277.6 (5.4)	145.5 (2.8)	352.6 ([6.9])	435.4 (8.5)	279.9 (5.5)	10.0 (0.2)	827.7 (16.1)
Central east	48,343.0	10,155.0 (21.0)	3,589 (7.4)	4755.2 (9.8)	4,424.9 (9.2)	1,094.5 (2.3)	4,793.6 (9.9)	[1,838.7] ([3.8])	2,103.5 (4.4)	7,690.2 (15.9)	1,921.0 (4.0)	7,816.1 (16.2)
Southeast	25,845.3[c]	10,150.0 (39.3)	765.4 (3.0)	3,007.1 (11.6)	1,295.4 (5.0)	129.7 (0.5)	142.0 (0.6)	467.5 (1.8)	820.4 (3.2)	3,929.4 (15.2)	385.9 (1.5)	5,220.0 (20.2)
Southwest	2,429.0[b]	936.2 (38.5)	70.5 (2.9)	81.9 (3.4)	300.5 (12.4)	73.8 (3.0)	23.2 (1.0)	103.8 (4.3)	118.1 (4.9)	478.8 (19.7)	11.4 (0.5)	334.6 (13.8)
Total	98,612	28,369.5 (28.8)	5,754.3 (5.8)	8,880.4 (9.0)	8,651.0 (8.8)	2,389.7 (2.4)	6,824.9 (6.9)	2,981.3 (3.0)	3,828.2 (3.90)	13,545.8 (13.7)	2,540.8 (2.6)	17,713.0 (18.0)

[a]The estimates of FDI from the EU understate reality by virtue of excluding relatively small flows of investment not recorded in official provincial data.
[b]The figure for Central China is derived from estimates of utilized FDI in Henan, Jiangxi, and Hunan provinces; similarly, that for Southwest China embodies an estimate of utilized FDI in Sichuan province. I have been unable to find the corresponding estimates of contractual FDI for these four provinces.
[c]Excluding Hainan, for which a breakdown of the geographical origins of FDI is not available.

NOTE: Except where stated, the estimates are for approved contractual FDI.

TABLE 16. Regional Destinations of FDI Inflows into China, 2002

	Contractual value of FDI (US$ million)	Share of each region in total FDI inflows to China (%)
North	6,421.5	6.5
Northwest	1,660.7	1.7
Northeast	8,781.1	8.9
Central-Interior	5,131.1	5.2
Central-Coastal	48,343.0	49.0
Southeast	25,845.3	26.2
Southwest	2,429.0	2.5
Total	98,612.0	100.0

SOURCES: Appendix III and table 16.

economies of its land-based neighbors than the reverse[44] (lack of data unfortunately makes it difficult to test this). Meanwhile, a priori reasoning based on simple geographical propinquity might lead one to expect a bias among Korean and Japanese investors toward engagement in the economies of northern and northeastern China, or among Hong Kong and Taiwanese entrepreneurs in southeastern and central-eastern provinces. As we shall see, the evidence in favor of these propositions is far from unambiguous.

Nevertheless, table 15 confirms that FDI inflows are still disproportionately oriented toward central-eastern and southeastern China—that is, toward provinces[45] whose infrastructural bases have offered overseas investors a favorable environment. In 2002, these provinces received three-quarters of all FDI officially recorded as having entered China. Next in importance was the Northeast and North, which together accounted for a further 15 percent of total FDI. By contrast, central-inland provinces (Anhui, Jiangxi, Hubei, and Hunan) received just 5 percent of FDI, while western regions— the focus, since 2001, of a major new development strategy—absorbed a mere 4.2 percent of FDI receipts. Such estimates afford little evidence that border regions have yet derived any significant benefit from policies that were supposedly designed to help facilitate FDI flows to such areas.[46]

Table 17 indicates, as expected, that in 2002 the Northeast was a favored destination of FDI—the second most important—from Japan and South Korea, while the North was also a major recipient of investment funds from these two countries. Such findings do not, however, support the notion of the overwhelming dominance of truly transnational linkages in making FDI available. Further consideration of table 17 will, for example, reveal that a surprisingly large share of ASEAN FDI disbursements was directed toward

TABLE 17. FDI Disbursements among China's Regions, by Source, 2002

	Hong Kong	Japan	Taiwan	U.S.	EU	ROK	ASEAN	Singapore	Virgin and Cayman Islands	Other
North	5.7	7.5	1.6	8.0	19.8	8.0	8.2	6.9	7.3	4.6
Northwest	2.7	0.9	0.7	2.9	2.2	0.4	0.7	—	1.2	1.3
Northeast	8.7	13.8	4.1	15.4	12.1	16.8	0.3	.4	—	13.9
Central-Interior	8.1	0.9	5.3	4.0	11.6	2.1	11.4	11.8	1.8	4.7
Central-Coastal	35.8	62.4	53.5	51.1	45.8	70.2	54.9	61.7	59.7	44.1
Southeast	35.8	13.3	33.9	15.0	5.4	2.1	21.4	15.7	26.8	29.5
Southwest	3.3	1.2	0.9	3.5	3.1	0.3	2.7	3.5	3.0	1.9

SOURCES: Appendix III and table 16.

northern provinces; the Northeast, too, benefited from significant shares of U.S. and EU—and, to a lesser extent, Hong Kong—FDI flows to China. The extent to which central and southeastern coastal Chinese provinces (above all, the Pearl and Yangzi River Delta regions) have benefited from investment undertaken by entrepreneurs based in Hong Kong and Taiwan has been widely recognized. Such FDI activity no doubt reflects emerging transnational linkages, although, as the scale of FDI inflows from ASEAN member countries and the United States indicates, wider international links have also been important.

Perhaps the strongest transnational FDI link to have emerged in recent years is that between Taiwan and the Yangzi Delta region. Taken at face value, the figures in table 16 show that over half of Taiwanese FDI inflows to China were destined for Greater Shanghai. In fact, this is likely to understate reality significantly, since most of the large-scale investment that ostensibly derives from the British Virgin Islands and the Cayman Islands is a cover for FDI that originates in Taiwan.[47]

An authoritative official source in Taiwan reveals that in 2002 total investment (approved FDI) in mainland China was $6,723.06 million,[48] of which almost half ($3,172.31 million) was destined for Jiangsu alone.[49] Interestingly, the same source gives a detailed breakdown of such flows in terms of their provincial destinations within China. This information is reproduced in table 18.

Since 1991, Jiangsu has absorbed the largest share (virtually 40 percent) of cumulative approved FDI from Taiwan, with Guangdong in second place (32 percent).[50] Despite having the closest geographical and cultural links with Taiwan, Fujian secured less than 10 percent of FDI inflows during the same period. After deducting the further 10.5 percent shared, almost equally, by Zhejiang and Hebei, it emerges that between 1991 and 2002, the remaining twenty-six provinces, municipalities, and autonomous regions benefited from $3,754.4 million of Taiwanese FDI, or a mere 14 percent of the cumulative total.

Here, if anywhere, is evidence of the creation of growing economic integration through the forging of increasingly close transnational investment and, by implication, foreign trade links.[51] The driving force behind this process is twofold: first, the relocation, by small and medium-scale Taiwanese enterprises, of labor-intensive manufacturing activities to Guangdong; second, the transfer of much larger-scale high-tech electronics and IT production to the Yangzi Delta Region (predominantly Jiangsu and Shanghai). It is the latter development that has become the defining feature of transnational Taiwan-mainland linkages in the most recent past. In this respect, analysis of the functional distribution of Taiwan's investment in China toward the end of the 1990s is revealing: in 1997–98, the share of electronics and associated production activities in total Taiwanese FDI rose

TABLE 18. Provincial Distribution of Approved FDI from Taiwan to Mainland China

Level (US$ million) and share (%)

	Jiangsu	Guangdong	Fujian	Hebei	Zhejiang	Shandong	Liaoning	Sichuan	Hunan	Hubei	Other	Total
1991	24.40	73.33	55.96	7.47	0.19	2.06	0.31	0.17	0.14	0.80	9.33	174.16
	(14.0)	*(42.1)*	*(32.1)*	*(4.3)*	*(0.1)*	*(1.2)*	*(0.2)*	*(0.1)*	*(0.1)*	*(0.5)*	*(5.4)*	
1992	34.39	112.04	29.58	22.27	16.75	1.98	15.60	0.43	8.05	—	5.90	246.99
	(13.9)	*(46.4)*	*(12.0)*	*(9.0)*	*(6.8)*	*(0.6)*	*(6.3)*	*(0.2)*	*(3.3)*		*(2.4)*	
1993	833.31	1,047.81	473.80	194.30	124.84	95.03	49.32	61.67	21.93	35.93	230.47	3,168.41
	(26.3)	*(33.1)*	*(15.0)*	*(6.1)*	*(3.9)*	*(3.0)*	*(1.6)*	*(1.9)*	*(0.7)*	*(1.1)*	*(7.3)*	
1994	391.81	230.93	96.62	56.81	62.80	24.58	5.91	32.51	4.24	8.09	47.91	962.21
	(40.1)	*(24.0)*	*(10.0)*	*(5.9)*	*(6.5)*	*(2.6)*	*(0.6)*	*(3.4)*	*(0.4)*	*(0.8)*	*(5.0)*	
1995	394.77	222.75	121.66	83.19	57.43	24.04	36.61	6.50	31.56	24.44	89.76	1,092.71
	(36.1)	*(20.4)*	*(11.1)*	*(7.6)*	*(5.3)*	*(2.2)*	*(3.4)*	*(0.6)*	*(2.9)*	*(2.2)*	*(8.2)*	
1996	541.99	282.82	110.88	132.90	32.75	43.20	26.27	12.37	15.06	4.07	26.93	1,229.24
	(44.1)	*(23.0)*	*(9.0)*	*(10.8)*	*(2.7)*	*(3.5)*	*(2.1)*	*(1.0)*	*(1.2)*	*(0.3)*	*(2.2)*	
1997	1,247.30	1,720.90	472.23	233.56	195.28	109.17	52.94	49.81	29.85	50.71	172.56	4,334.31
	(28.8)	*(39.7)*	*(10.9)*	*(5.4)*	*(4.5)*	*(2.5)*	*(1.2)*	*(1.1)*	*(0.7)*	*(1.2)*	*(4.0)*	
1998	694.75	824.42	150.79	92.42	85.81	66.12	8.26	20.15	4.93	32.15	54.82	2,034.62
	(34.1)	*(40.5)*	*(7.4)*	*(4.5)*	*(4.2)*	*(3.2)*	*(0.4)*	*(1.0)*	*(0.2)*	*(1.6)*	*(2.7)*	
1999	475.01	500.11	58.90	57.28	78.98	4.14	4.02	38.15	0.88	17.80	17.51	1,252.78
	(37.9)	*(39.9)*	*(4.7)*	*(4.6)*	*(6.3)*	*(0.3)*	*(0.3)*	*(3.0)*	*(0.1)*	*(1.4)*	*(1.4)*	
2000	1,251.62	1,019.70	99.49	92.63	68.67	12.08	14.26	26.91	0.16	1.09	20.53	2,607.14
	(48.0)	*(39.1)*	*(3.8)*	*(3.6)*	*(2.6)*	*(0.5)*	*(0.5)*	*(1.0)*	*neg.*	*neg.*	*(0.8)*	
2001	1,422.59	787.97	120.12	125.23	208.48	28.26	18.19	19.23	8.86	28.09	17.13	2,784.15
	(51.1)	*(28.3)*	*(4.3)*	*(4.5)*	*(7.5)*	*(1.0)*	*(0.7)*	*(0.7)*	*(0.3)*	*(1.0)*	*(0.6)*	
2002	3,172.31	1,635.09	749.94	275.28	511.55	64.44	58.67	61.35	12.62	14.79	167.02	6,723.06
	(47.2)	*(24.3)*	*(11.2)*	*(4.1)*	*(7.6)*	*(1.0)*	*(0.9)*	*(0.9)*	*(0.2)*	*(0.2)*	*(2.5)*	
1991–2002	10,484.25	8,457.87	2,539.97	1,373.34	1,443.53	475.10	290.36	329.25	138.28	217.96	859.87	26,609.78
	(39.4)	*(31.8)*	*(9.5)*	*(5.1)*	*(5.4)*	*(1.8)*	*(1.1)*	*(1.2)*	*(0.5)*	*(0.8)*	*(3.2)*	

SOURCE: *Zhonghua mingui tongji nianjian, 2003* [Statistical yearbook of the Republic of China, 2003] (Taipei: Sanmin Publishing House, October 2003), 242.

from 22 percent to 41 percent; and by 2000, the corresponding figure had reached 61 percent. The inference is clear: since 1998, Taiwan's FDI in China has basically been driven by this single sector.[52]

CONCLUSION

The principal focus of this chapter is the extent to which transnational economic linkages have emerged as a distinctive feature of China's foreign economic relations under the impact of post-1978 reforms. On the one hand, the statistical analysis of China's regionally based trade and FDI relations do reveal clear transnational axes. Undoubtedly, the most important of these are those that exist between Guangdong (the Pearl River Delta) and Hong Kong—a transnational axis that has generated a true economic symbiosis; and between the Yangzi Delta region and Taiwan—a more recent phenomenon, characterized by growing economic integration. The contrast between these leading examples of closer transnational economic relations is interesting and telling. In the former, integration derived from the shared economic benefits of factor endowments that were highly complementary in the production of labor-intensive activities. Factor complementarity is also important in the development of the Taiwan–Yangzi Delta growth hub. But here, integrative forces have been driven by the relocation of high-tech, higher valued–added activities associated with the IT industry. A noteworthy feature, which both links share, is that FDI has been strongly linked to trade: that is, Hong Kong–funded and Taiwan-funded activities in China have had a robust export orientation.

On the other hand, data presented in this chapter also suggest the wider context in which China's foreign trade and FDI must be placed. If China's remarkable record of GDP growth since the early 1980s reflects its emergence as a major economic power within East and Southeast Asia, its more truly international, even *global* trading and investment links are an important part of the same story. While the regional and subregional economic axes highlighted here are of course important, the country that has the widest geographical representation, in terms of both foreign trade and FDI, in China is, significantly, the United States. EU and ASEAN member states also enjoy a significant presence throughout China

A special focus of the analysis in this chapter has been the extent to which significant economic relationships have emerged across China's land borders. The evidence presented does attest to the rapid growth of associated trade flows, although the aggregate value of exports and imports is still tiny when set in the context of national merchandise trade, or when compared with the scale of trade involving coastal Chinese regions. Nevertheless, cross-border trade ties are likely to grow, especially as development accelerates in Russia and Central, South, and Southeast Asia.[53] There is little doubt that the potential for such trade expansion involving, severally, these countries, Xinjiang, and Inner Mongolia is considerable.[54] The establishment of the Shanghai Cooperation Organization (SCO) is likely to encourage stronger trade and investment relations between China's Northwest (especially Xinjiang) and other SCO members.[55] The construction of the Russia-China oil pipeline similarly promises to confer benefits on border regions in North and Northwest China. Tibet is already cooperating with Tajikistan in power engineering, and is also negotiating with the same country for the supply of large-scale supplies of electricity. Meanwhile, at the Twelfth Ministerial Conference of the Greater Mekong Subregion Economic Cooperation Programme, held in Dali (Yunnan) in September 2003, China committed itself to strengthen cooperation and promote regional development within the GMS framework.[56]

Any assessment of these positive developments must, however, be tempered by a recognition of the constraints still facing western border regions in their efforts to attract large-scale FDI, especially from major international players in the United States and Europe. The reality is that these regions are seriously disadvantaged in their attempts to attract more FDI. They are poor, their markets are correspondingly undeveloped, they are situated far from major international trading routes, west-east migration has resulted in a decline in their human capital (especially skills) and, at least until recently, they have been the victims of discrimination.[57] Apart from resource-seeking FDI, capital inflows to China are likely to become even more motivated by the desire to capture its domestic markets—an area in which the border regions will remain at a disadvantage vis-à-vis other parts of the country.[58]

Overall, a complex mix of subregional, regional, and global forces has shaped China's foreign trade and FDI inflows. Without underestimating the local significance of cross-border trade and investment relations involving China's western and northern border provinces, it is clear that, for the time being and into the foreseeable future, by far the most important of all the transnational links are and will remain those that reflect economic integration between central and southeastern China, Taiwan, and Hong Kong. In an article published more than a decade ago, Harry Harding noted the emergence of a "transnational Chinese economy" based on economic complementarities that linked China, Hong Kong, and Taiwan.[59] This matrix remains the most striking example of transnational economic links involving China, even if the conceptual framework in which such relations are investigated demands refinement in order to allow for the separate and distinctive roles now played by Hong Kong and Taiwan. Even if China's border regions, especially those in the Northwest and Southwest, become more open, it will be a very long time indeed before these regions claim benefits similar to those that have so far disproportionately accrued to the maritime regions of coastal China.

APPENDIX 1. Value and Direction of Chinese Regional (Provincial) Exports (2002)

Region or province	Value of total regional (provincial) exports (US$ million)	Value (US$ million) and share (%) of exports to each of the five main export destinations of each Chinese region (province) as share of total exports from that region (province)				
North	23,750	USA 5,378.2 (21.3)	Japan 3,681.0 (14.6)	EU 2,630.7 (11.1) [Germany] [948.1] [(4.0)]	ROK 2,469.0 (9.8)	HK 1,696.6 (7.1)
Beijing	5,899ᵃ	Japan: 1,094.5 (18.6)	USA: 1,022.6 (17.3)	HK: 802.3 (13.6)	Germany: 448.1 (7.6)	ROK: 386.1 (6.5)
Tianjin	11,595	USA: 3,645 (31.4)	Japan: 1,667 (14.4)	ROK: 1,139 (9.8)	HK: 697 (6.0)	Germany: 500 (4.3)
Hebei	4,594	EU: 709.6 (15.4)	Japan: 686.5 (14.9)	ROK: 620.9 (13.5)	USA: 549.8 (12.0)	Taiwan: 312.5 (6.8)
Shanxi	1,662	ROK: 323.0 (19.4)	Japan: 233.0 (14.0)	USA: 160.8 (9.7)	Holland: 87.3 (5.3)	Brazil: 76.7 (4.6)
Northwest	4,520	Japan 493.6 (10.9)	Kazakhstan 445.4 (9.9)	ROK 445.0 (9.8)	USA 407.0 (9.0)	HK 314.3 (7.0)
Inner Mongolia	807	Japan: 163.1 (20.2)	ROK: 161. (20.0)	HK: 78.0 (9.6)	Malaysia: 46.0 (5.7)	Mongolia: 45.3 (5.6)
Shaanxi	1,377	USA: 191.4 (13.9)	Japan: 115.0 (8.4)	HK: 106.1 (7.7)	ROK: 95.9 (7.0)	Holland: 94.0 (6.8)
Gansu	549	Singapore: 122.8 (22.4)	Japan: 93.3 (17.0)	ROK: 73.7 (13.4)	HK: 46.7 (8.5)	USA: 33.5 (6.1)
Qinghai	151	ROK: 37.6 (24.9)	Japan: 29.6 (19.6)	HK: 19.1 (12.6)	USA: 16.2 (10.8)	Singapore: 12.6 (8.4)
Ningxia	328	Japan: 57.1 (17.4)	USA: 46.1 (14.1)	Singapore: 33.1 (10.1)	ROK: 30.4 (5.6)	Italy: 18.1 (5.5)

APPENDIX I (*continued*)

Region or province	Value of total regional (provincial) exports (US$ million)	Value (US$ million) and share (%) of exports to each of the five main export destinations of each Chinese region (province) as share of total exports from that region (province)				
Xinjiang	1,308	Kazakhstan: 442.0 (*33.8*)	Kyrgyzstan: 99.5 (*7.6*)	Azerbaijan: 86.3 (*6.6*)	Italy: 79.7 (*6.1*)	USA: 76.0 (*5.8*)
Northeast	16,122	Japan 5,118.8 (*31.8*)	ROK 2,042.2 (*12.7*)	USA 1,981.7 (*12.3*)	ASEAN 986.8 (6.1) [Singapore] [627.1] [(3.9)]	Russia 972.2 (*6.0*)
Liaoning	12,366	Japan: 4,680 (*37.8*)	USA: 1,813 (*14.7*)	ROK: 1,266 (*10.2*)	Singapore: 627.1 (*5.1*)	HK: 433.8 (*3.5*)
Jilin	1,769	ROK: 582.5 (*38.9*)	Japan: 264.0 (*14.9*)	Malaysia: 183.6 (*10.4*)	DPRK: 108.1 (*6.1*)	Indonesia: 96.3 (*5.4*)
Heilongjiang	1,987	Russia: 972.2 (*48.9*)	ROK: 193.7 (*9.7*)	Japan: 174.8 (*8.8*)	USA: 82.4 (*4.1*)	HK: 81.2 (*4.1*)
Central-Interior	9,515	USA: 1,475.4 (*15.5*)	HK: 1,276.9 (*13.4*)	Japan: 1,088.0 (*11.4*)	EU: 734.7 (*7.7*)	ROK: 607.7 (*6.4*)
Henan	2,119	USA: 334.0 (*15.8*)	HK: 277.0 (*13.1*)	EU: 252.3 (*11.9*)	ROK: 245.6 (*11.6*)	Japan: 226.3 (*10.7*)
Anhui	2,450	USA:[b] 493.2 (*20.1*)	EU: 412.2 (*16.8*)	Japan: 260.7 (*10.6*)	ASEAN 172.6 (*7.0*)	ROK: 121.8 (*5.0*)
Jiangxi	1,052	HK: 185.5 (*17.6*)	Japan: 131.7 (*12.5*)	USA: 128.2 (*12.2*)	ROK: 37.2 (*3.5*)	UAR: 28.8 (*2.7*)
Hubei	2,099	HK: 413.7 (*19.7*)	Japan: 304.8 (*14.5*)	USA: 230.6 (*11.0*)	Germany: 118.6 (*5.7*)	ROK: 94.6 (*4.5*)
Hunan	1,795	HK: 291.3 (*16.2*)	USA: 289.4 (*16.1*)	Japan: 164.5 (*9.2*)	ROK: 108.5 (*6.0*)	Germany: 62.6 (*3.5*)

APPENDIX I (*continued*)

Region or province	Value of total regional (provincial) exports (US$ million)	Value (US$ million) and share (%) of exports to each of the five main export destinations of each Chinese region (province) as share of total exports from that region (province)				

Region or province	Value of total regional (provincial) exports (US$ million)					
Central-Eastern	121,057	USA 24,949 (20.6)	Japan 23,980 (19.8)	EU 13,393.3 (11.1) Germany 4,711.4 (3.9)	HK 8,273.6 (6.9)	ROK 7,306.0 (6.0)
Shandong	21,120	Japan: 5,372 (25.4)	USA: 3,733 (17.7)	ROK: 3,273 (15.5)	Germany: 577.4 (2.7)	UK: 464.6 (2.2)
Shanghai	32,046	USA: 7,321 (22.9)	Japan: 6,999 (21.8)	HK: 3,118 (9.7)	Germany: 1,221 (3.8)	ROK: 1,160 (3.6)
Jiangsu	38,471	USA: 8,205 (21.3)	Japan: 7,599 (19.8)	HK: 3,281 (8.5)	ROK: 1,707 (4.4)	Germany: 1,643 (4.3)
Zhejiang	29,420	USA: 5,690 (19.3)	Japan: 4,010 (13.6)	HK: 1,410 (4.8)	Germany: 1,270 (4.3)	ROK: 1,166 (4.0)
Southeast	136,666	HK 44,524.9 (32.6)	USA 33,748.9 (24.7)	EU 17,987.2 (13.2)	Japan 13,008.9 (9.5)	ASEAN 7,119.7 (5.2)
Fujian	17,373	USA: 4,071 (23.4)	Japan: 3,572 (20.6)	HK: 1,822 (10.5)	Germany: 681 (3.9)	Holland: 438 (2.5)
Guangdong	118,474	HK: 42,391 (35.8)	USA: 29,582 (25.0)	EU: 15,434 (13.0)	Japan: 9,339 (7.9)	ASEAN: 6,111 (5.2)
Hainan	819	HK: 311.9 (38.1)	Japan: 97.9 (12.0)	USA: 95.9 (11.7)	ROK: 41.9 (5.1)	Germany: 25.4 (3.1)

APPENDIX I (*continued*)

Region or province	Value of total regional (provincial) exports (US$ million)	Value (US$ million) and share (%) of exports to each of the five main export destinations of each Chinese region (province) as share of total exports from that region (province)				
Southwest	7,265	USA 1,211.7 (16.7)	ASEAN 983.6 (13.5) Vietnam 613.2 (8.4)	HK 871.8 (12.0)	Japan 578.7 (8.0)	Burma 296.1 (4.1)
Guangxi	1,510	Vietnam: 340.3 (22.5)	HK: 257.4 (17.1)	USA: 157.2 (10.4)	Japan: 120.7 (8.0)	Taiwan: 63.3 (4.2)
Chongqing	1,091	Vietnam: 139.2 (12.8)	USA: 105.5 (9.7)	Japan: 73.4 (6.7)	HK 73.2 (6.7)	Iran: 69.7 (6.4)
Sichuan	2,711	USA: 892.9 (32.9)	HK: 294.5 (10.9)	Japan: 214.9 (7.9)	ROK: 125.4 (4.6)	Singapore: 120.4 (4.4)
Guizhou	442	ASEAN: 93.4 (21.1)	USA: 51.7 (11.7)	EU: 44.9 (10.2)	ROK: 42.0 (9.5)	Japan: 36.9 (8.4)
Yunnan	1,430	Burma: 296.1 (20.7)	HK: 242.7 (17.0)	Vietnam: 133.7 (9.4)	Japan: 130.1 (9.1)	Indonesia: 76.6 (5.4)
Tibet	81	Nepal: 56.7 (69.8)	USA: 4.4 (5.5)	HK: 4.0 (4.9)	India: 3.2 (4.0)	Japan: 2.7 (3.3)
Total	318,895	USA 69,151.9 (21.7)	HK 56,958.1 (17.9)	Japan 47,949.0 (15.0)	EU 34,745.9 (10.9)	ROK 13,037.3 (4.1)
Total (NBS)	325,570					

APPENDIX 11. Value and Origin of Chinese Regional (Provincial) Imports, 2002

Region or province	*Value of total regional (provincial) exports (US$ million)*	*Value (US$ million) and share (%) of imports to each Chinese region (province) associated with that region's (province's) five main points of import origin*				
		1	2	3	4	5
North	22,096	Japan 4,896.1 (22.2)	ROK 3,464.3 (15.7)	USA 2,642.2 (12.0)	EU 2,063.0 (9.3) [Germany] [1,122.1] [(5.1)]	Taiwan 912. 0 (2.5)
Beijing	8,143[a]	Japan 1,721.6 (21.1)	USA 1,049.8 (12.9)	HK 877.1 (10.8)	Germany 529.1 (6.5)	ROK 495.7 (6.1)
Tianjin	11,231	Japan 2,834 (25.2)	ROK 2,773 (24.7)	USA 1,291 (11.5)	Taiwan 912 (8.1)	Germany 593 (5.3)
Hebei	2,072	EU 425.4 (20.5)	Japan 340.5 (16.4)	USA 238.7 (11.5)	ROK 195.6 (9.4)	Brazil 168.0 (8.1)
Shanxi	650	Australia 139.2 (21.4)	Germany 101.5 (15.6)	France 78.2 (12.0)	USA 62.7 (9.7)	India 43.7 (6.7)
Northwest	3,147.1	Kazakhstan 923.6 (29.3)	EU 617.8 (19.6) [Germany] [314.9] [(10.0)]	USA 356.0 (11.3)	Australia 322.9 (10.3)	Japan 248.9 (7.9)
Inner Mongolia	1,634	Russia 1,134 (69.4)	Mongolia 163.7 (10.0)	USA 83.9 (5.1)	Germany 61.8 (3.8)	Australia 53.7 (3.3)
Shaanxi	848	Japan 165.3 (19.5)	USA 115.0 (17.0)	Germany 113.4 (13.4)	Belgium 65.5 (7.7)	Sweden 54.4 (6.8)
Gansu	328.5	Australia 118.1 (36.0)	USA 39.3 (12.0)	Germany 17.7 (13.4)	Chile 13.9 (4.2)	Peru 13.4 (4.1)
Qinghai	456.2	Australia 177.4 (38.9)	Germany 80.9 (17.7)	USA 50.0 (11.0)	Japan 39.5 (8.7)	HK 31.4 (6.9)

APPENDIX II (*continued*)

Region or province	Value of total regional (provincial) exports (US$ million)	Value (US$ million) and share (%) of imports to each Chinese region (province) associated with that region's (province's) five main points of import origin				
		1	2	3	4	5
Ningxia	114.7	Australia 26.9 (*23.4*)	USA 18.0 (*15.7*)	Japan 9.6 (*8.4*)	India 6.8 (*5.9*)	Germany 5.5 (*4.8*)
Xinjiang	1,383.4	Kazakhstan 923.6 (*66.8*)	Russia 168.2 (*12.2*)	Kyrgyzstan 54.4 (*3.9*)	USA 49.8 (*3.6*)	Germany 35.6 (*2.6*)
Northeast	13,669.4	Japan 3,693.1 (*27.0*)	ROK 1,812.2 (*13.3*)	EU 1,777.6 (*13.0*) [Germany] [1,769.8] [(*12.9*)]	Russia 1,360.4 (*10.0*)	USA 803.8 (*5.9*)
Liaoning	9,373	Japan 3,323.0 (*34.5*)	ROK 1,581.0 (*16.9*)	USA 576.2 (*6.2*)	Saudia Arabia 527.2 (*5.6*)	Germany 491.3 (*5.2*)
Jilin	1,934.4	Germany 1,199.2 (*62.0*)	Japan 172.2 (*8.9*)	USA 93.6 (*4.8*)	ROK 92.5 (*4.8*)	DPRK 44.0 (*2.3*)
Heilong-jiang	2,362	Russia 1,360.4 (*57.6*)	Japan 198.1 (*8.4*)	ROK 138.7 (*5.9*)	USA 134.0 (*5.7*)	Germany 79.3 (*3.4*)
Central Interior	6,394	EU 1,818.8 (*28.4*)	Japan 1,022.3 (*16.0*)	USA 640.3 (*10.0*)	ROK 563.6 (*8.8*)	Australia 178.0 (*2.8*)
Henan	1,084.8	USA 234.2 (*21.6*)	EU 185.2 (*17.1*)	Japan 149.0 (*13.7*)	Australia 124.0 (*11.4*)	Brazil 74.3 (*6.9*)
Anhui	1,730	EU 398.9 (*23.1*)	Japan 343.9 (*19.9*)	ROK 148.1 (*8.6*)	USA[b] 119.3 (*6.9*)	Taiwan 97.8 (*5.7*)
Jiangxi	642.4	USA 83.6 (*13.0*	Japan 79.1 (*12.3*)	HK 66.9 (*10.4*)	Switz'l'd 56.1 (*8.7*)	Taiwan 49.6 (*7.7*)
Hubei	1,856	Japan 273.4 (*14.7*)	HK 164.7 (*8.9*)	Germany 154.4 (*8.3*)	France 129.3 (*7.0*)	USA 129.1 (*7.0*)

APPENDIX II (*continued*)

Region or province	Value of total regional (provincial) exports (US$ million)	Value (US$ million) and share (%) of imports to each Chinese region (province) associated with that region's (province's) five main points of import origin				
		1	2	3	4	5
Hunan	1,080.8	ROK 294.8 (27.2)	Japan 176.9 (16.4)	Germany 74.5 (6.9)	USA 74.1 (6.9)	Australia 54.0 (5.0)
Central Eastern	*97,796*	*Japan 21,383.8 (21.9)*	*ROK 12,262.1 (12.5)*	*Taiwan 12,025.5 (12.3)*	*EU 10,786.2 (11.0) [Germany] [6,892.4] [(7.0)]*	*USA 10,224.3 (10.5)*
Shandong	12,830	ROK 4,144.0 (32.3)	Japan 1,996.6 (15.6)	EU 1,397.6 (10.9)	USA 1,205.5 (9.4)	Taiwan 538.2 (4.2)
Shanghai	40,595	Japan 8,779 (21.6)	USA 5,478 (13.5)	Germany 4,308 (10.6)	Taiwan 3,971 (9.8)	ROK 2,830 (7.0)
Jiangsu	31,826	Japan 7,887 (24.8)	Taiwan 6,036 (19.0)	ROK 3,403 (10.7)	USA 2,427 (7.6)	HK 1,201 (3.8)
Zhejiang	12,545	Japan 2,721.2 (21.7)	ROK 1,885.1 (15.0)	Taiwan 1,480.3 (11.8)	USA 1,113.8 (8.9)	Germany 700.5 (5.6)
Southeast	*114,722*	*Taiwan 22,814.2 (19.9)*	*Japan 19,106.8 (16.7)*	*EU 16,922.3 (14.8)*	*ASEAN 15,122.7 (13.2)*	*ROK 9,087.2 (3.5)*
Fujian	11,027	Taiwan 2,918 (26.4)	Japan 1,505 (13.6)	ROK 1,402 (12.7)	USA 889 (8.1)	Malaysia 496 (4.5)
Guangdong	102,647	Taiwan 19,868 (19.4)	Japan 17,368 (16.9)	ASEAN 13,740 (13.4)	EU 8,000 (7.8)	ROK 7,653 (7.5)
Hainan	1,048	USA 534.1 (51.1)	Japan 233.8 (22.3)	Germany 36.3 (3.5)	ROK 32.2 (3.1)	Taiwan 28.2 (2.7)

APPENDIX II (*continued*)

Region or province	Value of total regional (provincial) exports (US$ million)	Value (US$ million) and share (%) of imports to each Chinese region (province) associated with that region's (province's) five main points of import origin				
		1	2	3	4	5
Southwest	4,479.3	Japan 971.6 (21.7)	USA 612.7 (13.7)	EU 493.8 (11.0)	ROK 257.8 (5.8)	Taiwan 250.1 (5.6)
Guangxi	923	Brazil 155.2 (16.8)	Vietnam 145.6 (15.8)	USA 113.8 (12.3)	Japan 64.9 (7.0)	Taiwan 60.3 (6.5)
Chongqing	702.8	Japan 308.6 (43.9)	HK 62.4 (8.9)	ROK 40.1 (5.7)	USA 37.7 (5.4)	Taiwan 34.7 (5.0)
Sichuan	1,758	USA 397.8 (22.6)	Japan 394.8 (22.5)	Taiwan 155.1 (8.8)	Germany 125.0 (7.1)	ROK 96.0 (5.5)
Guizhou	249.6	ROK 65.0 (26.0)	India 27.8 (11.1)	Japan 26.3 (10.5)	EU 24.4 (9.8)	ASEAN 19.1 (7.7)
Yunnan	796.7	Japan 140.0 (17.6)	Burma 110.7 (13.9)	Germany 76.1 (9.5)	USA 63.4 (8.0)	Australia 43.0 (5.4)
Tibet	49.2	Japan 37.0 (75.1)	Nepal 5.0 (10.2)	Germany 2.1 (4.2)	ROK 1.6 (3.3)	—
TOTAL	262,303.8	Japan 51,322.8 (19.6)	Taiwan 36,001.8 (13.7)	EU 34,479.5 (13.1)	ROK 27,447.2 (10.5)	USA 23,397.4 (8.9)
TOTAL (NBS)	295,200					

APPENDIX III. Origins of Regional (Provincial) FDI (2002)

Value (US$ million) and origin (%) of FDI for each region (province), 2002

Region (province)	FDI (US$ million)	Hong Kong	Japan	Taiwan	USA	EU[a]	ROK	[Singapore]	ASEAN	British Virgin Islands	Cayman Islands	Residual
North	*6,421.5*	*1,603.3 (25.0)*	*431.0 (6.7)*	*144.6 (2.3)*	*693.7 (10.8)*	*472.2 (7.4)*	*546.2 (8.5)*	*[206.3] (3.2)*	*313.2 (4.9)*	*1,016.8 (15.8)*	*165.4 (2.6)*	*821.0 (12.8)*
Beijing	2,808.2	564.2	182.7	22.6	204.3	247.9	287.9	[151.5]	160.0	642.6	165.4	330.2
Tianjin	2,015.0	417.0	179.0	122.0	365.0	135.0	177.0			234.0		227.1
Hebei	1,279.3	494.0	69.3		99.8	89.3	71.4	[54.8]	142.8	85.6		172.3
Shanxi	319.0	128.1			24.6		9.9		10.4	54.6		91.4
North-West	*1,660.7*	*766.6 (46.2)*	*51.8 (3.1)*	*64.9 (3.9)*	*251.2 (15.1)*	*52.9 (3.2)*	*26.0 (1.6)*	*[1.4] [(0.1)]*	*26.6 (1.6)*	*150.7 (9.1)*	*47.1 (2.8)*	*222.9 (13.4)*
IMAR	195.8	127.3	11.1	1.4	16.4		12.3	[1.4]	3.2			24.1
Shaanxi	840.6	366.9	34.5	53.4	104.7	51.0				125.4	47.1	57.6
Gansu	110.3	42.0	2.7	0.5	43.6		12.8					8.7
Qinghai	241.6	153.8	0.3	5.0	75.5	0.1			1.4			5.5
Ningxia	147.1	15.0	1.8	1.2	6.7	1.3	0.9		11.5	24.9		83.8
Xinjiang	125.3	61.6	1.4	3.4	4.3	0.5			10.5	0.4		43.2e

North-East	8,781.1	2,468.9 (28.1)	796.8 (9.1)	359.8 (4.1)	1,336.5 (15.2)	289.0 (3.3)	1,148.4 (13.1)	[11.0] (0.1)	11.0 (0.1)			2,470.7 (28.1)
Liaoning	7,185.0	2,089.0	762.0	305.0	1,170.0	289.0	982.0	[11.0]	11.0			1,588.0
Jilin	573.1	154.7	34.8	17.5	53.6		125.7					175.8
H'jiang	1,123.0	225.2		37.3	112.9		40.7					706.9
Central	5,131.1	2,289.5 (44.60)	49.8 (1.0)	466.9 (9.1)	348.8 (6.8)	277.6 (5.4)	145.5 (2.8)	352.6 [(6.9)]	435.4 (8.5)	279.9 (5.5)	10.0 (0.2)	827.7 (16.1)
Henan	504.2[b]	202.4	12.9	30.7	51.9	15.2		[43.2]	43.2	55.0	10.0	82.9
Anhui	887.1	425.4	22.3	124.1	76.2	29.3	43.1	[20.3]	20.3	56.3		90.1
Jiangxi	1,247.3[b]	491.2		118.9	64.7	28.9		[187.7]	187.7	37.4		318.5
Hubei	1,421.6	693.7	14.6	97.8	91.9	145.8	7.4	[53.6]	98.5	88.2		183.7
Hunan	1,070.9[b]	476.8		95.4	64.1	58.4	95.0	[47.8]	85.7	43.0		152.5
Central East	48,343.0	10,155.0 (21.0)	3,589 (7.4)	4755.2 (9.8)	4,424. (9.2)	1,094. (2.3)	4,793. (9.9)	[1,838.7] [(3.8)]	2,103.5 (4.4)	7,690.2 (15.9)	1,921.0 (4.0)	7,816.1 (16.2)
Shandong	11,310.0	2,180.0	370.0	860.0	1,370.0		3,700.0		11.0	370.0		2,460.0

APPENDIX III (*continued*)

Value (US$ million) and origin (%) of FDI for each region (province), 2002

Region (province)	FDI (US$ million)	Hong Kong	Japan	Taiwan	USA	EU[a]	ROK	[Singapore]	ASEAN	British Virgin Islands	Cayman Islands	Residual
Shanghai	10,576.0	1,680.6	1,060.0	469.3	834.2	980.9		[526.7]	526.7	2,544.2	1,275.2	1,204.9
Jiangsu	19,667.9	3,993.0	1,698.0	2,561.0	1,532.0		900.0	[1,312.0]	1,312.0	4,114.0	400.0	3,157.9
Zhejiang	6,789.1	2,301.4	461.0	864.9	688.7	113.6	193.6		264.8	662.0	245.8	993.3
South East	*25,845.3[c]*	*10,150.0* (39.3)	*765.4* (3.0)	*3,007.1* (11.6)	*1,295.* (5.0)	*129.7* (0.5)	*142.0* (0.60)	*467.5* (1.8)	*820.4* (3.2)	*3,929.4* (15.2)	*385.9* (1.5)	*5,220.0* (20.2)
Fujian	6944.2	2,246.0	231.0	2,200	268.0			[88.1]	377.9	701.0	190.0	730.3
Guangdong	18,901.1	7,904.0	534.4	807.1	1,027.4	129.7	142.0	[379.4]	442.5	3,228.4	195.9	4,489.7
Hainan	231.0d											
South West	*2,429.0*	*936.2* (38.5)	*70.5* (2.9)	*81.9* (3.4)	*300.5* (12.4)	*73.8* (3.0)	*23.2* (1.0)	*103.8* (4.3)	*118.1* (4.9)	*478.8* (19.7)	*11.4* (0.5)	*334.6* (13.8)
Guangxi	737.6	430.0	47.5	41.2	84.1			[36.6]	36.6			98.2
Chongqing	505.1	154.5			23.2	26.1		[35.2]	35.2	203.2		62.9
Sichuan	659.3b	262.2	23.0	21.3	135.6	19.6		[32.0]	32.0	84.5		81.1
Guizhou	189.4	22.6		6.2	2.0					91.7		66.9
Yunnan	333.0	64.9		13.2	55.6	28.1	23.2		14.3	97.6	11.4	24.f
Tibet	4.6	2.0			0.02					1.8		0.8g
TOTAL	98,612	28,369.5 (28.8)	5,754.3 (5.8)	8,880.4 (9.0)	8,651.0 (8.8)	2,389.7 (2.4)	6,824.9 (6.9)	2,981.3 (3.0)	3,828.2 (3.90)	13,545.8 (13.7)	2,540.8 (2.6)	17,713.0 (18.0)

NOTES

1. Between 1990 and 2002, China's merchandise trade grew, on average, by 15 percent yearly, to reach more than $620 billion. During the same period, the cumulative value of foreign direct investment (FDI) was $431 billion. See National Bureau of Statistics (NBS), *Zhongguo tongji nianjian* [China statistical yearbook] (hereafter *TJNJ*), 2003, 654 and 671.

2. Data for 2002 were the most recent available at the time of writing.

3. In a chapter that is quite heavy with statistics, the absence of a separate section on data problems may seem perverse. I do not seek to be disingenuous in merely noting that problems of data reliability and interpretation are inherent in any attempt to disentangle national foreign trade and FDI flows. In China's case, the entrepôt role of Hong Kong, the widespread practice of investment "round-tripping," and the opaque nature of economic relations conducted through the British Virgin Islands and the Cayman Islands (hugely important in Taiwan's FDI in the mainland) lend substantial analytical difficulties. Where, as here, the exercise seeks to disaggregate macrotrends to provincial levels, the hazards are greatly magnified. To insist on quantitative exactitude would probably dictate abandoning the exercise. My belief is, however, that the quantitative matrix offered here is sufficiently robust to support the accompanying analysis.

4. *TJNJ*, 2003, 655. Imports have followed a similar but less pronounced trend (the share of manufactures was 83 percent in 2002, compared with 65 percent in 1980) (*TJNJ*, 2003, 656).

5. In 2002 more than $980 billion had been invested in China's 208,000 FFEs, of which 41 percent derived from foreign partners. FFEs absorbed 54 percent of Chinese imports (*TJNJ*, 2003, 653 and 670).

6. David Hale and Lyric Hughes Hale, "China Takes Off," *Foreign Affairs* 82, no. 6 (November–December 2003), note that China's electronics exports account for 30 percent of total exports of such products from Asia.

7. China's own experience since 1979—not least, the gains from increasingly close transnational economic integration between the two great Chinese river delta regions (those of the Pearl and Yangzi Rivers) and, respectively, Hong Kong and Taiwan—highlights the potential sacrifices associated with Mao Zedong's misconceived ideological preoccupations and their distorting effects on the economy. For the years since 1997, I use "transnational" in a de facto sense to describe economic relations between China and Hong Kong Special Administrative Region.

8. Thus, Dali Yang: "Comparative advantage is the central concept in post-Mao regional development policy" ("Patterns of China's Regional Development Strategy," *China Quarterly* 122 [June 1990]: 241–42).

9. Such variants include "subregional economic zones," "extended metropolitan regions," and "natural economic territories." A useful working definition of a growth triangle is given by the Asian Development Bank, as follows: "transnational economic zones spread over well-defined geographically proximate areas covering 3 or more countries where differences in factor endowments are exploited to promote external trade and development" (http://www.adb.org/Help/Index/G.asp, accessed on February 12, 2004). Note that "geographically proximate" does not necessarily mean geographically contiguous: e.g., coastal central-eastern China and Taiwan, which

constitute an increasingly identifiable transnational economic entity, are separated by the Taiwan Strait.

10. Compare Shaun Breslin and Glenn D. Hook's reference to "'spontaneous' microregionalism" as a phenomenon that "may develop without or beyond the formal will of institutionalised governmental arrangements . . . [and] . . . is driven by economic forces, production and finance, that do not acknowledge formal borders" ("Microregionalism and the World Order: Concepts, Approaches and Implications," in *Microregionalism and World Order,* ed. Shaun Breslin and Glenn D. Hook [New York: Palgrave Macmillan, 2003], 4). The essay by Breslin and Hook offers many valuable insights into microregionalism, its economic and political implications, and its relationship to higher regional and global levels of interactions. Françoise Mengin also observes that the establishment of transnational groupings tends to reflect "the primacy of economic interests over national identification" ("Taiwanese Politics and the Chinese Market: Business's Part in the Formation of a State, or the Border as a Stake of Negotiations," in *Politics in China: Moving Frontiers,* ed. Françoise Mengin and Jean-Louis Rocca [New York: Palgrave Macmillan, 2002], 234–35).

11. That is, "economic entities that cross political boundaries, taking advantage of the complementarity of neighbouring regions, combining resources, manpower, capital, technology and managerial skills" (Robert A. Scalapino, "The Changing Order in Northeast Asia and the Prospects for US-Japan-China-Korea Relations," Institute on Global Conflict and Cooperation [IGCC] Policy Papers, 1998, p. 47, available at http://repositories.cdlib.org/igcc/PP/pp47, accessed on February 12, 2003).

12. GMS embraces Yunnan province, Cambodia, Lao People's Democratic Republic, Myanmar, Thailand, and Vietnam, and has for some years been proposed as a growth hub for Southwest China and its Southeast Asian neighbors. TRADP comprises Yanbian Korean Autonomous Prefecture (Jilin province, China), the Rajin-Sonbong Economic and Trade Zones (Democratic Republic of North Korea), Hentii, Dornod, and Sukhbaatar provinces (Eastern Mongolia), and Primorsky Krai (Russia).

13. In 2002, with little more than a quarter of China's population, a mere six provinces—Shandong, Shanghai, Jiangsu, Zhejiang, Fujian, and Guangdong—generated 43 percent of its GDP and almost 80 percent (86 percent, if Beijing and Tianjin are included) of the value of its merchandise trade. By contrast, the provinces of the northwest and southwest, with almost 30 percent of total population, accounted for only 17 percent of national GDP and a minuscule 3.7 percent of trade.

14. A path-breaking investigation into provincial trading patterns at a much earlier stage in China's economic reforms from which I have benefited in writing this chapter is given by Brantly Womack and Guangzhi Zhao, "The Many Worlds of China's Provinces," in *China Deconstructs: Politics, Trade and Regionalism,* ed. David Goodman and Gerald Segal (London: Routledge, 1994).

15. Ministry of Trade of the PRC, *Zhongguo duiwai jingji maoyi nianjian* [Yearbook of China's foreign economic relations and trade] 2003 (Beijing: Foreign Economic Relations and Trade Publishing House, September 2003).

16. For example, note that the total value of China's exports, revealed by summing the provincial figures, is only about 2 percent below that of the aggregate fig-

ure available in official NBS sources, whereas the corresponding gap for imports is some 11 percent.

17. The internationalization, even globalization, of coastal China's economy is suggested by the finding that, by 1997, Guangdong exported to more than 160 countries and regions.

18. Those regions are North, Central-Interior, Central-East, and Southwest China.

19. Much the same can be said of FDI inflows (see below).

20. See Appendix I.

21. This will no doubt change under the impact of dual WTO accession by China and Taiwan.

22. *TJNJ*, 2003, 659.

23. Taiwan was the chief source of imports to Guangdong and Fujian, and the second most important source for Jiangsu.

24. Data published by Taiwan's Mainland Affairs Council suggest that by the end of 2002, the share of Taiwan's exports to China in its global exports had reached 22.6 percent, 15.4 percent for all merchandise trade (http://www.chinabiz.org.tw/maz/EcoMonth/133-2003-09/133-08/xls, accessed on February 13, 2004).

25. See, for example, R. F. Ash and Y. Y. Kueh, "Economic Integration within Greater China: Trade and Investment Flows between China, Hong Kong and Taiwan," in *Greater China: The Next Superpower?* ed. David Shambaugh (Oxford: Oxford University Press, 1995), 59–93. In the same volume, the chapter by Qi Luo and Christopher Howe is also relevant.

26. For example, Appendix I shows Hong Kong to have been an important source of imports (even if as an intermediary) to Inner Mongolia, Shaanxi, Gansu, and Ningxia (Northwest), Henan, Jiangxi, Hubei, and Hunan (Central-Interior), and Chongqing, Sichuan, Yunnan, and even Tibet (Southwest). Appendix II shows Hong Kong to have been an important destination for exports from Beijing, Chongqing, Hubei, and Jiangxi. ("Important" in these contexts means ranking within the top four immediate import origins or export destinations.)

27. In southwest China, Guangxi, Yunnan, and Tibet have a land border that runs for 8,600 kilometers. The length of Xinjiang and Inner Mongolia's combined land border with the Mongolian Republic, Russia, and various countries of Central Asia is even longer.

28. China's border regions embrace Liaoning, Jilin, Heilongjiang, Inner Mongolia, Gansu, Xinjiang, Tibet, Yunnan, and Guangxi. Their cross-border trading counterparts include North Korea, Russia, the Mongolian Republic, Kazakhstan, Kyrgyzstan, Tajikistan, Afghanistan, Pakistan, India, Nepal, Sikkim, Bhutan, Myanmar, Thailand, and Vietnam.

29. Such trade involved Yunnan, Guangxi, India, Myanmar, and Vietnam in the south, and Jilin, Heilongjiang, and North Korea in the north.

30. See Su-cheng Chao, *Zhongguo dalu xinan shengqu duiwai maoyi fazhan moshi* (The pattern of foreign trade in Southwest China) (hereafter *Xinan shengqu*) (Taipei: Yinke Publishing Company, 2002), 174 and 176.

31. The immediate origins of the rapid growth of such trade implied in these figures lie in policies adopted by the Chinese government in 1992, which designated a number of border cities, such as Pingyang and Dongxing (on Guangxi's border with

Vietnam) and Wanding and Ruili (on Yunnan's border with Myanmar), to facilitate the extension of border trade and simultaneously established economic cooperation zones and trading ports in border regions. These initiatives had a swift impact: in Xinjiang, for example, the number of border trading companies rose from 5 (1991) to 346 (1996); meanwhile, from Inner Mongolia, trade and technical cooperation with Russia, the Mongolian Republic, and other Asian countries rapidly expanded. Nineteen ninety-two was also the year in which Cambodia, the Lao People's Democratic Republic, Myanmar, Thailand, Vietnam, and Yunnan province formed the Greater Mekong Subregion (GMS) as a new growth area, based on enhanced regional economic integration.

32. *Xinan shengqu,* 180.

33. Detailed annual estimates of border trade in China's Southwest reveal an average growth of –43% percent in 1996 and 1997; during the next two years, however, the corresponding figure was +97 percent (*Xinan shengqu,* 197, table 5.1). This recovery was largely carried by an expansion in imports of 135 percent per year in 1998–99.

34. The growing importance of cross-border linkages is also apparent from other indicators. For example, by 1999 border trade in the Northeast had come to account for 35.2 percent of Heilongjiang's total foreign trade; in the Northwest, the corresponding figure for Xinjiang was a remarkable 55.8 percent (although this figure was below the 63.3 percent attained in 1993) (*Xinan shengqu,* 139–40).

35. That is, the remaining share of regional exports/imports to/from the rest of the world, after deducting those to/from the United States, EU, Hong Kong, Japan, South Korea, Taiwan, and ASEAN.

36. For example, in 2002 over 63 percent of exports from the Northwest—Inner Mongolia, Shaanxi, Gansu, Qinghai, Ningxia, and Xinjiang—were destined for countries and regions other than China's main trading partners.

37. Reference to Appendix I reveals that Kazakhstan was the second most important export destination for the Northwest. In Xinjiang, which accounted for almost 30 percent of all northwestern exports in 2002, one-third of its exports went to Kazakhstan, other important destinations being Kyrgyzstan (7.6 percent), Azerbaijan (6.6 percent), Pakistan (5.1 percent), and the Russian Federation (3.6 percent). Australia has also been a trading partner of some importance with provinces in the Northwest. On Xinjiang's trade and investment relations with Russia and its Central Asian neighbors in the 1980s and early 1990s, see Peter Ferdinand, "Xinjiang: Relations with China and Abroad," in *China Deconstructs,* esp. 279–84.

38. I deliberately exclude ASEAN member states because of the expected close trade relationship between the Southwest and ASEAN. In terms of individual provinces, the importance of Southeast and South Asian countries as export destinations is striking. For example, in 2002 21 percent of Yunnan's exports were shipped to Myanmar and a further 17 percent to ASEAN countries; 22.5 percent of Guangxi's exports were destined for Vietnam (which also took 13 percent of Chongqing's exports); and 21 percent of Guizhou's exports were purchased by ASEAN members. As for Tibet, some 70 percent of its exports were destined for Nepal (Ministry of Trade of the PRC, *Zhongguo duiwai jingji maoyi nianjian,* 2003). For time series data on the ranking of the export partners of southwestern Chinese provinces, see *Xinan shengqu,* 294–316.

39. *Xinan shengqu,* 271, table 7.2.

40. Between 1991 and 1999, the share of border trade in Guangxi's total foreign trade fell from 40 percent to 24 percent. In 1999, the corresponding figures for Yunnan and Tibet were 20 percent and 8.4 percent (*Xinan shengqu,* 211).

41. Measuring flows of foreign capital into China is extremely hazardous, and the estimates shown here should be regarded as approximations. The difficulty of determining FDI originating in the British Virgin Islands and the Cayman Islands without distortion is one challenge. Another is addressing FDI flows whose immediate, but not necessarily true, origin is Hong Kong. Such hidden data are a salutary reminder of the likely extent of any assumed margin of error for provincial FDI ($98.6 billion) shown here is some 19 percent higher than the national figure recorded by NBS (*TJNJ,* 2003, 653). To what extent this discrepancy reflects double counting or some other source of exaggeration by provincial sources, or underestimation by NBS sources, it is impossible to know.

42. Japan's overseas development assistance (ODA) has also been an important source of capital funding to China, although to what extent this will continue is sometimes questioned.

43. Recent years have seen an increasingly important role played by European and, especially, American multinational corporations (MNCs) as sources of FDI.

44. China itself is one of the most important sources of FDI in the world, although the extent of such involvement is extremely difficult to measure. (But see C. S. Tseng, "The Internationalisation of Enterprises from Guangdong," in *Guangdong: Preparing for the WTO Challenge,* ed. Joseph Y. S. Cheng [Hong Kong: Chinese University Press, 2003], 146, which cites an authoritative Chinese source to the effect that as of the end of 2002, the cumulative value of China's contractual investment was $9.34 billion.) A recent source also notes that in the last several years, Chinese transnational corporations (TNCs) have invested abroad in an attempt to "explore and open up new markets." For the purposes of the analysis here, it is noteworthy that in terms of project numbers (1979–2001), the second and third most favored destinations for Chinese outward investment are Hong Kong–Macau and Russia; the level of cumulative investment in cross-border countries is as follows: Hong Kong and Macau, $534 million; Thailand, $194 million; Russia, $130 million; Cambodia, $120 million; Vietnam, $56 million; Myanmar, $47 million; Laos, $30 million; and India, $18 million. See John Wong and Sarah Chan, "China's Outward Investment: Expanding Worldwide," East Asian Institute, National University of Singapore, *China: An International Journal* 1, no. 2 (September 2003): 273–201.

45. For example, Guangdong, Shanghai, Jiangsu, Fujian, Zhejiang, Shandong, and Tianjin.

46. See David Zweig, *Internationalizing China: Domestic Interests and Global Linkages* (Ithaca: Cornell University Press, 2002), 58. In talks with President Roh Moo-hyun during his visit to China in July 2003, Premier Wen Jiabao urged Korean businessmen to undertake investment in support of the development of Western China (Xinhua News Agency, July 8, 2003).

47. Most FDI from these British territories was disguised investment undertaken by Taiwanese entrepreneurs in an effort to circumvent discriminatory regulations against China by the government in Taipei. The Virgin and Cayman Islands have been used as tax havens and "risk buffers" for Taiwanese enterprises. By registering

in the Caribbean, Taiwanese companies have been able to transfer and subsequently reinvest capital in mainland China at little cost, while also securing the safety net of mutual protection agreements that normally apply to FDI transactions—and also, incidentally, distancing themselves from political arguments about sovereignty and associated risks. It is suggested that around 90 percent of FDI to China from the British Virgin Islands is Taiwanese investment in disguise. See Zhen-yuan Tong, "Global Division of Labor and Interdependence in Cross-Strait Economic Relations," *Quarterly Journal and Review of Economic Conditions* 7, no. 3 (December 2001). I am indebted to C. J. Wu for bringing this source to my attention, as well as for his insights into Taiwan's FDI behavior in China.

48. This figure is almost 17 percent higher than the cumulative figure shown in Appendix III. To what extent this difference is attributable to unrecorded FDI, and to what extent to small-scale FDI to individual provinces that does not appear in *Zhongguo duiwai jingji maoyi nianjian*, it is impossible to say.

49. Legislative Yuan, *Zhonghua minguo tongji nianjian, 2003* [Statistical yearbook of the Republic of China, 2003] (Taipei: Sanmin Publishing House, October 2003), 242. Estimates for Shanghai are not given separately in this source and are no doubt included in the figures for Jiangsu (before 1958, Shanghai was part of Jiangsu province).

50. The crude average rate of growth of inflows of FDI to Jiangsu was 73.5 percent yearly; for Guangdong, it was 54 percent yearly. But such figures take no account of the considerable annual fluctuations revealed in the table. Note that except for 1997–99, Jiangsu has consistently outstripped Guangdong as a recipient of Taiwanese FDI since 1994.

51. What table 18 does not show is the level of FDI flows to China that were not "approved" by Taipei. Estimating the scale of such flows is of course ultimately impossible, although an authoritative source cites sources in China to the effect that "at least US$10 bn. in unapproved investment flowed from Taiwan to China between 1991 and 2001" (Economic Intelligence Unit [EIU], *Country Forecast: Taiwan* [London: EIU, March 2003], 28).

52. To what extent this has generated an "irrationally" skewed structural distribution of Taiwanese FDI in China is beyond the confines of this chapter.

53. At the time of writing (February 2004), recent estimates indicate that as of third quarter 2003, year-on-year GDP growth was 8.4 percent (India), 6.5 percent (Thailand), 5.7 percent (Russia), and 5.1 percent (Pakistan) (*The Economist*, February 14–20, 2004, 114, available at http://www.economist.com/printedition, accessed on February 16, 2004). See also Jiang Xiaojuan, "The New Regional Patterns of FDI Inflow in China: Policy Orientation and Expected Performance," in Organization for Economic Cooperation and Development (OECD), *Foreign Direct Investment in China: Challenges and Prospects for Regional Development* (Paris: OECD, 2002), 68.

54. Inner Mongolia now has almost twenty "port" cities linking it with Russia (Xinhua News Agency, hereafter XHNA, July 17, 2001).

55. XHNA, July 29, 2001, urged Xinjiang to "adjust its export structure, improving competitiveness of exported commodities so as to turn geographic advantages into economic edges" vis-à-vis members, other than China, of the SCO (Russia, Kazkhstan, Kyrgyzstan, Tajikistan, and Uzbekistan), with which it has a 3,700-

kilometer-long border. Elsewhere, the same source noted that China's border trade with these countries was shifting from simple everyday manufactured goods toward machinery, electronics, and high-tech products; cooperation and investment projects in Russia and Central Asia had also been implemented in farm technology and the development of oil and gas resources (XHNA, October 14, 2001).

56. See XHNA, September 19, 2003.

57. "They are . . . burdened with the remnants of a faltering state-owned industry, handicapped by a reform and open door policy that has discriminated against them for at least 15 years" (Markus Taube and Mehmet Ögütçü, "Main Issues on Foreign Investment in China's Regional Development: Prospects and Policy Challenges," in OECD, *Foreign Direct Investment in China*, 35.

58. See OECD Investment Policy Review, *China: Progress and Reform Challenges* (Paris: OECD, 2003), especially chapter 2.

59. Harry Harding, "The Concept of 'Greater China': Themes, Variations and Reservations," *China Quarterly* 136 (December 1993), especially 664–72.

PART THREE

Politics and Diplomacy

5

China-Japan Relations

Downward Spiral or a New Equilibrium?

Mike M. Mochizuki

Recent bilateral frictions on a variety of economic, historical, and security issues have suggested that relations between China and Japan are becoming increasingly competitive and conflictual. With China on the rise and Japan in relative decline, some have argued that China and Japan are now engaged in an intense rivalry for regional leadership. Others believe that this relationship is now on a downward spiral and could even have destabilizing consequences for the Asia-Pacific region. In contrast to this pessimistic view, this chapter will argue that while China-Japan relations are now in a period of adjustment, these two major powers of East Asia are more likely to establish a new equilibrium than to slide into a downward spiral.

END OF THE "FRIENDSHIP DIPLOMACY" FRAMEWORK

After normalization of China-Japan relations in 1972, the two countries interacted in terms of what Benjamin Self has aptly called the "friendship diplomacy" framework. From the Japanese perspective, this paradigm entailed an obsequious attitude toward China motivated by guilt about the past. In its dealings with its giant neighbor, Japan tended to accommodate Chinese pressures, to shy away from strongly pressing Japanese concerns and interests, and to downplay bilateral differences. For example, Japan tightly restricted its relations with Taiwan and restrained its security policy for fear of upsetting China. It also sought to promote friendship with China by providing large amounts of economic assistance. From the Chinese perspective, this paradigm involved bilateral cooperation and cordiality based on a clear strategic calculus. Concerns about the Soviet threat pushed China to normalize relations with Japan in 1972 and to sign the Peace and Friendship Treaty in 1978 without pushing Japan very hard about unequivocal apologies and compensation for its past transgressions. The Chinese government even restrained scholars from documenting and publicizing the Chinese suffering caused by Japan in order to improve relations with Japan. Chinese leaders also accepted Japan's security alliance with the United States as a useful means to prevent Japan's remilitarization.

The improvement of relations with the Soviet Union during the early 1980s, however, weakened China's basic strategic rationale for friendship diplomacy with Japan. In this context, based on a false media report, Beijing strongly criticized Tokyo for compelling the revision of a progressive high school textbook to soften the wording regarding Japan's aggression against China.[1] Chinese protests against the dramatic increase in Japanese imports and Prime Minister Yasuhiro Nakasone's official visit to the Yasukuni Shrine in August 1985 also revealed the absence of broad support in China for cooperative relations with Japan. Nevertheless, conciliatory responses from Japan helped to sustain the friendship diplomacy framework. Cordial ties with Japan indeed served China's interest even after the collapse of the Soviet Union in 1989. Most notably, Japan played a major role in facilitating China's reintegration into the international community after the Tiananmen massacre. In many respects, the 1992 visit of the Japanese emperor to China, during which the host country graciously received Emperor Akihito and refrained from harshly criticizing Japan's militarist past, was the culmination of friendship diplomacy.[2]

On the Japanese side, generational change in the conservative political leadership undermined one of the key domestic foundations of the friendship framework. In the post-normalization era, powerful politicians like Kakuei Tanaka, Masayoshi Ohira, and Noboru Takeshita took the lead in managing relations with Beijing and prevented nationalistic criticisms of China from damaging the bilateral relationship. After their departure from the political scene, politicians like Ryutaro Hashimoto and Koichi Kato lacked the clout to play a comparable role. As a result, within the ruling Liberal Democratic Party (LDP), the post-normalization consensus began to wither away and the politics of China policy became more pluralistic and contentious.

Changes in party politics also altered the domestic political dynamics regarding Japan's China policy. In the past, the opposition camp led by the Social Democratic Party of Japan (SPDJ) backed friendly relations with China and served as allies of the pro-China forces in the LDP. But with the transformation of the party system that began in 1993 and led to the demise of the SPDJ, even the progressive forces became increasingly critical of Chinese behavior. In the wake of the Tiananmen massacre and Chinese nuclear tests in the mid-1990s, a tacit coalition emerged between conservative nationalists and some in the liberal camp to denounce the obsequious attitude of the Japanese government toward Japan. Moreover, Taiwan's democratization encouraged a more favorable view of Taiwan among politicians in the opposition camp. These domestic political changes removed the insu-lation that the so-called "China school" in the Japanese Foreign Ministry had enjoyed after 1972 to keep relations with China on an even keel.

Attitudinal shifts at the popular level in Japan further contributed to the demise of the friendship diplomacy framework. Even as the Japanese gov-ernment facilitated China's reintegration into the international community after the Tiananmen massacre, the repressive measures taken by the Chi-nese government against the democracy movement dramatically tarnished China's image among the Japanese people. The frequently cited annual public surveys of public attitudes toward foreign countries revealed a sharp drop in positive Japanese feelings toward China after 1989: in the October 1988 survey 66.3 percent of the Japanese had positive feelings toward China, but in the October 1989 survey this percentage fell to 50.1 percent. Although the positive feelings jumped back up to 57.2 percent after the 1992 emperor's visit to China, the Chinese missile tests against Taiwan in March 1996 caused another deterioration in Japanese opinion about China. According to the October 1996 survey, only 39.4 percent harbored positive feelings about China, while 51.0 percent had negative views about China. This result indicates the most critical opinion of China since these annual surveys began in 1978. As more and more Japanese began to see China's external behavior as threatening and its internal politics as repul-sive, the feelings of guilt the Japanese once harbored about their past behav-ior toward China began to fade.

On the Chinese side, the decline of communism and the rise of nation-alism have encouraged a critical examination of the normalization bargain that Chinese leaders struck with Japan back in 1972, accepting an equivo-cal Japanese apology and forgoing financial compensation for the past because of strategic calculations. After 1989, Chinese leaders increasingly used nationalism to legitimate their grip on power, and they often directed this nationalism against Japan. The government stressed "patriotic educa-tion" to sidestep domestic political, economic, and social contradictions, and numerous state-funded history museums were established that high-lighted the atrocities committed by Japan. This shift in policy, however, has been a double-edged sword. Although the mobilization of anti-Japanese sentiment may have helped to bolster the communist regime as it pursued rapid economic development through capitalist means, this approach has also spawned the rise of "history activists" who have effectively mobi-lized public opinion to pressure the Chinese government to be tougher on Japan, especially regarding history-related issues. The incremental steps toward political liberalization have also expanded the political and social space for public criticisms of Japan and the reproduction of hostile feelings toward Japan.[3]

The end of the friendship diplomacy framework was clearly evident during the November 1998 summit between President Jiang Zemin and Prime Minister Keizo Obuchi in Tokyo. Originally, this meeting was to be a celebratory affair commemorating the twentieth anniversary of the bilateral Peace and Friendship Treaty and unveiling a comprehensive program of China-Japan cooperation in thirty-three areas. But unfortunately for Sino-Japanese relations, floods in China caused the Jiang-Obuchi summit to be postponed until after the Japan–South Korea summit. The meeting between Obuchi and South Korean president Kim Dae Jung was truly historic, with Kim declaring that relations should be oriented toward the future without dwelling on the past and Obuchi providing an unequivocal written apology to the Korean people. Seeing this outcome, Jiang understandably wanted the same sort of written apology from Obuchi, but he appeared unwilling to offer a statement similar to Kim's about China's future orientation. After Obuchi's decision to provide an oral apology but not a written one, President Jiang used his state visit to Japan to harp on Japan's past transgressions toward China, much to the displeasure of his hosts. Although Jiang may have won some points with the Chinese military and anti-Japanese citizens with his tough rhetoric, the Japanese people were so irritated by this behavior that even progressive newspapers like *Asahi Shimbun* criticized the Chinese leader. So, rather than focusing attention on the sweeping declaration for cooperation in thirty-three areas, the media focused on why the declaration was not formally signed but simply enunciated. The summit was a nadir in Sino-Japanese relations in the post-normalization era.

TOWARD A NEW EQUILIBRIUM

If the November 1998 summit brought the curtain down on the friendship diplomacy era, is the China-Japan relationship now heading toward a dangerous rivalry as some have warned? Pessimists about China-Japan relations often make the following arguments.[4] First, the pessimists see a bilateral competition being fueled by what Benjamin Self has called "dueling nationalism and national identities."[5] As China develops economically, national pride could steer Chinese away from conciliatory gestures and policies toward Japan. In fact, this pride might lead China to adopt high-handed strategies and tactics to supplant Japan in Asia and even dominate Japan. The Japanese, on the other hand, are both frustrated by their economic stagnation and confident about their "democratic, nonmilitarist character." Whereas before the Japanese were contrite about the past and concerned about their ability to control the Japanese military, they now feel less hesitation about using the military with democratic legitimacy to protect Japan's interests and to contribute to international security. This new national identity promotes greater convergence between Japan and Taiwan rather than between Japan and China, raising the possibility that a Japanese tilt toward Taiwan would anger China. Moreover, the person-to-person exchanges that are increasing between the Japanese and Chinese may only exacerbate this problem by reinforcing their negative stereotypes of each other: Japan as cold and unfriendly and China as dirty and dangerous. The increase in crimes committed by Chinese nationals in Japan and the problematic recreational behavior of Japanese men in China have certainly not helped.[6]

Second, the pessimists argue that economic interests and economic interdependence may aggravate rather than stabilize China-Japan relations. The Japanese are becoming more concerned about differential growth rates and about relative (as opposed to absolute) gains from bilateral trade. The Japanese are anxious about a hollowing out of their economy as more investments are being pulled into China; and the Chinese probably believe that the benefits of bilateral economic cooperation have already peaked. Given the problems in the Japanese economy, Japanese aid and investments to China are likely to decline. Furthermore, a Chinese economic slowdown that will inevitably exacerbate internal social problems could cause Chinese to scapegoat Japan. In other words, great expectations could lead to great disappointment and a lashing out toward Japan.

Finally, the pessimists stress the incipient strategic rivalry between Japan and China. Japan is now clearly on the American side regarding defense strategies vis-à-vis Taiwan, and this posture will be viewed by China as going against its core national interests. Moreover, Benjamin Self argues that Japanese participation in peacekeeping operations in Southeast Asia is "part of a plan to fill the strategic vacuum in the region and prevent China from exercising influence." Whereas the Japanese are worried about strengthening Chinese naval and air capabilities that could strangle Japan's vital shipping lanes, as well as Chinese modernization of their nuclear weapons and missile capabilities, the Chinese are concerned about Japan's cooperation with the United States on ballistic missile defense and the possible acquisition of a naval theater missile defense system that could be used in a Taiwan scenario.[7]

As compelling as these arguments are, there are also countervailing factors that could work to stabilize China-Japan relations. Those who are cautiously optimistic about China-Japan relations emphasize the following points.[8] First, the dynamics of bilateral economic interaction are on balance more positive than negative. Because both China and Japan are currently focused on domestic economic challenges, they are likely to continue to see the benefits of economic cooperation. China desires peaceful and cooperative relations with its Asian neighbors, including Japan, and it continues to rely on Japan for economic aid, technology, investments, and markets. And despite Japanese concerns about hollowing out and the influx of Chinese imports, China is becoming more important as an export market and an off-shore production base.

Second, the increase in people-to-people exchanges, through govern-ment-sponsored student exchange programs and the two-way flow of tourists and workers, may be promoting more realistic perceptions of each other even though they may not be engendering positive feelings. In the long run, realism may be healthier than romantic notions of the other that could lead to disappointment. And realism is more likely to yield mutual understanding and respect.

Finally, the cautious optimists note that external forces will serve to keep Japan-China relations from deteriorating into a downward spiral. The United States will seek to maintain a balance in its policies toward Japan and China by strengthening its alliance with Japan on the one hand, while developing a constructive relationship with China on the other. And even in the post-9/11 world, China is likely to be concerned enough about the United States that it will seek to contain disputes with Japan in order to pre-vent Japan from becoming a more active American ally for balancing against a rising China. According to Robert Sutter, China may even attempt "to woo Japan away from a close alignment with the United States toward positions more favorable to China."[9] In addition to American and Chinese strategic calculations, one might also add the keen interest of most coun-tries in the Asia-Pacific region in a stable Sino-Japanese relationship. Indeed, the embedding of China-Japan interactions in a variety of regional multilateral processes and institutions can contribute to checking a dra-matic deterioration in Sino-Japanese relations.

In this debate between pessimists and cautious optimists, I tend to side with the optimists. Rather than the end of friendship diplomacy leading to a period of dangerous rivalry, what is more probable is the emergence of a new equilibrium, a relationship based on common interests, on frankness, and on mutual respect and understanding rather than a façade of friend-ship. China-Japan relations are likely to interweave elements of both "coop-eration and coexistence" and "competition and friction."[10] But in the end, the centripetal forces are likely to counter the centrifugal forces.

In addition to the stabilizing factors that the cautious optimists empha-size, I would add the following. First, there has been a significant tactical, if not strategic, shift in how China deals with Japan since the November 1998 Jiang-Obuchi summit. That meeting was in some ways a personal catharsis for Jiang, a leader with negative personal memories of Japanese military expansion. But after the summit, foreign policy advisors (especially those with long experience dealing with Japan) convinced Jiang and the top polit-ical leadership that treating Japan harshly would go against Chinese inter-ests, as it would only drive Japan to support strategic cooperation with the

United States to contain China. They also argued that China should not focus solely on relations with the United States to promote Chinese interests in the Asia-Pacific region. China should instead pursue an omnidirectional foreign policy that is multilayered (both bilateral and multilateral) and that involves stable and cooperative relations with Japan. An indicator of this shift in approach came in April 1999, when Jiang gave an especially warm reception for a visiting Japanese parliamentary delegation and a large group of Japanese tourists. On this occasion, Jiang issued an important statement in the *People's Daily* highlighting China-Japan cooperation. The problems in U.S.-China relations in the wake of the May 1999 mistaken U.S. bombing of the Chinese embassy in Belgrade and during the first year of the Bush administration reinforced this change in policy and posture toward Japan. Moreover, the increasing sense of confidence among Chinese elites appeared to promote magnanimity rather than arrogance. Therefore, rather than trying to dominate or berate Japan, Chinese leaders have become more accommodative of Japanese complaints and concerns.

Second, during recent years, mid-level officials in both China and Japan who are in charge of managing bilateral relations have developed relatively effective ways to deal with bilateral disputes and frictions in a constructive manner as well as to deal with common challenges in the region. This problem-solving mechanism is now evident in a variety of areas relating to the issues of economic relations, security, the history issue, and the territorial dispute. In fact, some prominent Chinese analysts of Japan acknowledge that Japanese ideas and initiatives played an important role in encouraging China to embrace multilateral dialogues to address pressing regional issues.[11]

Third, although China and Japan appear to be competing on various fronts, this competition does not necessarily entail a rivalry for regional domination or hegemony. China would certainly like to enhance its economic (and military) power and its regional influence. And it seeks to exercise regional leadership by making diplomatic initiatives. But these initiatives are not alarming to Japan because they do not suggest that China is trying to impose its will on other states in the region. By the same token, the notion that Japan seeks to dominate East Asia appears to be farfetched at a time when Japan's economic position in the region is in relative decline. Japan is therefore likely to continue to "lead from behind," preferring to promote its substantive security and economic interests rather than maximize its international status in the region. The other countries in the region prefer a balance between Chinese and Japanese power and influence. As long as neither China nor Japan has a hegemonic agenda, a certain degree of Sino-Japanese competition to enhance their appeal and influence in the rest of the region might have a positive effect on promoting regional economic integration and security stability.

Lu Zhongwei, former president of the China Institute of Contemporary International Relations and one of China's leading analysts of Japan, provided this remarkably rosy assessment of China-Japan relations:

> We are justified to say the two sides [China and Japan] are in the best of their relations for the past three decades [sic]. . . . Beijing believes that Tokyo has embarked on the path of peaceful development and that the Japanese people love peace, thus negating her earlier assessment of Japan's possible remilitarization. This signifies that over the past decade China's diplomatic action has already revolutionized her relations with Japan. In other words, China's diplomacy and Japan policy have ushered in a new stage in her relations with the close neighbor. This has been a "quiet revolution." . . . Today the two sides no longer talk about "friendship" alone. They lay stress on "interests" by turning the courteous slogan of friendship into interests-oriented [sic] practices that give consideration to common interests and strive for a win-win situation.[12]

Lu's view of Japan echoes the December 2002 essay by the Chinese commentator Ma Licheng, who admonished his fellow citizens to abandon anti-Japanese sentiments, to acknowledge Japan's economic assistance, and to be relaxed about Japanese participation in overseas peacekeeping mechanisms. Ma writes, "China and Japan are the heart of Asia. Both of our peoples must check their nationalistic impulses, abandon their narrow-minded prejudices, and march forward toward regional unification, the emerging goal toward which the hearts of Asians and the tide of the times are now turning."[13]

Of course, it would be misleading to claim that Lu and Ma's views represent the mainstream opinion of the Chinese leadership, much less the Chinese people. But given that both are well placed in China's elite circles and their opinions are widely circulated, one should not underestimate the change in Chinese policy toward Japan and the restabilization of China-Japan relations.

THE MANAGEMENT OF BILATERAL ISSUES

Although there are numerous areas of friction between China and Japan, a review of the major issues in bilateral relations suggests that the two countries are managing problems well enough to prevent a downward spiral and to establish what might be called a "new equilibrium."

Economics

When Japan invoked safeguard measures against Chinese agricultural imports in April 2001, China retaliated with tariffs against Japanese automobiles, cellular phones, and air conditioners. But rather than letting this trade dispute escalate, the two sides resolved the dispute, with Beijing agreeing to a form of voluntary export restraints and with Tokyo lifting its safeguard measures.[14] In April 2002, Japan and China agreed to institutionalize a dialogue to manage bilateral economic problems in a cooperative manner. Trade frictions are bound to occur given the rapid increase in bilateral trade. Two-way trade between China and Japan now exceeds $100 billion, and Japan is China's largest trading partner while China is Japan's second largest trading partner after the United States.

At a time when China's economy is booming and China is becoming an aid provider while the Japanese economy has stagnated, Japanese domestic opposition to large amounts of official development assistance to China has increased sharply. In this political climate, Japanese diplomats worked quietly to convince Chinese officials of the need to reevaluate the old yen loan programs. In addition to cutting dramatically the amount of overseas development assistance (ODA) to China, Japan has shifted from a multiyear to a single-year pledge system for its yen loans, refocused its assistance away from large-scale infrastructure projects toward environmental protection and social development programs, and asked China to assume primary responsibility for infrastructure development in the coastal areas.[15] This change in Japanese policy did not provoke any meaningful protest or resentment among the Chinese. In fact, Chinese and Japanese officials discussed the changing priorities of Japanese yen loans in a constructive and businesslike manner.

Many American analysts interpret the China-ASEAN (Association of Southeast Asian Nations) agreement to forge a free trade agreement (FTA) as a major blow to Japan's influence in Asia—and one that has provoked Japanese resentment of China. But such an interpretation is misleading. First, one should remember that it was Japan that began to ride the FTA wave before China by initiating discussions with South Korea and Singapore. Second, from ASEAN's viewpoint, China was becoming increasingly attractive as an export market (given the weakness of the Japanese market) and ASEAN was worried about redirection of new Japanese investments from ASEAN to China. Therefore, an FTA with China would yield two benefits for ASEAN: freer access to the China market and greater attractiveness of ASEAN as a destination of Japanese foreign investments. In short, rather than a Chinese victory over Japan regarding Southeast Asia, the China-ASEAN FTA goal should be a Southeast Asian effort to restore some balance in regional economic trends (including checking Japan's bypassing of ASEAN for the China market).[16] Finally, Japanese analysts now see that competitive bilateralism (in the form of FTAs) can help promote regional economic integration. They see a balance among Japan, China, ASEAN, South Korea, and Australia / New Zealand as the most suitable framework for East Asian integration.

There is certainly much discussion in Japan about how the gravitational pull of the Chinese economy might hollow out the Japanese economy.[17] But in the last year, the Japanese business community and political leadership have begun to view China as more of an economic opportunity than an economic threat, and for good reason. China is now the fastest growing export market for Japan; Japanese investments in China are beginning to yield larger profits, and Japanese companies are forging more successful business ventures with their local Chinese counterparts. As Naoko Munakata has pointed out, "Japanese manufacturers have avoided head-to-head price competition with producers in China and shifted domestic production to higher value added devices and materials. Successful companies have been able to compensate for hollowing-out of lower added operations and to boost overall sales through strong exports."[18]

During the 1997 East Asian financial crisis, the United States and China were the two countries that opposed Japan's proposal for an Asian Monetary Fund. But afterwards Japanese finance officials worked hard to persuade their Chinese counterparts about China's stake in regional financial stability. The Chinese were responsive and ultimately endorsed regional financial cooperation with Japan and supported Japan's Chiang Mai initiative, which involved a multilateral currency swap arrangement.[19] A forward-looking Chinese and Japanese dialogue about a regional financial architecture is continuing in the context of the ASEAN Plus Three process.

Security

Japanese defense officials have been keeping a watchful eye on China's modernization of its nuclear arsenal, its efforts to develop a "blue-water" navy, and increasingly frequent Chinese naval movements in international waters near the Japanese archipelago.[20] Their Chinese counterparts are concerned about how the promotion of U.S.-Japan defense cooperation, joint U.S.-Japan research on ballistic missile defense, and the planned Japanese deployment of the PAC-3 antimissile battery and upgrade of destroyers' air defense capabilities in 2007 might affect a Taiwan contingency. But these concerns do not amount to an interactive arms race so far. Although some alarmist analyses of Chinese military capabilities and intentions have appeared in Japan, most Japanese defense analysts do not see a major military threat from China *for the time being*.[21] Even without the United States, Japan has enough capability to resist direct conventional military threats from China because of its superior air and naval capabilities. The Japanese feel that America's security commitment to Japan is robust enough to deter nuclear threats from China. And a Chinese threat to Japan's vital sea-lanes could be countered jointly by U.S. and Japanese forces.

The intrusion of Chinese oceanographic research vessels into the exclusive economic zone (EEZ) claimed by Japan has irritated the Japanese. After Japanese complaints, China and Japan agreed in February 2001 to a mutual prior notification framework for marine research in areas near each country in the East China Sea. Although this framework got off to a bumpy start, with Japan charging that China had violated the prior notification agreement, the Chinese responded by confirming its commitment to the framework in July 2001. Related to the EEZ issue, China demonstrated its accommodative posture toward Japan in June 2002 when it allowed Japan to lift the North Korean spy boat that sunk during a gun battle with a Japanese Coast Guard gunboat. This boat had sunk in the EEZ claimed by China.[22]

Japanese participation in peacekeeping operations in Asia is motivated primarily by what the Japanese increasingly see as an obligation to contribute to international security, not by a desire to fill regional strategic vacuums or to counter the Chinese. In fact, during the preliminary Japanese discussions about the revised U.S.-Japan defense cooperation guidelines, many Japanese officials favored Japanese-Chinese cooperation on UN peacekeeping activities; China, however, was not responsive at that time. China has been remarkably understanding about Japan's overseas deployments of Self-Defense Forces to assist U.S. military operations against Afghanistan.[23] But Chinese acquiescence to such Japanese activity may depend on Japan's adherence to Article 9 of the constitution and a continuing reluctance to participate in combat missions.

Defense exchanges between Japan and China have lagged behind those between the United States and China. During their 1998 summit, Jiang and Obuchi did agree to expand bilateral security dialogues and defense exchanges. But in response to Prime Minister Koizumi's visit to the Yasukuni Shrine, China postponed a scheduled visit by the Japanese state minister for defense to China in April 2002 and a planned visit by a Chinese ship to Japan in May 2002. Defense Minister Shigeru Ishiba's visit to China in September 2003 (the first such visit by a Japan defense minister since 1998) yielded an agreement to boost defense exchanges, including mutual visits of naval ships. Chinese analysts now see such exchanges as valuable mechanisms for fostering mutual trust at a time when the security policies of both Japan and China are in transition.[24]

Regarding territorial dispute about the Senkaku/Diaoyu Islands, the Deng Xiaoping strategy to prevent the sovereignty dispute from blocking the development of China-Japan relations has been sustained. Periodic gestures by Japanese nationalistic groups, such as the erection of a light tower on the disputed islands, have strained bilateral relations. But so far, the Japanese government has been able to check these nationalistic forces. Problems over the territorial dispute flared up again when the Japanese government renewed its lease of three of the contested islands in January 2003.

Although the Chinese government lodged a formal protest, this lease iron-ically enables the Japanese government to prevent Japanese nationalists as well as Chinese and Hong Kong activists from landing on these islands and thereby aggravating Sino-Japanese relations.

Taiwan

For the Japanese, Taiwan's appeal has risen dramatically since its democra-tization. Across the political spectrum, politicians have become more favor-ably disposed toward Taiwan than toward mainland China. In fact, the opposition Democratic Party of Japan views the Democratic Progressive Party's ascendancy in Taiwan with both admiration and envy. And Lee Teng-hui, a fluent speaker of Japanese, is viewed as a hero among most Japanese conservatives. Because of this shift in Japanese opinion, there is now a grow-ing consensus in favor of upgrading Japan-Taiwan relations. Nevertheless, Japan's relations with Taiwan will not go beyond the parameters of U.S. rela-tions with Taiwan.

Despite Japan's increasing affinity for Taiwan, there is little Japanese support for a departure from the one-China policy or for Taiwan's formal independence. In the past, the ruling Liberal Democratic Party was divided between the pro-Taiwan and pro-China groups. Today, the pro-Taiwan and pro-China groups have overlapping memberships, indicating that Japanese political elites no longer see relations with China and Taiwan in zero-sum terms. They desire good relations with both China and Taiwan and good relations between China and Taiwan.

The Japanese government has continued to be sensitive about China's opposition to high-profile official and political visits between Japan and Taiwan. For example, Japan denied a visa to Taiwan Presidential Office secretary-general Chang Chun-hsuing, who wanted to attend Prime Minister Obuchi's funeral in June 2000. Although domestic political and public pres-sure forced the Japan Foreign Ministry to allow Lee Teng-hui to visit Japan in April 2001 for a heart checkup, Ministry of Foreign Affairs officials in charge of Asia policy imposed tight restrictions on Lee's activities while in Japan.[25] They were also successful in discouraging Lee from applying for a visa to attend a student festival at Keio University in fall 2002. When LDP Diet member Kenichi Mizuno wanted to visit Taiwan after becoming parliamen-tary secretary of foreign affairs (a third-level political appointee), Foreign Minister Kawaguchi refused the request even though Mizuno had visited Tai-wan in December 2001 as a Diet member. Despite these restrictions on high-level official visits, at the unofficial political level, Taiwan has become a pop-ular destination for Japanese politicians.

Japan has neither explicitly included nor explicitly excluded Taiwan from the revised 1997 U.S.-Japan defense cooperation guidelines. But there are signs of implicit Japanese support for Taiwan's security. First, the U.S.-Japan defense cooperation guidelines and the antiterrorism measures do open the way for possible Japanese "rear area" support in a Taiwan contingency. Second, Japan could take an expansive view of its "right of individual self-defense" by deploying Self-Defense Forces to protect Okinawa in the context of a Taiwan crisis. Third, informal and nonofficial dialogues have taken place between Taiwan and Japan via retired Japanese Self-Defense Force officers and nongovernment defense analysts. And finally, even opposition leaders like Naoto Kan have openly favored letting the United States use its military assets in Japan to help defend Taiwan. But there appears to be some willingness to accommodate partially Chinese concerns about missile defense and Taiwan. For example, some Japanese officials are open to the idea of explicitly restricting the use of missile defense systems to the defense of Japan or explicitly excluding their use for Taiwan's defense.

Japan has extensive trade and investment ties with Taiwan, and Taiwan is likely to be the first purchaser of Japan's high-speed railway system. But Japan has not responded positively to Taiwan's overtures for official talks concerning a Japan-Taiwan free trade agreement. In September 2002, Foreign Minister Kawaguchi assured the Chinese that Japan had no intention of concluding such an agreement with Taiwan, and that only private-sector studies have been conducted about the matter. Japan would prefer that the United States lead the way by negotiating an FTA with Taiwan. In the meantime, Japan would like to avoid politicizing the FTA issue with Taiwan and pursue a low-key approach in the context of Asia-Pacific Economic Cooperation (APEC) or perhaps its vision of an East Asian economic community.

History

The history issue continues to be a thorn in China-Japan relations. The approval of a Japanese nationalistic history textbook, Koizumi's repeated visits to the Yasukuni Shrine, and provocative statements by conservative Japanese politicians have caused frictions in Sino-Japanese relations. But since 1999, Chinese leaders have been notably restrained in their criticisms of Japan about the history issue. Their public statements appear to be carefully crafted to be responsive to Chinese popular sentiments critical of Japan while trying not to inflame anti-Japanese views. Nevertheless, Koizumi's bold behavior regarding the Yasukuni Shrine visits has impeded the exchange of visits by the top leaders of the two countries, even on the occasion of the thirtieth anniversary of Sino-Japanese normalization and the twenty-fifth anniversary of the bilateral Peace and Friendship Treaty.

Koizumi's brashness regarding Yasukuni, however, has not prevented him from making conciliatory gestures on the history issue. To repair some of the damage caused by his first visit to the Yasukuni Shrine, Koizumi made a historic visit to Marco Polo Bridge. After a leak of mustard gas containers left behind by Japanese troops killed one Chinese and injured forty-three in Qiqihar City of Heilongjiang province in August 2003, Japan provided medical assistance to help treat the victims and agreed to pay 300 million yen in compensation. Although similar incidents have harmed more than two thousand Chinese in the past, Japan did not accept legal liability for them. This time around, however, Japan acknowledged its responsibility and decided to compensate the victims.[26] Will this compensation contribute to deeper reconciliation between China and Japan, or will it exacerbate the situation by stimulating Chinese demands for individual compensation for Japan's past transgressions?

CONCLUSION

Although this chapter has argued for a new equilibrium in China-Japan relations based on mutual interests and frankness, one should not be Pollyannaish about this relationship. As the above review of key issues demonstrates, there are numerous areas of friction and disagreement that require careful and attentive management by leaders in both countries. Thus far, bilateral problem solving at the state level has prevented a clash of nationalisms. But a lot of the credit has to go to the softer and more conciliatory approach of Chinese leaders toward Japan since 1999. Unfortunately, Japanese public awareness and acknowledgment of this Chinese shift has been meager. Negative portrayals of China and pessimistic prognoses of Sino-Japanese relations continue to gain popularity in Japan. There is only so much that state officials on both sides can do to promote stability and cooperation between the two countries. Positive attitudes about the other country have to develop much more at the societal level before one can be confident about Sino-Japanese stability, much less a Sino-Japanese partnership for East Asian regional integration. People-to-people exchanges might ultimately nurture such feelings; but in the meantime, it would be helpful if Japan were to give more positive feedback to China about its shift in Japan policy.

In the meantime, two imperatives are likely to steer the Japanese government toward keeping relations with China cordial and stable. The first is the commercial imperative. Japan's own economic fortunes are now increasingly tied to the continuing expansion of the Chinese economy. Therefore, the Japanese business community will do what it can to dampen public hostility toward China and support the government's effort prevent a downward spiral in Sino-Japanese relations. The second is the strategic imperative. Although Japan is now strengthening its security alliance with the United States, it wants to avoid an international situation in which it has to choose between its alliance with the United States and stable relations with China. As Eric Heginbotham and Richard J. Samuels have argued,

Japan is pursuing a "double hedge" strategy. While promoting security cooperation with the United States and expanding its defense capabilities to counter the rise of China, it is also developing diplomatic and economic links with China to enhance its global position relative to both the United States and Europe.[27]

NOTES

The author would like to thank the Smith Richardson Foundation for its support of his project on Japan-China-U.S. relations, on which this chapter is based.

1. Hidemori Ijiri, "Sino-Japanese Controversy Since the 1972 Diplomatic Normalization," in *China and Japan: History, Trends, and Prospects*, ed. Christopher Howe (Oxford: Clarendon Press, 1996), 64–73.

2. Mike Mochizuki, "Terms of Engagement: The U.S.-Japan Alliance and the Rise of China," in *Beyond Bilateralism: U.S.-Japan Relations in the New Asia-Pacific*, ed. Ellis S. Krauss and T. J. Pempel (Stanford, CA: Stanford University Press, 2004), 96–100.

3. James Reilly, "China's History Activists and the War of Resistance Against Japan," *Asian Survey* 44, no. 2 (March/April 2004): 276–94; and Kokubun Ryosei, "Beyond Normalization: Thirty Years of Sino-Japanese Diplomacy," *Gaiko Forum* (Winter 2003): 35–36.

4. For a leading example of this pessimism, see Benjamin Self, "China and Japan: A Façade of Friendship," *Washington Quarterly* 26, no. 1 (Winter 2002/2003): 77–88. Other works in this school of thought include Masahiko Sasajima, "Japan's Domestic Politics and China Policymaking," in *An Alliance for Engagement: Building Cooperation in Security Relations with China*, ed. Benjamin L. Self and Jeffrey W. Thompson (Washington, DC: Henry L. Stimson Center, 2002), 79–110; and Yoshihisa Komori, *Nit-chu yuko no maboroshi* [Japan and China: Illusion of friendship] (Tokyo: Shogakkan, 2002).

5. Self, "China and Japan," 81–82.

6. Satoshi Tomisaka, *Sen-nyu: Zai-Nichi Chugokujin no Hanzai* [Infiltration: The crimes of Chinese residents in Japan] (Tokyo: Bungei Shunju Sha, 2001); Joseph Kahn, "China Angered Over Reported Japanese Orgy," *New York Times*, September 30, 2003, A9; and John Pomfret, "Wild Weekend's Hangover: Outrage Follows Japanese Tourists' Orgy with Chinese Prostitutes," *Washington Post*, October 3, 2003, A14.

7. See also Thomas J. Christensen, "China, the US-Japan Alliance, and the Security Dilemma in East Asia," *International Security* 23, no. 4 (Spring 1999): 49–80.

8. For a leading example of this cautious optimism, see Robert Sutter, "China and Japan: Trouble Ahead?" *Washington Quarterly* 25, no. 4 (Autumn 2002): 37–49. Other works in this school of thought include Toshiya Tsugami, *Chugoku Taito: Nihon wa nani o nasu beki ka* [The rise of China: What should Japan do?] (Tokyo: Nihon Keizai Shimbunsha, 2003); and Zhu Jianrong, *Chugoku Dai San no Kakumei* [China's third revolution] (Tokyo: Chuo Koronsha, 2002).

9. Sutter, "China and Japan."

10. This is the language used in the November 2002 report by the Prime Minister's Task Force on "Basic Strategies for Japan's Foreign Policy in the 21st Century: New Era, New Vision, New Diplomacy."

11. Lu Zhongwei, "Sino-Japanese Relations: Understanding and Promoting," in *Contemporary International Relations* 12, no. 10 (October 2003): 5–6.

12. Ibid., 4, 7, and 8.

13. Ma Licheng, "New Thinking on Sino-Japanese Relations," *Japan Echo*, June 2003, 35–40. The original essay was published in Chinese in the December 2002 issue of *Zhanlue yu Guanli* [Strategy and management].

14. Tsugami, *Chugoku Taito*, 178–84.

15. The Ministry of Foreign Affairs of Japan, "Review on Japan's ODA to China," available at http://www.mofa.go.jp/policy/oda/region/e_asia/china-1.html.

16. Tsugami, *Chugoku Taito*, 210–16.

17. Naoko Munakata, ed., *Nit-Chu Kankei no Tenki* [Turning point in Japan-China relations] (Tokyo: Toyo Keizai Shimbunsha, 2001).

18. Naoko Munakata, "China's Impact and Regional Economic Integration—A Japanese Perspective," Statement before the U.S.-China Economic and Security Review Commission, December 4, 2003. See also Ken Belson, "Japanese Capital and Jobs Flowing to China," *New York Times*, February 17, 2004, C1, C4.

19. Saori N. Katada, "Japan's Counterweight Strategy: U.S.-Japan Cooperation and Competition in International Finance," and Jennifer A. Amyx, "Japan and the Evolution of Regional Financial Arrangements in East Asia," both in *Beyond Bilateralism*, 176–218.

20. Japan Defense Agency, *2002 Defense of Japan* (Tokyo: Urban Connections, 2002), 55–64; and National Institute for Defense Studies Japan, *East Asian Strategic Review 2003* (Tokyo: Japan Times, 2003), 181–94.

21. Satoshi Morimoto, *Anzen Hosho Ron: 21 Seiki Sekai no Kiki Kanri* [Discourse on security: Crisis management in the 21st-century world] (Tokyo: PHP Kenkyujo, 2000), 243–64; and Hisahiko Okazaki and Keitaro Hasegawa, *Chugoku Hatsu no Kiki to Nihon* [A China crisis and Japan] (Tokyo: Tokuma Shobo, 1998), 117–212. For different Japanese views about China's military, see Ikuo Kayahara, *Anzen Hosho kara Mita Chugoku: Nit-chu Kyozon—Kyoei ni Muketa Shikaku* [China from a security perspective: Aiming toward Japan-China coexistence and coprosperity] (Tokyo: Keiso Shobo, 1998); and Shigeo Hiramatsu, *Chugoku no Kyoi* [The Chinese threat] (Tokyo: Jiji Tsushin Sha, 1995).

22. National Institute for Defense Studies Japan, *East Asian Strategic Review 2003*, 176–77.

23. Paul Midford, "Japan's Response to Terror: Dispatching the SDF to the Arabian Sea," *Asian Survey* 63, no. 2 (March–April 2003): 345–46.

24. Yuan Yang, "Japan's Military Transformation and Sino-Japanese Military Relations," *Contemporary International Relations* 13, no. 11 (November 2003): 27–33.

25. Okazaki Hisahiko, et al., *"Taiwan mondai" no saki ni aru Nihon no kiki* [Japan's crisis that lies before the "Taiwan problem"] (Tokyo: Bijinesu Sha, 2001), 36–42, 52–57.

26. Frank Ching, "'History' Bedevils China-Japan Relations," *Japan Times*, September 4, 2003.

27. Eric Heginbotham and Richard J. Samuels, "Japan," in *Strategic Asia 2002–03: Asian Aftershocks*, ed. Richard J. Ellings and Aaron L. Friedberg (Seattle: National Bureau of Asian Research, 2002), 111–16.

6

China's Ascendancy and the Korean Peninsula

From Interest Reevaluation to Strategic Realignment?

Jae Ho Chung

China has so far pulled off one of the most successful economic reforms recorded in the twentieth century. Its success has been so remarkable that China has been elevated to the status of an "economic giant" (*jingji daguo*), if not the "biggest new variable in the global equation."[1] In accordance with its growing power, China has assumed increasing responsibilities in regional affairs. Beijing attracted international attention with its responsible fiscal policy during the Asian financial crisis of the late 1990s, when China maintained the value of its currency.[2] And, by hosting the three- and six-party talks in 2003, China also demonstrated a more proactive position on the management of a near-crisis situation induced by North Korea's nuclear brinkmanship.[3]

In tandem with the growing literature on the "rise" of China, an increasing number of studies regarding how to respond to it have also been produced.[4] Certainly, these studies vary significantly according to the country concerned. That is, responses by the Taiwanese and Japanese have been qualitatively different than reactions by those from Singapore and Myanmar.[5] Even within Southeast Asia, the *modi operandi* have varied between the islands and continental areas of the region.[6] Perhaps no nation has been as receptive as South Korea, where China has managed to win the hearts of many, the elite and the public alike.[7]

South Korea's "China fever" has been closely monitored in the United States. In particular, Washington has paid special attention to a possible connection between "China fever" and the upsurge of anti-American sentiment in South Korea in recent years.[8] This possible—but as yet unproven—connection has led to the revival of America's earlier suspicion that Seoul might eventually enter into Beijing's diplomatic orbit, thus abandoning the Washington-based alliance structure.[9]

This chapter argues that some readjustment is already taking place with respect to South Korea's relations with the United States, due in part to the rapidly expanding bilateralism between Seoul and Beijing. The core question, then, concerns whether that readjustment will remain in the realm of interest reevaluation or perhaps develop into some sort of strategic realignment. This chapter suggests that realignment may be inevitable, but that it will not likely occur in the near future, both due to the enduring gap in capabilities between the United States and China and because of the uncertainties involving North Korea. More importantly, in the longer run, America's efforts to reduce the tensions between Washington and Seoul may help to restrain, if not reverse, the pace of South Korea's strategic realignment with China.

The remainder of this chapter consists of four sections. The first describes the politico-economic background against which China has emerged as a crucial partner of South Korea since the early 1990s. The second section examines Beijing's evolving position on the North Korean nuclear conundrum, in which China has risen as an indispensable broker for the peace and stability of the region. The third section traces the process by which the relationships of the two Koreas with their major allies—China and the United States—have shifted over time from those of loyalty to those of voice and possibly even of exit.[10] The chapter will conclude with some observations regarding the prospects for a Sinocentric system on the Korean peninsula.

DRIVERS OF CHINA–SOUTH KOREA BILATERALISM

China's normalization of relations with South Korea was one of the most astonishing developments of the 1990s. Furthermore, the dramatic growth in Sino–South Korean relations in the post-normalization phase was so dramatic that Washington began to question the future of its alliance relationship with Seoul.[11] At least four factors may jointly account for the remarkable expansion of South Korea–China bilateralism and "comprehensive cooperative partnership."[12]

First, the political atmosphere of East-West rapprochement on a global scale since the mid-1980s was an important contributing factor. The "détente spirit" among the United States, the USSR, and China—facilitated in large part by Mikhail Gorbachev's overtures to China—created the space for similar conciliatory moves between China and South Korea. Furthermore, several fortuitous events and episodes—most importantly, the landing in South Korea of a hijacked Chinese civil airliner in 1983, the 1986 Asian Games and the 1988 Olympic Games in Seoul, and the 1990 Asian Games in Beijing—led to closer encounters between Beijing and Seoul.[13]

A more far-reaching change in the structure of the international system took place in the early 1990s with the collapse of global communism and the

TABLE 19. China's Trade with North and South Korea, 1980–2002

	With North Korea (US$ million)	With South Korea (US$ million)	Share of China's total (%)	Share of South Korea's total (%)
1980	678	188	0.5	0.5
1985	473	1,161	1.9	1.9
1990	483	3,821	3.3	2.8
1995	550	16,540	5.9	6.4
2000	488	31,250	6.6	9.4
2001	740	31,490	6.2	10.8
2002	738	41,152	6.6	13.1

SOURCES: http://www.stats.gov.cn and http://www.kotis.or.kr.

Soviet Union in particular. With the virtual demise of the Cold War, both China and South Korea became much less restrained by their junior allies—North Korea and Taiwan, respectively—and more proactive in their dealings with each other. Subsequently, they decided to normalize their relations in 1992 and announced their "comprehensive cooperative partnership" in 2003. In short, crucial system-level changes provided valuable opportunities for regional actors.[14]

Second, Sino–South Korean bilateralism was also facilitated by the convergence of the economic interests of the two developing economies. The search for low-cost labor—and profitable overseas markets—on the part of Seoul coincided with Beijing's will to join the international economic system. China also hoped that its search for capital and technology could be helped significantly by South Korea, which, unlike the United States and Japan, was much more forthcoming and willing to provide both with few political strings attached.[15]

Once bilateral exchanges gained a foothold, both South Korea and China immediately realized the value of cooperation in trade, investment, tourism, education, and so on. The mutual recognition of the benefits of cooperation was another incentive to expand the bilateralism, leading to the establishment of semigovernmental trade offices in 1991 and to the diplomatic normalization in 1992. The expansion of bilateral cooperation in the post-normalization phase has been dramatic.

Table 19 demonstrates the central importance of China in South Korea's foreign trade. By 2002, trade with China accounted for over 13 percent of South Korea's total trade. In 2003, China had overtaken the United States to become the largest export market for South Korea while continuing to be the number one destination for South Korea's outbound investment.[16] Trade and investment are only part of the story. More people travel between China and South Korea than between the United States and South Korea.[17] At the end of 2002, South Korean students in China numbered 36,093, accounting for 42.1 percent of all foreign students in China.[18]

Third, Sino–South Korean bilateralism has also benefited from China's implicit "disengagement" from North Korea since the early 1990s. Beijing's distancing from Pyongyang was facilitated by the fundamental shift in China's spirit of foreign policy from vulnerability, contention, and rigidity to confidence, reconciliation, and flexibility.[19] More specifically, China's conviction that North Korea would never tilt too heavily toward the Soviet Union (and Russia) was a key contributing factor.[20] China's confident foreign policy was reflected in its changing perception of South Korea as well. As one Chinese analyst has put it, "China no longer views the United States as wanting to use Korea as a springboard to attack her . . . [and] the Korean contradiction is now less one between the East and the West than one between rival political forces in Korea."[21]

One may even speculate that by 1991, when both Koreas joined the United Nations, China had already come to the conclusion that inter-Korean relations were qualitatively different from cross-strait relations.[22] Subsequently, the Korean issue became a more maneuverable game for China than it had been previously, when it had been directly linked to ideological dogmatism and superpower rivalry. The improved Seoul-Beijing relationship was therefore based in significant part upon China's ability to distinguish the North Korean issue from the "Taiwan problem."

Once the trilateral dynamics between China, North Korea, and South Korea were transformed from a "stable marriage" into a sort of "romantic triangle,"[23] North Korea had to seek a mechanism—if not a pretext—to guarantee its security and survival, hence the first nuclear crisis of 1993–94. Yet that was precisely the time when Beijing's relations with Pyongyang began to cool off rather significantly, China's sustained economic assistance for the survival of North Korea notwithstanding.[24]

While stability on the Korean peninsula remained a high priority for Beijing, in support of which China offered the DPRK economic assistance of various sorts, Beijing's distancing from North Korea also began around this time. High-level visits were considerably reduced. A spokesperson from China's foreign ministry commented in 1995 that "China does not believe the friendship treaty with North Korea is one that requires the dispatch of military forces." In 1997, Tang Jiaxuan, then vice foreign minister, said in a public forum in Seoul that China was not willing automatically to intervene if North Korea were to start a war.[25] Although there was a small increase in North Korea's trade with China during the mid-1990s, it was more a function of China filling the void caused by Russia's withdrawal from providing assistance to North Korea than of Beijing actively helping Pyongyang with economic recovery.[26]

Fourth, China's infatuation with South Korea and its disengagement from North Korea have had much to do with so-called "socialization effects." That is to say, over the decades of reform and opening, China has come to appreciate global norms of trade and diplomacy.[27] While it does not mean that China has completely shed its hypersensitivity to sovereignty, certain changes are easily discernible in its dealings with the outside world. Gradually, China's evolving norms of international relations have made South Korea more attractive than North Korea.[28] In a nutshell, shared interests and norms have been the locomotives of South Korea–China bilateralism.

CHINA'S ASCENDANCY OVER THE NUCLEAR CRISIS

China's evolving position with respect to the North Korean nuclear problem became more visible during the second nuclear crisis since October 2002. From October 2002 to February 2003 China's official position remained largely unchanged, although some "unconventional" commentaries appeared in the online version of *People's Daily* at the turn of the year.[29] In this earlier phase, the Chinese were apparently still reluctant to join the United States in accepting its intelligence assessments and condemning North Korea's nuclear brinkmanship.

During this phase, the Chinese government repeated three of its official principles: (1) permitting "no nuclear weapons" on the Korean peninsula; (2) maintaining peace and stability; and (3) resolving the dilemma through dialogue and negotiation.[30] Initially, China did not quite buy the American perspective, but rather suggested that "[South] Korea cannot blindly follow the United States."[31] Chinese officials continued to argue that Beijing had only limited influence over Pyongyang and that it was Washington that should do more to solve the problem at hand.[32] Yet, at the same time, the officials seemed to enjoy the world's assessment of China's potential role in the resolution of the looming crisis.[33]

China's position made a significant turnaround in the spring of 2003. According to Chinese analysts, it was around this time that Beijing began to accept American intelligence assessments regarding the progress in North Korea's nuclear weapons programs.[34] The change was also facilitated by China's perception that North Korea's relationship with the United States was heading toward a certain clash that would be disastrous for China. The Chinese not only expressed grave concerns about the increasingly hostile exchanges between Washington and Pyongyang, but they were also extremely alarmed by the March 2 close encounter between North Korea's MiG fighters and America's RC-135S reconnaissance plane against the backdrop of the looming war in Iraq.[35]

China's deputy foreign minister, Wang Yi, went to Pyongyang in February to meet with Paik Nam-soon, North Korea's foreign minister. At the meeting, Wang reportedly made a direct plea that Pyongyang terminate its nuclear provocation immediately. China allegedly even hinted about the possibility that Beijing might drop its long-standing opposition to international sanctions if Pyongyang should fail to do so. In March, Qian Qichen—China's foreign policy guru—flew to Pyongyang to demand again that North Korea stop its nuclear provocations.[36]

In early March, the Central Committee of the Chinese Communist Party (CCP) reportedly set up the Leadership Small Group on the North Korean Problem, headed by Hu Jintao. Upon its establishment, according to media reports, the first thing Hu did was to summon China's top Korea specialists to solicit their opinions on the issue.[37] This coincided with the flourishing of debates and discussions in Beijing with regard to the need to readjust China's policy toward North Korea.[38]

During the first nuclear crisis of 1993–94, China had mostly stayed on the fence and threatened to veto a United Nations condemnation of Pyongyang. In stark contrast, this time around, Beijing even chose to support a resolution adopted by the International Atomic Energy Agency (IAEA) in January 2003 demanding the immediate termination of North Korea's nuclear weapons programs. Furthermore, in February, China went so far as to vote in favor of referring the North Korean case to the United Nations Security Council.[39]

A puzzling episode took place in late February 2003 whereby oil pipelines from China to North Korea were shut down for three days. Although the incident was officially attributed to "technical problems," one could not help wonder if it were instead a veiled warning from Beijing to Pyongyang.[40] When China subsequently offered to host a three-party dialogue, which would provide Washington and Pyongyang the invaluable opportunity to communicate face to face, North Korea did not hesitate to accept the invitation. Although the three-way meeting in April did not produce any tangible results, China nevertheless emerged from the scene as a major peace broker for the region.[41]

China once again showed off its diplomatic capacity by hosting six-party talks in August 2003, during which, for the first time, the United States, China, Japan, Russia, and the two Koreas gathered to exchange views. At this meeting, Beijing pressed the participants to sign a communiqué that could serve as a foundation for a peaceful solution to the North Korean conundrum. Although the communiqué was not signed because of a lack of consensus between the United States and North Korea, China emerged as a crucial mediator in the region, boosting its image as a great power. China's official publications lost no time in publicizing the constructive role performed by Beijing.[42] Interestingly, every time Pyongyang came to the

TABLE 20. Chinese Delegations to North Korea before Major Events

Date of delegation	Head of Chinese delegation	Major decision
March 2003	Qian Qichen	Three-party talks (April)
July 2003	Dai Bingguo	Six-party talks, first round (August)
October 2003	Wu Bangguo	Six-party talks, second round (December)[a]

[a]The second round of the Six-Party talks was initially scheduled for December 2003, but it was later put off.

negotiating table, high-level Chinese delegations to Pyongyang seem to have just preceded the dialogues (see table 20).[43]

If ideological and strategic factors had facilitated the bifurcation of Korea-China ties into South Korea–Taiwan and North Korea–China relations, the Korean War (1950–53) solidified the Cold War structure in Northeast Asia. So long as survival was the ultimate objective, security concerns carried the most weight in any country's strategic calculations.[44] At the time, for most states the line between survival and demise was ideologically drawn, and the alignment with the Soviet Union and China (in the case of North Korea) or with the United States (in the case of South Korea) was not a deliberate choice but mostly a given. .

The relationships of the two Koreas with other countries during the 1950s can best be described as loyalty-based. That is, both Koreas maintained "stable marriages" with their key allies: relationships were amicable between patrons and clients (China and North Korea, on the one hand, and the United States and South Korea, on the other), although relationships between each patron (China and the United States) and the third players (South Korea and North Korea, respectively) were characterized by enmity.[45] Ideology played a crucial, if not exclusive, role, permitting little room for benign relations between China and South Korea, on the one hand, and the United States and North Korea, on the other.[46]

The 1960s began with the Sino-Soviet split, facilitated in part by China's unwillingness to swallow Soviet direction. The breakup of the socialist bloc—or the rise of the "third" camp—generated a starkly different context for Korea-China relations. During the 1960s, while Pyongyang often sided with Beijing in ideological terms, it nevertheless had to solicit economic and military assistance from Moscow. During this era of Sino-Soviet schism, North Korea managed to develop its own *modus operandi* in dealing with both the Soviet Union and China, although Pyongyang's loyalty-based relationship with Beijing—often dubbed an "alliance sealed in blood"—remained largely intact.[47]

Throughout the 1960s, South Korea's relations with China remained deeply antagonistic due to the enmity generated during the Korean War and perpetuated by South Korea's firm anticommunist stance. In brief, ideology continued to constrain Sino–South Korean relations throughout the 1960s. Furthermore, unlike the Beijing-Pyongyang ties, which became more flexible due to the Sino-Soviet schism, the solid Washington-Seoul relationship remained mostly unchanged. Loyalty was the defining factor of the bilateral ties.

China's perennial preoccupation with survival necessitated a radical break with its isolationist policy of the late 1960s. The outcome was its strategic alignment with the United States against the Soviet Union, or the united front against Moscow during the 1970s. North Korea responded to China's new stance by breaking out of its traditional loyalty-based relationship. First, to maximize its chances of attaining military and economic assistance from both Beijing and Moscow, Pyongyang fine-tuned its "equidistance" policy. Second, North Korea actively sought to elevate the Juche ideology to the level of Marxism, Leninism, and Maoism.[48] Third, North Korea also tried to improve its relations with the South and to expand its trade with Japan and Western Europe.[49] For North Korea, loyalty to China became increasingly difficult.

During the 1980s, South Korea–China relations began a decade-long process of "de-ideologization" through the creation of trading networks.[50] This was also the period when, following the reduction of U.S. forces and the Kwangju tragedy, friction between South Korea and the United States started to build up. Although South Korea's loyalty to the United States was still intact, at least on the surface, popular criticism of the United States was already being expressed. [51] North Korea, on the other hand, kept a wary eye on the expansion of South Korea–China bilateralism while intermittently voicing its discomfort with the situation.[52]

During the 1990s, the Cold War structure was largely dismantled as both the Soviet Union and China normalized relations with South Korea in 1990 and 1992, respectively, further reducing the space for North Korea to maneuver. These sea changes meant that neither the Soviet Union/Russia nor China was to constitute a reliable patron or protector for North Korea. Naturally, Pyongyang expressed its security concerns by making an explicit statement—namely, the threat of nuclear proliferation. Although North Korea's nuclear ambition was designed to attain a minimum level of security against external threats, as well as to deal directly with the United States under the pretext of the nuclear Non-Proliferation Treaty (NPT), it was at the same time an affront to its traditional allies, most notably China.[53]

In retrospect, Pyongyang's statement does not appear to have been very effective, at least vis-à-vis Beijing. China gradually phased out the use of the term "alliance sealed in blood" when describing its relationship with North Korea, preferring instead the less dramatic term "traditionally amicable ties." Although China officially continues to display concern for North Korea, the intensity of its support has certainly declined over the years, as discussed in the earlier section.[54] Although it may be a truism that Beijing will not sacrifice Pyongyang for the sake of Seoul, China's *modus operandi* in dealing with both Koreas is increasingly shifting in favor of the South at the expense of the North.[55]

Despite the Agreed Framework and the Korean Energy Development Organization (KEDO) project, North Korea's ultimate security dilemma has not been resolved from Pyongyang's perspective. As some analysts have put it, North Korea's relations with China are neither allied abandonment nor allied entrapment.[56] Such an ambiguous cul-de-sac might have prompted Pyongyang to pursue another measure of nuclear brinkmanship, the highly enriched uranium (HEU) program, which it hoped might possibly link itself again with Washington in a more direct way. Whether North Korea will actually take the final step of declaring itself a nuclear weapons state remains unclear, however.

South Korea, too, has taken a winding path in its attempt to move beyond a patron-client relationship based solely on loyalty to the United States. With the attainment of economic modernization and a democratic transition in the late 1980s, South Korea made strenuous efforts for diplomatic "pluralization," dubbed *nordpolitik* (northern diplomacy toward socialist states). One crucial goal of South Korea's *nordpolitik* was to "expand the horizons of South Korea's foreign policy, which were hitherto limited to the countries like the United States and Japan."[57] The rapprochement with China in 1992 in particular introduced a new variable, since it had been pursued by Seoul fairly independently of American direction.[58]

With more power, wealth, prestige, and influence than ever before, China has gradually become an indispensable regional presence to be reckoned with concerning the Korean question. Yet few South Koreans talk publicly and negatively about the security implications of the "rise of China." Strategic ambiguity aptly describes Seoul's position on China as a potential threat.[59] Most importantly, the South Korean view of China has become increasingly favorable, while U.S. opinion of China has deteriorated substantially (see table 21).

Although it was widely believed that there existed a fine line between elite and public views of China—that is, that the South Korean elite have generally been more concerned about the "rise of China" than the general public—a significant shift may be underway.[60] In a rare survey of South

TABLE 21. Public Perceptions of China
and the United States, 1996–2002

	chose China (%)	*chose United States (%)*
1996	47	24
1997	56	31
1999	33	22
2000	45	43
2002	41	30

NOTE: The figures do not add up as the balance refers to the percentages of those who chose countries other than China and the United
States.

SOURCES: *Ministry of Information Survey* (Seoul: MOI, 1995), 354; *1997
Sejong Survey* (Seoul: Dongseo Research, December 1997), 11–13; *Dong-A
Ilbo*, January 1, 1999; *Hangook Ilbo*, June 9, 2000; and *Sisa Journal*, March
2002, cited in *Korean Journal* (December 2002), 30.

Korean elite perceptions conducted by an American think tank in 2002
(see table 22), it was discovered that the younger South Korean elite, like
their public counterparts, appear to display high hopes for Sino–South
Korean ties, possibly at the expense of South Korea's relationship with the
United States.[61] This perceptual shift can be attributed in large part to generational changes, since younger Koreans are more hopeful about the
future role of China.[62]

With respect to perceptions of Japan, a huge gap exists between those of
the United States, on the one hand, and those of China and South Korea
(and North Korea, for that matter), on the other. Americans generally view
Japan, which they consider unique among Asian countries, very favorably.[63]
According to a survey conducted in the United States in 1999, 46 percent
of the public and 62 percent of the elite (represented by the Luce Foundation Fellows) were in favor of Japan's rearmament.[64] Two nationwide surveys done in South Korea in 1997 and 2000, however, reveal that more than
90 percent of the South Korean public believed that preventing Japan's
militarism should be Seoul's top foreign policy priority.[65] Of the fifty-six
American experts interviewed by the author in Washington, D.C., during
2002–2003, 63 percent projected that an enhanced strategic role for Japan
in Asia would push South Korea closer to China.[66]

Washington and Seoul have also diverged in their assessment of the
threat posed by Pyongyang's nuclear brinkmanship. Not only has South
Korea persistently differed from the United States in its strategic assessment
of the North, but it has also found more common ground with China in

TABLE 22. Projections for South Korea's Future Ties
with Major Powers

(%)

	U.S.	China	Russia	Japan
Closer	14	86	45	39
Unchanged	78	14	47	55
Weaker	8	0	8	6

SOURCE: William Watts, Next Generation Leaders in the Republic of Korea: Opinion Survey Report and Analysis (Washington, DC: Potomac Associates, April 2002), 12.

dealing with the nuclear problem.[67] The Seoul-Washington relationship has been going through a process that is revealing the loss of trust between the two allies. Washington is finding it difficult to adjust to Seoul's increasingly independent voice.[68]

The crux of the problem is the disparity of attention given by South Korea and the United States to the other. Very few Americans, experts and the public alike, are aware that South Korea is America's seventh largest trading partner. According to a 1995 Gallup survey, fewer than 10 percent of American respondents knew the name of South Korea's president (Kim Young Sam), while the comparable figure for Chinese respondents was 66 percent. The survey revealed that 58 percent of American respondents showed no interest at all in South Korea, and only 6 percent expressed a substantial interest in knowing about the country.[69] In 2001 another survey by Harris Interactive also found that 60 percent of American respondents had no opinion whatsoever when asked "how do you perceive South Korea?"[70]

THE KOREAN PENINSULA, CHINA, AND THE UNITED STATES:
TOWARD REALIGNMENT?

Irrespective of the changes in the foreign policy orientations of the two Koreas, an inevitable dilemma looms large for both Pyongyang and Seoul. In order for North Korea to get on the track of genuine reform and opening, its compliance with minimum international norms of nonproliferation—and improved relations with the United States as a result—are indispensable. The precedent set by China, and China's increasing valuation of its relationship with the United States, are highly supportive of the point. Yet, if North Korea were to "exit"—that is, if it were to declare itself a nuclear state—it would introduce a new variable to the already very complicated dynamics of Northeast Asia, with complex implications for its domestic politics as well.

The upcoming dilemma for Seoul is no less serious. South Korea's economic and geopolitical stakes in China are increasing rapidly, quite to the point of surpassing those in the United States. Yet South Korea's unabated reservations about China's intentions for the region, particularly on the part of some elite, may sustain a resilient hope for the United States.[71] While the state of U.S.-China relations holds a key to South Korea's strategic stance, to Seoul's insurmountable frustration, the Washington-Beijing relationship is far beyond Seoul's independent control. If the relationship should become conflict-ridden, either because of a power transition or a clash of civilizations, South Korea will be put in a very difficult situation.[72]

In the short run—for ten years, at least, during which the capability gap between the United States and China will be both clear and unbridgeable—South Korea's optimal choice will be to stick with the U.S.-centered alliance structure and, at the same time, to further expand its burgeoning ties with China.[73] During this period, however, South Korea's strategy will increasingly resemble that of hedging since China's regional influence over the Korean peninsula is inevitably larger than its overall (i.e., global) capabilities.

Despite prevailing concerns and speculation that South Korea might eventually depart from the U.S.-based alliance system, such an event will take a substantial amount of time—at least twenty years, if it should occur at all—before South Korea comes to the strategic assessment that China's overall capabilities—both global and regional—have surpassed those of the United States.[74] Even then, a significant amount of psychological and perceptual inertia may continue to operate to constrain the acceleration of China's emergence as South Korea's "strategic supplement."

On the other hand, the gradual manifestation of China's "imperial" attitude toward South Korea—a side effect of a new Sinocentric order—may work as a crucial restraint on South Korea's exclusive reliance on China at the expense of the United States.[75] Of course, the persistent rationale that America—because of its sheer physical distance from the Korean peninsula—has no immediate geopolitical stake, as China and Japan do, and therefore may serve as a more honest broker for peace and stability in the Korean peninsula, may continue to persuade many.

In conclusion, China's ascendancy may produce the most immediate and far-reaching impact on the Korean peninsula, where the residue of the Cold War remains. Although strategic realignment is unlikely in the near term, the same cannot be said of the mid- and long term. Strategic realignment will depend upon whether China is able to manage its rise peacefully and whether the United States continues with its controversial unilateralism.

Will China even succeed in generating its own normative appeal to replace that of the United States?[76] Viewed in this vein, realignment is likely to be slow, if it occurs at all. Yet both North and South Korea are reconsidering their interests and are recalibrating their relationships with each other, with China, and with the United States.

NOTES

1. While China does not yet have a per capita GNP of a developed country, this does not deprive it of the ability and opportunity to become a global presence to be reckoned with (if the precedent set by the Soviet Union is any guide). The term "economic giant" was used by Lee Hsien Loong, then deputy prime minister of Singapore. See *South China Morning Post,* August 3, 2001. For China's own aspirations to become a world-class power, see Ye Zicheng, *Zhongguo dazhanlue* [The grand strategy of China] (Beijing: Zhongguo shehui kexue chubanshe, 2003).

2. Barry Naughton, "China: Domestic Restructuring and a New Role in Asia," in *The Politics of the Asian Economic Crisis,* ed. T. J. Pempel (Ithaca, NY: Cornell University Press, 1999), 203–23.

3. For China's assumption of more responsibility on a par with its power, see Yongjin Zhang and Greg Austin, eds., *Power and Responsibility in Chinese Foreign Policy* (Canberra: Asia Pacific Press, 2001).

4. Limited space here does not permit a detailed discussion of the scenarios concerning the future of China. For a review of this growing literature, see Jae Ho Chung, "China's Reforms at Twenty-Five: Challenges for the New Leadership," *China: An International Journal* 1, no. 1 (March 2003): 127–32.

5. See Alastair I. Johnston and Robert S. Ross, eds., *Engaging China: The Management of an Emerging Power* (London: Routledge, 1999); Herbert Yee and Ian Storey, eds., *China Threat: Perceptions, Myths and Reality* (London: Routledge Curzon, 2002); and Zainal A. Yusof, "Malaysia's Response to the China Challenge," Tain-Jy Chen, "Will Taiwan Be Marginalized by China," and Shigeyuki Abe, "Is 'China Fear' Warranted?" all in *Asian Economic Papers* 2, no. 2 (Spring–Summer 2003): 46–131.

6. See the contribution by Wang Gungwu to this volume.

7. See Jae Ho Chung, "South Korea between Eagle and Dragon: Perceptual Ambivalence and Strategic Dilemma," *Asian Survey* 41, no. 5 (September–October 2001): 783–88; and William Watts, *Next Generation Leaders in the Republic of Korea: Opinion Survey Report and Analysis* (Washington, DC: Potomac Associates, 2002), 12.

8. This observation is based on the author's year-long interviews in Washington, D.C., during 2002–2003. See, for instance, Jae Ho Chung, "How America Views South Korea–China Bilateralism," Brookings CNAPS Working Paper (September 2003), available at http://www.brookings.edu.

9. For the earlier suspicion, see Kurt M. Campbell and Mitchell B. Reiss, "Korean Changes, Asian Challenges and the US Role," *Survival* 43, no. 1 (Spring 2001): 59–60, 63; and Eric A. McVadon, "China's Goals and Strategies for the Korean Peninsula," in *Planning for a Peaceful Korea,* ed. Henry D. Sokolski (Carlisle, PA: U.S. Army War College Strategic Studies Institute, February 2001), 149, 169.

10. The analogies of "loyalty, voice, and exit" used here and subsequently have been adapted from Albert Hirschman, *Exit, Voice, and Loyalty: Responses to Decline in Firms, Organizations, and States* (Cambridge: Harvard University Press, 1970).

11. See, for instance, Zbigniew Brzezinski, Lee Hamilton, and Richard Lugar, *Foreign Policy into the 21st Century: The United States Leadership Challenges* (Washington, DC: CSIS, 1996), 49.

12. South Korea–China relations had initially been officially designated a "cooperative partnership" during President Kim Dae Jung's state visit to China in 1998. Although an agreement on upgrading it to a "comprehensive cooperative partnership" had been reached during Premier Zhu Rongji's visit to Seoul in 2000, the agreement was officially announced and endorsed in July 2003, when President Roh Moo-Hyun visited China. For the terms, see Zhang Jianhua, *Jiejue zhongguo zaidu mianlin de jinyao wenti* [On the resolution of the urgent problems China has faced again] (Beijing: Jingji ribao chubanshe, 2000), 523–24.

13. For the East-West rapprochement, see Joan E. Spero and Jeffrey A. Hart, *The Politics of International Economic Relations* (New York: Wadsworth, 1996), chapter 10. For the importance of the hijacking incident and international sporting events, see Chae-jin Lee, *China and Korea: Dynamic Relations* (Palo Alto, CA: Hoover Press, 1996), 106–8.

14. For studies that discuss this volatile period from the perspectives of South Korea, the Soviet Union, and China, see, respectively, Robert E. Bedeski, *The Transformation of South Korea: Reform and Reconstruction in the Sixth Republic under Roh Tae Woo, 1987–1992* (London: Routledge, 1994), chapter 7; Charles E. Ziegler, *Foreign Policy and East Asia: Learning and Adaptation in the Gorbachev Era* (Cambridge: Cambridge University Press, 1993), chapter 6; and Samuel S. Kim, "The Making of China's Korea Policy in the Era of Reform," in *The Making of Chinese Foreign and Security Policy in the Era of Reform,* ed. David M. Lampton (Stanford, CA: Stanford University Press, 2001), 374–84.

15. See Eul Young Park, "Foreign Economic Policies and Economic Development," in *The Foreign Policy of the Republic of Korea,* ed. Youngnok Koo and Sung-joo Han (New York: Columbia University Press, 1985), 125–27; Jae Ho Chung, "The Political Economy of South Korea–China Bilateralism: Origins, Progress and Prospects," in *Korea and China in a New World: Beyond Normalization,* ed. Ilpyong J. Kim and Hong Pyo Lee (Seoul: Sejong Institution, 1993), 264–74; and David Zweig, *Internationalizing China: Domestic Interests and Global Linkages* (Ithaca, NY: Cornell University Press 2003), chapters 1–2.

16. Of 4,129 factories that have moved from South Korea since 1998, 71 percent chose China for their new sites. See *Chosun Ilbo* [Chosun daily], October 24, 2003.

17. In 2001, the number of airline passengers on Korea-China routes surpassed those on Korea-U.S. routes for the first time. It was also in 2001 that the total number of Korean visitors to China outnumbered those to the United States. *Chosun Ilbo,* January 15, 2003.

18. See *Hangook Ilbo* [Korea daily], U.S. edition, March 18, 2003.

19. See Wang Xuhe and Ren Xiangqun, *Guo zhi zun—xin zhongguo waijiao jishi* [The prestige of China: Chronicles of new China's diplomacy] (Hangzhou: Zhejiang renmin chubanshe, 1999), chapter 5; and Wang Taiping, *Xinzhongguo waijiao*

wushinian [Fifty years of new China's foreign affairs] (Beijing: Beijing renmin chubanshe, 1999), 1: 33–37.

20. See Hao Yufan, "China and the Korean Peninsula," in *The Chinese View of the World*, ed. Hao Yufan and Huan Guocang (New York: Paragon, 1989), 198.

21. Gu Weiqun, "Security in the Asia-Pacific Region," in *The Chinese View of the World*, 25–26. Also see Jianwei Wang and Xinbo Wu, *Against US or with US: The Chinese Perspective of America's Alliances with Japan and Korea* (Stanford, CA: Asia/Pacific Research Center, Stanford University, 1998), 34–35.

22. For this view, see Qian Qichen, *Waijiao shiji* [Ten episodes in Chinese diplomacy] (Beijing: Shijie zhishi chubanshe, 2003), 154–55.

23. A "romantic triangle" refers to a relationship of amity between one pivotal player (China) and two "wing" players and enmity between each of the latter. See Hong Yung Lee, "The Emerging Triangle among China and Two Koreas," in *Korea and the World: Beyond the Cold War*, ed. Young Whan Kihl (Boulder, CO: Westview, 1994), 97–110.

24. Pertinent data and interviews alike suggest that the visible downgrading of the bilateral relationship began in 1994, not in 1992, when China normalized its relations with South Korea.

25. Eric McVadon, "Chinese Military Strategy for the Korean Peninsula," in *China's Military Faces the Future*, ed. James Lilley and David Shambaugh (Armonk, NY: M. E. Sharpe, 1999), 280.

26. See Ilpyong J. Kim, "China in North Korean Foreign Policy," in *North Korean Foreign Relations in the Post–Cold War Era*, ed. Samuel S. Kim (Hong Kong: Oxford University Press, 1998), 105–9.

27. For China's adaptation to global norms and responsibilities, see Margaret Pearson, "China's Integration into the International Trade and Investment Regimes," in *China Joins the World: Progress and Prospects,* ed. Elizabeth Economy and Michel Oksenberg (New York: Council on Foreign Relations, 1999), 161–205; and Bates Gill and Evan S. Medeiros, "Foreign and Domestic Influences on China's Arms Control and Nonproliferation Policies," *China Quarterly* 161 (March 2000): 66, 68, 71.

28. See "North Korea's Decline and China's Strategic Dilemmas," United States Institute for Peace Special Report, October 1997, p. 6.

29. Some of these commentaries went so far as to describe "nuclear North Korea" as a serious trouble (*youhuan*) for China, to demand Pyongyang's "complete severing" (*jueyuan*) of any nuclear weapons program, and even to cast doubt on the possibility of peaceful dialogue. See, for instance, "Xinwen fenxi: Chaoxian heweiji yu zhongguo zhanlue anquan" [News analysis: North Korea's nuclear crisis and China's strategic security], *Renmin ribao* [People's daily], online version, January 23, 2003, available at http://www.peopledaily.com.cn/GB/junshi/62/20030123/913517.html.

30. See, for instance, *Renmin ribao,* October 25, 2002, January 10 and 22, 2003, and February 19, 2003. While a majority of these reports list the "no nuclear weapons" principle as the first priority, some do list "peace and stability" as such. Whether these variations mean anything remains unclear.

31. "Hanguo wending zhong qiu gaige" [Korea seeking changes in the midst of stability], *Renmin ribao,* January 8, 2003.

32. For the complaints by George Bush and Colin Powell that China should do more to defuse the crisis, see Elisabeth Rosenthal, "China Asserts It Has Worked to End Nuclear Crisis," *New York Times,* February 13, 2003. For Beijing's snubbing of Seoul's request that China send delegations to Pyongyang to express concerns, see John Pomfret and Glenn Kessler, "China's Reluctance Irks US: Beijing Shows No Inclination to Intervene in North Korea Crisis," *Washington Post,* February 4, 2003. Also see David Shambaugh, "China and the Korean Peninsula: Playing for the Long Term," *Washington Quarterly* 26, no. 2 (Spring 2003): 43–56.

33. *People's Daily* reported in January 2003, "Within a dozen days, five delegations came to seek China's cooperation. . . . The world is watching our position." See *Renmin ribao,* January 20, 2003, available at http://www.peopledaily.com.cn/GB/junshi/20030120/910932.html.

34. This according to the author's interviews in Washington in 2003. Also see *Renmin ribao,* February 8, 2003; and Joseph Kahn, "Turnaround by China: Center Stage as a Diplomatic Power," *New York Times,* August 28, 2003.

35. See *Renmin ribao,* February 20 and March 11 and 13, 2003. Kurt Campbell and others have suggested that, in its effort to enlist China's support, Washington scared China about the possibility of a disastrous outcome on the Korean peninsula. Such efforts presumably changed Beijing's calculation of the differences of the risks involved in noninterference and certain involvement.

36. For these reports, see Gady A. Epstein, "China Seen Toughening Stance against North Korea Nuclear Developments," *Baltimore Sun,* March 28, 2003; and David M. Lampton, "China: Fed up with North Korea," *Washington Post,* June 4, 2003.

37. On this group, see Willy Wo-Lap Lam, "China Looks Ahead to Korea Crisis," *CNN,* March 18, 2003, available at http://cnn.com/world; Morton Abramowitz and James T. Laney, *Meeting the North Korean Nuclear Challenge* (New York: Council on Foreign Relations, June 2003), 28; and *Dong-A Ilbo* [Dong-A daily], September 8, 2003. Some hold the contrary view that no such group was established.

38. See, for instance, Shen Jiru, "Weihu dongbeiya anquan de dangwu zhi ji" [The urgent mission to protect the security of Northeast Asia], *Shijie jingji yu zhengzhi* [World economy and politics] 9 (2003): 57.

39. See Charles Hutzler and Gordon Fairclough, "The Koreas: China Breaks with Its Wartime Past," *Far Eastern Economic Review,* August 7, 2003.

40. See "China Seen Toughening Stance against North Korea Nuclear Developments," *Baltimore Sun,* March 28, 2003. For an interpretation that accepts the official excuse but highlights Beijing's strategic use of the incident, see Andrew Scobell, "China and North Korea: The Limits of Influence," *Current History,* September 2003, 277.

41. In April, when Hu Jintao met with General Cho Myung-rok, the highest-ranking military officer with the exception of Kim Jung Il, their rhetoric was different. Whereas Cho emphasized the "blood and bullets" North Korea and China had gone through together, Hu remained more, sober stressing their "traditional friendship" *(chuantong youyi).* See *Renmin ribao,* April 23, 2003.

42. See *Renmin ribao,* April 23 and 28 and July 8, 2003. What China offered (or how it threatened) North Korea in order to bring it to the negotiating table is not known. Wu Bangguo, for instance, is alleged to have pledged the supply of 500,000 tons of heavy oil.

43. See *Chosun Ilbo,* November 13, 2003.

44. See David A. Baldwin, "Neoliberalism, Neorealism, and World Politics," in *Neorealism and Neoliberalism: The Contemporary Debate,* ed. David A. Baldwin (New York: Columbia University Press, 1993), 3–25.

45. For the concepts of "strategic triangle" and "stable marriage," see Lowell Dittmer, "The Strategic Triangle: An Elementary Game-Theoretical Analysis," *World Politics* 33, no. 4 (July 1981): 489.

46. The Chinese term for its foreign policy stance during this period was "leaning to one side" *(yibiandao),* referring to aligning unconditionally with the Soviet Union for its socialist leadership. The South Korean catchphrase at the time was "anti-Communist reunification" *(ban'gong tong'il).*

47. See Chin O. Chung, *Pyongyang Between Peking and Moscow: North Korea's Involvement in the Sino-Soviet Dispute, 1958–1975* (Mobile: University of Alabama Press, 1978). Except for 1967–69, when the radicalization of ideology and xenophobia reached its zenith during the Cultural Revolution, North Korea generally maintained a more amicable relationship with China than with the Soviet Union. See Liu Jinzhi, Zhang Minqiu, and Zhang Xiaoming, *Dangdai zhonghan guanxi* [Contemporary China-Korea relations] (Beijing: Zhongguo shehuikexue chubanshe, 1998), 41–44.

48. See Tai Sung An, *North Korea: A Political Handbook* (Wilmington, DE: Scholarly Resources, 1983), 79, 85–87; and Bruce Cumings, *Korea's Place in the Sun: A Modern History* (New York: W. W. Norton, 1997), 402–5.

49. The National Unification Board, ed., *Bukhan pyonlam* [Survey of North Korea] (Seoul: National Unification Board, 1984), 129–31.

50. For the "trading world" as an alternative to the "military world," see Richard Rosecrance, *The Rise of the Trading State: Commerce and Conquest in the Modern World* (New York: Basic Books, 1986). Also see Jae Ho Chung, "South Korea–China Economic Relations: The Current Situation and Its Implications," *Asian Survey* 28, no. 10 (October 1988): 1031–48.

51. See, for instance, William H. Gleysteen Jr., *Massive Entanglement, Marginal Influence: Carter and Korea in Crisis* (Washington, DC: Brookings Institution, 1999).

52. Pyongyang often filed complaints with Beijing regarding the burgeoning ties between South Korea and China. For informal complaints and Chinese responses, see Jae Ho Chung, "Sino-South Korea Economic Cooperation: An Analysis of Domestic and Foreign Entanglements," *Journal of Northeast Asian Studies* 9, no. 2 (Summer 1990): 69–70.

53. It should be noted that the conspicuous decline in the high-level official exchanges between North Korea and China since 1994 began with the first nuclear crisis.

54. A Chinese official's comment is interesting in this regard: "Even a thin lip could still be better than nothing in protecting one's teeth." Personal communication.

55. See, for instance, Chae-Jin Lee and Stephanie Hsieh, "China's Two-Korea Policy at Trial: The Hwang Chang Yop Crisis," *Pacific Affairs* 74, no. 3 (Fall 2001).

56. See Samuel S. Kim and Tae Hwan Lee, "Chinese–North Korean Relations: Managing Asymmetrical Interdependence," in *North Korea and Northeast Asia,* ed. Samuel S. Kim and Tae Hwan Lee (Lanham, MD: Rowman and Littlefield, 2002), 117.

57. See the Ministry of Information, "Great Strides Made during the First Five Years of the Roh Tae Woo Presidency," *Backgrounder* 94 (February 8, 1992): 10.

58. Edward A. Olsen writes, "Leaders in Seoul display a new appreciation that security means more than perpetuating the US connection. . . . [It] still remains vital but so are Seoul's new-found diplomatic levers." See "Korean Security: Is Japan's Comprehensive Security Model a Viable Alternative?" in *The US-Korean Alliance: Time for A Change*, ed. Doug Bandow and Ted Galen Carpenter (New Brunswick, NJ: Transactions, 1992), 146, 148.

59. *The Defense White Paper*, published annually by South Korea's Ministry of National Defense, generally devotes four to five pages to briefly outlining China's military modernization and intermilitary exchanges. No trace of concern for security is evident in these publications. The corresponding Japanese publication, on the other hand, in 2000 spent sixty-six pages on China's weapons programs and military policy. See *East Asian Strategic Review* (Tokyo: National Institute for Defense Studies, 2000), 67–69, 77–79, 83–88, 104–7, 139–41, 191–237.

60. For this elite-public divergence, see Chung, "South Korea between Eagle and Dragon," 785–87.

61. There are, of course, a significant number of South Korean elites who are increasingly uneasy about China's growing economic and political power in the region. See *US-Korea Relations: Opinion Leaders Seminar* (Washington, DC: Korea Economic Institute, July 2003), 16.

62. See Chung, "South Korea between Eagle and Dragon," 783–85. Although South Koreans have generally demonstrated a realist mindset, relative-gains diplomacy, and reactive nationalism in their relationship with the United States, this has been much less true of their dealings with China. This crucial disparity remains to be explained. For these three characteristics, see Victor Cha, "The Security Domain of South Korea's Globalization," in *Korea's Globalization*, ed. Samuel S. Kim (Cambridge: Cambridge University Press, 2000), 236–40.

63. See Seymour Martin Lipset, *American Exceptionalism: A Double-Edged Sword* (New York: W. W. Norton, 1996), chapter 7.

64. See William Watts, *Americans Look at Asia* (Washington, DC: Asia Society Washington Center, 1999), 42.

65. See *1997 Sejong Survey* (Seoul: Sejong Press, 1997), 12; and *Dong-a Ilbo*, December 5, 2000. Harris Poll no. 8, January 31, 2001, table 2; and Harris Poll no. 8, January 31, 2001, table 3 also support this point.

66. See Chung, "How America Views South Korea–China Bilateralism."

67. Abramowitz and Laney, *Meeting the North Korean Nuclear Challenge*, 4, 13, 25–27.

68. *US-Korea Relations: Opinion Leaders Seminar*, 3, 6–8.

69. See *Chosun Ilbo*, July 23, 1995.

70. Harris Poll no. 8, January 31, 2001.

71. The State Department's own surveys on South Koreans' perceptions suggest that China's "attractiveness" is so far mainly economic in nature. See Office of Research, "For South Koreans, China's Draw Is Mainly Economic," *Opinion Analysis*, September 30, 2003.

72. For the possibility of a conflict-ridden relationship between Washington and Beijing, see Nicholas Eberstadt and Richard J. Ellings, "Assessing Interests and

Objectives of Major Actors in the Korean Drama," in *Korea's Future and the Great Powers,* ed. Nicholas Eberstadt and Richard J. Ellings (Seattle: University of Washington Press, 2001), 338–40. For South Korea's menu of choices, see Chung, "South Korea between Eagle and Dragon," 788–93.

73. This was the conclusion drawn by the majority of the South Korean and American policy elite interviewed by the author. See Chung, "South Korea between Eagle and Dragon," 786, and Chung, "How America Views South Korea–China Bilateralism."

74. Such a forecast for the military sphere is provided in Harold Brown et al., *Chinese Military Power* (New York: Council on Foreign Relations, 2003). In the context of the Korean peninsula, China's influence may become irresistible in less than ten years.

75. The controversy over China's alleged "whitewashing" of ancient Korean history produced a huge stir in South Korea in 2003–2004.

76. See, for instance, Michael Mastanduno, "Incomplete Hegemony: The United States and Security Order in Asia," in *Asian Security Order: Instrumental and Normative Features,* ed. Muthiah Alagappa (Stanford, CA: Stanford University Press, 2003), chapter 4. Also see Fang Ning, *Xindiguozhuyi shidai yu zhongguo zhanlue* [The new era of new imperialism and China's strategy] (Beijing: Beijing chubanshe, 2003), chapters 8–10.

7

Taiwan Faces China

Attraction and Repulsion

Richard Bush

In May 1996, on the occasion of his second inauguration as president of the Republic of China, Lee Teng-hui offered a unique view on how Taiwan mattered for China. He recalled that China had suffered a series of shocks in its encounter with the West, despite an excellent traditional culture. He expressed the hope that the people of Taiwan would foster a new Chinese culture that combined the best of the West with Chinese heritage. He went so far as to draw an analogy between the seminal role that the Wei River valley (the central plains, *zhongyuan*) had played in the flowering of traditional Chinese culture and the role that Taiwan (which he termed the new central plains, *xinzhongyuan*) would play in fostering that new Chinese culture. For Lee, Taiwan represented the *best* part of China in the modern world, and China would again become a great civilization only if it followed Taiwan's lead.[1]

It is a mark of how rapidly the PRC's wealth and power have grown since Lee's second inaugural that his act of historical entrepreneurship seems so quaint. Although Taiwan may be on the right side of history in the realm of political values, it, like other countries in Asia, has had to adjust to the PRC's growing prowess in other dimensions. And despite growing economic interdependence between the island and the mainland, in most other respects Taiwan has refused to accommodate Beijing's growing influence as its neighbors have. If East Asia is indeed becoming more Sinocentric, Taiwan is in critical ways the exception that proves the rule, for reasons that are unique to Taiwan itself.[2]

THE PRC'S ECONOMIC CENTRALITY

The Taiwan Strait used to be a military no-man's-land. Since the mid-1980s, however, it has become an economic and human superhighway. The mainland has become a magnet for the Taiwanese in a wide variety of sectors. Take, for example, the contacts reported in the press in the single month of June 2001.

There were, of course, a variety of business initiatives. Taiwan banks were preparing to set up representative offices on the mainland. State-owned oil companies in the PRC sought the technical cooperation of their Taiwanese counterparts on a project in Shenzhen. Leaders of the Taiwan pharmaceutical industry visited the mainland to investigate investment opportunities. PRC executives in the areas of information, communications, and banking attended a conference in Taiwan. Companies in mobile communications set up an organization to conduct exchanges. There were calls to set up an arbitration body to resolve business disputes. The Taipei government lifted some restrictions on people from the mainland working in Taiwan, while a poll of the island's residents found that 64 percent of respondents were either "willing" or "strongly willing" to work in the PRC.

In areas other than business a lot was happening in just the month of June 2001. Museum curators from Taiwan and Henan jointly produced a catalogue of bronze objects from the tomb of Western Zhou nobleman Prince Zeng. Pilgrims from a Taoist temple in Yunlin county made a pilgrimage to the mother temple in Quanzhou, Fujian province. Educators from both sides held a conference on adult education in Taipei, reflecting the extensive exchange relationships that Taiwan universities have with mainland counterparts. More than three thousand young Taiwanese were studying at mainland universities in the fields of law, finance, accounting, Chinese literature, history, religion, and Chinese medicine. Through the facilitation of Ciji Gongdehui, the major charitable organization in Taiwan, the Taiwanese people provided bone marrow for transplant to mainland patients suffering from leukemia. In the latest example of varied sports exchanges, athletes from the PRC and Taiwan participated in a long-distance race to promote Beijing's bid to host the 2008 Olympics. The Taipei and Shanghai municipalities held a nine-day city cultural exchange. Taiwan rescued fishermen from a missing mainland freighter. Through the cooperation of the Red Cross societies of the two sides, Taiwan repatriated illegal immigrants from the mainland and extradited eight hijackers. The PRC also repatriated four criminals sought by police in Taiwan.[3] All of these interactions occurred in the short space of a single month, belying the myth of little contact across the strait.

Powerful economic imperatives on both the mainland and Taiwan made possible this rich array of interactions and muted the military and ideological conflicts that had dominated cross-strait relations since 1949. The Chinese Communist Party, facing public alienation after the disaster of the Cultural Revolution, had decided in the late 1970s that fostering economic growth was the only way to restore its legitimacy. Economic growth that would employ the growing Chinese workforce required massive amounts of foreign investment, and Taiwan businessmen were an obvious source, both because they had capital and because they were culturally Chinese. In Taiwan, companies that had produced manufactured goods for the international market were becoming less competitive because of the rising costs of land and labor, a growing emphasis on environmental protection, and the appreciation of the New Taiwan Dollar. Moving production offshore was an obvious way to prevent their goods from being priced out of the global market, and the mainland presented a good alternative production platform because it was also a Chinese society, local governments were providing special investment incentives, and the cost of land and labor was low. Someday, moreover, it might become a place to sell finished goods from Taiwan. Of course there was a political dimension as well. Beijing hoped that Taiwan's investment in China would improve the climate for reunification as well as create disincentives to independence. Taipei feared that it would increase the island's political vulnerability.

The movement of production west across the Taiwan Strait occurred in several waves. The first, in the late 1980s, was dominated by small and medium enterprises (SMEs) in labor-intensive industries like garments, shoes, and basic consumer electronics. The second wave occurred in the mid-1990s, as larger Taiwan firms in sectors like petrochemicals and food processing joined the SMEs. One reason for companies to make the move was to get behind the Chinese tariff walls, which would enable them to provide cheap raw materials to their Taiwanese SME customers or, in the case of food processing, to the Chinese market itself. The third wave surged in the late 1990s as information technology firms that had become the dominant sector of the Taiwan economy moved to the mainland to maintain the competitiveness of their low-end products.

And investment drove trade. The bulk of the products that Taiwan shipped to the mainland were components for assembly and operations; most of the products that went from the mainland to Taiwan were finished or almost-finished goods. Two-way cross-strait trade was about $41 billion in 2002 ($31.1 billion in Taiwan exports, $7.95 billion in imports). In 2002, 25.3 percent of Taiwan's exports went to the PRC, making China the island's number one export market, displacing the United States from that position.[4]

The personal computer industry offers a good example of the process in the second and third waves, as described by Chin Chung.[5] Taiwan PC companies are the middle links in a complex and evolving global supply chain that is headed by American firms that provide the brands, the sophisticated technology and components, and the marketing. In the 1980s, production of most components and assembly of the PCs were done on the island. Taiwan PC companies did not attempt to manufacture all of the necessary components in house, but instead created an "extensive network of vertical linkages within the industry . . . ranging from upstream electronic components and parts (logic integrated circuits [IC], memory IC, chip sets, smaller liquid crystal displays, cathode ray tubes, and motherboards), midstream peripheral items (keyboards, monitors, image scanners, PC mice, and power supply units), to the final assembly of desktop and portable PCs." In the early to mid-1990s, because of constant pressures to cut costs, the main Taiwan PC firms moved some of the elements of their networks to the mainland and other places in order to remain competitive and maintain their middle position in the supply chain. Small suppliers producing only a few items on a limited scale moved first. More differentiated, medium-sized firms moved some operations and upgraded others on the island. The large-scale manufacturers who make a great variety of items, and for whom production outside Taiwan is an integral yet supplemental part of their overall strategy, were the last to move, and they did so on a selective basis.

The shift of production from Taiwan in the IT industry and other sectors accelerated with the recession that began in 2000. By 2003, half of the top one thousand Taiwan companies had investments in the PRC. Investment projects approved by the Taiwan government surpassed $30 billion, and some experts estimated that the amount is actually at least double the approved figure, if not triple. By one estimate, the PRC accounted for 74 percent of Taiwan's total foreign direct investment from 1991 to 2002. Two-way trade is around $40 billion a year.[6]

With investment comes human interaction. Several hundred thousand Taiwanese are now living in Shanghai and its suburb Kunshan, in Dongguan in Guangdong province, and in other Chinese urban areas. According to Taiwanese government estimates, there have been more than 190,000 cross-strait marriages. Taiwanese schools have been established in Dongguan and Kunshan to cater to the children of Taiwanese in those areas. More significant is the flow of sophisticated talent, much of it made up of ethnic Chinese, among Silicon Valley in California, Hsinchu in Taiwan, and Kunshan. U.S.-educated Taiwanese engineers have fostered the movement of technology, capital, and expertise between the United States and Taiwan, as well as fostered productive business partnerships. As Taiwan companies move more production to the mainland, they put their second-generation Taiwanese executives in charge of the mainland operations and recruit talented Chinese engineers. Young Taiwanese IT entrepreneurs build relationships with the PRC's young capitalists and children of high-ranking officials, and they may attend Chinese business schools. In turn, Silicon Valley is a magnet for talented engineers from both the mainland and Taiwan.[7]

It is easy to exaggerate the extent of cross-strait human interaction. Emerson Niou has discovered that a significant majority of the Taiwan population have little or no direct exposure to the PRC. According to a recent poll, 67.8 percent have not traveled to the mainland at all since 1987, and an additional 12.7 percent have visited only once. Only 13.1 percent of Taiwan residents or their family members have gone to study, work, do business, or reside in the PRC.[8]

Nor does everyone in Taiwan believe that growing economic interdependence is beneficial for Taiwan. Concerns take three forms. First, some worry about the "hostage effect," believing that Taiwan companies will become so dependent on the mainland that the island will become vulnerable to economic leverage from Beijing. The second concern is about the "fifth column effect." According to this theory, Taiwan businessmen on the mainland will become a lobby for the PRC and a tool that will help China accomplish its political agenda. The third is the "hollowing-out effect," or the concern that the movement of manufacturing across the Taiwan Strait will leave Taiwan economically weak. These concerns, which manifest themselves in political debates—about whether semiconductor manufacturers may move eight-inch wafer fabs to the mainland, for example—are understandable, but they are also either exaggerated or misplaced. The movement of production from Taiwan is inevitable, and it presents a challenge to create new forms of high-wage employment for the people who remain. Were the PRC to try to exert economic leverage, it would probably have as much to lose as Taiwan would. And there is little evidence that Taiwan executives have been agents of influence, except on the margins.[9]

Like it or not, Taiwan has been pulled into the PRC's economic orbit, and its companies have long since accepted the centrality of the mainland for their future. The island can balance its dependence to an extent by enhancing its economic ties with the United States, Japan, Southeast Asia, and so on. But it cannot disregard the PRC's challenge. Former premier Vincent Siew, for example, asserts that cross-strait relations are critical to Taiwan's medium- and long-term survival, claiming, "Taiwan cannot afford to ignore the immense mainland market."[10]

Economics is one thing; politics is another. Whatever the mainland's importance for Taiwan companies, and however much influence China exerts on the rest of East Asia, politically Taiwan is an outlier. Relying on the United States, it seeks to balance Beijing rather than bandwagon with it. It is a special case for special reasons. First of all, the two sides are caught in a security dilemma. Second, they are deadlocked over the legal identity of the government in Taipei. Third, because of Taiwan's history, the Taiwanese are continually suspect of Beijing's intentions. And fourth, even if Beijing were to make Taiwan an acceptable political offer that accommodates its other concerns, the island's rather dysfunctional political system will make it hard to "take yes for an answer."

SECURITY DILEMMA

Taiwan is profoundly vulnerable in its relationship with the PRC, in spite of the vibrant cross-strait economic relationship. And, in fact, the feeling is mutual. Taiwan and the PRC each focus upon the power of the other and how it might be used. They each take steps to guard against the threat posed by the other, only to trigger a hedging response from the other side. Thus Beijing and Taipei have continually added new systems to their respective arsenals to counter the acquisitions of the other. In the 1990s, the PRC acquired advanced fighter aircraft from Russia (the Sukhoi-27s and -30s), and Taiwan secured F-16s from the United States and Mirage 2000s from France. Over that same decade, Beijing bought Kilo-class submarines from Russia, and Taiwan requested diesel-powered submarines from the United States. The PRC indigenously produced a growing force of short- and medium-range ballistic missiles, and Taiwan sought to acquire missile defense capabilities—and received Patriot batteries—from the United States. In addition, the Taiwan armed forces worked to improve institutional ties with their American counterparts.

This state of affairs has a long history, of course, but the current impasse began in the early 1990s. This was a time when both the PRC and Taiwan sought to take advantage of the buyers' market in advanced weapons systems created by the collapse of the Soviet Union. Politically, there were growing conflicts over Taiwan's approach to the unification of China. Lee Teng-hui grew increasingly frustrated over the constraints of the one country, two systems framework and Beijing's refusal to adjust its approach to the legal and political status of the ROC government (see below for more on this subject). The PRC saw Lee's domestic policies and his effort to reinsert Taiwan into the international system as a serious threat.

The conflict of the mid-1990s demonstrates that this is not the classic security dilemma as described in the international relations literature, even though the two sides of the strait are engaged in something of an arms race. It is not a simple case of Beijing fearing that Taipei's arms acquisitions will make it more vulnerable to attack. Instead, what Beijing dreads are Taiwanese political initiatives that would permanently separate the island from China, or, as the Chinese might put it, Taiwan seizing Chinese national territory by fiat rather than by force. Taiwan's military power and its de facto alliance with the United States become relevant not because they are inherently threatening, but rather because they are seen as useful in defending those political initiatives (in this case, Taiwan's defensive capabilities increase the security dilemma). It is to, at a minimum, deter those steps and counter Taiwan's defensive military buildup that the People's Liberation Army acquires new capabilities. And it is supposedly to allay fears of independence that Beijing has asked Taipei to reaffirm the One China Principle. The central political dimension of this security dilemma gives it an asymmetrical and perhaps unique character. As Thomas Christensen so elegantly puts it:

> Security dilemma theorists have assumed that international security politics concerns merely defending sovereign territory from invasion and foreign acquisition. [But] to a large degree, the Taiwan question is one more of the island's political identity than of the PRC's territorial expansion. The danger to the PRC is that Taiwan might eventually move from de facto independence to legal independence, thus posing an affront to Chinese nationalism and a danger to regime stability in Beijing.[11]

It was these political vectors that created the crises of 1995 and 1996, which, at its core, was a coercive PRC response to a series of political initiatives undertaken by Lee Teng-hui. Beijing was similarly alarmed in July 1999, when Lee Teng-hui declared that cross-strait relations were special "state-to-state relations," and in March 2000, when it became clear that Chen Shui-bian, whose Democratic Progressive Party had stated its goal of independence in its charter, was about to win the Taiwan presidency. The PRC repeated its coercive diplomacy to restrain what it saw as threats to its interests. And it has continued to build up its military power, in order to at least deter Taiwan from declaring independence, if not to compel it to accept unification. Taiwan seeks to acquire its own deterrent, but ultimately it depends on the protection of the United States.

This security dilemma has another political dimension, which is the PRC's use of united-front tactics within Taiwan to try to prevent what China most seeks to avoid (Taiwan's independence) and perhaps secure what it seeks (unification on its own terms). The PRC has sought to capitalize on the business community's interest in better cross-strait economic relations. During Chen Shui-bian's 2000–2004 term, it aligned with the Kuomintang (KMT) and the People's First Party and used the prounification media on the island to project its message. The point here is that Beijing's efforts to manipulate Taiwan politics intensify the anxiety felt by some segments of the Taiwan public and lead them to suspect the worst of PRC intentions. (Note the asymmetrical nature of this situation; Taipei doesn't have the option of meddling in Chinese politics.)

An important dimension of this dilemma is the atmosphere that is heavy with mistrust. Each side not only watches the actions of the other and takes steps to deter the worst, but it also assumes that the other will not keep its word should the two sides actually come to mutual agreement. This is the problem with the proposed "dual renunciation" solution, that Taiwan would renounce independence if the PRC would renounce the use of force. Hammering out the content of such an agreement would be a difficult but not impossible task. Harder still would be overcoming the ingrained fear on each side that the other will find some way to renege on its agreements and exploit the other's good will.

For Taipei, the dilemma is even more profound. Because it is in an increasingly weak position, it must rely on the United States for its security. Prudence requires that Taipei assume that Beijing would require, in any resolution of the Taiwan Strait issue, that Taipei cut the security cord to Washington in a meaningful way (after all, this is what Beijing tried to do in 1978 and 1981–82). From Taipei's point of view, then, the PRC must make an extremely attractive offer for it to cut the cord (an unlikely prospect). The logic of the situation requires that Taiwan's default position is to balance with the United States rather than bandwagon with Beijing.

SOVEREIGNTY AND THE TAIWAN GOVERNMENT'S STATUS

The second reason that Taiwan resists the PRC's growing influence is a profound disagreement over the legal status of the governing authority in Taiwan, specifically whether it possesses sovereignty. Discussion usually focuses on the issue of *whether* Taiwan is a part of China (that is, whether the state known as China owns the territory of Taiwan). The heart of the matter, however, is *how* Taiwan might be a part of China, or, to be more precise, whether the ROC government might be part of the Chinese state.

Ever since 1949, the PRC has asserted that the ROC ceased to exist and the "Taiwan authorities" are not a sovereign entity. On the island, in contrast, there is a broad political consensus, from the People's First Party to the Taiwan Solidarity Union, that the government does possess sovereignty. The standard formulation is that "the ROC (or Taiwan) is an independent sovereign state." All major political actors on the island have consistently held that if unification is to occur, then the sovereign character of the Taipei government must be preserved within the context of that national union. Somehow, that government would be part of the state called China. Under the PRC's reunification formula of one country, two systems, however, Taiwan, like Hong Kong and Macau already, would possess autonomy or home rule but not sovereignty. The government in Beijing would remain the exclusive sovereign.

The legal identity of the governing authority on Taiwan keeps popping up in most cross-strait disputes. During the 2000–2004 presidency of Chen Shui-bian, the PRC demanded that he accept the One China Principle in return for dialogue. Chen believed that to accept the One China Principle as Beijing understood it would be to concede that his government did not possess sovereignty. To agree to the dialogue, then, would be tantamount to conceding a fundamental issue before the negotiations even began. (Chen may have exaggerated the danger of PRC deceit, but a PRC willingness to talk without preconditions would have been the best way to reassure him.) Similarly, there was no progress on opening direct transportation links between the two sides due to an argument about how to discuss bringing them about. Beijing said that private associations should organize the discussions. Chen said that governments should either conduct the talks or play the principal role. Chen saw in the PRC proposal a not-so-subtle ploy to undermine the legitimacy of his government and deny him face. The PRC regarded his proposal as a way of making gains that it wished to deny him.

What would it mean for Taiwan's government to possess sovereignty within a unified China? First of all, it would probably mean that the government in Taipei was fundamentally equal in legal status to the government in Beijing. Second, it would mean that the Taipei government would have the absolute right to rule over the territory under its jurisdiction. This might imply, for example, that the PRC would have to tolerate the continuation of parties and speech advocating Taiwan independence. And third, a sovereign Taiwan would have the right to participate as a member of the international community, a right that it does not in most cases now have. Indeed, Taiwan has claimed that right since the late 1980s and has taken actions in order to assert that right, but Beijing has vigorously resisted these actions for obvious reasons.

Exacerbating this disagreement is Beijing's perception of Lee Teng-hui's and Chen Shui-bian's goals during their respective presidencies. The PRC regarded their claim that the Taiwan government possessed sovereignty as ipso facto proof that they were separatists. To be sure, both Lee and Chen vigorously opposed the "one country, two systems" framework because it was antithetical to their basic view of the legal character of the government that they successively headed. They refused to accept a formula that would create a Taiwan special administrative region subordinate to the central sovereign government in Beijing (as is the case with Hong Kong and Macau). A careful reading of their statements indicates clearly that Lee did not oppose unification per se, but rather Beijing's consistent approach to the problem. At least during the early part of his administration, Chen hinted that there were modes of unification other than "one country, two systems" method that he thought had promise.

Some national unions are made up of sovereign entities. The United States, for example, started out as a confederation, and then became a federation. The increasing integration of the European Union has been accompanied by a progressive pooling and delegation of sovereignty. These systems, however, are difficult to design and maintain. Whether the entities that form the union maintain the right of withdrawal is a delicate issue, but, in the abstract at least, these examples provide a model for the PRC to fulfill its historic mission of unification while Taiwan preserves the sovereignty of its government. Many in Taiwan have found the idea of forming some type of confederation attractive, and the Kuomintang floated a proposal along those lines in 2001. Beijing shot down the idea, however, on the grounds that it was antithetical to its vision of unification. There was also probably some concern that acknowledging Taiwan's sovereignty under a confederation model would stimulate claims by Hong Kong and Macau for similar treatment. In cross-strait relations, therefore, the issue at stake is not China's growing role in East Asia, but rather the PRC government's centrality within the Chinese state.

TAIWAN IDENTITY

Complicating these core issues of security and sovereignty is the impact of history of the relationship between Taiwan and the PRC. KMT authoritarian rule fostered a belief among long-term residents of Taiwan that they had a unique identity and that mainlanders were the Other. Thus in the late 1940s Taiwanese summed up the situation using a metaphor referring to two animals unpopular in Chinese culture, "the dogs [the Japanese] had left, but the pigs [mainland Chinese] had come."

This Taiwanese identity was created in a variety of ways: though the brutality with which the Nationalist army repressed the February 28 Incident; the harsh and systematic "white terror" of the early 1950s; the KMT's restrictions on Taiwanese political participation and political power until the 1980s; its efforts to carry out a cultural revolution on the island that would mould its residents into good Chinese after five decades of Japanese colonial rule; and the social and economic segregation of mainlanders and Taiwanese that was the urban norm into the 1970s. The result was that many Taiwanese, to one degree or another, translated their harsh experience of KMT rule into the claim that their homeland was a separate country and culture. Democratization in the 1990s allowed this identity to emerge and become an overt political force. And Lee Teng-hui found it useful to strengthen that sense of identity in order to prevent a too-easy accommodation with Beijing.

Yet it is important to understand that this nationalist Taiwanese identity does not have a long history. As Alan Wachman notes, "The cultural identity of Taiwanese appears to have been 'invented' in reaction to the efforts of the mainland elite to make residents of Taiwan cleave to the Chinese motherland, its culture, and its people."[12] What is significant for cross-strait relations today, moreover, is not just the existence of this Taiwanese identity, but also the profound fear of outsiders—including PRC outsiders—that stems from it. KMT repression thus made it more difficult for Beijing to make its case to the Taiwan public.

Virtually all Taiwan residents today consider themselves to possess at least two and probably as many as three identities at once. One of these identities—emerging over the last fifty-plus years—is native Taiwanese, which even immigrant mainlanders possess. The second is a Chinese identity, at least in an ethnic and cultural sense. The third is a dual cosmopolitan identity. Since the 1990s, there has been extensive polling in Taiwan on levels of identification with Taiwan and China. A comprehensive survey of that data found a gradual yet clear trend toward a stronger and more exclusive identification with native Taiwanese identity. Some of those who originally identified themselves as Chinese only have more recently developed a "double identity." Those who began with a double identity have tended to identify more strongly as Taiwanese. This shift has occurred irrespective of ethnic background, age, educational level, gender, and party affiliation. External forces, particularly actions by the PRC, can shape the balance of Chinese and Taiwanese identities.[13]

Yet the consensus of a number of scholars is that the growth, or even dominance, of a Taiwanese identity does not ipso facto lead to a quest for independence. Wachman finds the growth of Taiwanese identity to be a function of the KMT's prior monopoly of power. Christopher Hughes distinguishes between political and cultural identity and defines rising Taiwanese sentiment as a postnationalist mentality. Rwei-Ren Wu finds a pragmatic nationalism that is the product of democratization and is "civic, liberal, and above all, pacifist" in its character. Yun-han Chu notes that an exclusive Taiwanese identity may have peaked, and that in fact younger residents of the island are more likely to see themselves as both Chinese and Taiwanese than their elders do. A fundamental pragmatism continues to guide Taiwanese choices.[14]

Identity is thus both complicated and malleable. Whether Taiwan nationalists are correct that their homeland is a separate country is immaterial. What is important is that a significant percentage of the population believes that Taiwan is distinct from (but not necessarily exclusive of) China. That KMT repression was the principal cause of this invented identity remains a point of departure for those Taiwanese who experienced it in some fashion and also an analytic reminder that external forces can shift the balance among identities. Taiwanese consciousness does not necessarily translate into a drive to legal independence, but it both constitutes a powerful bulwark against acceptance of the one country, two systems, formula and reinforces the more substantive concerns about sovereignty and security.

DOMESTIC POLITICS

Taiwan's domestic politics also affects its approach to Beijing, in two different ways. The first is the shifting impact of competitive politics on the Democratic Progressive Party. Some of the DPP's factions have believed that the way to gain power was to emphasize Taiwan's independence as a political goal. The appeal of this strategy reached its first peak in 1991, when the goal of the creation of a Republic of Taiwan was inserted into the DPP's charter. Through the 1990s, however, the party gradually shifted its emphasis from outcome to process. (Actually, this was a return to the approach of the 1980s and the calls for democracy and self-determination.) In the DPP's resolution on Taiwan's future, passed in May 1999, the goal of an independent Republic of Taiwan disappeared and was replaced by a formulation of Taiwan's status that was pretty close to that of the KMT *and*, for the first time, a backhanded acceptance of the term "the Republic of China." The resolution also emphasized caution and gradualism. The purpose of this new position, which was reaffirmed in most of Chen Shui-bian's statements in the 2000 presidential campaign, was to remedy the vulnerability that had dogged the DPP for almost a decade, the perception that it could not be trusted with power. As Shelley Rigger summarizes the DPP's evolution through the 1990s, "A careful reading of DPP statements on the [independence] issue reveals a party struggling through a protracted search for a position that both preserves its commitment to Taiwan's autonomy and identity while acknowledging the political realities beyond the party's control. Many DPP members still dream of an independent Taiwan, but individually and collectively they now recognize that this is not a dream they can realize unilaterally or soon."[15] More generally, Taiwan scholar Wu Yu-shan has demonstrated that this imperative compelled both the KMT and the DPP to converge during the 1990s. The former became more cautious on unification, while the latter distanced itself from independence. Each accepted the need to allow significant economic interdependence with the mainland. "Because Taiwan's mainstream public opinion is located in the middle of the identity and interest spectra," Wu writes, "presidential candidates rushed to the middle ground to capture votes."[16]

The evolution of DPP thinking on Taiwan independence, away from rigid adherence to the principles of the party's true believers and toward a pragmatism that would appeal to the middle of Taiwan's electoral spectrum, is clearer in retrospect than it was in execution. At every step of the way, DPP "fundamentalists" would engage in rearguard actions. Moderates knew that they could not totally ignore the fervor of their comrades' views, even as they continued to adjust tactically. This tension did not disappear when the DPP became the party in power, and it resurfaced with a vengeance during the 2004 presidential campaign. Chen Shui-bian returned to old DPP proposals for referenda and a new constitution in order to rally a disaffected base. He also sought to provoke China and intensify the strength of a Taiwanese identity. One of the reasons he felt he could focus on his base was, ironically, the failure of the opposition KMT and PFP to make the case to mainstream voters that economics should take precedence over politics in mainland policy.

The inability of Taiwan's political system of Taiwan's political system to facilitate clear-cut decisions on controversial issues also affects the island's approach toward the PRC.[17] Several factors related to the limitations of Taiwan's system work together to limit political accommodation.

The first factor is the multiple-member, single-vote electoral system for seats in representative bodies. Because parties run more than one candidate in each district, campaigns focus on personalities rather than issues. Parties tend toward factionalism and become fragmented. Because each candidate needs to secure only a small share of the vote to win a seat, extreme views secure greater representation in the Legislative Yuan than would be the case if there were single-member districts. By and large, radical views are anti-PRC views.

Reinforcing the impact of the electoral system are more fundamental defects in the constitutional and institutional structures.[18] Taiwan's system is rather like the French system, with both a president and a premier, but it lacks the mechanisms that the French have developed to ensure effective government when cohabitation between two power centers is necessary. The checks and balances both *within* the executive and *between* the executive and the legislature, which were introduced through several constitutional amendments in the 1990s, have created too many checks and too few balances. The president may appoint the premier without securing the Legislative Yuan's approval, but he does not have the power to veto legislation that he does not like. He may dissolve the legislature only after it exercises its right of a vote of no confidence in the premier. The Taiwan system functions at least adequately when the same party controls both the executive and legislature *and* when that party, through the exercise of party discipline, can coordinate interbranch relations from behind the scenes. When government is divided or the ruling party is weak, the checks and balances are dysfunctional.

The legislature itself has a number of problems. Party discipline has been weak because the electoral system dictates that individual legislators rely on their own efforts to get elected. Once they do, there is an incentive is to promote their individual popularity rather than public support for the party with which they are affiliated. Corruption and conflicts of interest are common. There is no tradition of party discipline to ensure that individual legislators will vote with their caucus leadership. Nor does the institution encourage policy specialization and expertise, as the committee and seniority systems do in the U.S. Congress. Instead, Taiwan legislators are free to join whatever committees they believe will be useful in terms of publicity and campaign contributions. Legislation is developed on the basis of coordination among party caucuses and smaller ad hoc groups. As a result, only those bills that command broad consensus secure passage, and no one is accountable for the result. Obstructionism is relatively easy. (The alternative would be to subject legislation to votes, in which case the majority must take responsibility—or credit—for the outcome. In this sense, the Legislative Yuan is more like the U.S. Senate than the House of Representatives.)

Because of these problems, and because there have emerged two political blocs with almost equal power in the legislature (the DPP and the Taiwan Solidarity Union, on the one hand, and the KMT and People's First Party, on the other), it will be extremely difficult to secure broad consensus on delicate issues concerning mainland policy. Any changes that would take the form of a constitutional amendment would, under the provisions in place at the time of this writing, require a three-quarters majority of the National Assembly. That a significant percentage of the population shares a strong Taiwanese identity and a fear of outsiders only exacerbates the paralysis of the political system.[19]

THE FUTURE

There are several basic directions in which this deadlocked situation might evolve. First of all, the situation might simply continue as it is. The various factors that encourage stalemate would remain salient, and the mainland's economic strength would have no political impact on Taiwan. Second, the PRC strategy of winning Taiwan over through economic attraction would succeed, and a consensus would emerge on the island to sacrifice political principles in favor of economic prosperity, in spite of a lingering sense of military insecurity. Third, Beijing would reverse course and decide to concede to Taiwan on the issues of sovereignty and security. Negotiations would produce an agreement that created a national union in which Beijing and Taipei were equal sovereign units and set forth a series of reciprocal and conditional steps designed to attenuate the security dilemma. Fourth, Beijing would grow increasingly impatient and move toward coercing Taiwan into negotiating on its terms. Fifth, leaders in Taiwan could embark on a course that Beijing finds increasingly provocative, leading Beijing to conclude that it must respond coercively in order to preserve its credibility.

Each of these scenarios has attendant problems. In the first, instability across the strait and on Taiwan persists. The danger that conflict could occur through accident or miscalculation would not disappear, and Taiwan's vulnerability would only increase. In the second scenario, Beijing's victory might be only superficial, since there is no guarantee that those who identify themselves predominantly as Taiwanese most strongly would approve a settlement in the first place or quietly accommodate to it thereafter. In the third, an agreement that Taiwan would accept might foster pressures within the PRC political system. The fourth and fifth scenarios would produce a conflict that severely damages the economic cooperation that has occurred over the last two decades. The fourth would likely draw the United States into the conflict and transform Beijing's relations with its neighbors for the worse. In the fifth, that fact that Taipei had provoked the conflict would leave it with little international sympathy.

Whatever happens, and whatever choice Taiwan makes (including avoiding a choice), it will be less able to adjust to the PRC's growing strength unless it takes steps to fortify itself. First, it should strengthen itself economically, establishing a new global competitive niche—a knowledge-based economy—as manufacturing continues to move to the mainland and elsewhere. Second, it should strengthen itself militarily, in order better to deter Beijing from using force or, if deterrence fails, to hold on until U.S. forces arrive to defend the island. Third, it should strengthen itself internationally, less by high-profile campaigns to enter or reenter international organizations, but instead by enhancing its substantive participation in those organizations to which it has access. Fourth, whatever administration is in power must strengthen public understanding of the government's legal identity, so that any concessions on the sovereignty issue are made consciously. Fifth, Taiwan must strengthen its democracy so that it can maintain a more coherent mainland policy should the current stalemate continue and so that it can minimize any efforts by the PRC to influence the island's politics. Finally, should the stalemate dissolve, the political system must enable leaders to make a decision about whatever settlement might be proposed, a decision that accurately reflects Taiwan's economic, political, and security interests.

NOTES

1. "Text of President Li Teng-hui's Inaugural Speech," May 20, 1996, Foreign Broadcast Information Service (hereafter FBIS) CH-96–098.

2. This chapter is based on a volume tentatively titled *Untying the Knot: Making Peace in the Taiwan Strait* (Washington, DC: Brookings Institution Press, 2005).

3. *Taipei Times,* June 1, 2001, FBIS CPP20010601000048; Central News Agency (hereafter CNA), June 3, 2001, FBIS CPP20010603000038; CNA, June 19, 2001, FBIS CPP20010619000197; CNA, June 4, 2001, FBIS CPP20010604000106; *China Daily,* June 1, 2001, FBIS CPP20010601000045; *China Daily,* June 13, 2001, FBIS CPP20010613000099; CNA, June 15, 2001, FBIS CPP20010615000155; CNA, June 29, 2001, FBIS CPP20010629000091; CNA, June 8, 2001, FBIS CPP20010608000072; CNA, June 8, 2001, FBIS CPP20010608000085; CNA, June 14, 2001, FBIS CPP20010614000201; CNA, June 13, 2001, FBIS

CPP20010613000152; CNA, June 6, 2001, FBIS CPP20010606000147; Xinhua, June 13, 2001, FBIS CPP20010613000132; CNA, June 18, 2001, FBIS CPP20010618000108; CNA, June 24, 2001, FBIS CPP20010624000056; CNA, June 23, 2001, FBIS CPP20010623000054; CNA, June 7, 2001, FBIS CPP20010607000076; CNA, June 25, 2001, FBIS CPP20010625000075; CNA, June 27, 2001, FBIS CPP20010627000138; Xinhua, June 28, FBIS CPP20010628000106; *Renmin Ribao* [People's daily], June 28, CPP20010628000073.

4. "New Statistics Show Taiwanese Dependence on China for Exports," *Agence France-Presse*, March 16, 2003, FBIS CPP20030316000047.

5. Chin Chung, "Division of Labor across the Taiwan Strait: Macro Overview and Analysis of the Electronics Industry," in *The China Circle: Economics and Technology in the PRC, Taiwan, and Hong Kong*, ed. Barry Naughton (Washington, DC: Brookings Institution Press, 1997), especially pp. 181–82, 189–90; Rupert Hammond-Chambers, "The Emerging Technology Triumvirate: China, Taiwan, and the United States," speech to the China Forum, Johns Hopkins School of Advanced International Studies, February 20, 2002. You-tien Hsing's study of the migration of the Taiwan shoe industry to China is an excellent description of one aspect of the initial phase of this transition; see You Tien Hsing, *Making Capitalism in China: The Taiwan Connection* (New York: Oxford University Press, 1998).

6. "Survey Shows Half of Top 1000 Taiwan Companies Investing in Mainland," *China Post*, April 24, 2003, FBIS CPP20030424000231; Tain-Jy Chen and C. Y. Cyrus Chu, "Cross-Strait Economic Relations: Can They Ameliorate the Political Problem?" in *Taiwan's Presidential Politics: Democratization and Cross-Strait Relations in the 21st Century*, ed. Muthiah Alagappa (Armonk, NY: M. E. Sharpe, 2001), 218.

7. Tse-Kang Leng, "Economic Globalization and IT Talent Flows Across the Taiwan Strait," *Asian Survey* 42, no. 2 (March–April 2002): 230–50.

8. Communication from Emerson Niou, Duke University, October 20, 2003.

9. T. J. Cheng, "China-Taiwan Economic Linkage: Between Insulation and Superconductivity," in *Dangerous Strait: The U.S.-Taiwan-China Crisis*, ed. Nancy Bernkopf Tucker (New York: Columbia University Press, 2005).

10. "Don't Let 'One China Spell' Hinder Cross-Strait Ties: Adviser," CNA, June 23, 2003, FBIS CPP20030623000147.

11. Thomas J. Christensen, "The Contemporary Security Dilemma: Deterring a Taiwan Conflict," *Washington Quarterly* 25, no. 4 (Autumn 2002): 12–13.

12. Alan M. Wachman, *Taiwan: National Identity and Democratization* (Armonk, NY: M. E. Sharpe, 1994), 119.

13. Ho Szu-yin and Liu I-chou, "The Taiwanese/Chinese Identity of the Taiwan People in the 1990s," *American Asian Review* (Summer 2002). On cosmopolitan identity, see Christopher Hughes and Robert Stone, "Nation-Building and Curriculum Reform in Hong Kong and Taiwan," *China Quarterly* 160 (December 1999): 977–91.

14. Wachman, *Taiwan: National Identity and Democratization;* Christopher Hughes, *Taiwan and Chinese Nationalism: National Identity and Status in International Society* (New York: Routledge, 1997), 103–4, 127–28; Rwei-Ren Wu, "Toward a Pragmatic Nationalism, Democratization and Taiwan's Passive Revolution," in *Memories of the Future: National Identity Issues and the Search for a New Taiwan*, ed. Stéphane Corcuff

(Armonk, NY: M. E. Sharpe, 2002), 211; Yun-han Chu, "Taiwan's Security Dilemma: Military Rivalry, Economic Dependence, and the Struggle over National Identity," paper presented at the International Conference on Democracy, Nationalism, and Security in the Asia Pacific, Taipei, November 12, 2003.

15. Shelly Rigger, *From Opposition to Power: Taiwan's Democratic Progressive Party* (Boulder, CO: Lynne Rienner, 2001), 121–22.

16. Yu-Shan Wu, "Does Chen's Election Make Any Difference? Domestic and International Constraints on Taipei, Washington, and Beijing," in *Taiwan's Presidential Politics,* 167–79.

17. Shelley Rigger has heavily influenced my thinking on these issues.

18. See Yun-han Chu, "Democratic Consolidation in the Post-KMT Era: The Challenge of Governance," in *Taiwan's Presidential Politics,* 88–114.

19. Chen Shui-bian proposed during the 2004 presidential campaign that there be a new constitution, to be approved by a referendum rather than by the National Assembly. Absent more details on the new charter, it is impossible to predict whether it would improve the efficiency of the political system. China's immediate concern was that constitutional revision would make it easier for Chen to pursue a separatist project.

8

China and Southeast Asia

The Context of a New Beginning

Wang Gungwu

At the outset of the twenty-first century, Southeast Asia's relations with China appear to be the best they have been in at least half a century. In some countries, "China fever" seems to be replacing "China fear," and many look forward to the new "strategic partnership" and Free Trade Area being forged between China and ASEAN. Although this turn of events is significant, future relationships do not only depend on contemporary developments, but they must also be placed in the larger historical context (chapters 1–4 in this volume capably and sufficiently cover contemporary China–Southeast Asian relations).

On the surface, China's relations with the region's new nations have been totally transformed since the end of the Second World War. Two thousand years of history, however, have established a deeply ingrained pattern that it would be difficult to dismiss as irrelevant. During most of that time, Southeast Asia was a part of China's larger realm, especially when it came to the trade and tribute zones that were divided between polities that sent their envoys by sea and those that did so overland. Even that division fails to capture the differences between the lands that bordered South China from the Han dynasty and those that came into China's orbit much later on. For example, the areas that became Vietnam had a different relationship with China than states like Burma and Laos, which became neighbors only after Yunnan was made a province of the empire more than a thousand years later.[1] As for the maritime port kingdoms of Southeast Asia, the Chinese rarely differentiated them from those in what we would today call East Asia and South Asia. Up until the nineteenth century, many Chinese mandarins subscribed to the view that there existed an east-west division, with the Philippines, Borneo, and the islands east of Java part of the "Eastern Ocean," and the rest of the Malay archipelago part of the "Western Ocean," a geographical concept that encompassed not only the lands of the Indian Ocean to the Red Sea but also, between the sixteenth and nineteenth centuries, the European kingdoms of the Atlantic coasts. Also, in contrast with overland relations, which were invariably linked with political and territorial tensions, relationships with the seafaring peoples to the southeast were focused on trade and considered on the whole unthreatening before the nineteenth century.[2]

Much of the political landscape changed during the twentieth century. But the shadow of the former tributary system, often anachronistically interpreted as a kind of imperial dominance, remained long. When Western powers began to lose their colonies after Japan had failed to build its "Co-Prosperity Sphere" in Southeast Asia, this decolonization coincided with the near total unification of China by the Chinese Communist Party in 1949 (Hong Kong, Macau, and Taiwan remained outside the fold). The specter of future Chinese dominance after the West retreated was raised in the larger context of the Cold War. The late eminent historian John King Fairbank even spoke of a "Chinese world order," although he stressed that this network of "feudal" relationships was in fact relatively benign and defensive.[3] Others, however, portrayed the Chinese world order as similar to Western imperialism, and this interpretation was used by many Western analysts and Southeast Asian leaders in their anticommunist propaganda from the 1950s until the 1990s.

Recent positive changes in Chinese–Southeast Asian relations have eased concerns about the future of China's policy, but they have not erased the memories of Cold War propaganda.[4] Yet certain historical legacies endure. One major question is how much weight should currently be given to the facts of geography and the lessons of history. In that context, China still tends to view the region as unintegrated and broadly divided into three parts—namely, Vietnam and its immediate neighbors; Myanmar, bordering the strategic Chinese province of Yunnan and the Tibetan world; and the fluid and changeable maritime states.

Taking Southeast Asia as a whole, China's relations with the postcolonial nations could be regarded as a new beginning. There was one exception. China's ancient relationship with Thailand, whereby the Kingdom of Siam dealt with a Confucian state, was transformed to a modern diplomatic relationship with Republican China from 1912 to 1949. The fact of Thailand's independence throughout the colonial period has helped to make the country a pivot for Southeast Asia in the strategic thinking of China and countries like the United States and Japan that would like to limit China's influence in the region.[5] As for the other nine countries in Southeast Asia, China has had to face the products of colonial state building, new countries that the Spanish, Dutch, British, French, and Americans had done much to transform en route to modernity.[6] The British and French tried to do even more to protect their interests when they returned to their colonies in 1945 after the three and a half years of Japanese occupation, but the end of their rule was never in doubt. China, however, was in no position to take advantage of their withdrawal. For one thing, as the struggling government in Nanjing prepared for the new states to emerge from the decolonization process, it had to face a bitter civil war. No sustained diplomatic negotiation was possible, and by 1949 a revolutionary regime was established in Beijing under the shadow of an internationalist communist order.[7] As a result, decolonization in Southeast Asia became less the result of local nationalist leaders determining the kind of nations they wanted and more a result of these leaders determining which set of powers they could count on to enable them to establish independent sovereign states.

China could only play a subordinate and marginal role in the developments that followed. The Nationalist government, first in Nanjing and then in Taipei, was primarily concerned with its legitimacy and concentrated on asking all compatriots in the region to confirm their loyalty to China. The new communist government in Beijing countered this policy by encouraging these same overseas Chinese to support the forces of anticolonialism and work against the representatives of Western imperialism. Beijing's policy was actually counterproductive, and ultimately it contributed little to the shape of the new regional system now emerging. The mixed experiences of the nine new countries (apart from Thailand), whether communist, capitalist, or nonaligned, have left their legacy. Although they all looked to the system of United Nations–based states, they found that the system by itself was inadequate to protect their newly won sovereignty. They all needed powerful allies in an unstable and volatile world. This was also true for the regimes in Beijing and Taipei, for whom sovereignty was no more secure in the midst of superpower rivalry.[8] By 1975, the Vietnam War had demonstrated that fresh diplomatic starts were necessary for all.

China's adjustments to the changing circumstances of the 1970s did not evoke the same responses from the ten Southeast Asian states. It is, therefore, still useful to recall the older relationships between China and its overland neighbors and those across the South China Sea. On land, the Chinese state had consolidated its power along the borders of Yunnan province, putting great pressure on the kingdoms of Burma and Vietnam during the eighteenth and nineteenth centuries.[9] Elsewhere, however, China was relatively passive. Its coastal defense forces had been adequate only for dealing with local piracy. In its trading relations, it was often the littoral states from Japan to the Indian Ocean that took the initiative. Official policy required that trade be conducted within a framework based on tribute and security concerns, but enterprising merchants made their own connections, notably from the middle of the sixteenth century down to the nineteenth.[10]

In the following pages, China's relations with Southeast Asia are examined in four parts. The first two cover Vietnam (with Laos) and Myanmar separately, while the third focuses on Thailand and the region's heartland. The fourth part examines the archipelago world where the Chinese are very conscious of the differences between Filipinos and Indonesians and the peoples of the Malay peninsula. But it is also along this archipelagic arc that ASEAN was born. China's awareness of the sets of relationships and institutions that have been created to override the region's immediate interests is a major landmark in the new beginning for China that this volume of essays seeks to describe.

VIETNAM AND LAOS

Vietnam clearly stands as a special case, based on two thousand years of a close—but unequal—relationship with China. Although the French ended Vietnam's tributary relations with China and, for about seventy years, offered a kind of liberation, it was one that ultimately humiliated its people. The French tried to keep the Vietnamese separated from the Chinese, but they could not prevent close associations between the political leaders on both sides. Since the Chinese invasion of February 1979, the Vietnamese have learned that help from any faraway power—for example, the Soviet Union—cannot provide a guarantee of national security, especially if China is strong and Vietnam itself is seen as ambitious. Ultimately, a good relationship with China and other neighbors is the key to security.[11] The presence of a prosperous and united China has clear consequences. The fact that Vietnam and China share a political system has made it easier for their leaders to appeal for common policies by using familiar rhetoric and devices to ameliorate the problems left over from the past. This affords regular meetings of senior party and government leaders in Beijing and Hanoi, encouraging freer trade, and settling border disputes in an orderly way. The Vietnamese have also recovered their ability to express their unique identity without denying its similarities with Chinese political culture.

Nevertheless, Vietnam needs ASEAN to help affirm its national independence as much as ASEAN needs Vietnam to help forge a meaningful presence next door to China. This does not obviate Vietnam's traditional position in its historical relationship with China. But Vietnam's problems with China should not be exaggerated, nor should its long-term success in dealing with a powerful neighbor be underestimated. While the new Vietnam finds comfort in the ASEAN framework, it does not depend on that alone. It has also cultivated close bilateral relations with China, especially where trade and ethnic affairs along its long border with China are concerned.[12]

There is also the question of their relationships with Laos, an area in which feudal kingdoms and shifting populations have established a modern state. China and Vietnam are both sensitive to the local dynamics that are integrating the economies across the borders, especially key sections of the Mekong Valley that link China and Myanmar with Laos, Thailand, Cambodia, and, finally, the Vietnam delta provinces. Although progress is slow, all the countries involved have agreed to bring interested international players to join the Mekong Valley development, and to limit the damage that conflicts over human and natural resources would produce.[13]

China's interests, whether in improving transportation lines to its south or in reestablishing normal relations, are clear. But for ASEAN, the picture is less clear. Its existing mechanisms for regional economic cooperation are not well suited for quick responses to issues at the region's periphery. Vietnam and Laos have found that the best way to make progress in their links with southwest China is to find high-level support from the central authorities in Beijing wherever possible. ASEAN can provide backup support that emphasizes a responsibility to consult the other members of the organization and not harm their common interests, and this would normally be protection enough. Under that umbrella, other sources of international assistance could play an important part in infrastructure development, and there is evidence that China would welcome that as something from which local Chinese organizations could also benefit.[14]

The key here is that China knows Vietnam well, and the Vietnamese have a rich store of experience in dealing with Chinese authorities that enables them to play a distinctive role in China-ASEAN relations if and when necessary. This includes the knotty problems of the South China Sea. Much has been made of China's claims to sovereignty over all the islands, shoals, and reefs down to the northern coast of the island of Borneo and the eastern coasts of the Philippines. These claims stem mainly from an earlier nationalist response to French and British claims before the Second World War. The issues now have a totally different focus, and good relations with ASEAN have minimized the dangers of open conflict. What remain difficult, however, are the disputes between China and Vietnam over the Paracels and certain parts of the Spratlys. Vietnam finds the support of ASEAN reassuring, but it has always known that, ultimately, this is a matter that can only be settled directly with China. The regular bilateral talks proceeding on all remaining disputes for the past decade have made steady progress, and China's recent policies should be even more helpful.[15]

THE ISOLATION OF MYANMAR (BURMA)

Myanmar's traditional ties with China were cut off by the British in the 1880s. Unlike the rulers of Vietnam, the Burmese kings have never been under close scrutiny by Chinese mandarins. China, in turn, has never had great expectations of Theravada Buddhist Myanmar, a polity outside the Confucian realm. But the decision by the British to administer Burma

largely from New Delhi as part of their Indian empire led to much bitter-
ness among the Burmese. The nationalist Burmese elites after independence spurned membership in the British Commonwealth and forged a go-
it-alone nonaligned stance. China's support for Burma's communist rebels
only pushed the country into a deeper isolation. Then followed the Cultural
Revolution, and the ideas that the Chinese tried to export to Burma between 1966 and 1976, in particular, were disastrous for bilateral relations.[16]
It was only after the beginning of the economic reforms of Deng Xiaoping
in the early 1980s that the leaders of Myanmar began to build up a new level
of trust. By that time, the military junta had become unpopular, and a
national opposition had coalesced to fight for democracy. The sympathy
generated for its leader, Aung San Suu Kyi, and the fierce criticisms of the
regime by the West drove the leadership even further away from normal
diplomatic relations.

Thus, the invitation to Myanmar to join ASEAN in 1997 came at a time
when China was one of Myanmar's few friends in the world. The fact that
China understood Myanmar's desire to become a member of ASEAN is
important and marks the fresh awareness of ASEAN's potential as a group
friendly toward China. ASEAN was strengthened by having all the countries
in the region inside the organization. China realized that the eclectic membership of ASEAN reduced the chances of unfriendly neighbors to its south.
The Western hostility toward Myanmar over the suppression of democracy
and human rights is so intense that some ASEAN members are embarrassed
by the negative attention the region has received. But with its strict policy of
nonintervention in each other's internal politics, ASEAN has continued to
give Myanmar ample time to resolve the question of political normalcy
(although some member states are frustrated at Yangon's intransigence).

China is not committed to the ASEAN position, though it, too, has
affirmed the principle of noninterference in the internal affairs of other
countries. It sees the attacks on Myanmar by the West differently. For its own
political and economic reasons, it has cultivated a special relationship with
Myanmar for at least two decades, especially since 1988, when China finally
stopped supporting the pro-Beijing faction of the Burmese Communist
Party.[17] The Beijing government is aware that, outside the region, there is
concern that Myanmar has become one of China's "client states," and that
this is strategically important if China is to become active in the Indian
Ocean.[18] To be sure, Myanmar is entirely dependent on China's military
assistance, trade, and aid. As a member of ASEAN, Myanmar could be less
dependent on China, but if the country continues to be ostracized by too
many countries, Myanmar could tilt even more closely towards China. In
this context, India's recent efforts to have closer relations with ASEAN and
to cultivate Myanmar are clearly justified.[19]

THE THAI HEARTLAND

For more than a century, the heartland of the Hindu-Buddhist world of mainland Southeast Asia was divided. French incursions into Cochin-China and Cambodia and British advances in Lower Burma, plus an Anglo-French understanding to leave the Kingdom of Siam as a buffer zone between their respective empires, masked the deep fissures that had grown between the ancient Khmer and Burmese polities between the Mekong and the Salween and the Thai forces that had swept steadily southward since the thirteenth century. French rule helped to save the weakened kingdom of Cambodia, the center of an extended Khmer empire, but it also heightened the historic rivalries between the Khmers and their neighbors. The Thais had destroyed their empire and sought to absorb the territories west of the Mekong. From the north, Vietnam had steadily moved south at the expense of the Cham kingdom to take all the lands east of the Mekong.

The Cambodian state was saved by the French intervention. With the departure of the French after the fall of Dien Bien Phu in 1954, that state was given a new chance to restore itself. For fifty years, Prince Sihanouk managed, with great difficulty, to provide symbolic unity for the country's survival.[20] Among the measures available to him was to turn to Beijing for assistance, where his complaints fell on willing ears. These complaints included fears not only of a Thailand that sided with the capitalist enemies of communist China, but also of China's communist comrades in Vietnam. Despite Sihanouk's political agility, his weakness was accompanied by the rise of the Khmer Rouge and the tragic years of the killing fields. Nevertheless, his durability has been a factor in the country's ability to survive, and it was crucial in Cambodia's ability to obtain support from China, the United States, Japan, and Australia during the 1980s.[21] It is too early to say how soon Cambodia (Kampuchea) will regain prosperity with international help, but it is clear that, preferably through ASEAN, Cambodia is likely to strengthen its links with China.

Recent developments highlight the central position of the lands between the Mekong and the Salween in Southeast Asian history. They also underline the vital importance of Thailand in any regional development. The record shows that it was no accident that Britain and France recognized their function as a buffer in the nineteenth century, that Japan persuaded the Thai military regime to lean to its side early in the twentieth, and that the United States found Bangkok crucial during the Vietnam War.[22] Since the Second World War, the region has often pivoted on a Thai-based diplomatic axle, and China since the 1970s has increasingly appreciated the dynamic role that Thailand can play in the region and beyond.[23] This is not a question of merely acting the role of dependent ally, or acting as a temporarily useful instrument of foreign political maneuvers, but rather a question of having a steady hand to provide a sense of direction in a complex and fluid situation. The region has come to see that Thai moves toward or away from China may provide a valuable indicator of how to read the future. For example, Thailand under its present prime minister, Thaksin Shinawatra, has demonstrated that it knows how to find a comfortable position between the United States and China.[24] That both China and the United States appreciate this suggests that factors of history and geography will be an important factor in political and strategic calculations in the region. One of the reasons for this success is the way Thailand has been managed by skilful diplomats whose work has been an inspiration for their younger regional counterparts. Thailand's success was by no means inevitable. It was hard won and has contributed to the forging of a valuable instrument for regional cooperation.[25] It also explains why China recognizes that Thailand has the potential to serve as the anchor for a new Southeast Asian identity.

MARITIME SOUTHEAST ASIA AND ASEAN REGIONALISM

Maritime Southeast Asia is more like an extended periphery, part of the arc that begins with Japan, and includes all the Malay archipelago nations through the Straits of Malacca and the Sunda Straits into the Indian Ocean.[26] In contrast to continental Southeast Asia, China's maritime relations with Southeast Asia did not have the same importance until the twentieth century. The continuous pressure since the end of the nineteenth century on China's coastal provinces to respond to new dangers and opportunities, however, has been a spur to review its policies about its long-neglected navy. This has been further heightened by United States support for Taiwan since 1949, something that China sees as a challenge to its sovereignty. In response, the Chinese have turned more attention to naval power, and this has ramifications for maritime Southeast Asia.[27] Nevertheless, this perspective from the China coasts does not mesh with the one from Yunnan and Guangxi provinces, and it makes it difficult for China to see Southeast Asia as an integrated region.

The historical background supports the prospect of increased Chinese attention to maritime Southeast Asia. Formal relations between the Malay states and the Ming and Qing dynasties had ended centuries earlier. In the case of Malacca and other Malay states, including those in Java, relations had stopped in the early sixteenth century. These differences mattered little at the time. The Qing rulers paid little attention to affairs to the south of their empire, and the first two emperors in the nineteenth century were genuinely surprised by British power off the China coast. What did become clear was that, while the mainland states like Burma and Vietnam provided something of a defense bulwark for China, the port kingdoms were wide open to European dominance.[28] In the island world, local Malay rulers and their European partners were conscious that Chinese private traders and their ships played a useful part in helping European trading fleets establish their economic dominance. But the Qing rulers were either unaware of the role of those Chinese or cared too little to try to influence what they were doing. Their only concern was that these Chinese who defied the ban to trade overseas did not bring their illegal ventures back to China's own ports.

The gulf that grew between China and much of this maritime world extends also to cultural spheres. Buddhism and the Indian linkages of that religion had provided some common values when the first contacts were recorded. This was no longer true for the Malay world, notably after a sinicized Buddhism had drawn China away from the religion's Indian roots and when Islam advanced into the archipelago after the thirteenth century. As a result, the wide range of links across the South China Sea that once thrived on the religious and cultural connection was further weakened. In contrast, Theravada Buddhism spread from Sri Lanka to the mainland kingdoms up to the borders of the Song and Yuan empires and helped to ease relations with the Chinese state as Chinese traders and settlers moved toward those land borders. Although religious policy has never been its strength, China remains sensitive to the differences in faith that have grown over the centuries in the island world. China pays close attention to common Islamic concerns in countries like Malaysia, Indonesia, and Brunei.

Nevertheless, China's maritime relations in Southeast Asia became less marginal when both China and the region shared the experience of postindustrial European expansion. Because of the dramatic impact of the West, China has now reevaluated the significance of the region as the passageway toward its southern coast, its soft underbelly. Its leaders have learned the hard lesson that weak and unstable polities in the region could allow foreign powers to threaten China.

It is important to highlight to what extent China has transformed its relations with this maritime world during this past century. Until the end of the nineteenth century, port cities and riverine kingdoms were rarely able to sustain themselves for long as stable states. Now the archipelago has five stable states (East Timor is excluded here) that have successfully weathered decades of nation building.[29] Although none can be said to have assumed a definite final form, China knows that the heritage of colonial methods of state formation has given them the means to affirm their respective sovereignty. Chinese officials have also learned what a mixed group these states are. The two with clear Muslim majority populations, Brunei and Indonesia, are totally unlike each other. The one that is based on Christian communities, the Philippines, strains at understanding its neighbors. Malaysia is an exceptional kind of Muslim monarchy, with its Malay majority divided between modernizers and the tradition-bound, whereas Singapore, which might have acted as a balancing member of the Malaysian Federation, now serves as the only genuinely secular state. It is therefore not surprising that none of the five see China in the same way, and that, in its recent bilateral relations, China has worked very hard to respond to the varying needs and expectations of each of these states.[30]

China has also learned a sharp lesson from its early dealings with the region's largest country, Indonesia. The country was created in 1945–50 out of revolution, and leaders of the country had hoped that China would be an ally in a nonaligned world. The Bandung Conference in 1955 was a landmark for that cause, as President Sukarno wanted real independence from the capitalist West. China's keen support for that ambition, however, was to cost the Chinese dearly. The president's flirtation with the Parti Kommunist Indonesia (PKI), the October 1 coup in 1965 and the killings of alleged "communists" and hundred of thousands of ethnic Chinese that followed, and the rise of President Suharto soon afterward were followed by twenty-five years of Indonesian hostility and suspicion.[31] That turnaround gave a major impetus to the establishment of ASEAN, with Indonesia acting as the organization's anchor. Accompanied by the country's impressive economic development for the next thirty years, this initial grouping of five nations (later six, with the addition of Brunei) gave the region a common sense of purpose that no one had predicted was possible. Indonesia was helped in its axial role by the mature monarchy of Thailand and the relatively stable Philippines state. Together, in 1967, they provided a protective shield for a riot-torn Malaysia and the former colony of Singapore, which Malaysia had just shed to become the region's newest republic.[32]

Despite strong support from the United States, Britain, and Australia, the formation of ASEAN was far from convincing at the time, and, insofar as it was seen as a group directed against China, it was certainly not something the Chinese wanted to succeed. But China was in a poor position to deal with the new organization. It was then in the grip of the Cultural Revolution. Its foreign policy was incomprehensible even to China's friends, and its foreign ministry had been dysfunctional for years. No one, in any case, anticipated that ASEAN would later provide a framework for the kind of communication and interaction that began to change the region's political and security environment.[33] ASEAN members in turn did not know how desperate China had become when it faced a hostile Soviet Union during the height of the Vietnam War. It took the bold steps by President Richard Nixon and Secretary of State Henry Kissinger to cut through the "bamboo curtain" that divided Asia at the time.

The ramifications of that ideological war in the Southeast Asian jungles and padi fields have been great. The war changed the expectations that most Asian leaders had of the benefits of decolonization, the ideal that independent nations should be free of any kind of external interference. The fact that this was somewhat utopian and unrealistic could be ignored during the struggle for sovereign freedoms. By the start of the war in Indo-China in the mid-1960s, however, no one could pretend that each nation could shape its own destiny all by itself. The twenty years of development from the 1970s to the 1990s for both China and Southeast Asia have created completely new conditions for the future. This was even more striking after the start of the economic reforms in China, followed by the end of the Cold War and the disintegration of the Soviet Union.

The decades of moving toward interdependence in the world have reached a phase when a new generation of leaders has come on the scene in both China and Southeast Asia. Most notably, the financial crisis that led to the fall of President Suharto was accompanied by experiments in democracy, a succession of transitional leaders, and sharp challenges to Indonesia's commitment to secularism. This has weakened the thrusting advances that ASEAN had achieved before 1997.[34] Fortunately, leadership in the other original member-states remained strong under former president Fidel Ramos of the Philippines and Prime Ministers Mahathir Mohamad of Malaysia and Goh Chok Tong of Singapore. Thailand now has a strong leader in Prime Minister Thaksin Shinawatra, and new leaders in Malaysia and Singapore are ready to be tested.[35] All this coincides with the emergence of a technocratic Politburo in Beijing under President Hu Jintao. Since the late 1990s, China has engaged the region through the ARF, not only on matters of trade and investment, but also increasingly on security issues.[36] These initiatives have begun to bear fruit, not least in giving fresh vigor to ASEAN in the larger context of East Asian regionalism. That body now has the opportunity to consolidate both its economic and security concerns as well as explore what it can do beyond Eastern Asia in a larger Asia.

Have these recent changes fundamentally rewritten the script for both China and ASEAN? Will the new regionalism lead to a different kind of sharing altogether, or will it ultimately revert to older patterns of relationships? On the one hand, China is nearly reunified, in almost a return to China of the Qing dynasty in 1911. On the other hand, there is a clearly incomplete regional effort to integrate the ten countries of Southeast Asia into ASEAN. This has evoked many different responses. For many leaders, this is an unequal relationship, but a united ASEAN should do much better than each country having to face China alone. To others, ASEAN was first brought together by fear of a common enemy, international communism, and would need a common enemy to bind the four new countries to the original members. That condition is no longer there, and it is unlikely that China will allow itself to be portrayed as a potential enemy in the future. Yet others see a new regionalism as a challenge to making ASEAN a major regional actor. This would be possible if ASEAN plays an instrumental role in shaping the larger regionalism that promises to bring prosperity all round.[37] If that succeeds, it could seek to act as something of a bridge between power groups in the Asia-Pacific and Indian Ocean worlds. In getting China to sign the Treaty of Amity and Cooperation in Bali in 2003, ASEAN has certainly made a major breakthrough.[38]

This brings us back to the context of the larger region in which China has invariably seen itself as placed at the center. There are two perspectives here. From the point of view of its Southeast Asian neighbors, there is historical baggage for all to carry. The geographic proximity of Vietnam, Laos, and Myanmar to both Southwest and South-Central China, and the almost continuous trade and tribute diplomacy between Thailand and China for centuries, cannot be easily set aside. The special local reasons for Cambodia to look beyond its immediate neighbors for support of its independence remain relevant to its future. This collection of relationships was severely disrupted during the past century, but it has not been broken. Some national leaders expect parts of the old relationships to be revived whether they like it or not. Others, notably the archipelagic countries, believe that long-distance interventions from outside the region may protect them from any possible Chinese ambitions. Yet others know that they need to be flexible in arranging their bilateral and multilateral links if they are to survive the rapidly globalizing world.

China's larger perspective reflects some of the same factors. It is not only Southeast Asian countries that are challenged in ways never encountered before. China's decisive moves to engage ASEAN form part of an effort to establish new parameters for a new Asia in which China hopes it may act as a responsible great power. As several other chapters in this volume show, China still faces powerful neighbors, unstable states, and potentially unfriendly alliances in almost every direction around its long land and sea boundaries. Although being the target of external forces is a familiar situation for China, evident since ancient times, China has learned over the last thousand years that, at every stage of growth, the power and determination of their neighbors have been harder to deal with. Most of all, the Chinese know, at each succeeding stage, how their past economic and technological advantages have been reduced. As each set of neighbors mastered whatever the Chinese had developed, the dangers to the "center" have been all the greater.

There are now no illusions about what advantages some of its neighbors have over China, and how much these can override considerations of history and geography. As China sees its position today, a hardheaded realism, free from outdated rhetoric, is necessary until China feels secure and confident enough to redefine itself distinctively in ways that the modern world would respect. From that perspective, Southeast Asia has its rightful place as a cornerstone of a larger East Asian arc of safety that stretches into the Indian Ocean. If the "ASEAN Way" can enable the region to be the first part of that arc to make China feel safe, after more than a century of turmoil and anguish, it is likely that future Chinese leaders will remember the debt that they owe to the initiatives ASEAN first took in the latter half of the twentieth century.

NOTES

1. This contrast became clear during the Ming dynasty (1368–1644). See Wang Gungwu, "Early Ming Relations with Southeast Asia: A Background Essay," in *The Chinese World Order: Traditional China's Foreign Relations,* ed. John K. Fairbank (Cambridge, MA: Harvard University Press, 1968), 34–62, 293–99; and "Ming Foreign Relations: Southeast Asia," in *The Cambridge History of China,* vol. 8, *The Ming Dynasty, 1368–1644, Part 2,* ed. Denis Twitchett and Frederick W. Mote (Cambridge: Cambridge University Press, 1998), 301–32.

2. This distinction was systematically employed after the sixteenth century. See Zhang Xie, *Dong Xi Yang Kao* [On the Eastern and Western Oceans] (Beijing: Zhonghua shuju, [1618] 1981). The contrast with overland relations is brought out sharply in essays by Joseph F. Fletcher in Fairbank, ed., *The Chinese World Order,* 206–24; and Morris Rossabi, "The Ming and Inner Asia," in *The Cambridge History, Ming Dynasty,* 221–71.

3. Fairbank, ed., *The Chinese World Order,* 1–19.

4. The chapters in this volume by Robert Sutter, Tang Shiping, and Bates Gill, as well as the editor's introduction, reflect some of these residual concerns.

5. The two research reports by Khien Theeravit draw interesting comparisons of Thai perceptions of China and Japan after the Vietnam War: *Japan in Thai Perspective* and *China in Thai Perspective* (Bangkok: Chulalongkorn Asian Studies Monographs, nos. 26 and 27, 1980). More details about the changing course of the China connection is given in R. K. Jain, ed., *China and Thailand, 1949–1983* (London: Sangam, 1987). A more recent review that brings out Thailand's central position is Gerrit W. Gong, ed., *Southeast Asia's Changing Landscape: Implications for U.S.-Japan Relations on the Eve of the Twenty-first Century* (Washington, DC: Center for Strategic and International Studies, 1999), 29–38, 67–82.

6. The limits to state building and decolonization are closely examined in Marc Frey, Ronald W. Pruessen, and Tan Tai Yong, eds., *The Transformation of Southeast Asia: International Perspectives on Decolonization* (Armonk, NY: M. E. Sharpe, 2003), with essays by Hugues Tertrais, Karl Hack, and Robert J. McMahon.

7. Diplomatic relations were established early with countries that either considered themselves neutral and refused to take sides between the Western allies and the Soviet bloc, like Indonesia (1950) and Myanmar (1950), or that needed comradely support, like the Vietnamese government of Ho Chi Minh (1950). When Thailand and the Philippines did not follow suit, this established the foundation for a tense superpower rivalry for the next two decades. A valuable contemporary record is George McTurnan Kahin, ed., *Governments and Politics in Southeast Asia* (Ithaca, NY: Cornell University Press, 1959). A longer view is outlined in C. P. Fitzgerald, *China and Southeast Asia since 1945* (Camberwell, Victoria: Longman, 1973).

8. All postcolonial states were left with untidy boundaries and multiple ethnic communities, and many in Southeast Asia had to fight territorial claims from neighbors and secessionist groups as soon as the colonial powers departed, for example,

between Malaysia and the Philippines, Thailand and Cambodia, China and Myanmar, and various claimants in the South China Sea. The initial faith in post-Westphalian ideals has been diluted by many new challenges, not least the pressures of economic globalization. There is renewed interest in the region in the new efforts to reexamine the concept itself: see Stephen D. Krasner, ed., *Problematic Sovereignty: Contested Rules and Political Possibilities* (New York: Columbia University Press, 2001); and Daniel Philpott, *Revolutions in Sovereignty: How Ideas Shaped Modern International Relations* (Princeton, NJ: Princeton University Press, 2001).

9. Trung Buu Lam, "Intervention versus Tribute in Sino-Vietnamese Relations, 1788–1790," in Fairbank, *The Chinese World Order*, 165–79; G. H. Luce, "Chinese Invasions of Burma in the Eighteenth Century," *Journal of the Burma Research Society* 15 (1925): 115–28.

10. Wang Gungwu, *The Nanhai Trade: Early Chinese Trade in the South China Sea*, 2nd ed. (Singapore: Eastern Universities Press, 2003), 136–42, 151–55; and Wang Gungwu, "Merchants without Empires: The Hokkien Sojourning Communities," in *The Rise of Merchant Empires: Long-distance Trade in the Early Modern World, 1350–1750*, ed. James D. Tracy (Cambridge: Cambridge University Press, 1990), 400–421.

11. Stephen J. Hood, *Dragons Entangled: Indochina and the China-Vietnam War* (Armonk, NY: M. E. Sharpe, 1992), 155–60. Vietnam's actions in Cambodia were seen as expansionist, and the treaty with the Soviet Union was threatening not only to China but also to the region.

12. Since 1991 officials at all levels of the respective communist parties and the government have had regular meetings; see Gu Xiaosong and Brantly Womack, "Border Cooperation between China and Vietnam in the 1990s," *Asian Survey* 40, no. 6 (2000): 1042–58. A fuller analysis of the relationship in the 1970s is Brantly Womack, "Asymmetry and Systemic Misperception: China, Vietnam and Cambodia during the 1970s," *Journal of Strategic Studies* 26, no. 2: 92–119.

13. A study that traces the efforts down to the late 1990s is Nguyen Thi Dieu, *The Mekong River and the Struggle for Indochina: Water, War, and Peace* (Westport, CT: Praeger, 1999), with a useful summary on the greater Mekong region on pp. 199–227. Also see Nick J. Freeman, "Greater Mekong Sub-Region and the 'Asian Crisis': Caught between Scylla and Charybdis," *Southeast Asian Affairs 1999* (Singapore: Institute of Southeast Asian Studies, 1999), 32–51. Since the late 1980s, many national and international agencies have tried to cooperate on the development of the Mekong Valley, and there are numerous reports, especially on the sections in Laos, Cambodia, and Thailand. The ADB, UNESCO, UNDP, and the WHO have all been active, but there have also been national efforts to cooperate in that development. The renewal of interest following the Kunming Initiative in 1999 has prompted India to be more active, notably with its Mekong-Ganga Project. But the ADB's Greater Mekong Subregion Economic Cooperation Program was invigorated in Bali in November 2003 following a meeting of the six heads of states most directly concerned. The six seemed to have a strong China focus that had not been obvious before. See "Mekong versus Metookong," November 13, 2003, available at http://www.asiasource.org/trade/fifteen.cfm.

14. China has several projects involving the upper reaches of what the Chinese call the Lanchang River, and attention is being paid to the ramifications of these projects on downstream countries. Qinghua University and the Geographical

Research Institute of Yunnan province, for example, have been asked to develop a support system for the upper reaches of the valley (*People's Daily*, November 17, 2001).

15. After the Vietnamese withdrew completely from Cambodia, Hanoi was invited to join ASEAN, after which tensions with China began to ease. Gradually the Chinese and Vietnamese leaders met more regularly, increasingly on a bilateral basis. One of the most significant meetings was that of Premier Zhu Rongji to Hanoi in 1999 to announce that the two countries had resolved their outstanding land boundary disputes (*People's Daily*, December 4, 1999). When Nong Duc Manh was appointed the new general secretary of the Communist Party of Vietnam in 2001, his visit to Beijing was hailed, and Jiang Zemin called on him in Hanoi soon afterwards (*People's Daily*, February 28, 2002). In 2003, Nong visited Beijing to congratulate the new president of China, Hu Jintao, which was also acclaimed as another major step in bilateral relations (*People's Daily*, April 8, 2003). General Secretary Nong also made highly publicized visits to Japan and India, but no other country in Southeast Asia had received as much attention by the most senior leaders of China since 1999.

16. Ralph Pettman, *China in Burma's Foreign Policy* (Canberra: Australian National University Press, 1973).

17. Liang Chi-shad, "Burma's Relations with the People's Republic of China: From Delicate Friendship to Genuine Cooperation," in *Burma: The Challenge of Change in a Divided Society*, ed. Peter Carey (New York: Macmillan; London: St. Martin's Press, 1997), 77–90.

18. Tin Maung Maung Than, "Myanmar and China: A Special Relationship?" in *Southeast Asian Affairs 2003* (Singapore: Institute of Southeast Asian Studies, 2003), 189–210; David I. Steinberg, "Myanmar: Regional Relationships and Internal Concerns," *Southeast Asian Affairs 1998* (Singapore: Institute of Southeast Asian Studies, 1998), 179–88.

19. John W. Garver, *Protracted Contest: Sino-Indian Rivalry in the Twentieth Century* (Seattle: University of Washington Press, 2001), has two excellent chapters that sum up the issues that have led to some recent Indian actions, "Burma: The Backdoor to China," 243–74, and "The Indian Ocean in Sino-Indian Relations," 275–312; S. D. Muni, *China's Strategic Engagement with the New ASEAN: An Exploratory Study of China's Post–Cold War Political, Strategic and Economic Relations with Myanmar, Laos, Cambodia and Vietnam* (Singapore: Institute of Defence and Strategic Studies, Nanyang Technological University, 2002), 77–88, 119–33.

20. Marie Alexandrine Martin, *Cambodia: A Shattered Society*, rev. ed., trans. Mark W. McLeod (Berkeley: University of California Press, 1994), 61–77, 110–20, 135–38. On the beginning of Prince Sihanouk's dependence on China, see pp. 88–95. See also Milton Osborne, *Sihanouk: Prince of Light, Prince of Darkness* (St. Leonards, N.S.W.: Allen and Unwin, 1994), 72–84, 151–55.

21. Osborne, *Sihanouk*, 248–63.

22. Kobkua Suwannathat-Pian, *Thailand's Durable Premier: Phibun through Three Decades, 1932–1957* (Kuala Lumpur: Oxford University Press, 1995), 240–43, 283–91; Daniel Fineman, *Special Relationship: The United States and Military Government in Thailand, 1947–1958* (Honolulu: University of Hawaii Press, 1997), 259–63.

23. Sukhumbhand Paribatra, *From Enmity to Alignment: Thailand's Evolving Relations with China* (Bangkok: Institute of Security and International Studies, Chula-

longkorn University, 1987), 34–49; Arne Kislenko, "Bending with the Wind: The Continuity and Flexibility of Thai Foreign Policy," *International Journal* 57, no. 4 (2002): 537–61. But, rather as with China, being in the center also means that Thailand is vulnerable and its policies are seen as ineffective; Chayachoke Chulasiriwongs, "Thailand's Relations with the New ASEAN Members: Solving Problems and Creating Images," *Southeast Asian Affairs 2001* (Singapore: Institute of Southeast Asian Affairs, 2001), 337–54.

24. Michael R. J. Vatikiotis, "Catching the Dragon's Tail: China and Southeast Asia in the 21st Century," *Contemporary Southeast Asia* 25, no. 1 (2003): 77. In 2003, the United States reconfirmed Thailand's partner status while Prime Minister Thaksin carefully reaffirmed its "strategic cooperation" with China (as in the China-Thailand Joint Communiqué, August 29, 2001); *Straits Times,* October 19, 2003. Rapid progress followed immediately with a free trade agreement with India in October.

25. Thailand's diplomatic contributions to the ASEAN Way began with one of the founding foreign ministers, Thanat Khoman, in 1967. See "ASEAN: Conception and Evolution" (foreword), in K. S. Sandhu et al., comp., *The ASEAN Reader* (Singapore: Institute of Southeast Asian Studies, 1992), xvii–xxii. Thailand's contributions to ASEAN have been well sustained into the 1990s; see John Funston, "Thai Foreign Policy: Seeking Influence," *Southeast Asian Affairs 1998* (Singapore: Institute of Southeast Asian Affairs, 1998), 292–306.

26. The historical evolution of this maritime periphery has been described in two stimulating studies by Hamashita Takeshi, "The Intraregional System in East Asia in Modern Times," in *Network Power: Japan and Asia,* ed. Peter J. Katzenstein and Takashi Shiraishi (Ithaca, NY: Cornell University Press, 1996), 113–35; and "The Tribute Trade System and Modern Asia," in A. J. H. Latham and Heita Kawakatsu, eds., *Japanese Industrialization and the Asian Economy* (London: Routledge, 1994), 91–107.

27. Lee Jae-Hyung, "China's Expanding Maritime Ambitions in the Western Pacific and the Indian Ocean," *Contemporary Southeast Asia* 24, no. 3 (2002): 557–64.

28. The port kingdoms were wide open insofar as *"mare liberum"* (free seas) seemed to have been taken for granted by the Malay seafaring peoples and their trading partners. Hugo Grotius thought through the legal principle as "a navigable body of water, such as a sea, that is open to navigation by vessels of all nations"; Hugo Grotius, *The Freedom of the Seas; or, The Right which Belongs to the Dutch to Take Part in the East Indian Trade,* trans. Ralph Van Deman Magoflin, ed. James Brown Scot (New York: Oxford University Press, 1916).

29. The nation-building history project at the Institute of Southeast Asian Studies has stressed that the task begun some fifty years earlier is far from done, but at least two generations of leaders and officials have learned what the most difficult problems are. See Wang Gungwu, "Introduction," in Cheah Boon Kheng, *Malaysia: The Making of a Nation* (Singapore: Institute of Southeast Asian Studies, 2002), xi–xviii. This is the first of a five-volume series on Malaysia, Indonesia, the Philippines, Thailand, and Singapore.

30. Brunei is a monarchy of 360,000 people, while the Indonesian Republic has a population of 235 million. The Philippines is a well-established democracy of 85 million, of whom more than 80 million are Christians, and the thirteen states of

Malaysia form a special kind of Islam-based federation, with nine sultans acting as heads of state in rotation. Singapore is unique as the only state in the world in which immigrant Chinese form a 75 percent majority of its people. During the past two decades, China has published dozens of books on Southeast Asia and scores of articles on relations with ASEAN and each of its member countries. See, for example, Liu Yongzhuo, *Zhongguo Dongnanya yanjiu de huigu yu qianzhan* [Southeast Asian studies in China: Retrospect and prospect] (Guangzhou: Guangdong Remin Chuban she, 1994). This work is updated by Liu Hong, "Southeast Asian Studies in Greater China," *Kyoto Review of Southeast Asia* 3 (March 2003), available at http://www .kyotoreview.cseas.kyoto-u.ac.jp.

31. On the 1965 upheaval, see John Hughes, *The End of Sukarno: A Coup That Misfired, a Purge That Ran Wild* (London: Angus and Robertson, 1968); Benedict R. O'G. Anderson and Ruth McVey, *A Preliminary Analysis of the October 1, 1965 Coup in Indonesia* (Ithaca, NY: Modern Indonesia Project, Cornell University, 1971). For Suharto's policy toward China, see Rizal Sukma, *Indonesia and China: The Politics of a Troubled Relationship* (New York: Routledge, 1999), 104–65; Leo Suryadinata, *Indonesia's Foreign Policy under Suharto: Aspiring to International Leadership* (Singapore: Times Academic Press, 1996), 101–21.

32. For more on the most hopeful and difficult formative years, see Michael Leifer, *ASEAN and the Security of South-East Asia* (London: Routledge, 1989); and Roger Irvine, "The Formative Years of ASEAN: 1967–1975," in Alison Broinowski, ed., *Understanding ASEAN* (London: Macmillan, in association with the Australian Institute of International Affairs, 1982), 8–36. For the longer perspective, see Shaun Narine, *Explaining ASEAN: Regionalism in Southeast Asia* (Boulder, CO: Lynne Rienner, 2002), with a short introduction on the organization's formation, pp. 9–38.

33. Sharon Siddique and Sree Kumar, comps., *The 2nd ASEAN Reader* (Singapore: Institute of Southeast Asian Studies, 2003), 263–309; and Frank Frost, "Introduction: ASEAN Since 1967—Origins, Evolution and Recent Developments," in *ASEAN into the 1990s*, ed. Alison Broinowski (New York: St. Martin's Press, 1990), 10–28.

34. Siddique and Kumar, comps., *2nd ASEAN Reader,* 471–508; Simon S. C. Tay, "Institutions and Processes: Dilemmas and Possibilities," in *Reinventing ASEAN,* ed. Simon S. C. Tay, Jesus P. Estanislao, and Hadi Soesastro (Singapore: Institute of Southeast Asian Studies, 2001), 243–55, 261–69; Narine, *Explaining ASEAN,* 193–209; Amitav Acharya, *Seeking Security in the Dragon's Shadow: China and Southeast Asia in the Emerging Asian Order* (Singapore: Institute of Defence and Strategic Studies, 2003).

35. All four leaders named here maintained close relations with China by making regular visits to China and inviting senior Chinese leaders to visit their respective countries. President Ramos continued to maintain his China links after retirement. A manifestation of one of the warmest relationships in recent years was the visit of the new leader of Malaysia, Prime Minister Abdullah Ahmad Badawi, in September 2003, on the eve of his taking over from Dr. Mahathir Mohamad; see Karim Raslan, "Engagement with China," available at http://www.inq7.net/opi/2003/ oct/01/opi_commentary1–1.htm. Lee Hsien Loong of Singapore, of course, is well known in China, not only as the son of Minister Mentor Lee Kuan Yew, but also as Singapore's new prime minister.

36. Joseph Y. S. Cheng, "China's ASEAN Policy in the 1990s: Pushing for Regional Multipolarity," *Contemporary Southeast Asia* 21, no. 2 (1999): 183–200. The move toward an ASEAN-China Free Trade Agreement began in Manila in 1999, was pursued further in Singapore in 2000, and was endorsed in Brunei in November 2001; see Kevin G. Cai, "The ASEAN-China Free Trade Agreement and East Asian Regional Grouping," *Contemporary Southeast Asia* 25, no. 3 (2003): 387–402.

37. Following the final report of the East Asia Study Group presented to the ASEAN Plus Three summit in Phnom Penh, November 4, 2002, rapid steps were taken in 2003 to deepen the relationships of ASEAN Plus Three (involving China, Japan, and South Korea) and to work toward regional integration and an economic community. East Asia Study Group Report and the Phnom Penh Communiqué of ASEAN Foreign Ministers of June 17, 2003, available at http://www.aseansec.org/14833.htm and http://www.mofa.go.jp/region/asia-paci/asean/pmv0211/report.pdf.

38. Chinese initiatives at the Bali Summit in October 2003 were widely reported, notably China's signing of the Instrument of Accession to the Treaty of Amity and Cooperation in Southeast Asia. Also significant was the Joint Declaration of the Heads of State/Government of the Association of Southeast Asian Nations and the People's Republic of China on Strategic Partnership for Peace and Prosperity, October 8, 2003, signed in Bali at the Ninth ASEAN Summit; see http://www.aseansec.org/15265.htm. The framework agreements for comprehensive economic cooperation with India and for comprehensive economic partnership with Japan were signed on the same day.

9

China's Influence in Central and South Asia

Is It Increasing?

John W. Garver

Has China's relative influence in Central and South Asia increased since 1978? If so, to what extent? How have the major shifts in the international system since 1978—the breakup of the USSR in 1991 and the U.S. response to the September 11, 2001, attacks—affected China's relative influence? These are the questions addressed by this chapter.[1]

No attempt will be made to evaluate the ends for which Chinese influence has been used. The focus, rather, will be on the instruments of Chinese influence—on the things that China has done that give it the ability to influence developments in Central and South Asia, or which might give China's leaders that ability. Influence is always relative, however, so China's capabilities in these two regions must be compared to those of other state actors.

THE STRUCTURAL UPHEAVAL OF 1991

An obvious but extremely important point is that the breakup of the USSR and the resulting establishment of a number of sovereign, independent states in Central Asia greatly increased China's relative influence in that region. Each of the five post-Soviet Central Asian states possessed capabilities relative to China far inferior to those possessed by the former USSR. Instead of one powerful state actor, China now faced five far weaker ones. In terms of relative influence, the upheaval of 1991 was a windfall for China.

Moreover, the new Central Asian states desired expanded relations with China as an alternative to complete dependence on the Russian Federation, the USSR's successor state and the dominant extraregional power in Central Asia, at least until September 11. Although the leaders of the new Central Asian states felt comfortable with familiar Russian leaders and methods, and although the Central Asian states had not wrested independence from reluctant Russian/Soviet leaders, the Central Asian states nonetheless began groping for increased room for maneuver from Russia. China quickly came into view in this regard. China offered attractive economic opportunities for the new Central Asian states. As early as June 1992, China's premier Li Peng convened a meeting of provincial leaders from China's northwest and urged them to seize the opportunity to expand economic cooperation with the new Central Asian states.[2] This expanded economic cooperation between China and Central Asia depended on the development of physical infrastructure.

GROWTH OF CHINA'S TRANSPORT LINKS WITH CENTRAL AND SOUTH ASIA

Transport links being built between Xinjiang province and Central Asia will significantly increase China's influence in that region. In 1984 China and the Soviet Union agreed to build the first railroad directly linking Xinjiang and Soviet Central Asia. This project was expanded in scope after Mikhail Gorbachev took power and he and Deng Xiaoping strove to expand Sino-Soviet economic cooperation. In 1990 the rail line between Urumqi, Xinjiang, and Aqtoghay, Kazakhstan, opened. The next year it was upgraded to a Eurasian land bridge. Computer systems were introduced to control the movement of trains, and facilities were built at the border to change the wheels on rail carriages an entire train at a time. The rail line between Lanzhou and Urumqi was also double-tracked.[3]

During the Fifth Five-Year Plan (1996–2000), a rail line was pushed south along the west edge of the Tarim desert to Kashgar. That line, called the South Xinjiang railway, was opened in 1999. As construction of the South Xinjiang line progressed, Beijing lobbied the Asian Development Bank (ADB) for support for a rail line running westward from Kashgar through Kyrgyzstan to link up with the Soviet-era Central Asian rail net at Tashkent, capital of Uzbekistan. China and Kyrgyzstan disagreed about the best route for such a line, although both proposed routes linked up with existing rail lines at Andijan, Uzbekistan.[4] China has also proposed to the ADB construction of a "North Xinjiang railway" diverging from the Urumqi-Aqtoghay line at Jinghe and proceeding southwest to Almaty. This would have the advantage of paralleling the Urumqi-Tashkent truck corridor. If the line were built entirely on the Chinese gauge, the need to change wheel carriages at the border would be eliminated. This North Xinjiang railway will probably be completed before a Kashgar-Andijan line because the terrain is much less of a hindrance to construction and existing volumes of commerce are much higher. The various transportation links between Xinjiang and Central Asia are illustrated by map 1.

Highway links between Xinjiang and Central Asia improved rapidly after 1991. By 1999 there were five hard-surfaced roads crossing between Xin-

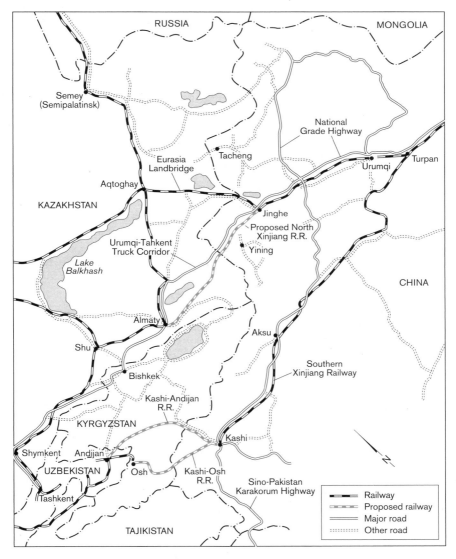

MAP 1. Development of transport links between Western Xinjiang and Central Asia.

jiang and Kazakhstan.[5] A major highway linking Kashgar with Bishkek and then heading north to Almaty was also constructed.[6] China has also invested heavily in improving the Urumqi-Horgos-Almaty-Bishkek highway. According to the ADB, this road is heavily used by trucks carrying international freight and constitutes the main truck line in Central Asia. Beijing has also proposed to the ADB that improvement of the road is a high priority, ranking above improvement of existing roads from Kashgar west via either the Irkeshtam pass to Osh and Tashkent, or via Torugart pass to Bishkek.[7]

Regarding pipelines, in 1997 China and Kazakhstan agreed to construct a 3,100-kilometer pipeline from western Kazakhstan to Urumqi in association with the Chinese purchase of a $4.4 billion interest in the Aktyubinsk and Aktobe oil fields on the Caspian Sea littoral of western Kazakhstan.[8] Plans for this pipeline encountered many difficulties, however, and as of fall 2003 construction had apparently not begun. In spite of these setbacks, Beijing remains committed to the pipeline project. As of 2003 China had linked by pipeline its two western Kazakh oilfields, which will make it possible one day to pump the output of both those fields into a future pipeline to Urumqi.[9] Moreover, during the Kazakh-China summit in June 2003, the two countries signed an agreement to proceed with the construction of the pipeline once conditions are propitious. The Joint Declaration on Cooperation signed by Presidents Hu Jintao and Nazarbayev during that summit stipulated that the two sides will "continue the feasibility studies on the PRC-Kazakhstan oil pipeline project and the related oilfield development project. . . . Kazakhstan supports China's participation in prospecting and developing the oilfields in the seabed of the Caspian Sea in Kazakhstan."[10] It appears, however, that the Aktyubinsk-Urumqi pipeline is a long-term project, and it will not be realized for a number of years.

In accord with the precept that all influence is relative, it is necessary to compare lines of communication between China and Central Asia with westward-running lines inherited from the Soviet era, when "all roads led to Moscow." In contrast to the two railways connecting China and Central Asia (the Eurasian land bridge and the North Xinjiang railway—that will probably soon be built), there are twenty-two rail lines crossing between Kazakhstan and the Russian Federation.[11] In contrast to the absence of any direct rail connection between Kyrgyzstan and China, there four rail lines linking Kyrgyzstan to the west (one from Bishkek via Kazakhstan, and three via Uzbekistan's Andijan, although the latter three lines terminate very short distances inside Kyrgyzstan's borders).[12] Uzbekistan has two railway trunk lines linking it with Russia to the west and three linking it with Turkistan to the south, with two of the latter three lines leading further south to Iran. In terms of roads, there are twenty-three border crossing points between Kazakhstan and Russia, compared to the four between China and Kazakhstan.[13] Regarding Kyrgyzstan, eleven roads link that country with its western Central Asian neighbors, while two roads link it with China.[14] In contrast with the one Kazakhstan-Xinjiang pipeline under construction, there are already four pipelines running from Kazakhstan to Russia.[15] Completion of the U.S.-supported line running southwest from Baku on the Caspian Sea via Azerbaijan and Georgia to Turkey's Mediterranean port of Ceyhan would also balance a Kazakh-China pipeline.

The conclusion is clear. While China is improving the infrastructural basis for its presence in Central Asia, it has a long way to go before it becomes the major transportation presence in the region. Lines of communication westward and northward from Central Asia are still far more robust than lines running eastward to China. This legacy of a century of Russian and Soviet imperial policy is changing, but only very slowly. These transportation facts are closely linked to the dominance of Russia and European countries in Central Asian trade—a matter discussed below. To foreshadow the argument presented in that section, the European Union countries have been able to exploit Soviet-era lines of transportation to expand their trade with post-Soviet Central Asia.

Turning to South Asia, China has undertaken three very large-scale infrastructural projects since 1978 that will, when complete, qualitatively boost its capabilities to move goods and people to and from South Asia. These three projects are:

1. The Irrawaddy Corridor in Myanmar
2. The Sino-Pakistan Friendship Highway–Gwadar Project in Pakistan
3. The Qinghai-Tibet railway to Lhasa

The general alignment and spatial relationship of these three projects is depicted in map 2. This map is inverted, that is, south is at the top, in order to lessen the perceptual bias that accustoms us to seeing South Asia at the bottom. Seen from a more unusual perspective, it becomes clearer that, from China's point of view, South Asia constitutes a littoral giving its westernmost regions access to the high-seas highways of the global economy.

Taken together, these three projects constitute a major augmentation of China's transportation infrastructure with South Asia, resulting in a significant increase in China's ability to move cargo and people to and from South Asia. India's response to these developments—perhaps the most important political issue related to the projects—is discussed later in this chapter.

CENTRAL ASIA AND 9/11

The vigorous response of the United States to the attacks of September 11, 2001, produced a second upheaval for Central Asia nearly as fundamental, though perhaps not as long lasting, as that of 1991. The 9/11 upheaval brought the United States into Central Asia as a major political-military

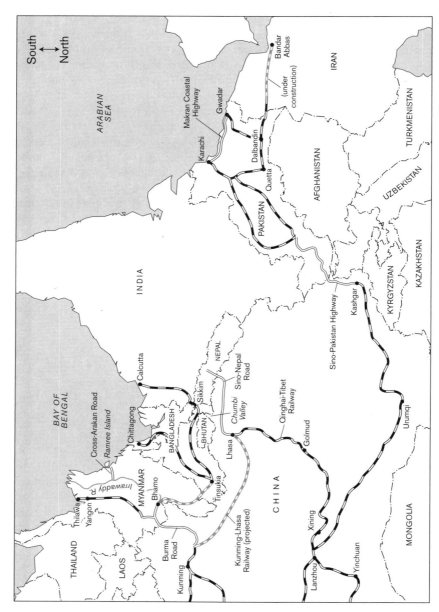

MAP 2. Expansion of China's transportation infrastructure links with South Asia.

player, thereby marking a major setback for China's relative influence in Central Asia.

From 1991 to 2001, Russia and China were the leading extra–Central Asia players in the rivalry for political and military influence in that region. After 1991 Turkey, Iran, Saudi Arabia, Pakistan, the Gulf States, India, the United States, Japan, and the European countries all established diplomatic relations with, and began trading with, the new Central Asian states. The Islamic countries tapped into the revival of Islam across the region, sending missionaries, advisors, and money in a search for converts to their own brand of Islam.[16] The economic role of Europe and the United States became quite significant. The United States and its Western allies (the EU countries and Turkey) also pushed to involve the new Central Asian states in Western military organizations, including NATO's Partnership for Peace, joint peacekeeping operations under the U.S. Central Command, and the U.S. Army's Marshall Center in Germany. These Western security activities, however, were basically an effort to prevent the region from coming under Russian domination once again, and were dwarfed by Russia's continuing security role in the region.[17]

Both China and Russia are faced with Islamic terrorist and / or secessionist movements within their boundaries. Both realized the transnational character of these movements and the need for international cooperation in their suppression. Both Beijing and Moscow looked favorably on the secular, postcommunist states of Central Asia, and saw them as more sympathetic to Chinese and Russian perspectives than either Western-linked or Islamicist states would be. For these reasons Beijing and Moscow began cooperating with the new Central Asian states to deal with these security threats. Common concern with Islamic fundamentalism was a central factor inspiring formation of the Shanghai Five (Russia, China, Kazakhstan, Kyrgyzstan, and Tajikistan) in June 1996. The concerns of Russia, China, and the Central Asian states about Islamic fundamentalism mounted in 1999, when jihad activity increased dramatically in Uzbekistan and Kyrgyzstan. Cooperation between Russia, the Central Asian states, and China intensified further. A number of measures were intended to counteract the growing Islamic threat: conclusion of the Commonwealth of Independent States Collective Security Treaty in June 2000 with a joint antiterrorist center and a rapid-reaction force in Kyrgyzstan, and the establishment in June 2001 of the Shanghai Cooperative Organization with a permanent secretariat in Shanghai.[18] Areas of cooperation between Russia, China, and the Central Asian states under these arrangements and prior to 9/11 included: exchange of intelligence about fundamentalist activities; arrests, extradition, and suppression of groups objectionable to other friendly states; strict control of borders and inspection for subversive activities; and supply of technology and training useful for internal security purposes. In 2000 and

2001 Beijing gave military and technical assistance (sniper rifles and other equipment and supplies for border guards) worth $1.3 million each to Kyrgyzstan and Uzbekistan. China also funded the construction of bunkers for Kyrgyz border guards and flew in flak jackets, night vision goggles, and sniper rifles for Kyrgyz and Uzbek border guards.[19]

A key factor that enabled the Russian-Chinese condominium in Central Asia prior to September 2001 was American disinterest in playing a major security, military, or even political role in the region. Until 9/11, successive governments in Washington deemed Central Asia outside the strategic interests of the United States.[20] That changed abruptly with 9/11, after which the United States began to play a major security and military role in Central Asia for the first time. Washington swiftly sought and secured permission from Central Asian governments to base U.S. forces in Uzbekistan, Tajikistan, and Kyrgyzstan for purposes of combat operations in Afghanistan, to overfly national airspace, and to operate air bases in Kazakhstan and Turkmenistan. In October 2001 Washington concluded a classified agreement providing for a long-term strategic and security partnership between the United States and Uzbekistan.[21] High-level U.S. officials also increasingly visited Central Asia for the purposes of coalition building, improved coordination with CENTCOM, intelligence sharing, and increased assistance.[22] U.S. assistance to the Central Asian countries also increased dramatically, from a total of $244 million in fiscal year 2001 to $408 million in 2002.[23] In Afghanistan the dramatic demonstration of the efficacy of U.S. military power in ending in a period of eight weeks the Taliban scourge that had plagued the Central Asian countries for years demonstrated the efficacy of U.S. military power. The United States was able and willing to provide generously for military cooperation. Cooperation with the United States yielded greater ancillary benefits than did cooperation with China or Russia; Washington simply had more money to give, plus more potent and flexible military power. As a consequence of these factors, the United States quickly became the favored security partner, and the major security actor, in post–September 11 Central Asia—except in Tajikistan, where Russian troops still guarded the southern border with Afghanistan. The Central Asian countries did not, of course, abandon cooperation with China, which remained very important in dealing with these challenges, but the relative role of China diminished.

As the importance of the United States increased, China struggled to maintain its hard-won political influence in the region. In 2002 the Chinese agreed to provide aid to Kazakhstan worth $3 million (compared to U.S. aid of $82 million) and to Kyrgyzstan worth $1.2 million (compared to U.S. aid of $50 million).[24] President Jiang Zemin undertook a "major diplomatic move," according to foreign minister Tang Jiaxuan, by holding bilateral meetings with all Shanghai Cooperation Organization (SCO) heads of state during the SCO summit meeting in St. Petersburg in early 2002.[25] In October 2002 the PLA conducted its "first ever" exercise with the armed forces of another country. The two-day exercise with Kyrgyzstan took place along their common border, under the framework of the SCO, and was designed so that the PLA could practice dealing with a hypothetical terrorist threat.[26] A year later, in August 2003, China, Kazakhstan, Kyrgyzstan, and Russia undertook antiterrorist military exercises. Chinese troops were not mixed with those of the other countries, but they practiced releasing hostages and destroying terrorist bases on the Chinese side of the border.[27]

In October 2002 China also initiated an unprecedented dialogue with NATO to discuss, inter alia, NATO activities in Central Asia.[28] All of these Chinese military activities were efforts to limit the erosion of China's position in Central Asia. The real question in Chinese minds was how preeminent the U.S. role in Central Asia would become, and how long that U.S. preeminence would last. Chinese officials repeatedly expressed their expectation that the U.S. military presence in Central Asia would not be permanent.[29] Viewed from the perspective of this chapter's central concern, a decrease in the U.S. presence in Central Asia is a precondition for the growth of China's relative influence in that region.

China's Relative Economic Role in Central Asia

China's trade with Kazakhstan, Kyrgyzstan, and Uzbekistan has grown rapidly since 1978, as shown by figures 1–3. While China's trade importance relative to all the Central Asian countries has increased, and while Russia's role has generally declined, Russia is still a far more important trading partner than China. Moreover, it is the European Union countries that have accomplished the largest and most rapid growth of trade with the new Central Asian countries. The broad picture is that as Central Asia moves out of Russia's economic orbit, it is moving into the Western economic sphere, and not China's.

SOUTH ASIA AND 9/11: DID U.S.-PAKISTAN REENGAGEMENT WEAKEN CHINA'S INFLUENCE WITH PAKISTAN?

Since 1964 Pakistan has been China's closest strategic partner in South Asia. Assuming, then, the great importance of Beijing's link to Islamabad for China's overall position of influence in South Asia, what has been the impact on that link of U.S. reengagement with Pakistan since 9/11? Has restored U.S.-Pakistan strategic cooperation diminished China's influence with Pakistan, and thus China's overall influence in South Asia?

To begin with, there is considerable evidence that China's representatives encouraged Pakistan to cooperate with the United States at that critical juncture. Official statements from China quickly endorsed President's

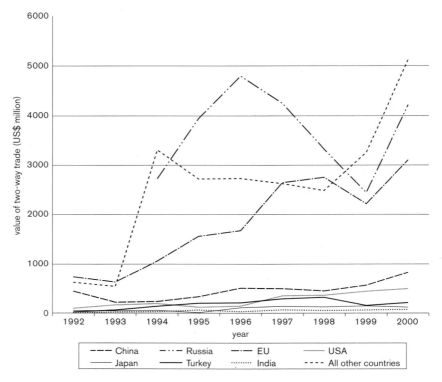

FIGURE 1. Kazakhstan foreign trade trends, 1992–2000.

Musharraf's decision to cooperate with the United States, and Beijing urged Islamabad to cooperate with the United States and dispatched Vice Foreign Minister Wang Yi to Islamabad within one week of 9/11 for this purpose. Western academics in Beijing at the time were also told by Chinese officials and analysts that China supported Pakistan's new tact.[30]

The events of 2001 are merely the most recent example of Chinese acceptance of U.S. support for Pakistan. There had been two previous instances of this phenomenon: at the Bandung Afro-Asian conference in 1955, when Zhou Enlai was understanding of Pakistan's recent decision to ally with the United States, ostensibly against communist China;[31] and in 1980, when Beijing approved renewed Pakistan-U.S. strategic cooperation in the aftermath of the Soviet invasion of Afghanistan.[32] In all three cases, China's fundamental interests in South Asia explain, I believe, Beijing's support for Pakistan's engagement with the United States. China's basic geopolitical interest in Pakistan and South Asia is to keep Pakistan strong enough

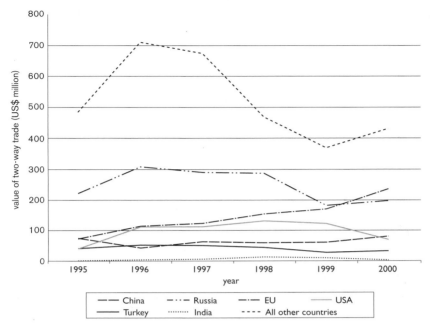

FIGURE 2. Kyrgyzstan foreign trade trends, 1995–2000.

and confident enough to continue serving as a counterweight to India. A strong, independent-minded Pakistan forces India to divide its military strength between two fronts (Pakistan and China), keeps Indian attention focused on South Asian issues, and hobbles India whenever it attempts to act on the global stage as China's equal. Simultaneously, however, China has sought to forge improved relations with India, even though Chinese assistance for the development of Pakistan's military-industrial capabilities (such as the current Gwadar project) has constituted a perennial stumbling block to Sino-Indian rapprochement. U.S. support for Pakistan serves both Chinese purposes: it helps keep Pakistan strong while simultaneously dissipating Indian anger at Chinese support for Pakistan by directing at least some of that anger toward Washington. These interests underlie a recurring pattern of Chinese acceptance of U.S. support for Pakistan. At a geopolitical level, then, China's influence in South Asia was not diminished by U.S.-Pakistan reengagement. In fact, that reengagement helped sustain a fundamental condition for China's position of influence in South Asia.

Might China's leaders worry that Pakistan will drift away from its close partnership with China as a result of a renewed strategic partnership with

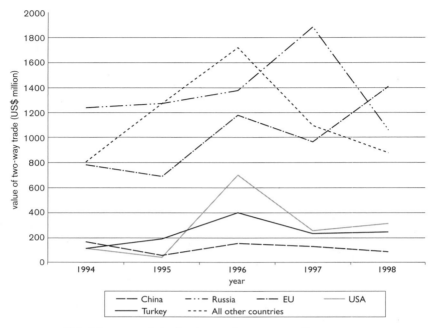

FIGURE 3. Uzbekistan trends in foreign trade, 1994–1998.

the United States? Press commentary in Pakistan has occasionally suggested such apprehensions.[33] This analyst's sense is that although China's leaders may have anxieties about a possible Pakistani defection, this concern is off-set by a deep underlying trust. Pakistan's long partnership with China has served Pakistan very well, or at least there seems to be a consensus to this effect in Pakistan. There is also a corresponding perception in Pakistan that the United States is unreliable. While China has stood by Pakistan during all sorts of circumstances, there is a sense that the United States "abandoned" Pakistan in 1965, again in the mid-1970s, and yet again in 1990. This per-ception of Chinese reliability juxtaposed to American unreliability makes it unlikely that the Pakistan leadership would choose to draw away from a strategic partnership with China.

This is not to say that Beijing has not had to increase its support for Pak-istan to counter increased U.S. aid to Pakistan. To some extent China's gen-erous assistance to Pakistan's Gwadar and railway modernization projects after 9/11 was informed by a desire to demonstrate that China's generosity and economic capabilities were comparable to those of the United States. To a degree, it does make sense to say that post–9/11 Beijing faces increased

TABLE 23. PLA Navy Ship Visits to Indian Ocean Ports

Date	Port visited	Composition of squadron
November 1985–Jan. 1986	Karachi, Colombo, Chittagong	3,500-ton Luda destroyer, 7,500-ton replenishment ship
November 1993	Bombay, Chittagong	4,500-ton training ship
March 1997	Lumut	guided missile destroyer, guided missile frigate
July–August 2000	Kelang, Dar es Salaam, Simonstown	guided missile destroyer, replenishment ship
March 2001	Sittwe	submarine
May 2001	Karachi, Bombay	guided missile destroyer, replenishment ship

U.S. competition for influence in Islamabad. Beijing has been willing to pay the premiums in that competition, however, and it has not lost out to Washington. And U.S. engagement with Pakistan helps maintain the very basis of China's position of influence in South Asia: a balance of power constraining India.

China's Naval Presence and Potential Military Capabilities in South Asia

China has steadily expanded its naval presence in the Indian Ocean since 1978. PLA Navy warships made their first-ever visits to foreign ports—Karachi, Columbo, and Chittagong, all in the Indian Ocean—from November 1985 to January 1986. As indicated by table 23, subsequent port calls around the Indian Ocean littoral continued at a slow but steady pace.

This increasing Chinese naval activity was paralleled by robust Chinese involvement in the expansion and modernization of Myanmar's maritime and overland transportation infrastructure, plus development of a military-strategic partnership with Yangon. China's strategic partnership with Pakistan remained strong, and the transport links between Xinjiang and Pakistan grew steadily better. This raises the possibility that Chinese-supported dual-use infrastructure in Myanmar and Pakistan might in the future be used to support PLA Navy operations in the Bay of Bengal and the Arabian Sea, that is, on either flank of India. This scenario has not yet occurred, but the physical prerequisites for its realization have been, and are being, put into place.

Viewed in relative terms, China's growing naval presence in the Indian Ocean pales in comparison to that of the United States Navy or even the far smaller Indian Navy. U.S. naval activity in the Indian Ocean began growing at about the same time as China's. The Iranian revolution of early 1979 followed by the Soviet invasion of Afghanistan at the end of the same year forced a basic reorientation of U.S. policy toward the Persian Gulf and the Indian Ocean region. Although U.S. leaders had recognized since 1940 the vital importance of the rich oil resources of the Gulf region, they had preferred to rely on other powers to protect access to those resources. Prior to London's 1968 decision to withdraw militarily from "east of Suez," the preferred proxy power was Britain. After Britain's withdrawal, the Nixon administration looked to Iran under the Pahlavi dynasty. The events of 1979 forced the U.S. to itself assume for the first time responsibility for the security of access to Persian Gulf resources, which it did reluctantly. The Carter administration thought through this problem in 1979–80, reoriented U.S. policy, and began building requisite U.S. military capabilities in the region. This U.S. military buildup was accelerated under the Reagan administration. By 1987, when Iran began attacking tankers carrying oil through the Persian Gulf as part of its bitter war with Iraq, the United States had in place in the Indian Ocean powerful military capabilities.

Compared with these powerful U.S. military capabilities, the post-1984 expansion of China's naval forces in the Indian Ocean was extremely modest. In 1985, the year a PLA Navy squadron first visited the Indian Ocean, for instance, U.S. aircraft carriers, with their powerful accompanying battle groups, accumulated 475 ship days of duty in that ocean. Total surface ship days accumulated by the U.S. Navy in the Indian Ocean in 1985 numbered 5,236.[34] The latter number contrasted with the 110 ship days—only 2.1 percent of the U.S. Navy total—accumulated by the two-ship PLA Navy squadron in the Indian Ocean between November 16, 1985, and January 9, 1986.

CHINA'S PARTNERSHIP WITH MYANMAR (BURMA)

While, strictly speaking, Myanmar is a Southeast Asian—not South Asian—nation, Sino-Burmese relations still merit consideration here. The formation of a political-military partnership with Myanmar in the 1990s represented a significant advance for China's position at the eastern flank of South Asia. After Myanmar's post–Ne Win junta (which seized power from the ailing dictator in 1988, and then proceeded to repress a large prodemocracy movement) became the target of U.S., European, and Japanese sanctions as well as criticism by India and Southeast Asian, China stepped in to fill the vacuum. Beijing defended Yangon in international forums, and provided it with military equipment and training, trade, investment, and generous developmental aid (much of it tied to the transportation projects mentioned earlier). Trade with China flourished and investment from China flooded into Myanmar as Western economic interest in Myanmar evaporated. Myanmar's new rulers scrapped the policies of economic statism and isolation that Ne Win had long enforced, and Chinese businessmen rushed into newly opened areas unfettered by U.S., Japanese, or European competition. Foreign hostility convinced Myanmar's new rulers that a major military expansion and modernization effort was required, and China became Yangon's partner in that effort. Beijing also helped Yangon end the Burma Communist Party (BCP) insurrection and several ethnic rebellions that had plagued Burma's central government since independence in 1947.

Myanmar's post-1988 alignment with China was to some degree a marriage of convenience. Nonetheless, Beijing demonstrated to Myanmar's rulers China's willingness to work cooperatively and its ability to deal effectively with major problems identified by Myanmar's government. This translated into a Burmese willingness to cooperate with China in ways conducive to the further expansion of Chinese power in South Asia. The construction of road, rail, and maritime links, and the joint naval intelligence activities conducted by China and Myanmar discussed earlier, were the fruits of Myanmar's willingness to cooperate with China. This willingness, combined with the potential military use of Chinese-supported transport and maritime projects in Myanmar, suggest a significant enhancement of Chinese military potential in the Bay of Bengal region.

Yet there are several reasons to conclude that China's entente with Myanmar is fragile. First, the Burmese (referring here to the ethnic Burmese who inhabit the central valley of Burma, not the non-Burmese minorities who dwell in the mountainous fringes of that valley) are intensely nationalistic and suspicious of China. As noted by Wang Gungwu in the previous chapter, Burma's national consciousness, like Vietnam's, has been deeply influenced by a history of national resistance to Chinese invaders. Chinese support for the BCP rebellion during the Maoist era reinforced these fears—as has the flood of Chinese immigrants and investment into northern Myanmar since 1988. Under certain conditions, this popular anti-China sentiment could easily be roused. There is nothing comparable to this popular anti-China animus in Pakistan, China's other strategic partner in South Asia.

A second vulnerability *might* arise from Beijing's close association with Myanmar's post-1988 military junta. Were the democracy movement led by Aung San Suu Kyi to take power in Yangon, Beijing might bear the onus of its earlier support for dictatorship. Beijing would certainly press for continued Sino-Myanmar partnership regardless of regime changes in either country. Beijing's model would be its relationship with Pakistan, which has been characterized by continued cooperation despite repeated changes from military to civilian rule and back again. Beijing would stress its willingness to cooperate with any Myanmar government and attempt to demonstrate the utility of such cooperation to whatever government ruled in Yangon. Yet such an approach might not work. Unlike Sino-Pakistan relations, which are bolstered by both countries' fear of India, the relationship between China and Myanmar is not supported by a fundamental convergence of geostrategic interests. Popular anti-China sentiments could easily push a democratic Yangon government to distance itself from Beijing.

A third vulnerability is that the Sino-Myanmar partnership is, to a significant degree, a function of Yangon's isolation. Yangon turned to China in the face of Western pressure and general international isolation. India and ASEAN soon realized this, and both began working to improve ties with Yangon to check still closer China-Myanmar links. Were an international solution to Myanmar's domestic deadlock (pitting the army against the democracy movement) to be found, U.S., European, and Japanese assistance to Myanmar could well be restored. The government in Yangon might then find that these Western nations could simply offer Myanmar more than China in the way of capital, technology, and market access.

Finally, and perhaps most importantly, it is difficult to see what Myanmar would gain by entering an active military alliance with China, perhaps by allowing PLA forces to conduct operations in the Indian Ocean from Myanmar territory. Yangon's military rulers did fear U.S. and Indian military intervention in 1989, and this fear was instrumental in pushing Yangon toward Beijing, but that fear seems to have passed. If this is indeed the case, it is difficult to see what benefits Yangon might receive from an alliance with China that would be adequate to offset the significant risks and costs of such an alliance. Myanmar significantly departed from its traditional neutralism in 1988, but fear of having Burmese "grass" trampled by two fighting "elephants" is still part of Burma's culture. What power might Myanmar fear deeply enough for its rulers to subject their nation to the dangers of genuine alliance with China? Again, a comparison with the Pakistan-China relationship is germane: the entente between those two powers is premised on a common fear of India. In the case of Myanmar and China there is no common foe that might underpin a genuine military alliance. In the absence of such a foe, the costs associated with such an alliance would be unlikely to outweigh the costs to Myanmar.

In sum, although China has significantly enhanced its position in South Asia via partnership with Myanmar since 1988, that partnership may well rest on fragile foundations.

CHINA'S INFLUENCE WITH INDIA

Assuming that India is the preeminent political, economic, and military power in South Asia, China's ability to work constructively with India is central to China's overall influence in that region. Strong Indian opposition to Chinese policies would make it more difficult for China to achieve its goals, while Indian nonopposition, or even active cooperation with China, would facilitate China's achievement of its objectives. We can think of India's relationship to Chinese influence in South Asia as a continuum, depicted below. At one extreme would be intense Indian opposition to virtually any Chinese move in South Asia. At the other extreme would be Indian cooperation with China as an ally, with India using its own influence to help China achieve its goals in South Asia. From Beijing's perspective, the purpose of Sino-Indian rapprochement is to move India as far as possible toward the positive end of this continuum.

Negative	*Positive*
Inveterate and intense Indian opposition to Chinese moves in South Asia	Indian cooperation with China as an ally in the South Asia region

If New Delhi could be persuaded to facilitate the accomplishment of Chinese goals, Beijing's position would be much enhanced. For example, the construction of an extension of the Lhasa rail line through the Chumbi Valley to link up with Bangladesh's rail system, or the extension to Chittagong of a Kunming-Bhamo railway, is feasible only if New Delhi could be persuaded to agree to them. Or, if India could be persuaded to look upon the presence of the PLA Navy in the Indian Ocean as advantageous to Indian security by restraining an aggressive U.S. Navy that would otherwise threaten India, China's naval presence in the Indian Ocean could expand more freely. On the other hand, if India used its very considerable leverage with Bangladesh, Sri Lanka, or other South Asian countries to pressure those countries to abstain from cooperation with PLA Navy activities, the expansion of such activities would become far more difficult.

Viewed from the standpoint of this continuum, China's position in South Asia improved considerably between 1978 and 2003. In 1978 Sino-Indian relations were still quite tense. Although ambassadorial relations had been restored in 1976, substantive improvement of Sino-Indian relations did not begin until Prime Minister Rajiv Gandhi's visit to Beijing in late 1988. Over the next fifteen years there was considerable progress in Sino-Indian rapprochement. By the time of Prime Minister A. B. Vajpayee's landmark visit to China in June 2003, the two sides were able to issue a Joint Declaration of Principles that proclaimed that "the common interests of the two sides outweigh their differences."[35]

Beijing was able to accomplish the post-1988 rapprochement with India without diminishing China's position in South Asia. Most importantly, Beijing was able to persuade India to move forward with Sino-Indian rapprochement while maintaining China's close strategic partnership with Pakistan. Improvement of Sino-Indian relations paralleled continued Chinese assistance to Pakistan's efforts to augment its national capabilities. At the time of Prime Minister Gandhi's 1988 visit, China was providing assistance to Pakistan's missile and nuclear weapons programs. As Sino-Indian rapprochement progressed in the 1990s, China's assistance to Pakistan's missile and aircraft development programs continued unabated.[36] China suspended its covert assistance to Pakistan's nuclear weapons program in the early 1990s, but it insisted on continuing its cooperation with Pakistan's "civilian" nuclear programs. The Gwadar project is the most recent example of this uncoupling of Sino-Indian rapprochement and Sino-Pakistan entente. Between 2001 and 2003 China committed approximately $2 billion to develop Gwadar harbor and modernize Pakistan's railway system. Creating "strategic depth" for Pakistan in the event of a war with India was a major reason why Pakistan's leaders decided to begin the Gwadar project in 2001,[37] while modernization of Pakistan's railways would considerably increase that country's war-fighting capabilities in the event of another India-Pakistan war. Yet in spite of this, India's leaders moved forward with Sino-Indian rapprochement. One cannot say that Beijing's insistence on continuing strategic entente with Pakistan has had no effect on Sino-Indian rapprochement. It *has* had the effect of slowing down the development of that rapprochement, but it is indisputable that continuing Sino-Pakistan strategic partnership has not prevented Sino-Indian rapprochement.

In an act of diplomatic jujitsu, China has been able to transform a potential diplomatic liability into leverage with India. Pakistan's continuing strength, due in no small part to China's assistance, and periodic confrontations between Indian and Pakistan, suggesting the prospect of another major India-Pakistan war, have lead to Indian leaders' concern about China's possible role in the event of such a war. Indian leaders have generally seen improved relations with China as a way of diminishing China's support for Pakistan in the event of another India-Pakistan war. In this way, China's continuing strategic support for Pakistan has been transformed into leverage, not obstructing further Sino-Indian rapprochement, but pushing India toward progress in that direction.

Indian strategists hope that China's improved relations with India will give Beijing greater incentive to diminish its strategic cooperation with Pakistan. China's interests will be better served, however, by insisting on developing friendly, cooperative ties in all areas, including military and security areas, with all countries of South Asia ("multifaceted" is the diplomatic euphemism used to describe cooperation that includes the military sort). China's strategic cooperation with Pakistan should continue, even while China and India develop strategic and military cooperation. Since 1978, Beijing has gone a considerable distance in securing India's acceptance of this line.

Beijing has used both negative and positive incentives to persuade New Delhi to accept China's line regarding China-Pakistan-India relations. The key negative leverage has been to ensure that India has a sober appreciation of China's military power. The positive incentives have been an emphasis on two themes continually stressed in Chinese propaganda directed toward India and that have great appeal to the Indian elite: third-world identity and suspicion of the United States. According to China's pitch to India, the United States is an arrogant hegemonic power threatening to both China and India and, indeed, to the rest of the world. Washington relies on power politics and bullying, and arrogates to itself the right to ignore principles of state sovereignty, interfering in the internal affairs of other states. Kosovo in 1999 and Iraq in 2003 are offered as examples. India and China should stand together to restrain U.S. unipolar, unilateralist, hegemonic behavior. This line is less effective than the third-world identity, but both have substantial appeal in India. Together these propaganda themes have contributed significantly to the success of China's efforts to forge multifaceted, cooperative relations with all the countries of South Asia.

The evolution of India's position in the South Asian power equation has not been entirely in China's favor. The most adverse development for Beijing has been the formation of an India-U.S. strategic partnership late in the second Clinton administration, and the expansion of that partnership to the military and security areas since the Bush administration took office in early 2001.[38] The beginning of India-U.S. military cooperation and the formation of a strategic partnership between those two countries has greatly strengthened India's bargaining position with Beijing. With U.S. backing, India will be more confident of its ability to resist Chinese demands and to press Indian demands on Beijing. Beijing is deeply apprehensive of India working with various U.S.-concocted "anti-China schemes," and may become more willing to make concessions to New Delhi to keep it out of closer alignment with Washington. Fortunately for Beijing, the loss represented by U.S.-Indian engagement is offset by new tensions in India-U.S. relations resulting from Washington's post–9/11 reengagement with Pakistan.

CONCLUSION: THE RISE OF CHINA AND THE
RISE OF WESTERN UNIPOLARITY

China's ability to influence events in Central Asia increased dramatically with the replacement in 1991 of a single state actor by five smaller, weaker state actors. Several of those five new actors, as well as Russia, found reason to seek Chinese cooperation in various fields. China also improved the transportation structure linking it to Central Asia, thereby diminishing the tyranny of distance that had determined China's relations with Central Asia for centuries. Economically, however, China's gains were far less impressive.

China's trade with the new Central Asian countries expanded while that of Russia generally declined. But it was the European countries, not China, that were becoming the dominant new trading partners of the region. The European countries, like China, had played virtually no role in Soviet-era Central Asia. But it was European economic prowess, not China's, that drew post-Soviet Central Asia into its orbit.

Then, after 9/11, the relatively influential political position that Beijing had carefully constructed over the previous decade was swept away. Central Asia was transformed overnight from an area of peripheral U.S. concern to the front line in the war on international terrorism. U.S. military, economic, technological, and political capabilities offered far more to the Central Asian states than they could hope to obtain from China. China was quickly pushed into a marginal role in Central Asia and struggled to avoid being reduced to irrelevance in the region

In South Asia, China's influence has grown in several ways since 1978. Construction of modern transportation links between Yunnan and Myanmar has substantially boosted China's capabilities. Completion in 1999 of the South Xinjiang railway to Kashgar—now the new railhead of the Sino-Pakistan Karakorum Highway—did so as well, and combined with completion of the Gwadar harbor and modernization of Pakistan's railway network, it will further increase China's ability to move goods and people to and from South Asia. Completion of the Xining-Lhasa railway in 2006 and of the Dali-Lhasa rail line perhaps in the 2010s will strengthen China's overland links with South Asia further still. In short, China is developing robust overland transport links with the Indian Ocean littoral that are unprecedented.

Economically, China's position in South Asia is far less impressive. China's trade with Bangladesh has increased only marginally, while European and U.S. trade have grown far more rapidly. China's trade role with Myanmar has been more impressive, but it is still surpassed by Thailand's and dwarfed by Singapore's. Politically, China has engineered a significant improvement of relations with India, thereby marginally reducing Indian opposition to Chinese moves in South Asia. Moreover, Beijing has been able to accomplish this without weakening its strategic support for Pakistan that focuses India's attention to its west. China has also expanded its military presence in the Indian Ocean region, deploying its warships to the area with increasing frequency since its first port calls in 1985. China has also developed with Myanmar a close military supply and advisory relationship, as well as a maritime intelligence cooperation relationship.

We cannot conclude from this distinct but modest growth of Chinese influence that a Sinocentric order is emerging in South Asia. India remains the overwhelmingly dominant power in the region. The large gap between Chinese and Indian capabilities may eventually alter this situation, but this event remains many decades in the future. The expansion of Chinese influence has also paled beside the expansion of Western influence. U.S. military capabilities in the Indian Ocean utterly dwarf those of China.

The broad conclusion is that while China's capabilities in Central and South Asia are growing, that growth is taking place in the shadow of the far more vigorous growth of United States and Western influence. It is often said these days that we are witnessing "the rise of China," but we are also witnessing the unchecked and even more rapid growth of U.S. global influence. After 1979 the United States built up within a very few years an extremely powerful military position in the Indian Ocean region. Then, after 9/11, Central Asia, a region in which U.S. power had never before been exercised, was drawn into the U.S. political-military sphere. These events came on top of a growing economic dominance in the Central Asian region by European allies of the United States. In the Indian Ocean region, U.S. military prowess was demonstrated repeatedly: against Iran in 1987, against Iraq in 1991 and 2003, and in Afghanistan in 2001. Compared with these powerful U.S. operations, the dozen or so visits by Chinese warships to the Indian Ocean seem insignificant. Juxtaposed with the modest improvement in Sino-Indian relations is the new Indo-U.S. strategic partnership initiated by President Bill Clinton's 2000 visit to India and advanced into the military area under the presidency of George Bush. Indo-U.S. cooperation is in many areas is far deeper than Indo-Chinese cooperation.

China is rising, but that rise is occurring in the shadow of immense and still expanding U.S. power. By coincidence, both powers pushed to expand their influence in the same regions at about the same time. That this process has not generated great friction in Sino-U.S. relations is probably due to the fact that neither the U.S. nor the PRC views Central or South Asia as a primary sphere of interest, nor has either sought to build an exclusive sphere of influence in either region. As a result, neither power has sought to exclude the other from either Central or South Asia. Both powers have sought an open international order in both regions.

NOTES

1. Central Asia is defined here as the five new sovereign states that emerged in December 1991: Kazakhstan, Kyrgyzstan, Uzbekistan, Turkmenistan, and Tajikistan. South Asia is defined as the area extending from Myanmar's eastern border westward through Pakistan and south of the crests of the Himalayan-Karakorum mountain chain. The Indian Ocean will be included here as part of South Asia since maritime capabilities in a sea very often translate into influence in adjacent continental landmasses.

2. Guangcheng Xing, "China and Central Asia: Toward a New Relationship," in *Ethnic Challenges beyond Borders: Chinese and Russian Perspectives on the Central Asian*

Conundrum, ed. Yongjin Zhang and Rouben Azizian (London: Macmillan, 1998), 32–49. Xing reviews efforts by China in the 1990s to expand cooperation with the new Central Asian states.

3. "'Oriental Express' Will Start Here," *Beijing Review*, October 5–11, 1992, 20–21.

4. Presentations by country delegations at the Asian Development Bank, First Workshop on Economic Cooperation in Central Asia: Challenges and Opportunities in Transportation, Manila, February 1998, available at http://www.adb.org.

5. All maps in this chapter were constructed by the author with data from the following maps: National Geographic Maps, "Caspian Region," May 1999, and "Afghanistan and Pakistan," December 2001; Central Intelligence Agency Maps, "Kyrgyzstan" (R00184) and "Kazakhstan" (C00217); "Zhongguo tielu jiaotong ditu" [Map of China's railway transportation] (Beijing: Zhongguo tiedao chubanshe [China railway publishing company], 1999); "Zhongguo jiaotong quantu" [Complete map of China's transportation] (Hebei: Zhongguo ditu chubanshe [China cartographic publishing company], 2004).

6. Samina Yasmeen, "Sino-Pakistan Relations and the Middle East," in *China and the Middle East: The Quest for Influence*, ed. P. R. Kumaraswamy (New Delhi: Sage Publications, 1999), 98.

7. ADB, *The 2020 Project: Policy Support in the People's Republic of China*, part II, "Strengthening the Competitiveness of the Western Region," chapter 6, "Transport Policies," available at http://www.adb.org/Documents/Reports/2020_Project/chap06.pdf.

8. David Murphy, "Asian Pipeline Politics," *Far Eastern Economic Review*, July 24, 2003, available at http://www.feer. See also Barry Rubin, "China's Mideast Strategy," in *China and the Middle East*, ed. Kumaraswamy, 112–13.

9. Michael Lelyveld, "Kazakhstan: China Seeks Oil Investment with an Eye on Pipeline," *Radio Free Europe*, March 11, 2003, available at http://www.rferl.ort/nca/features/2003/03/11032003212209.asp.

10. "'Text' of Hu Jintao–Nazarbayev Joint Declaration on Cooperation," *Xinhua*, June 3, 2003.

11. National Geographic Maps, "Caspian Region."

12. Central Intelligence Agency Maps, "Kyrgyzstan."

13. National Geographic Maps, "Caspian Region."

14. Central Intelligence Agency Maps, "Kyrgyzstan."

15. National Geographic Maps, "Caspian Region."

16. Ahmed Rashid, *Jihad: The Rise of Militant Islam in Central Asia* (New York: Penguin Books, 200).

17. Elizabeth Wishnick, *Growing U.S. Security Interests in Central Asia* (Carlisle, PA: Strategic Studies Institute, U.S. Army War College, October 2002), 10.

18. Mark A. Smith, *Russia, the USA and Central Asia* (Surrey, UK: Conflict Studies Research Centre, Royal Military Academy Sandhurst, May 2002), 2.

19. Rashid, *Jihad*, 172, 204.

20. Wishnick, *Growing U.S. Security Interests*. See also Eugene B. Rumer, "Flashman's Revenge: Central Asia after September 11," *Strategic Forum* no. 195, National Institute for Strategic Studies, National Defense University, December 2002.

21. David Stern, "Historic Pact Signed with U.S.," *Financial Times,* October 13, 2001.

22. Wishnick, *Growing U.S. Interests,* 13.

23. Smith, *Russia, the USA and Central Asia,* p. 8.

24. "Chinese Politics: China Uses Separatists to Influence Central Asia," STRATFOR, May 29, 2002, available at http://www.securities.com and cited in Wishnick, *Growing U.S. Security Interests.* The figures for the United States are from Smith, *Russia, the USA and Central Asia.*

25. *Xinhua,* June 18, 2002, FBIS-CHI-2002–0618.

26. "China, Kyrgyzstan Hold Joint Anti-Terrorism Exercise, 10–11 October," *Xinhua,* October 11, 2002.

27. Nadya Osira, Radio Free Asia, personal communication with author, August 11, 2003.

28. Jonathan Marcus, "China Seeks Dialogue with NATO," *BBC News,* November 14, 2002, available at http://news.bbc.co.uk.

29. See statements by foreign ministry spokesman on April 18 and 23, 2002, in *Beijing Review,* May 9, 2002, 15, and statements made on March 11, 2003, in *Renmin ribao,* overseas edition, March 12, 2003, 1.

30. This author happened to be part of a delegation visiting various Chinese think tanks in Beijing when the Anglo-American offensive against the Taliban began. The unanimous response to a half-dozen queries about Pakistan's new foreign policy orientation was approval and endorsement of Pakistan's approach.

31. Regarding the Sino-Pakistan understanding at Bandung regarding Pakistan's alliance with the United States, see Anwar H. Syed, *China and Pakistan: Diplomacy of an Entente Cordiale* (Amherst: University of Massachusetts Press, 1974), 61–62.

32. Regarding the reorientation of U.S. policy in 1980, including the renewal of U.S.-Pakistan cooperation, see, Zbigniew Brzezinski, *Power and Principle: Memoirs of the National Security Advisor, 1977–1981* (New York: Farrar, Straus and Giroux, 1985), 426–69.

33. A report in *The Nation of Islamabad* in March 2003 during Jamali's visit to China stated, for example, that China was "not entirely comfortable" with the presence of U.S. troops in the region and that Pakistan "had been careful to take China into confidence on the issue." "Pakistani Daily Highlights Importance of Jamali's Visit to China," *The Nation of Islamabad* (Lahore edition), March 24, 2003.

34. Michael A. Palmer, *Guardians of the Gulf: A History of America's Expanding Role in the Persian Gulf, 1833–1992* (New York: Free Press, 1992), 107.

35. "Comparative Version of Full Text of Sino-Indian Declaration on Bilateral Ties," *Xinhua,* June 24, 2003.

36. John W. Garver, "The Future of the Sino-Pakistan Entente," in *South Asia in 2020: Future Strategic Balances and Alliances,* ed. Michael K. Chambers (Carlisle, PA: Strategic Studies Institute, U.S. Army War College, November 2002), 385–447.

37. John W. Garver, "The Security Dilemma in Sino-Indian Relations," *India Review* 1, no. 4 (October 2002): 1–38.

38. John W. Garver, *The China-India-U.S. Triangle: Strategic Relations in the Post-Cold War Era* (Seattle: NBR Analysis 13, no. 5, October 2002).

10

China and Russia

Normalizing Their Strategic Partnership

Yu Bin

For China, normal relations with Russia have been both the precursor to, and the underpinning of, its regional policy during the reform decades.[1] This is in sharp contrast to the Sino-Soviet rivalry during the Cold War, when China was widely described as "a regional power without a regional policy," or an Asian power without an Asian policy.[2] It is within this broad context of China's relations with its neighbors that recent Sino-Russian relations are examined. This chapter briefly examines how China forever lost its "periphery" in modern times, and why it was unable to formulate any meaningful regional policy during most of the hot and cold wars of the twentieth century. I argue that China's effort to normalize relations with Russia in the 1980s was an integral part of China's conception and conduct of a genuine regional policy. Such a policy took some definitive shape during the post–Cold War decade with the signing of the Treaty of Good Neighborliness and Friendly Cooperation (TGNFC) in 2001. The post–September 11 years have seriously tested their strategic partnership as both nations have adapted their regional policies in this era of preemption and unilateralism.

Ironically, the current Sino-Russian strategic partnership seems to have entered a qualitatively different phase from the past. Both sides realize that their strategic ties are incomplete unless they can manage their growing interactions in some nonsecurity and nonpolitical areas. At the onset of the twenty-first century, China and Russia are therefore "normalizing" their "strategic partnerships." In a broad sense, this occurs against the backdrop of China's historical rise and the unprecedented decline of Russia since 1991.

THE EROSION OF CHINA'S "PERIPHERY"

Historical interactions between the two large land powers have always seemed zero-sum and asymmetrical. If the current decline of Russia is one of the major factors favoring stable and normal bilateral relations between Beijing and Moscow, it is Russia's historical expansion to the Far East that marked the beginning of the end of a Sinocentric East Asian system of tributary states.[3] Indeed, long before the European powers made any serious inroads into China's coastal region from the south and east, Russia began its relentless advance to China's north through military operations, diplomatic treaties, and commercial expansion.[4] As a result of Russia's and Europe's encroachment on China, the nineteenth century witnessed China being gradually reduced to semicolonial status by foreign concessions, extraterritoriality, and the so-called "open door."

Russia's expansion at China's expense continued into the early twentieth century, when it joined other imperial and colonial powers in 1900 to forcibly suppress the xenophobic Boxer Rebellion; when it fought Japan in Korea and on the Liaodong Peninsula in China's northeast (1904–5); and when Stalin instigated the independence of Outer Mongolia from Chinese suzerainty during the 1920s. In retrospect, Russia's territorial gain along China's periphery has proven enduring, despite the fact that other Western powers and Japan may have scored some of the most notable and memorable military victories and diplomatic deals in the past two hundred years.[5]

The Absence of China's Regional Policy and the "Russian Factor"

In addition to their physical impact on China, Russia and the Soviet Union have exerted a less tangible influence on China that has been unparalleled by that of any other power during the twentieth century. In the early twentieth century, for example, Lenin's unilateral declaration to end Russia's special privileges in China was perhaps the single most powerful catalyst to inspire Chinese intellectuals to abandon their infatuation with Western liberalism in favor of Bolshevism.[6] Both the Chinese Communist Party (CCP) and the Nationalist Party (KMT) were modeled on the Soviet Communist Party and epitomized Leninist principles, ideologically and organizationally, at least in their early days.

During the twentieth century, China was so consumed by its internal chaos and external threats that the government had no chance to formulate a meaningful regional policy. In the first half of the century, China remained divided and weak, as it was totally consumed by warlordism (1916–27), the CCP-KMT rivalry and civil war (1927–49), and Japan's invasion (1937–45). Engulfed by civil and foreign wars, China did not have the coherence to develop a regional Asian policy, much less a global foreign policy. The Chinese saying *"ruo guo wu waijiao"* (weak nations have no diplomacy) captured China's predicament.

In this environment even the Soviet Union, the CCP's ideological soul mate, took advantage of China's weakness in the case of Mongolia and in Stalin's insistence on Russian "rights" in Manchuria. During the second half of the twentieth century, Sino-Soviet relations, both for better and for worse, distracted and deprived China from developing its own regional Asian policy that served its own interests. In 1949, the Cold War was well on its way to dividing the world into two spheres. Both sides of the Iron Curtain saw everything in terms of two camps. Conflicts were globalized, militarized, zero-sum, and ideological. There were, in fact, no "peripheries" at this stage of the Cold War and bipolar world (this did emerge during the 1970s and 1980s). As a result, China's cooperative and confrontational interactions with almost all of its neighbors were regarded by both China and its superpower allies/ antagonists as part of the grand strategies of the opposing side. China's "lean-toward-one-side" policy with respect to Moscow in the 1950s and its de facto alliance with Washington in the 1970s and 1980s dominated China's diplomatic and security calculus.

There were two distinctive exceptions to this rule in China's foreign policy. One was Beijing's brief flirtation with the Nonaligned Movement in the 1950s as a "third way" in international relations,[7] but this "Bandung Spirit" was short-lived and inconsequential at best. In the 1960s, China was a victim of its own "splendid isolation" when Mao's radical Cultural Revolution ideology led to a strategy of confronting both Moscow and Washington simultaneously. Although Beijing claimed to have "friends from all over the world" at this time, it was a period when China could count on only a few friendly nations in the world and pursued a dual adversary strategy vis-à-vis the superpowers. Beijing's two Asian allies, North Korea and Vietnam, were not entirely on China's side either, but maneuvered between Moscow and Beijing to maximize their own national interests.

The Emergence of China's Peripheral Policy and the Process of Normalizing Relations with Russia

As other chapters in this volume make clear, China's regional policy has emerged over a protracted period of diplomatic experimentation during the reform decades (1978 to the present). This process began immediately after the Cultural Revolution with a subtle, but steady, reassessment of the Soviet system, leading to more balanced views of Moscow. Meanwhile, the Sino-U.S. "honeymoon" in early 1979 quickly ran into obstacles because of the Taiwan Relations Act, signed into law by the Carter administration in March 1979. China subsequently adopted an "independent" foreign policy in 1982, with the goal of a more balanced posture between the two superpowers.

Once relations with the superpowers were redefined to expand China's strategic space and flexibility, foreign policy analysts started to move down the list of priorities. The concept of a "peripheral policy" emerged from a series of policy deliberations and evolved into a set of pronouncements and diplomatic initiatives. The consensus was intended to provide an across-the-board improvement of relations with neighboring states to produce a more stable and peaceful regional environment.

The actual conduct of China's peripheral policy, however, evolved only gradually, and not without twists and turns. In the case of China's Soviet/Russia policy, it too was conducted in a more pragmatic manner in the 1980s. Although Beijing appeared unwilling to compromise on its preconditions for normalizing relations with Moscow,[8] it managed to keep the talks alive at the deputy foreign minister level, participating in twelve rounds in six years (1982–88). Meanwhile, the lack of progress in political relations did not prevent exchanges in other areas such as culture, sports, and commerce.

It is hard to say which aspect of China's policy—regional or Soviet—drove the other. The process of normalizing relations with Moscow in 1989, however, constituted a crucial step toward defusing the once highly charged and tense relationship along China's periphery.

The 1990s: Different Beds, Same Dream

No sooner had China rediscovered some virtues of the Soviet system than the Russians started to dispose of some of their seventy-year-old communist practices. Events in the Soviet Union led to at least three challenges for China. The first was a growing ideological gap between Gorbachev's radical political reforms and China's incremental economic experiments. The Soviet leader's visit to Beijing in May 1989 to officially normalize relations with China coincided with the student-led demonstrations that caused a serious challenge to the ruling Communist Party. At least for the short term, the energetic and confident Gorbachev captured the imagination of those who aspired to political change in China.

China's strategic environment, too, was radically altered. Western sanctions after the 1989 Beijing crackdown aside, the subsequent collapse of the Berlin Wall, East European communist regimes, and finally the Soviet Union itself left China as the only major communist system in the world. The Soviet implosion created several smaller Central Asian states. China therefore had to cope with a far more fluid periphery in the north and west, while waiting for the post-Soviet state to emerge.

In the midst of the sea changes in internal and external affairs, China's ruling elite confronted the classic Leninist question: "What is to be done?" Ironically, the answers to that question were produced by Jiang Zemin, Li

Peng, and Zhu Rongji, the generation of leaders who were either educated in the former Soviet Union or in China during the Sino-Soviet alliance. The ensuing policy debate in China about the causes and consequences of the Soviet collapse produced a consensus to pursue a pragmatic policy of establishing ties with the fragmenting former Soviet republics, while continuing the decade-long regional policy.[9]

In a review of China's post-Tiananmen foreign relations after the Soviet collapse, foreign minister Qian Qichen, a veteran in Russian and Soviet affairs, made Beijing's peripheral policy the top priority in China's overall foreign relations. The goal was to maintain a stable and peaceful periphery around China.[10] This policy enabled China to restore or establish diplomatic relations with several influential nations in the region, including Mongolia (December 1989), Indonesia (August 1990), Singapore (October 1990), Brunei (September 1991), Vietnam (November 1991), and South Korea (August 1992). The continuation of China's peripheral policy also paralleled China's effort to stabilize its relations with Russia and the former Soviet republics along China's northern and western borders.[11] If anything, China's post-Tiananmen and post-Soviet foreign policies seemed to have accelerated its peripheral policy of peace, stability, and development. China's policy toward Russia and its former Soviet republics, administered by China's Soviet-trained generation of leaders, was part of this broad regional strategy.

The successes in China's regional policy, however, could hardly conceal the geostrategic reality that China's external environment was being radically altered in the 1990s. Relations with Russia, too, were influenced by the fact that the two continental powers were now divided by a growing gap in domestic political systems and ideologies. Despite Jiang's strong background in Russian affairs, it was unclear whether he could smooth his relationship with Yeltsin, the most pro-Western Russian politician. In retrospect, the 1990s turned out to be a decade of "cold peace," during which China and Russia, whose differences in domestic political systems were perhaps the greatest they had been in a century, mutually probed and adjusted to the other.

There were two broad phases of bilateral relations in the Jiang-Yeltsin era (1991–99). In the first phase (1991–95), the two sides avoided entanglement with each other's domestic changes and continued to institutionalize regular contacts at the presidential level—between bureaucracies and in various areas of economics, science and technology, foreign affairs, and societal exchanges—even while the countries' perceptions of one another were becoming increasingly negative. President Yeltsin's 1992 visit to China indicated that the two sides were starting to escape the shadow of their divergent domestic politics. In their signed communiqué, Jiang and Yeltsin pledged not to enter into treaties "prejudicing the sovereignty and security interests of the other party." They also renounced the use of a nuclear first strike against the other.[12] Upon Yeltsin's suggestion, in 1994 the two sides for the first time defined their burgeoning relationship as a "constructive partnership." In May 1995, Yeltsin invited Jiang to join the fiftieth V-E Day anniversary in Moscow, an unusual gesture toward a non-European partici-pant in World War II.

Given the disparity between Russia's and China's political systems and economic fortunes, it was difficult to predict at the time whether the Sino-Russian "constructive partnership" would evolve by itself into a "strategic partnership" in the second half of the 1990s. By 1996, however, there were enough pressing geostrategic needs—the Gulf War, the 1995–96 Taiwan Strait crises, NATO expansion, Chechnya, Tibet, Kosovo, and the prospect of U.S. missile defense systems, for example—for both sides to deepen their bilateral ties. In early 1996 the idea of a "strategic partnership" was first con-sidered by Russia,[13] and it then became official when Yeltsin visited China in April that year.

Yeltsin's visit turned out to be significant for both bilateral relations and the PRC's regional policy. Exchanges accelerated, a hot line was connected, and military sales and military technology transfers expanded. At the same time, the "Shanghai Five" regional security regime (composed of Russia, China, and the three Central Asian states) made its debut.[14] In the next few years, the strategic partnership continued to broaden and deepen, particu-larly in the areas of border confidence-building measures and demilitariza-tion, military hardware sales, and military exchanges. Meanwhile, both sides openly echoed each other's rhetoric espousing a multipolar world. In his last foreign trip as Russian president in December 1999, Yeltsin found him-self in Beijing. The man who had brought down the mighty Soviet Union went so far as to remind his hosts that Russia "possesses a full arsenal of nuclear arms."

Yeltsin's sudden exit from power at the end of 1999 was quite a surprise to the Chinese, who were by then quite used to Yeltsin's rough but straight-forward style. His handpicked successor Vladimir Putin, however, seemed unwilling to continue Yeltsin's apparent overdependence on China. In the first six months of 2000, Putin overlooked several of China's requests for an early summit, claiming constitutional constraints,[15] which turned out to apply only to trips to China.[16] Meanwhile, Putin was extremely busy with his *ostpolitik* foreign tour of Western Europe. Within a few months Putin's "de-Yeltsinization" initiatives had reconnected Russia with the trans-Atlantic world by ridding Russia of its image as an antiquated nuclear power. Pri-vately, Putin confided to visiting U.S. secretary of state Madeleine Albright in early 2001 that he was the type of Russian with a European outlook (who shared Western thinking and values) who outwardly seemed Asian (he enjoyed Chinese food and practiced Japanese judo).

For a while, it seemed as if bilateral relations would repeat the pattern of younger men in the Kremlin challenging the old guard in the Zhongnan-hai, as Khrushchev challenged Mao and Gorbachev challenged Deng. Putin did, however, turn his attention back to China in July 2000 with a short "working visit" to Beijing. His stopover, however, was only one stop on a whirlwind diplomatic tour that also took him to Dushanbe, Seoul, Pyongyang, and Tokyo. It seemed that Russia's China policy was balanced not only between the Atlantic (West) and Pacific (East), but it was also embedded in fostering an overall East Asia equilibrium among major players such as Japan, China, and the two Koreas.

Despite Putin's *ostpolitik* outlook, some of Yeltsin's legacies were preserved. China and Russia hammered out the historic Treaty of Good Neighborliness and Friendly Cooperation during Jiang's July 2001 visit to Russia.[17] The document is unique in both style and essence. On the one hand, the twenty-five-article treaty, which was initiated by Jiang in 1996, covers almost every aspect of bilateral ties. It includes, among other things, the basic principles of bilateral relations,[18] security issues,[19] economic cooperation, societal interactions, regional affairs,[20] and border issues. On the other hand, the document leaves one with the impression that it is not directed toward any third party. There were reasons, however, to hail this treaty as a milestone. The perceived unilateralism of the new Bush administration was the key to moving the two rather reluctant strategic partners toward closer policy coordination. During the first few months in office, the Bush team was busy undoing international treaties,[21] as well as playing hardball with both Beijing and Moscow, though for different reasons. Within ten days, fifty Russian diplomats were expelled from the United States for "spying" (March 21, 2001), and a U.S. surveillance plane collided with a Chinese jet fighter (April 1). These events were followed by Bush's public statement that "the United States would do whatever it takes to help Taiwan defend itself," including an $18 billion arms sale package. Dealing with the new administration of George W. Bush was precarious for both Beijing and Moscow.

In addition to accelerating the pace of drafting the Friendship Treaty, Beijing and Moscow also gave a face-lift in July 2001 to the five-year-old "Shanghai Five" regional security regime by redefining it as the Shanghai Cooperation Organization (SCO) and by admitting a new member (Uzbekistan). Until a few months later, the SCO, which acted as an important interface between China and its northern periphery, including Russia, was the only regional security mechanism in which Washington did not directly participate. Things, however, were soon to change.

9/11 for China and Russia

After September 11, 2001, both Russia and China quickly came to assist the U.S. antiterrorist operation with moral support, intelligence sharing, security coordination, and diplomatic efforts, though to different degrees and with different results. Hoping to improve their difficult relations with the lone superpower, Jiang and Putin did not even contact each other until a week after 9/11. It was unclear if their newly upgraded strategic partnership and regional security mechanism would be able to survive the strategic return of the United States to Central Asia. Within a month of the demise of the Taliban regime in Afghanistan, the Anti-Ballistic Missile Treaty was cancelled (December 13, 2001). This was quickly followed by a new, proactive nuclear strategy (Nuclear Posture Review) on January 8, 2002, which established both China and Russia as some of the seven candidates for possible U.S. nuclear strikes. In May 2002, the Bush doctrine of preemption made its debut. Within a year, U.S.-led coalition forces took Baghdad.

Slowly, China and Russia recovered from the 9/11 shockwaves and adapted themselves to the post–9/11 world. Top leaders and bureaucrats of both nations also actively coordinated their policies toward the U.S. and many other issues. Bush seemed convinced that Putin could be trusted because he detected, even before 9/11, a "soul mate" in the eyes of the former KGB colonel. Bush also traveled to China twice in four months (October 2001 and February 2002), while both Putin (in November 2002) and Jiang (in October 2003) were entertained at Bush's Texas ranch. It was in St. Petersburg, Russia, however, that the flurry of summitry culminated in May 2003, when Putin hosted forty-four heads of state from around the world, including China's new president, Hu Jintao.

THROUGH RUSSIA, TO THE WORLD

By the time the "fourth generation" of Chinese leaders emerged in late 2002 and early 2003, similar generational transitions had occurred in Russia under Putin and the United States under Clinton and Bush. Yet this generation of Chinese leaders had the least exposure to Russia of any over nearly the last century. If anything, they were politically socialized during the height of the Sino-Soviet schism. There was no doubt that the Sino-Russian relationship they inherited was perhaps the most balanced and the most mutually beneficial in the three hundred years since the 1689 Treaty of Nerchinsk.

It was under these circumstances that China's "fourth generation" of leaders set out to shape and reshape China's foreign and regional policies, and Hu's first foreign stopover as China's head of state was Russia. The Moscow summit in May 2003, either by desire or design, was by no means an annual ritual. For the new non-Russian-speaking Chinese leader, Putin carefully arranged an informal, private "2 + 2" dinner (the two presidents and two first ladies) in his dacha in a western suburb of Moscow on May 26. This was immediately followed by the SCO's third meeting in Moscow. Hu then traveled to St. Petersburg for the city's tricentennial festivities. Soon after that, both Hu and Putin joined the G-8 Summit in France.

Perhaps the most substantial outcome of Hu's trip through Russia was the revival of the SCO, which had been plagued by both the impact of 9/11 and its own internal inefficiency. Major steps were taken to move the regional security mechanism forward. These steps included putting into operation, in early 2004, the SCO Secretariat in Beijing and a regional antiterrorist structure in Bishkek; approving procedures for drafting the SCO's budget; appointing China's ambassador to Moscow, Zhang Deguang, the SCO's first executive secretary; approving rules on SCO's councils of heads of state, heads of government, and foreign ministers, and on conferences of the heads of various agencies; conducting the first SCO antiterror exercise in August 2003; holding the SCO's second prime ministerial meeting in Beijing a month after that to promote economic cooperation and to finalize its operating budget; and establishing principles and regulations for linking with other international organizations and countries. Already Iran, Pakistan, India, Mongolia, and Turkey have expressed their intentions to join the SCO.[22]

The durability of the SCO can be partially explained by China's and Russia's overlapping interests in Central Asia. Despite a growing U.S. presence there, Moscow needs the SCO as a means to preserve and advance its interests. For Beijing, the SCO is highly desirable for stabilizing its western borders. Economic interests, too, become both the ends and the means for Beijing to interact with the region. In bilateral terms, the SCO is also a useful mechanism for Russia and China to regulate their interests in this highly volatile region. As a result, the SCO, which started as an ad hoc security forum in 1996, made the first crucial step in 2003 toward becoming a regional political forum, a security mechanism, and, possibly, an economic bloc.

China's effort to speed up the SCO's institutionalization was part of broader moves toward shaping a more stable regional order in the age of American unipolar preemption. By late June 2003, the long-smoldering Sino-Indian-Russian triangle started to take shape when Indian prime minister Atal Bihari Vajpayee paid a weeklong visit to China, the first in ten years. The vision of this triangle previously articulated by Russia's former foreign minister Yevgeny Primakov was finally becoming a reality. Now three foreign ministers regularly meet in the UN.

The Korean peninsula is also an area where China and Russia have overlapping and competing interests. The second North Korean nuclear crisis, which began in October 2002, however, has demonstrated both their differences and their ability to manage the crisis. Korea has a special place in Putin's strategic calculus. Over the course of two years, Putin and Kim Jung Il met three times, including once during the first official visit by a Russian head of state to the Democratic People's Republic of Korea (DPRK) in July 2000, and another time during Kim's August 2002 visit to Russia's far east.[23] South Korea is also significant for Putin as an economic counterforce to a quickly rising China. Time and again the Russian president has expressed his preference that Russia's trans-Siberia railroad be linked with Korea, thus bypassing China.[24]

This special attention to the DPRK prompted Russian officials to act quickly in the early period of the nuclear crisis. In January 2003, Deputy Foreign Minister Alexander Losyukov launched a much-publicized mini–shuttle diplomacy between Beijing, Pyongyang, and Moscow, including a meeting with Kim Jung Il. China remained low-key as Losyukov flew in and out of Beijing on his mission. Three months later, Beijing hosted a U.S.-DPRK-PRC trilateral talk without Russian participation. Although Russia officially welcomed the Beijing talks, it clearly revealed its displeasure at being left out of the process.[25]

To be fair, China and Russia face quite different consequences with respect to the current crisis. A peninsula with nuclear capabilities in both North and South Korea certainly constitutes a bigger threat to China than to Russia due to China's smaller nuclear force. Nuclear proliferation in East Asia, which is highly likely if the DPRK goes nuclear, would immediately complicate China's security calculus. A final consideration is Taiwan's potential to acquire nuclear weapons. For these reasons, Beijing may have a stronger desire than Moscow to see a nuclear-free Korean peninsula. Russia, on the other hand, may be more interested in preserving its foothold in the peninsula and its special relationship with Kim Jung Il.

In a broader perspective, the regional strategy followed by China's new leaders has clearly reached north (to Russia) and south (to India and ASEAN), at a time when China's strategic space is being squeezed by pressure from the west (Central Asia) and from the east (a restless Taiwanese agitating for independence, a Japan determined to convert its economic power into military might, and a Korea that is on the brink of a nuclear capability). China's regional and Russia policies, therefore, are closely integrated into what one Chinese analyst has described as the country's "ideal security environment."[26]

THE FUTURE: MOSCOW'S STRATEGIC CONCERN FOR ITS STRATEGIC PARTNER

The newfound Sino-Russian "strategic love" in the post–9/11 era is only part of their complex relationship. Current leaders in Moscow and Beijing are still "sleeping in different beds and dreaming different dreams." The continuous rise of China as an economic powerhouse and Russia's relatively weak and sluggish economy is the weakest link in bilateral ties. To be fair, not all developments in the economic area are disappointing. Bilateral trade in 2003 reached about $16 billion, up from $12 billion in 2002.[27] This figure, though much smaller than China's trade with some of its largest trade partners, was actually larger than Russian-U.S. trade, which reached less than $10 billion for 2003. Russia and China are also increasingly cooperating in banking, credit insurance, and currency conversions.[28] The first unit of a Russian-built nuclear power plant in eastern China started tests for operation at full capacity in 2004. Transfer of the technology necessary to construct nuclear power plants in China in the future is also under way.[29]

Despite the progress in their economic relations, the issue of an oil pipeline between Russia and China (Angarsk-Daqing), a project initiated by Yeltsin in 1994, remains uncertain, and decision deadlines continue to be extended.[30] Numerous documents have been signed at various levels—by oil companies, by bureaucracies, and at presidential summits. Though these documents have not necessarily been binding or final, they all reaffirm China's and Russia's intention and willingness to proceed with the construction of the 2,400-kilometer pipeline with an annual capacity of 20 to 30 million tons of oil from resource-rich Russia to energy-thirsty China.[31]

In April 2002, some Russian officials started to question whether the pipeline deal with China was in Russia's strategic interests. The rapid rise of China's energy needs has meant that Russia's vast petroleum deposits have quickly assumed a strategic dimension. For Moscow, energy relations with both Beijing and Tokyo have strategic and economic dimensions. It was against this backdrop that Japan's intense lobbying for a Russian pipeline to Russia's Pacific coast city of Nakhodka started to lure Russia away from China.[32] For some in Russia, the Angarsk-Nakhodka oil pipeline has several advantages, including total Russian control, the creation of numerous jobs for port and shipping business, and flexibility in accessing a larger market (including China, Japan, South Korea, and the United States). The most attractive advantage is the $5 billion of Japanese credit available for constructing the pipeline, $2 billion to develop the eastern Siberian oil fields, and $1 billion for renovating Russian cities along the pipeline leading to Nakhodka.[33] In contrast, earlier documents signed with China before July 2003 specified that each side would construct its own portion of the pipeline (1,452 and 920 kilometers for Russia and China, respectively). Accordingly, Russia would have to find $1.7 billion for constructing its own portion of the Angarsk-Daqing line, and Russia would have only one end user, China.[34] Since March 2003, Russia has toyed with a compromised third route, with a branch line running to China from the middle of the Angarsk-Nakhodka line. This proposal, however, was rejected by Japan.[35] Nor would Russia have a sufficient supply of oil for both lines. Prime Minister Kasyanov was still speculating on the "dual-track" plan when he visited Japan in late 2003.[36]

Russia's indecision on the pipeline issue reflects its mixed perception of China, which is rooted in a muted, but serious, concern about a rising China.[37] Although the Russian economy has stabilized and even grew well above the world average in its first three years under Putin, it continues to be dwarfed by the galloping Chinese economy. Many in Russia believe that an oil pipeline to China would further fuel China's almost unstoppable rise.

The China threat perception is particularly strong in Russia's far east, where the Russian population in the past decade has declined by one million, or 13 percent, to 6.7 million. Meanwhile China has 140 million people living in the three adjacent northeastern provinces alone.[38] This has led to a rather exaggerated fear about the influx of Chinese into Russia. The actual number of Chinese in Siberia is about 200,000, and only twenty-nine Chinese visitors illegally stayed in Siberia in 2003. The popular belief among the Russians is that the real total is well above one million.

President Putin may not share such a deep concern. His envoy to the Far East Federal District, Konstantin Pulikovsky, was in Beijing in October 2003, actively soliciting China's economic inputs, in both labor and capital formats, into his vast region.[39] Most local Russian officials are nonetheless "China unfriendly." They would rather take immigrants from the DPRK than from China.[40] Even Pulikovsky himself lobbies hard for the Japan pipeline.[41]

Russia's mixed attitude toward China reflects a dual reality in Russia's far east. On one hand, the region is closely related to China economically. Eighty percent of the consumer products in Russia's far east come from China, and 10 percent of the regional economic growth was linked to the region's trade with China—now constituting 50 percent of Russia's total exports to China. During the SARS crisis in early 2003, when economic interactions with China were minimal, the Russians bitterly complained about short supply and high prices. Russia's far east is heavily dependent on China's inputs. On the other hand, the shadow of historical territorial disputes remains long and contributes to distrust of, and bias against, the Chinese.[42]

Concerns about a rising and threatening China may even come from those sectors of the Russia that have had close relations with China. The Russian military, which has supplied China with billions of dollars of weaponry over the past decade, is said to be strongly opposed to a China oil pipeline. The Russian General Staff reportedly vetoed the Angarsk-Daqing pipeline because it would give China access to Russia's strategic fuel stocks. While Beijing was eager to figure out any strategic implications for the pipeline deal behind the arrest of Russian oil tycoon Khodorkovsky, President Putin seems to have a broader blueprint in mind. That is, his goal is to use energy as a strategic lever in Russia's relations with the vast Asia-Pacific, or to make Russia "a pan-regional energy infrastructure."[43] For Russia, China is only part of this grand strategy to make Russia the linchpin for regional development.

Russia's obsession with its strategic interests as well as its vulnerability is also reflected in the way it conducts military-military relations with China. In retrospect, the two main areas of Sino-Russian military relations have been asymmetrical. In the area of border demarcation, territorial security, and confidence-building measures, Moscow and Beijing have gone a long way in converting what was once the world's longest militarized border into an area of peace, stability, and commerce. In the case of Russian arms sales and technology transfers to China, however, Moscow has so far refrained from treating Beijing as a "normal customer." Its arms supplies to China have been inferior to those for other nations, such as India, despite the fact that both Asian nations are Moscow's "strategic partners."[44]

Nonetheless, over the past decade, Russia has been China's principal supplier of military hardware and technology. The major arms sold to China include seventy-five Su-27SK fighters (as well as licensed production of two hundred Su-27s), sixty Su-30 MKK fighters, four Kilo-class submarines (eight more are being built), S-300 Tor-M1 SAM missile systems, two Sovremenny-class destroyers (two more are being built), and T-80 main battle tanks.[45] These weapon systems are at least twenty years ahead of China's aging inventory. For its part, China also contributed to the survival of the Russian arms industry as Russia's domestic demand shrank in the post-Soviet period. In the 1990s, Beijing purchased more than $4 billion worth of Russian arms. Current accounts show $5 billion worth of existing contracts,[46] and 2004 was a record year for Russia's arms transfers to China, exceeding $2 billion.[47]

The current asymmetrical military relationship between Beijing and Moscow is perhaps natural in the enduring geopolitical games nations play. In the absence of other major arms suppliers,[48] Beijing has no choice but to accept the second best. But Russian policy has forced China to actively search for alternative sources (such as the European Union), as it has in the case of Russia's indecision to construct the oil pipeline to China.

China's predicament may not change significantly in the near future due to U.S. pressure on the Europeans and Israelis not to see arms to China. Since early 2004, the active deliberation by the European Union (EU), particularly by France and Germany, to end the embargo has nonetheless put some psychological pressure on Russia to end its "discrimination" against China.[49] In early 2004, meetings between high-ranking civilian and military officers—Russian defense minister Sergey Ivanov visited China on April 20–23 and PLA chief of general staff Liang Guanglie visited Russia on May

17–23—clearly indicated that both sides are ready to promote military cooperation "to a qualitatively new level."[50]

LIVING WITH ONE ANOTHER

Not all of Russia's deep concerns regarding its strategic partner to the south are warranted, given systemic causes such as the steady rise of China and the historical decline of Russia. The deepening and broadening of bilateral exchanges, too, has led to more "normal" frictions. Both sides, however, realize that there are limits for these things to go unchecked. In the longer term, these nonpolitical/strategic issues could erode ties and even make the current strategic partnership unsustainable. For these reasons, among others, Moscow has thus far tried to alleviate the concerns about the perceived excessive influx of Chinese. China, in turn, has worked hard with Russia to regulate the number of Chinese crossing the border into Russia.[51] A joint working group for migration was set up, and security forces on both sides of the border are actively coordinating to minimize illegal border crossings. Beyond these current preoccupations, Beijing and Moscow also have eyes for the future, and they established 2004 a "year of friendship between the young people of the two countries."[52]

Even Russia's prolonged indecision about the pipeline route may not be based on "zero-sum" calculations, as many would argue. The stalled Angarsk-Nakhodka pipeline will not prevent oil from being shipped to China. At the strategic level, it is unlikely that President Putin would decisively tilt toward either Japan or China. What Moscow seems to be maneuvering for is milking maximum profit from both rich Asian neighbors while maintaining a balanced posture between them, particularly while Russia is weak.

In the end, both Russia and China still need to learn how to manage normal interactions, despite their strategic partnership and improved level of trust. This is particularly needed after the two great continental powers have experienced the fluctuations of the past fifty years. The creation of a true strategic partnership therefore seems to be the real challenge for both.

NOTES

1. For a further exploration of the evolution of China's foreign policy, from revolutionary to pragmatic, from political-military issues to economics, and from global geopolitical maneuvering to areas closer to home, see Yu Bin, "China and Its Asian Neighbors: Implications for Sino-U.S. Relations," in *In the Eyes of the Dragon: China Views the World,* ed. Yong Deng and Fei-Ling Wang (Lanham, MD: Rowman and Littlefield, 1999), 183–210.

2. See Steven I. Levine, "China in Asia: The PRC as a Regional Power," in *China's Foreign Relations in the 1980s,* ed. Harry Harding (New Haven, CT: Yale University

Press, 1984), 107–14; Michael H. Hunt, "Chinese Foreign Relations in Historical Perspective," in ibid., 1–42; Samuel S. Kim, *China In and Out of the Changing World Order* (Princeton, NJ: Princeton University Press, 1991), 84.

3. Within this regional hierarchy, the "Middle Kingdom" presided over an expansive tributary system. Those peripheral states would acknowledge China's cultural supremacy in exchange for autonomous rule.

4. Russia and China signed the 1689 Treaty of Nerchinsk after several clashes. Russia renewed its incursion into China's periphery later. The 1860 Treaty of Peking opened China's entire northern frontier to Russia. See A. Doak Barnett, *China and the Major Powers in East Asia* (Washington, DC: Brookings Institution, 1977), 21–22.

5. European holdings in China ended in the twentieth century. Taiwan was returned to China in 1945 and is still considered by China as an integral part of its sovereign territory. In contrast, China recognizes existing borders with Russia and Mongolia.

6. Western democracies insisted that China's Shandong province be transferred from Germany to Japan, despite the fact that China joined the Allies in World War I.

7. The initiators of the movement included India, Egypt, Indonesia, Yugoslavia, and China.

8. This refers to Beijing's three major demands—Soviet withdrawal from Afghanistan, the suspension of assistance to Vietnam's occupation of Cambodia, and the reduction of Soviet troops along Sino-Soviet border and from Mongolia—as a precondition for normalizing relations with Moscow.

9. Deng, though retired, was able to divert the debate onto a more realist path. He argued that China should pursue a policy of coexistence regardless of what happened in the Soviet bloc. Ma Licheng and Ling Zhijun, *Jiao Feng* [Crossed swords] (Beijing: Jinri Zhongguo Chubanshe, 1998), 164–65 and 273–75.

10. See Qian's speech in *Renmin Ribao,* December 16, 1991.

11. This included Kazakhstan, Tajikistan, Kyrgyzstan, Uzbekistan, and Turkmenistan.

12. For Beijing, this represented the official end of hostilities, particularly at the time when Russia, for the first time since it had become a nuclear power, declared in late 1993 that it was dropping its long-standing commitment not to be the first to use nuclear weapons in a conflict.

13. The concept was first articulated by Russian deputy premier Davidov in March 28 and then by President Yeltsin on April 2.

14. The Shanghai Five consisted of China, Russia, Kazakhstan, Tajikistan, and Kyrgyzstan.

15. According to the Russian Constitution, Putin cannot travel abroad as both president and prime minister.

16. In the first half of 2000, Putin's foreign trips included those to Britain, Belarus, and Ukraine in April; to Uzbekistan and Turkmenistan in May; and to Italy, Germany, and Spain in June.

17. "Jiang, Putin Issue Joint Statement in Moscow," *China Daily,* July 17, 2001.

18. The principles include political equality, noninterference in each other's internal affairs, mutual economic benefit, mutual trust for security, coordination in world affairs, and the "one China" policy.

19. This included preserving "strategic stability," arms control, not targeting nuclear weapons against each other, military exchanges, and cooperation in aerospace areas.

20. This included matters related to the Shanghai Five and antiterrorist, separatist, and cross-border activities.

21. These included the Comprehensive Test Ban Treaty, a treaty on global warming, and the ABM Treaty.

22. "Roundup Views: SCO's Role as Model for Multilateral, Regional Cooperation," *Xinhua,* May 28, 2003; *Ta Kung Pao* (Hong Kong), "Shanghai Professor Pan Guang Interviewed on SCO," June 3, 2003.

23. Yu Bin, "China Is in No Position to Pressure North Korea," *International Herald Tribune,* February 27, 2003, available at http://www.iht.com/articles/87967 .html.

24. Putin urged Russian officials to speed up rail links with Korea. "I can assure you that if we do not implement this idea in good time our esteemed neighbors will steal a march on us," Putin stated. Vladislav Vorobyev, "Putin Visits Far East, Discusses Economy, Meets Kim Chong-il," *Moscow Rossiyskaya Gazet,* August 24, 2002.

25. "Russia, Japan Hail Upcoming DPRK-US-China Talks in Beijing," *Xinhua,* April 18, 2003.

26. Tang Shiping, *Shuozao Zhongguo de Lixiang Anquan Huanjing* [Constructing China's ideal security environment] (Beijing: Zhongguo shehui kexue chubanshe, 2003).

27. "Russia: FM Ivanov Says Trade with China Increased to $16 Billion," *Itar-Tass,* January 16, 2004.

28. "Second China-Russia Financial Forum Closes in Beijing," *Xinhua,* November 28, 2003; "Russian, Chinese Insurance Firms Agree to Expand Cooperation," *Itar-Tass,* November 13, 2003.

29. "Russia Ready to Transfer Nuclear Technologies to China," *Itar-Tass,* December 19, 2003.

30. "Decision on Oil Pipeline Route from Angarsk to Be Made in 2004," *Itar-Tass,* October 19, 2003.

31. China became an oil-exporting country in 1994. By 2002, a quarter of China's oil consumption (200 million tons) came from foreign sources.

32. Since late 2002 Japanese officials have frequented Moscow and Russia's far eastern cities, offering billions of dollars of Japanese credit and other incentives. Prime Minister Koizumi traveled to Russia twice in five months (January and May 2003) to influence the decision about the pipeline construction.

33. James Brooke, "Wary of China, Russia and Japan Build Trade," *International Herald Tribune,* January 24, 2004.

34. "China May Fund Laying Out of Russian Part of Pipeline to Daqing," *Itar-Tass,* July 29, 2003.

35. Li Yin, "Zhong-E shiyou guandao xiangmu you sheng shiduan" [Another hurdle in Sino-Russian oil pipeline business], *Huanqiu Shibao* [Global times], September 9, 2003.

36. "Russia to Cooperate with China, Japan, S. Korea in Oil Production," *Itar-Tass,* December 25, 2003.

37. "FMA 8 Dec: Russian, Chinese, and Japanese Media Discuss Far Eastern Pipeline," December 8, 2003, FBIS; also see James Brooke, "Wary of China, Russia and Japan Build Trade," *International Herald Tribune,* January 24, 2004.

38. "Russians in Vladivostok Express Alarm at Growing Chinese Presence," Agence France-Presse, January 26, 2004; Bai Hua, *Voice of America* from Moscow, "E danxin zhongguoren dapi yongru yuandong" [Russians fear influx of large number of Chinese into the Far East], cited by www2.chinesenewsnet.com, November 14, 2003.

39. "Far East Representative Pulikovskiy Sees His Role as 'Political,' Denies Chinese Immigration Problem," *Moscow Trud,* October 17, 2003.

40. James Brooke, "To Fill an Empty Far East Russians Look to Refugees," *New York Times,* December 7, 2003; "Far East Governor Says Russia Ready to Take Immigrants from N. Korea," *Itar-Tass,* December 16, 2003.

41. James Brooke, "Japan and China Battle for Russia's Oil and Gas," *New York Times,* January 3, 2004.

42. Shi Ding, "E yuandong dengdai kaifa, yuandong diqu que dui zhongguoren you pianjian" [Russia's far east waiting for development, yet the region demonstrates a bias against the Chinese], *Huanqiu Shibao* [Global times], December 15, 2003, available at www.people.com.cn/GB/guoji/14549/2250515.html.

43. Putin's speech at the 2003 annual APEC summit in Bangkok, "APEC Summit: Russia Claims Role as 'Connecting Link' in Region," *Moscow Rossiyskaya Gazeta,* October 24, 2003, 4.

44. India's Su-30 MKI fighters are superior to China's Su-30 MKKs. While Russia licensed China to build two hundred Su-27s, it licensed India to build one hundred Su-30MKs. Moscow has shown an interest in selling India, not China, weapons with more power projection capabilities such as nuclear submarines, Tu-22M Backfire bombers, and the aircraft carrier *Admiral Gorshkov.*

45. For details, see Yu Bin, "Historical Ironies, Dividing Ideologies and Accidental 'Alliance': Russian-Chinese Relations into the 21ˢᵗ Century," in *The Rise of China in Asia: Security Implications,* ed. Carolyn W. Pumphrey (Carlisle Barracks, PA: Strategic Studies Institute, U.S. Army War College, 2002), 137–44.

46. "Chinese Army's Chief of General Staff Arrives in Moscow for Cooperation Talks," Interfax (Moscow), May 17, 2004.

47. Alexander Konovalov, "Analyst Says Russia-China Military Trade to Be above 2 Billion Dollars in 2004," *Itar-Tass,* April 16, 2004.

48. European nations have imposed an arms embargo on China since the 1989 crackdown on students' demonstrations.

49. "Russia May Relax Restrictions on Sales of Advanced Weapons to China," *Wen Wei Po* (Hong Kong), May 1, 2004.

50. "Russian, Chinese Defense Ministers Focus on Forces' 'Collaboration,'" *Moscow Rossiyskaya Gazeta,* April 22, 2004, 4.

51. "Russian, Chinese Border Guards To Hold Joint Exercise," *Itar-Tass,* January 21, 2004.

52. "Ivanov Says 2004 Will Be 'Year of Friendship' Between Russia, China," *Itar-Tass,* January 14, 2004.

PART FOUR

Security

11

China's Evolving Regional Security Strategy

Bates Gill

This chapter examines China's evolving regional security strategy, which is defined principally as Beijing's contemporary political and diplomatic efforts (not strictly its military posture) with its immediate regional neighbors, which are devised to foster a long-term security environment consistent with Chinese interests. After a brief overview of the assumptions, goals, and principles of China's regional security strategy, the chapter examines how these are expressed in practice around China's periphery, with an emphasis on four important trends that define China's evolving regional security strategy. The chapter concludes that while current trends favor a strengthened regional security role for China, and China's relative strength and influence are likely to grow in Asia, this process is still open to contradictions and complications over the longer term. Nevertheless, China's increasing regional security influence has been overlooked by many analysts and deserves closer scrutiny.

CHINA'S REGIONAL SECURITY STRATEGY: THEORY, GOALS, AND PRINCIPLES

China's post–Cold War regional security strategy evolved from, and continues to be founded upon, a single consistent theory, or assumption, and three basic goals. The core assumption is that in spite of dramatic changes in the global security environment, Beijing continues to pronounce its adherence to the proposition that the overall tendency of world affairs is toward "peace and development," increasing multipolarity and economic globalization, and a general easing of tensions. This framework is rooted in the strategic verdict determined by the late Chinese leader Deng Xiaoping, who, in 1982, concluded that the world was tending toward peace and development, the possibility of a world war was remote, and China could expect a stable international environment in which it could carry out its much-needed domestic development.

Within this overarching security framework, China's regional security strategy has consistently pursued three major goals. First, it generally seeks to maintain a stable environment that defuses external challenges to Chinese interests so that Beijing can address domestic economic, political, and social reform challenges. Second, Beijing aims to carefully manage its growing wealth and power to extend its influence, but in a way that reassures its neighbors with pledges of mutually beneficial intentions. Third, Beijing must grapple with the challenges of a unipolar world, doing what it can to counter, co-opt, or circumvent what it perceives as excessive American "hegemony" and influence around the Chinese periphery, while avoiding overt confrontation with the United States.

In recent years, the principles of this regional security strategy have been best encapsulated in what Beijing has termed a "new security concept." In brief, the new security concept draws from principles formally advocated by the Chinese government since the 1950s, in particular the so-called Five Principles of Peaceful Coexistence[1] dating back to the Bandung Conference of developing world nations in 1955. The Chinese have for decades called on nations to observe these principles. However, around 1994–95, Beijing made higher-profile calls for establishing a "new" system for international and regional security. These formulations cohered more distinctly into the "new security concept" over the following several years.

In a major foreign policy speech delivered in Geneva in March 1999, Chinese leader Jiang Zemin elaborated the new security concept in four parts. In his speech, Jiang asserted that:

> The world is undergoing profound changes which require the discard [sic] of the Cold War mentality and the development of a new security concept and a new international political, economic, and security order responsive to the needs of our times. . . . The core of the new security concept should be mutual trust, mutual benefit, equality and cooperation. The UN Charter, the Five Principles of Peaceful Coexistence and other universally recognized principles governing international relations should serve as the political basis for safeguarding peace while mutually beneficial cooperation and common prosperity are its economic guarantee. To conduct dialogue, consultation and negotiation on an equal footing is the right way to solve disputes and safeguard peace. . . . Only by developing a new security concept and establishing a fair and reasonable new international order can world peace and security be fundamentally guaranteed.[2]

Thus, Jiang's speech joined the new security concept to Deng Xiaoping's earlier pronouncements as well as longstanding core values of Chinese diplomacy.

CHINA'S REGIONAL SECURITY STRATEGY: FOUR EMERGENT TRENDS

While the overall theory, goals, and principles of China's regional security strategy have remained relatively consistent since the mid-1980s, China's security environment has not. As a result, Chinese policies and tactics have evolved over time. China's evolving regional security strategy can be described with reference to four key trends. A closer look at these four trends shows that Beijing's approach has become steadily more subtle, nuanced, flexible and—most importantly—successful.

From Concern to Confidence

From the mid-1990s and into the early twenty-first century, China's vigorous promotion of a new security concept appeared less a reflection of its strength than a reflection of its self-perceived weakness and its frustration with an increasingly troubled global and regional security environment. These views derived primarily, though not entirely, from Beijing's negative perceptions of U.S. security policies in the Asian region and elsewhere around the globe. For example, in November 1995, China issued its white paper on arms control and disarmament. The document—China's first public white paper on national defense and security issues—stated that the "forces for world peace have grown rapidly since the 1980s, and peace and development have become the main issues of the day." It also notes China's opposition to "hegemonism and power politics in any form," as well as "the threat or use of force in international relations." The Chinese defense white paper of July 1998 paid due regard to the Dengist line that "peace and development are the major themes of the present era," that "the present international situation has continued to tend toward relaxation," that the trend toward multipolarity has further developed, and that "the factors for safeguarding world peace are growing constantly."[3]

Yet, while opening on a positive note, the 1998 white paper went on to note that although the political situation in the Asia-Pacific region is "relatively stable," there are several "factors of instability." Indirectly referring to the United States, the document expressed concern with continued hegemonism, power politics, and Cold War thinking as the source of problems for world peace, and denounced "the enlargement of military blocs [i.e., NATO] and the strengthening of military alliances [i.e., new U.S.-Japan defense guidelines]" as causing instability on the world scene. The white paper noted how some countries, taking advantage of their military superiority, "pose threats to other countries," including by participating in armed interventions.[4] Importantly, for many Chinese analysts at this time, the "inevitable trend" toward multipolarity, while a welcome development, had its downside: the United States would try to resist the trend of its relative decline inherent in a more multipolar world, and would lash out accordingly in an ultimately fruitless, but still dangerous, effort to preserve its unipolar status.[5] As David Finkelstein argues, Chinese analysts continued to support the long-standing and fundamental theory of world order, rendered as the "three no changes": peace and development remain the core trend in international relations; the movement toward a multipolar world continues and economic globalization continues to increase; and the world still tends toward a relaxation of international tensions. However, the "three new changes" reflected their steadily increasing concern with the current world order, characterized by increased hegemonism and power politics, a greater tendency toward military interventionism, and a growing gap between developed and developing countries.[6]

The Chinese defense white paper in 2000 went further still in describing China's increasingly troubled view of the international and regional security situation, especially with respect to the United States. The document noted that factors for instability in the world have "markedly increased" and that the world is "far from peaceful." Hegemonism and power politics were singled out more pointedly: "Certain big powers are pursuing 'neo-interventionism', new 'gunboat policy', and neo-economic colonialism, which are seriously damaging the sovereignty, independence, and development interests of many countries, and threatening world peace." Local wars were increasing, according to this assessment, and "some countries" have purposely undermined the authority of the United Nations under the "pretexts of 'humanitarianism' and 'human rights.'"[7] The United States was attacked as a "certain country" that continues to develop and introduce national and theater missile defense (TMD); seeks to enlarge military blocs, strengthen military alliances, and increase its military superiority; tries to strengthen its military presence in East Asia; and is the "root cause" for the tension across the Taiwan Strait.[8]

However, from the first years of the twenty-first century, and particularly from 2001, the Chinese approach to the new security concept and to its regional security strategy become less stridently reactive and concerned, and steadily more proactive and confident. This trend predated the global shifts brought on by the September 11, 2001, terrorist attacks, although it was, indeed, accelerated by them, as the new strategic concern about terrorism sidetracked overt contentiousness between the United States and China. China's entry into the WTO in December 2001 and a stable transition to the new "fourth generation" leadership in Beijing further strengthened China's more confident approach toward the international and regional security situation.

China's defense white paper of 2002 continued to express the view that "peace and development remain the themes of the present era," that a new world war is "unlikely in the foreseeable future," and that multipolarization and economic globalization continue apace, though "amid twists and turns."

The Asia-Pacific region was viewed with particular favor as the "most dynamic region economically with the greatest development potential in the world." The white paper added that "strengthening dialogue and cooperation, maintaining regional stability and promoting common development have become the mainstream policy of the Asian countries." References to "factors of instability," "hegemonism," and "power politics" were less prominent, while the emergence of "non-traditional security challenges," particularly terrorism, were frequently mentioned as challenges China and the world must increasingly face together. "China will unremittingly put the new security concept into practice, oppose all kinds of hegemonism and power politics, and combat terrorism in all forms and manifestations."[9]

The 2004 defense white paper generally continued and strengthened these trends in Chinese strategic thinking. Overall, the global security situation was seen as moving in a positive direction for Chinese interests. The white paper reiterated that "peace and development remain the dominating themes of the times" and "the international situation as a whole tends to be stable," but, as in the past, it also warned that "factors of uncertainty, instability and insecurity are on the increase." The document favorably underscored the advancing trend of multipolarization in the world and a more "democratized" international order, thanks to the increasing importance of the developing world. Developments in the Asia-Pacific in particular were singled out as evidence of the "peace and development" trend, with the multilateral efforts of the Asia Pacific Economic Cooperation (APEC) forum, the Association of Southeast Asian Nations Regional Forum (ARF), the Shanghai Cooperation Organization (SCO), and the Six Party Talks on Korean peninsula security—all organizations in which China plays an increasingly important role—receiving high marks. The 2004 white paper concluded its analysis of the international security situation by finding that "China's national security environment . . . has on the whole improved, but new challenges keep cropping up."[10]

Although generally positive, the 2004 white paper did emphasize certain problems—some old, some new—including the Taiwan situation, the widening economic gap between the developed and developing world, the tension between unipolarity and multipolarity, and the widening military technical gap between the United States and other powers, the technological gap resulting from a "revolution in military affairs" (RMA), the risks and challenges caused by the development of the trends toward economic globalization, and the prolonged existence of unipolarity vis-à-vis multipolarity." Unsurprisingly, the document noted that the Taiwan Strait situation is "grim" and condemned the "vicious rise of the 'Taiwan independence' forces." Perhaps of greatest note, this assessment of the international security situation devoted significant discussion to the global military-technical environment, noting that major powers such as the United States and Japan were "readjusting" their military postures and "stepping up transformation of their armed forces by way of developing high-tech weaponry and military equipment and putting forth new military doctrines." The defense white paper was particularly aware of the importance of "informationalization" of the battlefield and the need for China to respond with an RMA of its own. As to the world military situation, the document found that "tendencies of hegemonism and unilateralism have gained new ground, as struggles for strategic points, strategic resources and strategic dominance crop up from time to time" and that "the role played by military power in safeguarding national security is assuming greater prominence."[11]

Overall, however, across the spectrum of China's foreign policy elite, new calls emerged in 2001–2004 for a more "mature," "constructive," and "responsible" great power diplomacy for China. As Medeiros and Fravel found, such appeals call for abandoning China's long-held and reactive "victimhood" complex, putting memories of the country's "century of shame" to one side, and identifying more closely with a "great power mentality" befitting China's larger and more secure position in regional and global affairs.[12] Even in areas of security concern, recent defense white papers have interpreted them matter-of-factly and without rancor, spelling out China's intended course of action in response. This broad policy approach is both cause and effect of China's more confident perception of its regional and global situation.

A More Proactive Regional Security Strategy

Proactiveness is a second key aspect of China's evolving regional security strategy. Beijing has increasingly taken the initiative to foster a security environment that is consistent with its interests but also engages its neighbors more openly and beneficially. For example, since the mid-1990s, Beijing has reached out and sought "strategic partnerships" with major bilateral and multilateral partners, including Russia, the United States, the Association of Southeast Asian Nations (ASEAN), the European Union, India, Japan, and South Korea. All told, over the course of the 1990s, Beijing established at least sixteen such partnerships, more than half of them with Asia-Pacific neighbors (see table 24). In 2002, Beijing also saw to the establishment of an annual China-Africa summit, and in January 2004, during his visit to Cairo, Chinese president Hu Jintao met with the secretary general of the Arab League and announced the creation of the China–Arab States Cooperation Forum.[13]

In some cases, these arrangements have moved beyond symbolism to deeper, sustained, and institutionalized relationships. For example, having established a strategic partnership, China and Russia signed a twenty-five-article "friendship treaty" during the Jiang-Putin summit of June 2001.[14]

TABLE 24. China's Bilateral Partnerships

Date	Partner	Name
November 1993	Brazil	Long-term and Strategic Partnership
March 1996	Russia	Strategic Cooperative Partnership
November 1996	India	Constructive Partnership of Cooperation Oriented towards the 21st Century
December 1996	Pakistan	All-round Cooperative Partnership Oriented towards the 21st Century
December 1996	Nepal	Good-neighborly and Friendly Partnership Oriented toward the 21st Century
May 1997	France	Long-term Comprehensive Cooperative Partnership
October 1997	United States	Building toward a Constructive Strategic Partnership
November 1997	Canada	Cross-century Comprehensive Partnership
December 1997	Mexico	Cross-century Partnership of All-round Cooperation
December 1997	ASEAN	Good-neighborly Partnership of Mutual Trust
April 1998	European Union	Long-term and Stable Constructive Partnership
October 1998	United Kingdom	Enhanced Comprehensive Partnership
November 1998	Republic of Korea	Cooperative Partnership
November 1998	Japan	Friendly Cooperative Partnership
April 1999	Egypt	21st Century–oriented Strategic Cooperative Relationship
October 2003	ASEAN	Strategic Partnership for Peace and Prosperity

SOURCES: Revised and updated from Alexander C. Huang, "China's View of the World Order in the Post–Cold War Era: A China-centered Web of Bilateral Partnerships," unpublished paper, December 1998; and David M. Finkelstein, "China's New Security Concept: Reading Between the Lines," *Washington Journal of Modern China* 5, no. 1 (Spring 1999).

China and the ASEAN states also signed an agreement establishing the Strategic Partnership for Peace and Prosperity at their October 2003 summit, an agreement that commits the eleven countries to work together on international and regional political, economic, social, and security issues of mutual concern. The purpose of the partnership, according to the declaration, is to "foster friendly relations, mutually beneficial cooperation and good neighbourliness between ASEAN and China by deepening and expanding ASEAN-China cooperative relations in a comprehensive manner in the 21st century, thereby contributing further to the region's long-term peace, development and cooperation."[15] China-ASEAN relations further advanced with China acceding to the ASEAN Treaty of Amity and Cooperation (discussed further below).

The establishment of the European Union–China summitry in the mid-1990s has led to deeply institutionalized dialogue channels across a range of issues. The sixth EU-China summit, held in October 2003, concluded two major agreements on satellite navigation cooperation and tourism facilitation, as well as the establishment of a new mechanism for industrial policy dialogue.[16] During the visit of Chinese president Hu Jintao to France in January 2004, the two countries signed a joint declaration to deepen their "comprehensive strategic partnership" in political, economic, and cultural arenas.[17]

China also took the lead in establishing the Shanghai Five process as a way to manage security matters with its Central Asian neighbors, and then expanding and institutionalizing it as the Shanghai Cooperation Organization (SCO) in 2001. China funded the establishment of the group's new secretariat, which is located in Beijing and headed by a Chinese career diplomat. China also played a leading role in the formation in 1997 of the annual ASEAN Plus Three consultations, which entail security-related discussions among China, Japan, South Korea, and the ten states of the Association of Southeast Asian Nations. In spring 2002, Beijing quietly approached the North Atlantic Treaty Organization (NATO) to explore the possibility of initiating a security dialogue. That dialogue was announced in October of that year and held in January 2003. China has also taken the lead in establishing a range of important economic-related relationships with its neighbors, such as the ASEAN-China Free Trade Area and the Boao Forum. Although primarily focused on economic issues, these mechanisms nonetheless form part of Beijing's overall regional security strategy to the degree that they meet the goal of reassuring China's neighbors of the country's benign intentions. Perhaps most prominently, beginning in 2002–2003, China has been a far more active player in efforts to resolve differences between the United States and North Korea, initiating three-party consultations (between the United States, North Korea, and China) in April 2003, hosting six-party talks (with the United States, North Korea, China, South Korea, Japan, and Russia) in

August 2003, and orchestrating an active diplomatic effort with the key parties to keep the channels of dialogue open and the parties moving toward resolution.

Participation in Regional Security and Confidence-Building Mechanisms

A third important trend defining China's evolving regional security strategy concerns increased participation in and appreciation of regional security and confidence-building mechanisms. For example, in taking the lead to establish the SCO, Beijing has also actively seen to the institutionalization of the group as a regional, multilateral security and confidence-building mechanism. Under the auspices of the SCO, China and its Central Asian neighbors Russia, Kazakhstan, Kyrgyzstan, Tajikistan, and Uzbekistan engage in range of multilateral discussion and exchanges, from annual head-of-state and head-of-government summits, to regular meetings among senior counterparts in the fields of security, economics, and trade, to the establishment of the SCO counterterrorism center in Bishkek. Thus far, China and its SCO neighbors have participated in at least two joint military training exercises, the first in October 2002 between China and Kyrgyzstan, and the second in August 2003 involving China, Russia, Kazakhstan, Kyrgyzstan, and Tajikistan.[18] The Chinese navy also took part in back-to-back bilateral exercises with the Pakistan navy in late October 2003, and with the Indian navy in mid-November 2003. In its first-ever joint naval exercise, the Chinese navy conducted a search-and-rescue and counterterrorism simulation with naval forces from Pakistan off the coast of Shanghai. Three weeks later, three ships from the Indian navy joined Chinese naval forces off Shanghai for search-and-rescue exercises involving some 1,500 officers and sailors.[19]

China has been especially active in increasing its participation in regional security mechanisms in Southeast Asia. For example, China has deepened its interest and participation in the ASEAN Regional Forum (ARF) since the mid- to late 1990s, including by cohosting, with the Philippines, intersessional meetings on confidence-building measures in 1997; through the regular annual submission of defense policy white papers to the ARF; by hosting the ARF Seminar on Tropical Hygiene and Prevention and Treatment of Tropical Infectious Diseases, the ARF Professional Training Program on China's Security Policy, the Fourth ARF Meeting of Heads of Defense Colleges, the ARF Seminar on Defense Conversion Cooperation, and the September 2002 ARF seminar on military logistics outsourcing; and through participation in military college exchange programs within the ARF framework. Alongside its activities in ARF, Beijing has also become a more active participant in the ARF-related "track-two" dialogues under the auspices of the Council on Security and Cooperation in the Asia-Pacific (CSCAP), a group founded in 1993 and predating the formation of ARF (China joined

CSCAP in 1996). In this forum, Chinese scholars and officials, acting in their personal capacities, interact with their counterparts from eighteen other countries and the European Union to explore a range of multilateral regional security issues that are more difficult to address through official channels, including comprehensive and cooperative security, confidence- and security-building measures, maritime cooperation, transnational crime, and security issues affecting the North Pacific region.[20]

In another interesting development, at the July 2002 meeting of the ARF, the Chinese delegation submitted a formal position paper that provided a detailed explanation of the new security concept, the first time China had submitted such a document to the ARF. The position paper broke no new ground in describing the new security concept, but it explicitly linked the concept to the work of the ARF: "The line of thought of the [ASEAN Regional] Forum in promoting security through dialogue among equals suits the idea of the new security concept."[21] China proposed in 2001 that ARF members report on and send observers to multilateral joint military exercises. In another example of China's increased support for regional security mechanisms, Chinese foreign minister Li Zhaoxing proposed to the June 2003 ARF meeting in Phnom Penh that the organization establish a new ARF Security Policy Conference. This proposal was further refined and presented during a November 2003 ARF intersessional group (ISG) meeting on confidence-building measures, held in Beijing. In this proposal, China sought to establish an annual meeting, largely composed of senior military personnel from ARF participating governments, in order to open new channels of dialogue and increase mutual trust among regional defense officials. Issues considered for discussion by China included challenges to Asia-Pacific security, security and military strategies of ARF members, and topics such as the revolution in military affairs, defense modernization, defense conversion, and civil-military relations.[22] The first meeting of this grouping, known as the Security Policy Conference (SPC), convened in Beijing in November 2004.

But most interestingly for China's approach to security and confidence-building mechanisms in Southeast Asia, Beijing moved in the late 1990s and early 2000s to initiate numerous dialogue channels with ASEAN, but *outside* the ARF process. In 2002, China and ASEAN established a mechanism known as the Cooperative Operations in Response to Dangerous Drugs, which has included ministry-level meetings among China, Laos, Myanmar, and Thailand to deal with the challenge of drug smuggling in their shared border regions. During the China-ASEAN meeting of November 2002, the parties also agreed upon the Declaration on the Conduct of Parties in the South China Sea to govern the activities of claimants to various parts of the South China Sea, and to reduce the potential for tension and conflict in the disputed areas. This latter agreement with ASEAN was a significant change from previous Chinese attitudes: Chinese Foreign Ministry spokesman Zhang Qiyue, speaking at a news briefing at the annual ARF ministerial meeting in 1999, stated that "China is not in favor of discussing this issue [differences in the South China Sea] at any multilateral forum because this can only lead to further complication of the matter.... The consistent position of China on this issue is that the dispute in the South China Sea should be resolved through bilateral negotiations between countries concerned in peaceful means."[23]

Perhaps most importantly, in October 2003 China and ASEAN established the Strategic Partnership for Peace and Prosperity, and China signed on to the ASEAN Treaty of Amity and Cooperation. The declaration announcing the new strategic partnership stated that it "is non-aligned, non-military, and non-exclusive, and does not prevent the participants from developing their all-directional ties of friendship and cooperation with others." On security and confidence-building measures, the declaration commits the parties to "expedite the implementation of the Joint Statement on Cooperation in the Field of Non-Traditional Security Issues and actively expand and deepen cooperation in such areas," convene "ASEAN-China security-related dialogue to enhance mutual understanding and promote peace and security in the region," and "implement the Declaration on the Conduct of Parties in the South China Sea."[24] In signing and ratifying the ASEAN Treaty of Amity and Friendship, China agreed "faithfully to perform and carry out all the stipulations" of the treaty, which, among other points, calls for parties to "foster cooperation in the furtherance of the cause of peace, harmony, and stability in the region," to "not in any manner or form participate in any activity which shall constitute a threat to the political and economic stability, sovereignty, or territorial integrity" of the other parties, and to "refrain from the threat or use of force and ... at all times settle such disputes among themselves through friendly negotiations."[25]

China has also been increasingly open to participating as an observer of foreign military exercises in East Asia. Such Chinese participation has included the presence of an observer at the Rim of the Pacific (Rimpac) exercises in 1998 and at the first Pacific Reach 2000, a joint search-and-rescue exercise for submarine forces hosted by Singapore and involving Japan, South Korea, and the United States, in October 2000. In January 2002, Chinese military officers observed a naval mine clearance exercise in Singapore, and in April 2002 they observed a Japan-sponsored submarine search-and-rescue exercise. In May 2002, China also participated for the first time as an observer of U.S.-led Cobra Gold military exercises in Thailand, sending six military personnel.[26] In an unprecedented move, China in August 2003 allowed foreign military personnel from fifteen countries— including the United States, the United Kingdom, France, Russia, Germany, Canada, Tanzania, Thailand, and Turkey—to observe Chinese military exercises involving five thousand Chinese troops at the country's large tactical training base in Inner Mongolia.[27]

China has also become far more active in dispatching naval vessels abroad for friendly port visits and in expanding its programs of military-to-military exchanges. The country's first naval crossing of the Pacific took place in early 1997, with visits to the United States, Mexico, Chile, Peru, the Philippines, Malaysia, and Thailand; in 1998–99, Chinese naval vessels made friendly port calls to New Zealand, Australia, the Philippines, Malaysia, Tanzania, and South Africa; in a major first, the Chinese navy completed a circumnavigation of the globe in 2002, visiting ten countries along the way; and in October and November 2003, a Chinese missile destroyer and naval supply ship undertook a thirty-seven-day voyage paying port visits to Guam, Brunei, and Singapore.[28] In addition to port visits, China has an active program of military-to-military exchanges: in 2003, for example, the Chinese military conducted more than one hundred major exchanges, including forty-three important trips abroad to more than fifty countries, and sixty-eight visiting delegations from over fifty countries to China.[29]

In recent years, among other security-related discussions, China has held meetings of SCO defense ministers (June 2001, May 2002, and May 2003), several meetings of experts and the joint working groups on China-India border issues (June, July, and December 2001 and March, June, October, and November 2002), the first formal defense and security consultations between China and Thailand (December 2001), the China-Australia strategic dialogue (October 2001, October 2002, and October 2003), and the first China–United Kingdom and China-Germany defense consultations (both held in May 2002).[30] In 2003, according to an official report in the *PLA Daily*, China held strategic consultations and security dialogues with Australia, France, Germany, India, Mongolia, North Korea, Pakistan, Russia, South Africa, South Korea, Thailand, and the United States. At the same time, the Chinese military dispatched some 120 technical delegations involving some six thousand person-trips to conduct short-term cooperative exchanges with foreign militaries in such areas as equipment, logistics, and visits to defense colleges, and sent almost two hundred military officers abroad for training, including to such countries as France, Germany, Russia, the United Kingdom, and the United States.[31]

Further afield, China has also demonstrated its support for regional security mechanisms and multilateralism more generally. These measures have included its political and financial support for regime change in, and the rebuilding of, Afghanistan, and Beijing increased personnel contributions to United Nations peacekeeping activities in Africa, Asia, the Middle East, and Europe. Beginning in 2003, China significantly ramped up its contributions to United Nations peacekeeping missions: China has nearly three hundred observers, troops, and police serving in eight United Nations' missions, the highest number of Chinese personnel since the early 1990s, when China dispatched engineering troops to the United Nations mission to rebuild Cambodia. China has established counterterrorism dialogues with the United States, Russia, France, the United Kingdom, Pakistan, and India, acceded to ten of the twelve international counterterrorism conventions, and reached a number of bilateral counterterror agreements with the United States, resulting in China's membership in the Container Security Initiative announced in July 2003.[32]

Emphasizing Economic and Political Influence, Downplaying Military Might

A fourth key trend shaping Beijing's evolving regional security strategy relates to China's increased emphasis on economic and political influence while it downplays its growing military strength. China is certainly not abandoning its military modernization effort. Quite the contrary, in recent years China has made significant strides in building a more modern force through increased general and procurement budgets, major weapons imports and indigenous arms production programs, and an intensified focus on improved logistics and training. These steps have improved China's ability to exercise military power in the region, especially vis-à-vis Taiwan.[33]

However, it is clear that Beijing is recalibrating its overall regional security strategy to give greater emphasis to diplomatic and economic matters. In a prominent example of this tendency, China's role as host for the 2001 Asia Pacific Economic Cooperation (APEC) leaders summit in 2001 not only demonstrated its arrival as a major regional economic and political power, but it also showcased China's diplomatic adeptness in facilitating the meeting's joint counterterrorism statement. If and when China moves from observer status to full membership in a future "G-9," Beijing will likewise be able to leverage its growing economic and political might—as opposed to its military power—to weigh in on global and regional security matters.

In Northeast Asia, China is trying to exert its political and economic influence on North Korea. Similarly, South Korea's growing dependence on China as its principal trading and investment partner has helped strengthen relations between Seoul and Beijing. In Central Asia, China envisions an increasing role for economic and political ties with countries such as Kazakhstan and Kyrgyzstan for building upon and solidifying gains made in the security sphere since the late 1990s.

In Southeast Asia, disputed territorial claims in the South China Sea between China and its neighbors have been a source of tension, military muscle flexing, and sporadic clashes in the 1980s and 1990s. For example, China's military action in 1995 to secure the disputed Mischief Reef from the Philippines, and its steps to upgrade military facilities on Mischief Reef in 1998, created unease in Southeast Asia and among other Chinese neighbors, including the United States. However, Beijing has been adept in exercising its increasing economic and political influence in Southeast Asia to assuage such security concerns. This approach led to the Declaration on the Conduct of Parties in the South China Sea with ASEAN states in November 2003. Interestingly, according to Medeiros and Fravel, this agreement "included most of the draft language sought by ASEAN—and little of what was offered by China."[34] Furthermore, as noted above, in signing the ASEAN Treaty of Amity and Cooperation, Beijing took the significant step of pledging to resolve any future conflicts in the region through dialogue, again placing the emphasis for Sino-Southeast Asian relations on diplomatic and economic cooperation.

The increased Chinese emphasis on economic and political levers of regional power is best illustrated by China's more nuanced but still tough approach toward Taiwan that has emerged in recent years. In the late 1990s and into 2000, Beijing openly threatened Taiwan with military action, such as with the missile tests of 1995 and 1996 and the bellicose rhetoric during the run-up to the 2000 Taiwan presidential election suggesting that there was a timetable for forcible reunification. More recently, Beijing appears to see the wisdom of speaking softly with economic and political incentives, while still carrying (and continually sharpening) the military stick. Chinese leaders may be more willing to exercise economic and political levers—without abandoning the steady military buildup—to entice and co-opt different Taiwan-based constituencies into sharing a vision of cross-strait relations that is closer to Beijing. While considerable tension, uncertainty, and potential instability and conflict still weigh heavily in the cross-strait dynamic, Beijing's more sophisticated approach in recent years appears to be part and parcel of its more confident regional security strategy overall.

CHINA'S REGIONAL SECURITY STRATEGY: PROSPECTS AND IMPLICATIONS

How should we assess Beijing's evolving regional security strategy? Recall that for the past decade and beyond Beijing has consistently claimed that peace and development are the principal trends of the times, that multipolarity and economic globalization will continue, and that there is a general easing of tensions in the regional and international security situation. Moreover, Beijing has likewise been consistent in its goals: it has persistently sought a positive and stable external environment in order to focus on domestic challenges; it has carefully managed its growing wealth and power in ways that have extended its influence, but done so in a way that has reassured its neighbors; and it has cautiously balanced its concern about what it perceives as excessive American hegemony while avoiding overt confrontation with the United States. Overall, given China's current position in regional affairs, it appears that its understanding of the world situation and the goals it pursues have been correct and have met with success.

Looking ahead, however, at least two major points deserve closer scrutiny. First, the Chinese suppositions about peace and development and an easing of tensions are probably at a greater risk of being disproved today than they have been at any time over the past decade. The world may become an increasingly dangerous, uncertain, and unstable place for Chinese interests, forcing Beijing to reassess its security position and make some very difficult decisions. For example, Beijing has expressed its support of the war on terror in a number of basic ways. However, it was not supportive of American intervention in Iraq, and it would be extremely apprehensive about further expansion of American military action, not only for the disruption it might cause to the international and regional security situation, but also for what it might mean in terms of American unilateralism, hegemony, and military predominance. Indeed, many developments related to the counterterrorism effort exacerbate rather than alleviate long-standing Chinese concerns about the U.S.-led regional and global security order.

Similarly, intensified conflict on China's immediate periphery—up to and including war on the Korean peninsula or in the Taiwan Strait—would profoundly shake China's new confidence and, especially with regard to Taiwan, possibly bring it into conflict with the United States and its allies. Difficult choices lie ahead for Beijing regarding Taiwan, and these choices are likely to become even thornier. U.S.-Taiwan relations remain relatively strong, and many former taboos in the political and military relationship are slowly eroding. At the same time, the nature of Taiwan's politics remains divisive and incapable of agreeing on a basic package of measures that Beijing would deem acceptable to define the future cross-strait relationship. Such problems may challenge Beijing's currently positive and confident regional security strategy in the years ahead. As Chinese strategists pointed out in the 2002 defense white paper, "uncertainties impeding peace and development are also on the increase" and "the world is far from tranquil," while the 2004 white paper defined the Taiwan situation as "grim."[35]

Second, significant questions remain about the future of the U.S.-China relationship. For example, at what point does China's successful cultivation of influence with its regional neighbors significantly encroach upon spheres of influence enjoyed by the United States for decades? In many respects, the new security concept can be seen as Beijing's effort to propose a regional security system that is an alternative to Washington's framework of U.S. leadership, military alliances, and a forward-based presence. The stress China places upon equality and mutual respect can be interpreted in part as a call for Washington to act less high-handedly and unilaterally. Touting nonaggression, noninterference, and the need for disputes to be settled peacefully through dialogue reflects China's increased concern with U.S.-led armed intervention. Finally, by noting that the "Cold War mentality" needs to be abandoned, Chinese leaders are expressing their wariness of the U.S. alliance system, especially in East Asia.

Vague as the security concept may seem, it calls for a fundamental change in the way the world works. China's defense white papers warn that the current international political and economic order is "irrational," "unfair," and in need of change, that "democracy in international relations remains elusive," and that "there are new manifestations of hegemonism and power politics." For Beijing, the answer may lie in a "[a] new security concept and new international political, economic, and security order responsive to our times. . . . China's fundamental interests lie in . . . *the establishment and maintenance of a new regional security order*."[36] Moreover, as Vice Premier Qian Qichen noted a year after the September 2001 terrorist attacks in the United States, "Generally speaking Sino-U.S. relations are developing forward, but there are also many frictions and struggles. . . . There is no change in the basic contradictions between China and the United States."[37] Similarly, the 2001 Quadrennial Defense Review issued by the Pentagon stated that "the possibility exists that a military competitor with a formidable resource base will emerge in the region [East Asia]," and that among America's "enduring national interests" is "precluding hostile domination of critical areas," including Northeast Asia and the East Asian littoral, defined as "the region stretching from south of Japan through Australia and into the Bay of Bengal." These understandings on both sides of the U.S.-China relationship point to potentially contentious times ahead as China emerges as a more prominent player in Asia.

But whether China's regional security efforts continue smoothly along their currently successful trajectory, or whether they meet setbacks, one point seems certain: for better or worse, China is likely to become increasingly effective in pursuing its national goals and strategies, both within the region and among larger external powers with interests in the region, such as the United States.[38] That in itself is a relatively new and exceptional situation demanding great attention, and it points toward a different regional security system in the future.

NOTES

The author wishes to thank Ms. Jennifer Feltner for her excellent research assistance in the preparation of this chapter.

1. These principles are: mutual respect for sovereignty and territorial integrity, mutual nonaggression, mutual noninterference in each other's internal affairs, equality and mutual benefit, and peaceful coexistence.

2. See "Chinese President Calls for New Security Concept," summary of a March 26, 1999, speech by Jiang Zemin before the United Nations Conference on Disarmament in Geneva, available at http://nti.org/db/china/engdocs/jzmo399.htm.

These principles are reiterated in *China's National Defense 2000* (Beijing: Information Office of the State Council, October 2000), 8. See also an early presentation of the new security concept in *China's National Defense* (Beijing: Information Office of the State Council, July 1998), 6–7. David M. Finkelstein provides an excellent analysis of the new security concept in his "China's New Security Concept: Reading Between the Lines," *Washington Journal of Modern China* 5, no. 1 (Spring 1999): 37–49.

3. *China's National Defense 2000*, 3.

4. Ibid., 5.

5. See such views identified by Michael Pillsbury, *China Debates the Future Security Environment* (Washington, DC: National Defense University Press, 2000), 44–45, 64–65.

6. Discussion of this concept draws from David Finkelstein, *China Reconsiders Its National Security: "The Great Peace and Development Debate of 1999"* (Alexandria, VA: CNA Corporation, December 2000), 21–23.

7. *China's National Defense 2000*, 6.

8. Ibid., 7.

9. Quotations in this paragraph are from *China's National Defense in 2002* (Beijing: Information Office of the State Council, December 2002).

10. Quotations in this paragraph are from *China's National Defense in 2004* (Beijing: Information Office of the State Council, December 2004).

11. Ibid.

12. On China's more confident diplomacy, see Evan S. Medeiros and M. Taylor Fravel, "China's New Diplomacy," *Foreign Affairs* (November/December 2003).

13. "Chinese Premier Meets African Leaders at China-Africa Forum," *Xinhua*, December 16, 2003, available at http://news.xinhuanet.com/english/2003–12/16/content_1234649.htm; "President Hu Proposes Principles for Developing China-Arab Relations," January 30, 2004, available at http://www.china-embassy.org/eng/xw/t61176.htm.

14. For an English translation of the treaty, see "Treaty of Good Neighborly Friendship and Cooperation between the People's Republic of China and the Russian Federation," in Foreign Broadcast Information Service, document CPP20010716000104, July 16, 2001.

15. See "Joint Declaration of the Heads of State/Government of the Association of Southeast Asian Nations and the People's Republic of China on Strategic Partnership for Peace and Prosperity," October 8, 2003, available at http://www.aseansec.org/15265.htm.

16. See documents, joint statements, and other materials on the EU-China summit at http://europa.eu.int/comm/external_relations/china/summit/index.htm.

17. "Hu Jintao Proposes Steps to Boost Strategic Partnership with France," *People's Daily*, January 29, 2004, available at http://english.people.com.cn/200401/29/eng20040129_133455.shtml. See also "Declaration Conjointe Franco-Chinoise," January 27, 2004, available at http://www.elysee.fr/cgi-bin/auracom/aurweb/search/file?aur_file = discours/2004/DC040127.html.

18. On the SCO and China's relations with Central Asia more generally, see Bates Gill and Matthew Oresman, *China's New Journey to the West: China's Emergence in Central Asia and Implications for U.S. Interests* (Washington, DC: Center for Strategic and International Studies, August 2003).

19. "Yearender: Joint Military Drills Draw Attention Worldwide," *People's Liberation Army Daily,* December 15, 2003, available at http://english.pladaily.com.cn/english/pladaily/2003/12/15/20031215001011_TodayHeadlines.html.

20. See the CSCAP Web site, http://www.cscap.org.

21. See "Chinese Delegation Submits Position Document on New Security Concept to ASEAN Forum," *Beijing Xinhua Domestic Service,* August 1, 2002, translated in Foreign Broadcast Information Service, document CPP20020801000128, August 1, 2002.

22. See a summary of the November 2003 ARF ISG meeting at http://www.dfat.gov.au/arf/intersessional/report_interses_03_04.html. See also "FM Stresses Asian Security Issues in ASEAN Forum," *Xinhua,* June 19, 2003, available at http://www.china.org.cn/english/international/67429.htm.

23. Zhang quoted in "China Rejects ASEAN 'Code of Conduct' for Spratlys," *Kyodo News International,* August 2, 1999.

24. See "Joint Declaration of the Heads of State/Government."

25. See the "Instrument of Accession to the Treaty of Amity and Cooperation in Southeast Asia," October 8, 2003, available at http://www.aseansec.org/15271.htm; and the "Treaty of Amity and Cooperation in Southeast Asia," February 24, 1976, available at http://www.aseansec.org/1217.htm. See also "China, Southeast Asia Conclude Strategic Partnership Pact," *Xinhua,* October 8, 2003, available at http://www1.chinadaily.com.cn/en/doc/2003-10/08/content_270030.htm. For a further discussion on China joining the Treaty on Amity and Cooperation, see the chapter by Zhang Yunling and Tang Shiping in this volume.

26. Cobra Gold, the largest multinational exercise and movement of peacetime forces in the Pacific, is held annually by the United States, Thailand, and Singapore. In 2002, observers of the exercise included Australia, Cambodia, China, France, India, Indonesia, Japan, Malaysia, Mongolia, the Philippines, Russia, South Korea, Sri Lanka, and Tonga.

27. "Foreign Observers Attend Chinese War Games for the First Time," *Xinhuanet,* August 25, 2003, available at http://news.xinhuanet.com/english/2003-08/25/content_1044252.htm.

28. From *China's National Defense in 2002* (Beijing: Information Office of the State Council, December 2002). See also "Chinese Navy Fleet Back at Port after Overseas Visit," *Xinhuanet,* November 21, 2003, available at http://news.xinhuanet.com/english/2003-11/21/content_1192547.htm.

29. "China's Military Diplomacy in 2003," *PLA Daily,* December 29, 2003, available at http://english.pladaily.com.cn/english/pladaily/2003/12/29/20031229001013_MilitaryNews.html.

30. From *China National Defense 2002,* Appendix III.

31. "China's Military Diplomacy in 2003." On China's military diplomacy more broadly, see also Kenneth W. Allen and Eric A. McVadon, *China's Foreign Military Relations* (Washington, DC: Stimson Center, October 1999); and David Shambaugh, *Modernizing China's Military: Progress, Problems and Prospects* (Berkeley: University of California Press, 2003).

32. "China Formally Joins U.S. Container Security Initiative," Department of Homeland Security press release, July 29, 2003, available at http://usinfo.state.gov/topical/pol/terror/texts/03072900.htm.

33. For more details on China's military modernization effort, see Michael Swaine's chapter in this volume.

34. Medeiros and Fravel, "China's New Diplomacy."

35. *China's National Defense in 2002; China's National Defense in 2004.*

36. Quotes drawn from *China National Defense 2002* and *China's National Defense 2000* (emphasis added).

37. From a speech by Qian Qichen, "The International Situation and Sino-US Relations Since the 11 September Incident," in *Waijiao Xueyuan Xuebao* [Foreign affairs college journal] 3 (September 25, 2002): 1–6, translated in Foreign Broadcast Information Service, document CPP20021015000192, October 15, 2002.

38. With regard to Chinese inroads in Southeast Asia at the expense of U.S. influence, see, for example, Evelyn Goh, "A Chinese Lesson for the US: How to Charm South-east Asia," *Straits Times,* October 31, 2003, appearing in Foreign Broadcast Information Service, document SEP20031031000027, October 31, 2003; and Wayne Bert, *The United States, China, and Southeast Asian Security: A Changing of the Guard?* (Basingstoke, U.K.: Palgrave Macmillan, 2003).

12

China's Regional Military Posture

Michael D. Swaine

Some observers of Asia increasingly emphasize the growing importance of globalization and the forces of political, diplomatic, economic, social, and cultural change as key factors shaping the future of the region. Although such variables are unquestionably significant, the history of Asia, past experience concerning changes in the larger international system, and much of our conceptual understanding of how nations interact to shape their environment clearly indicate that military power remains a critical determinant of the security perceptions and behavior of all nations, and hence of the larger Asian and global systems.

In the case of China, military power has historically been regarded as a pragmatically essential, if not always ethically laudable, requirement for the maintenance of a secure and stable government. One of the primary goals of modern Chinese nationalism has been for the Chinese state to develop a sufficient level of military power to deter future aggression by other states, to support China's long-standing desire to achieve national wealth and power, and to attain international recognition and respect as a great nation. In addition, many outside observers measure the potential threat generated by China's rise as a modern nation-state in large part on the basis of the growing size, capabilities, and configuration of its military forces.

Thus, given China's expanse, its critical geostrategic location astride the Asian landmass, and its overall rapid rate of growth, there is little doubt that its future military posture will exert a decisive impact on the larger security environment and hence on the shape and tenor of those nonmilitary factors mentioned above. This impact will be most keenly felt in Asia. Indeed, China's current and likely near- to medium-term military posture is essentially limited to the Asian region. The only major exception involves those long-range strategic nuclear weapons systems of the People's Liberation

Army (PLA) that present a retaliatory, second-strike capability against targets outside Asia, for example, the United States homeland and European parts of the former Soviet Union. The rest of China's strategic forces, as well as all of its conventional forces, are oriented exclusively toward regional objectives.

In order to fully assess the current and future significance of China's regional military posture, one must first identify China's overall defense policy objectives and intended military capabilities relevant to Asia. This is covered in the first section of this chapter. The second section outlines the major features of China's current and likely future military capabilities and deployments in Asia. The third section assesses the possible implications of the preceding analysis for Asian security, including an evaluation of the impact of China's current and likely future capabilities and deployments upon key countries. The overall analysis strongly indicates that China's military posture in Asia is experiencing fairly rapid and significant change, marked most notably by a growing capacity to deploy forces along its maritime periphery. This expanding capability, along with China's overall growing regional military presence, will increasingly affect the diplomatic and security calculations of key Asian actors, and of the United States.

REGIONAL DEFENSE POLICY OBJECTIVES AND RELATED CAPABILITIES AND FORCE STRUCTURE

China's military posture in Asia is shaped by several fundamental defense policy objectives. First, and foremost, Chinese forces are deployed to deter or defeat possible threats or attacks directed against China's heartland, and especially its economically critical eastern coastline. The most likely sources of such threats or attacks include major regional powers such as Japan, India, and Russia, as well as U.S. forces based in Asia, in particular in Japan, South Korea, Guam, and Hawaii.

China's regional military posture is also designed to deal with a range of possible "local war" conflict scenarios that might occur along China's periphery, especially in maritime areas. Such conflicts would likely arise in response to Chinese efforts to defend an array of sovereignty and territorial interests, such as claims to the Diaoyutai/Senkaku Islands near Japan, to Taiwan, to areas along the border with India, and to the Spratly Islands in the South China Sea. They could also occur as a result of confrontations over hotspots affecting the broader regional balance, such as the Korean peninsula and the Indo-Pakistani imbroglio.

More broadly, China's regional military developments and deployments are also intended to support—either directly or indirectly—Beijing's overall foreign policy and security objectives in Asia. For example, the military supports in various ways (e.g., via senior military officer delegation visits) the development of more cooperative diplomatic and political relations between China and other regional states. The strengthening of the Chinese military also supports the expansion of Chinese diplomatic and military influence and leverage over nearby strategic territories claimed by Beijing, such as the Spratly Islands in the South China Sea; adds to Chinese influence within key regional entities, such as multinational economic, political, and military organizations; and enhances China's overall global and regional stature, particularly through the display of high-technology weaponry and efforts to establish a presence beyond China's borders. Over the long term, Chinese military power is presumably also intended to support critical strategic military objectives, such as the maintenance of access to vital oceanic routes in the event of conflict.

The above defense objectives clearly imply a significant transformation in China's past strategic outlook, from that of a continental power requiring large land forces for defense against threats to its internal borders, to that of a combined continental/maritime power with a diverse range of domestic and external security needs. Overall, in the conventional realm, China is shifting from a continental orientation requiring large land forces for "in-depth" defense of the homeland to a combined continental/maritime orientation requiring a smaller, more mobile, and more sophisticated "active peripheral defense" capability for both inland and especially coastal areas. Such notions are based, in turn, upon several new Chinese strategic principles and combat methods such as "strategic frontiers," "strategic deterrence," and "a greater stress on gaining the initiative by striking first."[1]

This shift requires three general types of capabilities for China's regionally oriented forces:

- The ability to respond rapidly, take the initiative, attain superiority quickly, prevent escalation, and resolve any conflict on favorable terms;
- The ability to conduct preemptive offensive strikes for self-defense as well as use forces for both conventional and nuclear deterrence and coercion;
- The eventual development of limited power projection capabilities in Asia, enabling a prolonged sea presence and limited land and sea area denial; sea area control is probably not a desired capability over the near- to medium-term.

Over the medium to long term, the above defense policy and capabilities objectives translate into a specific set of force structure requirements. In the area of conventional forces, these include:

- A smaller, more flexible, better motivated, highly trained and well-equipped ground force centered on rapid reaction units, with limited yet significant armored fixed-wing and helicopter transport and assault, airborne drop, and amphibious power projection capabilities, as well as a small but well-trained special operations force (SOF);[2]

· A robust green-to-blue-water naval capability centered on a new generation of surface combatants with improved air defense, anti-submarine warfare (ASW), and antiship capabilities, modern conventional attack submarines with advanced torpedoes and cruise missile capabilities, an improved naval air arm, and greatly improved replenishment-at-sea capabilities;[3]

· A more versatile, modern air force, with longer-range interceptor/ strike aircraft, improved early warning (EW) and air defense capabilities, extended and close air support, and longer-range transport, lift, and midair refueling capacities;[4]

· A joint service tactical operations doctrine utilizing more sophisticated command, control, communications, computers, intelligence, and strategic reconnaissance (C4ISR), early warning, and battle management systems, and the use of both airborne and satellite-based assets to improve detection, tracking, targeting, and strike capabilities, and to enhance operational coordination among the armed services.[5]

In the strategic realm, China possesses a small, retaliatory "countervalue" deterrent force, centered on a growing array of mobile short-, medium-, and intermediate-range ballistic missiles. A significant portion of these forces is oriented toward targets within Asia, most likely including Japan, India, Asian regions of Russia, and key forward U.S. air and naval bases in the Western Pacific such as Guam. China is currently seeking to improve the survivability and potency of these forces.[6] It is also likely contemplating the acquisition of a more sophisticated "counterforce" missile capability to defend against America's technologically superior conventional "in-theater" strike assets. This transition implies, over the medium to long term, the deployment in Asia of:

· A large number (possibly several hundred or more than one thousand)[7] of short-, medium-, and intermediate-range solid-fueled, mobile ballistic missiles (with a range of less than 5,500 kilometers) and short-range cruise missiles, with increased accuracy, and some with both nuclear and conventional capabilities;

· Smaller, more powerful nuclear warheads with potential multiple, independently targetable reentry vehicle (MIRV) or multiple reentry vehicle (MRV) capabilities;

· Modern strategic surveillance, early warning (EW), and battle management systems, with advanced land, airborne, and space-based C4ISR assets applicable to Asia and beyond.[8]

CURRENT AND LIKELY FUTURE REGIONAL CAPABILITIES

The Chinese military's current force structure, training, and deployment patterns suggest that the PLA is currently not fully configured or trained to realize most of the above aspirations and objectives guiding China's military posture in Asia. At present, the PLA possesses the following broad capabilities relevant to Asian contingencies:

- A highly effective capability to undertake "defense-in-depth" against any conceivable effort to invade and seize Chinese territory, especially by neighboring Asian countries; however, China does not have a very effective defense against precision long-range attacks against Chinese territory from more than 200 kilometers beyond China's borders;
- Effective ground force–based power projection across land borders against smaller regional powers to within approximately 100 kilometers, to inflict punishment and to deter attacks along China's periphery;
- Effective power projection to dislodge smaller regional powers from nearby disputed land and maritime territories such as various border areas in Northeast, Central, and Southeast Asia, and the Paracel and Spratly Islands; only a limited capability to hold and seize such territories, especially against combined regional forces;
- An extremely limited ability to project force against the territory or forces of the most militarily capable states near China, especially Russia, India, and Japan; the greatest potential threats to these countries are presented by ballistic and cruise missiles and, in the case of India and especially Russia, perhaps by air and ground forces deployed within contiguous border areas;
- The ability to undertake intensive, short-duration air and naval attacks on Taiwan, as well as more prolonged air, naval, and possibly ground attacks; China's ability to prevail under either scenario would be highly dependent on Taiwan's political and military response, and especially on any military actions taken by the United States and Japan;
- An effective second-strike, countervalue-based deterrent against nuclear or other WMD threats or attacks from within the region; China's confidence in this area has arguably been low in recent years, but is probably increasing as a result of ongoing improvements in missile capabilities.[9]

As these capabilities indicate, China's current military posture in Asia is primarily oriented toward defending Chinese territory (and in particular Beijing, China's economically dynamic eastern coastline, and major communications hubs) against a direct attack while deterring any WMD-based threats or pressures.

However, Beijing is also attempting to acquire a range of conventional offensive-oriented capabilities that, if attained, would likely enable the PLA not only to undertake sizable coordinated (i.e., joint) actions against nearby countries and territories such as Taiwan and the Spratly Islands, but also to achieve the more ambitious defense objectives outlined above. These desired capabilities apparently include:

- A multiregimental military air- and sea-lift capacity;
- A multiregimental amphibious attack capability;
- A demonstrated offshore medium-range bomber or strike aircraft capability;
- An operational in-flight refueling capacity for more than one hundred aircraft (approximately four regiments);
- The demonstrated ability to mount sustained naval operations;
- The demonstrated ability to deploy special operations force (SOF) and marine units beyond China's borders, probably totaling several brigades;
- The capability to undertake true joint operations or coordinated deployments across military regions;
- An airborne early warning and control capability and a strategic warning and real-time surveillance and reconnaissance capability.[10]

In order to attain such capabilities, the PLA must first overcome a variety of largely systemic obstacles that plague the entire military modernization effort. These include deficiencies in command and control, air defense, logistics, and communications; inadequate training for critical operators such as fighter pilots and for carrying out sizable offshore operations; persistent problems in the military education system; budget limitations; the lack of critical long-range support systems (e.g., surveillance and targeting); and nagging problems in defense research and development, technology, and the production of indigenous weaponry.[11]

Assuming that Beijing is able to overcome such problems and sustain or even accelerate somewhat the current tempo of its modernization program, one might expect that China could attain the following overall regional military capabilities by 2007–10:

- The ability to conduct limited[12] air and sea denial (as opposed to sea control) operations up to 250 miles from China's continental coastline;
- The ability to strike a wide range of civilian and military targets in East, Southeast, and South Asia[13] with a large number (perhaps more than one thousand) of nuclear or conventionally armed short- and medium-range ballistic missiles, as well as with several hundred medium-range bombers armed with conventional bombs and cruise missiles;

- The ability to transport and deploy one to two divisions (approximately 15,000–30,000 fully equipped soldiers) within one hundred miles of China's continental borders via land, sea, and air transport;
- The ability to survive a preemptive strike against China's nuclear facilities and retaliate within the region (and beyond) with a significant number of improved-accuracy intermediate- and long-range land- and sea-based ballistic and land-attack cruise missiles;
- The ability to overwhelm any likely space-based or air-breathing missile defense system deployed in Asia.

If one projects the above trends for another ten years or so, to the year 2020, one might expect the following general military capabilities:

- The ability to patrol a single non–carrier surface and subsurface battle group within one thousand nautical miles of China's continental coastline;
- The ability to conduct both sea and air denial operations within five hundred nautical miles of China's continental coastline;
- The ability to undertake a sizable naval blockade, with air support, of islands within two hundred nautical miles of China's continental coastline;
- The ability to transport and deploy three to four divisions (approximately 45,000–60,000 fully equipped soldiers) within two hundred miles of China's continental borders via land, sea, and air transport.

However, these are rough estimates.[14] Equally important, the ability to undertake the above military operations does not imply either intent or inevitable success. As indicated above, China's apparent objective, beyond deterring and defending against a direct attack on Chinese territory, is to protect Chinese territorial interests, to successfully prosecute a variety of possible "local war" scenarios that might emerge along China's periphery, and to possess sufficient capabilities to augment China's expanding political, economic, and diplomatic influence in Asia. None of these objectives necessarily implies an aggressive design. Moreover, China's ability to prevail in any application of military force in Asia will depend significantly on the specific threat perceptions, military doctrines, and capabilities of China's neighbors.

IMPLICATIONS FOR THE ASIAN SECURITY ENVIRONMENT

In the late 1990s, one American PLA expert observed that a concern about China's growing power and influence was only one, and usually not the primary, factor driving military modernization and deployment patterns in the region.[15] Moreover, PRC power projection capabilities at that time were viewed as quite rudimentary, and concerns about such capabilities were counterbalanced by China's strong emphasis on political accommodation, its increasing economic integration with the region, and the continued regionwide presence of and regional links with U.S. forces. These factors encouraged lower-cost, nonmilitary approaches to dealing with China's rise, such as emphases on more practicable, normalized bilateral relations, increasing economic interdependence, and the enmeshment of China in an increasing number of multilateral structures throughout Asia.[16]

These general observations remain largely true today for most countries of the region, despite a significant increase in Chinese defense spending and resulting military capabilities since the late 1990s. Looking at the region as a whole, there is little evidence that China's program of military modernization and its pattern of force deployments have thus far generated a broad-based military reaction from other Asian nations in the form of deliberate force buildups or other types of compensatory or anticipatory moves indicative of an arms race or security dilemma. In general, few Asian nations explicitly refer to China's expanding military acquisitions as a justification for their own military programs.

On the other hand, one can also perceive what appears to be a diffuse, albeit growing, impact of "the China factor" on regional threat perceptions, defense planning, and military acquisitions in certain areas and among specific nations (discussed below). Many regional strategists are particularly concerned with China's emerging maritime-oriented security priorities, the steady expansion of the PLA's operational capabilities—especially those relating to both naval and air power—and its foreign weapons and military technology acquisitions.

A more detailed understanding of the relationship between China's evolving military posture and regional perceptions and behavior can be gleaned from a closer examination of the most significant subregions and major states, in particular those key areas along China's maritime periphery, including Northeast Asia, maritime Southeast Asia, and India.[17]

Northeast Asia

Japan.   In the past, Japanese strategists focused far more attention on the prospects for social and economic instability in China than upon any potential Chinese military threat. In recent years, however, military analysts, some politicians, and even segments of the Japanese public have expressed concern over the possible adverse impact upon Japan's security of current trends in Chinese military modernization and deployments.

At present, Japan's air and naval capabilities are greatly superior to those of the PLA Air Force (PLAAF) and PLA Navy (PLAN). Its air force includes a large number of F-15s and a growing number of newer F-2 fighters, as well as several sophisticated airborne early warning (EW) aircraft that are unmatched by the Chinese. Moreover, Japanese pilots train between 50 and 100 percent more than their PLAAF counterparts, and their training system is more technologically sophisticated.[18] The Japanese navy operates several Aegis-equipped destroyers, while China's naval surface tonnage is reportedly only about three-quarters as large as Japan's and is far less sophisticated. Japan's Coast Guard is "almost as large as the entire Chinese surface combat fleet and in several respects better equipped." These Japanese capabilities resulted from significant increases in Tokyo's defense budget during the 1980s and 1990s.[19]

Thus, in general, China does not possess sufficient air and naval power projection capabilities to pose a major threat to Japanese forces or territory at present, nor will it in the foreseeable future. However, one notable exception is in the area of ballistic missiles. The PLA is deploying a growing number of increasingly accurate, mobile short- and medium-range ballistic missiles in South and Southeast China, many of them within range of Japan. Such weapons could be used to threaten or to attack Japanese targets or U.S. military bases located in the Japanese home islands, especially in the event of a serious crisis over Taiwan. This potential threat has added to Japan's existing incentives—based primarily on the growing security threat posed by North Korean missiles—to expand its program of research on a ballistic missile defense system.[20]

More broadly, Japanese statements and policies have been more critical of Chinese military behavior since the mid-1990s, in response to Beijing's nuclear tests, its clashes with the Philippines and Vietnam in the Spratly Islands, Sino-Japanese tensions over rival claims to the Diaoyutai/Senkaku Islands, and China's use of coercive force toward Taiwan. As a result, Tokyo's expanding definition of its security role in the Asia-Pacific—as envisioned by the U.S.-Japan Defense Guidelines Review of the mid-1990s—partly reflects a concern with China's growing military prowess. In response, China has expressed concern over the "buildup" of Japan's military and urged Tokyo to move with caution.[21]

In the final analysis, however, most informed observers in Japan believe that China remains at present only a hypothetical future military threat, albeit one that is of increasing concern to a growing number of Japanese citizens. Moreover, many Japanese—as many other Asians—hope that China's growing military capabilities can be constrained or blunted by successfully integrating Beijing into the multilateral international and regional security systems. Most Japanese appear to believe this effort has a good chance of succeeding, as long as China is not isolated or contained. Thus, the level of potential military threat from China has not been sufficient to dissuade Tokyo from seeking closer bilateral and multilateral cooperation with Beijing. Indeed, the search for such cooperation has arguably increased as Sino-Japanese economic ties have deepened in recent years.[22]

South Korea.   China's growing military capabilities have significant potential implications for South Korea, given Beijing's close proximity to South Korea's territorial borders, and China's historically close political, economic, and security ties with North Korea. In past decades, China's military posture in Northeast Asia was of great concern to Seoul largely because of the fear that the PLA might support Pyongyang in a conflict with the South. As recently as the mid-1990s, South Korean observers cited ongoing military-to-military contacts between China and North Korea as a significant security concern.[23] These security fears have declined greatly in recent years, however, in large part as a result of China's opening to the outside world, its reduced support for the North Korean regime, and especially the enormous improvement that has occurred in China's relations with South Korea.[24] Seoul fears that growing Chinese military capabilities might threaten the South in a future conflict on the Korean peninsula are also reduced by the fact that the chances of such a conflict are now regarded as very low by many South Korean citizens and politicians.[25]

Today, little evidence exists to suggest that enhanced Chinese ground, air, naval, or ballistic missile capabilities are either directed at South Korea or would be used against South Korea in the event of a Korean conflict. Even though South Korean defense planners have gradually downgraded their assessment of the urgency of the DPRK threat in recent years and have begun to plan for a "post-DPRK security environment" in which operational capacities beyond the peninsula will matter most, China has apparently not emerged as a major object of concern. In fact, some South Koreans view Japan as a more significant potential security concern than either Pyongyang or Beijing.[26]

Nonetheless, to some outside analysts, concern about growing Chinese power explains references by various South Korean military officials to the need for a more sophisticated "strategic force"—including AWACS, more indigenous submarines and destroyers, naval-launched attack helicopters, air-refueling aircraft, more sophisticated missiles, antimissile systems, and advanced fighters—to deal with deepening conflicts of interest in the region and threats outside the peninsula.[27] Yet even though South Korea is developing the ability to project force into Northeast Asia, "its capabilities are minimal in relation to its neighbors and are likely to remain minimal for some time to come."[28]

Taiwan.   China's military posture in Asia obviously provokes the greatest response from Taiwan, and for good reason. Since the mid- to late 1990s,

China's military has been heavily oriented toward developing a credible threat of force and a range of coercive measures that could be directed toward the island, both to deter what is viewed as an increasingly separatist-minded Taiwan from achieving de jure independence and, if necessary, to prevail in a military confrontation with Taiwan and possibly the United States.[29]

In response to this growing PLA capability, Taiwan is attempting—with the assistance of the United States—to carry out a fundamental restructuring and streamlining of its armed forces and to acquire a range of new capabilities and operational procedures. These efforts center on the attempt to create a smaller, more integrated, joint and balanced force, possessing smaller, lighter, more mobile ground units, greatly improved naval and air capabilities, better surveillance and battle management systems, quicker response times, increased survivability against missile and air attack, and enhanced deterrence capabilities. This highly ambitious modernization and reform program confronts many problems, however, and has shown only sporadic success to date, despite extensive and growing levels of U.S. assistance.[30]

Nonetheless, if Washington continues to press hard for change and the Taiwan government continues to respond positively, albeit incompletely, to such pressure, there is little doubt that advances will continue over the medium term, that is, within the next five to seven years, in areas such as C⁴ISR, jointness, and training, surface naval combatants, ballistic missile defense systems, long-distance radar, and ASW systems. In addition, the size, configuration, and orientation of the armed forces will continue to adjust to the demands of creating a more credible set of deterrence and defense capabilities. Yet it remains far from certain that such developments will together produce improvements in Taiwan's deterrent and war-fighting capabilities sufficient and timely enough to influence greatly both Beijing's overall political, diplomatic, and military strategy toward Taiwan and any specific Chinese decision to apply coercive measures or outright force in a crisis or military conflict. Specifically, the U.S. government worries that Taiwan's defense reforms and modernization will not take effect early enough to deal with the possible emergence of several major PRC military capabilities by 2007–10 or even earlier.[31]

Overall, the interactive military dynamic between China and Taiwan has produced a type of offensive-defensive arms race that arguably constitutes the most dangerous consequence of China's regional military posture to date.

Maritime Southeast Asia

Among Southeast Asian nations, China's developing military posture arguably exerts the greatest effect in the maritime arena. As suggested above, there is growing concern among some defense analysts and political leaders in Malaysia, Indonesia, Vietnam, and the Philippines that China will employ its growing naval and air capabilities to influence the security environment in adverse ways. The concern among these observers is not so much that China will apply a highly coercive strategy, but rather that China's size and aggregate capabilities will fundamentally alter strategic realities and power perceptions in its favor.[32] China already possesses the capability to overwhelm any combination of maritime Southeast Asian states in naval force-on-force encounters, assuming no extraregional assistance is forthcoming.

Many ASEAN countries have in recent years acquired some impressive combat aviation and antisurface warfare technologies, but these capabilities exist in relatively small numbers. Moreover, the integration of these technologies into the existing force structure will likely prove difficult (except in the case of Singapore), the combat proficiency of all Southeast Asian operators—barring the Singaporean Air Force—is an open question, and it is unlikely, in any case, that the more sophisticated aircraft and naval platforms of Southeast Asian states would ever face the PLAAF or the PLAN in any unified or coordinated fashion.[33]

In most contingencies that can be envisaged (e.g., territorial disputes in the South China Sea, or efforts to control vital maritime lines of communication or commerce), Chinese naval and air forces would have a considerable advantage vis-à-vis the forces of one or even several ASEAN states.[34] This will especially hold true once China acquires the ability to conduct routine in-flight refueling of fighter-bombers.

Despite this overall assessment, few Southeast Asian nations have exhibited any clear efforts to acquire new military capabilities in direct response to growing Chinese regional power, or to coordinate their military doctrines to deal collectively with a potential Chinese military threat. The only exception is the Philippines. The Mischief Reef incident of early 1995 provided an incentive to expand the Philippine defense budget to acquire warships and aircraft. Moreover, after the 1995–96 Taiwan Strait crisis, Philippine officials sought low-cost military equipment from the United States, including attack helicopters, air defense radars, multirole fighters, frigates, and coastal defense craft with Harpoon missiles.[35] The Mischief Reef incident also seemed to incite interest in Malaysia in acquiring diesel electric submarines. However, no clear military response to China's increasing regional capabilities or behavior has occurred in Vietnam and Indonesia,[36] and Beijing's relations with Singapore and Thailand remain extremely good. Indeed, the latter country has been a significant recipient of Chinese weaponry for many years. This is also true for Myanmar, which has arguably benefited the most among Southeast Asian nations from China's increasing military capabilities. Beginning in the early 1990s, Sino-Myanmar military links expanded significantly, and Beijing supplied well over $1 billion in

armaments, including fighter aircraft, patrol boats, artillery, tanks, antiair-
craft guns, and missiles. Some observers also believe that the Chinese military is involved in a Myanmar naval base at Hianggyik Island and a radar
station at Coco Island. Such a PLA presence could be used by China for signals intelligence (SIGINT) purposes and even to deploy forces in the
future, thereby greatly influencing traffic through the Strait of Malacca
and the strategic environment in the Indian Ocean.[37] Overall, most other
Southeast Asian states have sought to avoid offending China or suggesting
that their military procurement is in any way responsive to a "China
threat."[38]

India

Aside from Taiwan and perhaps the Philippines, China's expanding
regional military posture is arguably of greatest concern to India. Yet this
concern is certainly not new. New Delhi has been focused on the direct
potential threat posed by Chinese forces since the PLA decisively defeated
the Indian military in the Sino-Indian border conflict of 1962. Moreover,
since the 1970s, India's security concerns regarding China have been aug-
mented by its anxiety over the considerable conventional and nuclear assistance that Beijing has provided to Pakistan. India's subsequent program of
military modernization has thus resulted to a significant degree from such
concerns. During the late 1980s and the first half of the 1990s, this program
suffered considerably due to major economic and financial restructurings,
cutbacks in defense spending, declines in military research and development, and the collapse of the Soviet Union, India's major supplier of military hardware and technology.[39]

In more recent years, however, India has managed to devote a growing
number of resources to military modernization, partly to increase pressure
on Pakistan, partly to deal with China's recent program of military modernization, and partly in support of an overall strategy designed to raise its
strategic profile in Asia. New Delhi is now increasing its level of defense
spending by very significant amounts (with the air force receiving the lion's
share of new funding), developing larger numbers of indigenous weaponry,
and again acquiring major weapons systems and other forms of defense
assistance from Russia, as well as from new niche suppliers such as Israel.
This effort reflects a larger, ambitious military modernization program
affecting all of India's armed services.

Today, India's forces along its lengthy border with China are generally
regarded as superior in numbers and quality to Chinese border forces (as
shown in incidents with China in 1967 and 1986–87), and there is little sign
that this assessment will change in the foreseeable future. In part this is
because India continues to improve its most relevant capabilities for coun-

tering any potential Chinese thrust across the border by upgrading or acquiring new aircraft, missiles, artillery, command and communications facilities, and radars. Moreover, improvements in the Indian navy, including improvement to destroyers and submarines and even the acquisition of a new aircraft carrier, are being undertaken at least partly in order to counter the expected emergence of a more blue-water-capable Chinese navy.[40]

Because of these ongoing force developments, as well as the significant improvement in Sino-Indian political and diplomatic relations since the 1970s, few Indian defense analysts expect the PLA's modernization to alter the conventional balance of forces in South Asia or to result in a more assertive Chinese policy in the near to medium term. Moreover, China has for some time been most interested in developing cooperative ties with India, through high-level leadership dialogue, the pursuit of various political-military confidence-building measures (CBMs), and efforts to clarify much of the Line of Actual Control (LOAC) along the border.[41] Overall, from the Indian perspective, China seems far more interested than it once was in furthering good relations with New Delhi, maintaining domestic stability, improving its overall military capabilities, and handling security problems along its eastern and southeastern borders (i.e., regarding Taiwan and the Korean peninsula).

On the other hand, Indian analysts remain concerned about arms transfers from China into South Asia and nearby areas, including Pakistan, Myanmar, Bangladesh, Iran, Thailand, and Sri Lanka, as well as the development of air and defense ties with all of these Indian Ocean littoral countries.[42] According to at least one knowledgeable observer, China's post-1988 strategic ties and military relations with Myanmar in particular have "potential strategic implications almost as serious as Beijing's ties with Pakistan. It allows China to have two major allies on the two wings of India while it straddles the northern borders."[43]

However, of even greater concern to India are China's evolving strategic capabilities, centered on its nuclear weapons and ballistic missile programs. For many Indians, these programs constitute by far the most serious immediate as well as long-term security threat. In response to this threat, India has sought to expand its own nuclear weapons and ballistic missile capabilities. It reaffirmed to the world its nuclear weapons capability by exploding a nuclear weapon in 1998, and it is devoting considerable resources to the development of both medium- and intermediate-range ballistic missiles that are capable of delivering a nuclear warhead to any major city in China.[44]

IMPLICATIONS FOR THE FUTURE

From a broad perspective, the acquisition by China of even rough approximations of the kind of military capabilities projected above—and especially the development of the technical and operational capabilities to effectively control some battle spaces out to about 250 miles from China's frontiers— would have several significant implications for the overall security situation in the Asia Pacific.

First, if sustained over many years, China's military modernization program could prompt more Asian states to focus their own defense modernization efforts on potential vulnerabilities created by the Chinese buildup. In particular, the defense budgets, force structure plans, acquisition programs, and deployment patterns of key Asian militaries could more clearly reflect the need to counter growing Chinese power, especially air and naval power. Such a disturbing trend would become far more likely if China's political and economic integration into the region were to falter significantly or confidence in the ability of the United States to effectively counter advances in Chinese military capabilities and deployments were to drop. Without a continued strong U.S. presence, Asian alarm over growing Chinese capabilities could eventually fuel a destabilizing arms buildup in the region as countries such as Japan, the Philippines, Indonesia, India, and Vietnam seek to establish or maintain a military advantage over China in key areas. Such developments could significantly increase Chinese tensions with Japan over the U.S.-Japan security alliance, with ASEAN over the Spratly Islands, and with the United States and Western European states over continued access to Asian resources, technology, and markets. Alternatively, several Asian countries might gradually become more pro-Chinese in their foreign economic and diplomatic policies or less supportive of U.S. policies in the region, especially if Asian countries were unable to develop military forces to effectively counter the sort of increased Chinese capabilities described above.

Closely related to the previous factors, the acquisition by China of the above capabilities could significantly increase the costs and risks involved in deploying U.S. forces in East Asia, especially over the long term. For example, the acquisition by China of significant sea denial or control capabilities, or the continued deployment of both short- and medium-range missiles, possibly possessing both conventional and nuclear warheads, could complicate the U.S. calculus regarding whether, when, and how to deploy U.S. forces in the region to deter or reassure friends and allies, and more generally constrain Washington's freedom of action in a crisis. For some observers, such a situation would fundamentally weaken, if not destroy, the entire strategy of forward engagement and put major strains on U.S. relations with friends and allies in Asia. Of course, this problem would be made much worse if the United States were to reduce the physical presence or qualitative capabilities of its forward presence in Asia. Either reduction could seriously undermine confidence among regional states.

Obviously, the above developments would have extremely important implications for the future security of Taiwan. As a result of the 1995–96 tensions over Taiwan and former Taiwan president Lee Teng-hui's enunciation of the so-called "two states" theory of 1999,[45] China's weapons programs now place an increased emphasis on acquiring capabilities to strengthen the credibility of Beijing's military options against the island, and to deter the United States from deploying aircraft carriers and other forces in an effort to counter such options. As soon as 2010, the increased Chinese capabilities described above could lead China's leaders to attempt a variety of military actions against Taiwan, including another, more intensive round of military intimidation through various exercises and missile "tests," a naval blockade, a limited direct missile or air attack, and even perhaps limited ground incursions, all in an attempt to establish a fait accompli in Beijing's favor that the United States would find difficult to counter.

It is unlikely, however, that the Chinese leadership would attempt such actions unless they believed that Taiwan were about to achieve permanent independence. Moreover, it should be stressed that the ability of China to prevail in any deployment of military force against Taiwan, even by the year 2020, is by no means certain. As suggested above, China's *relative* military capabilities vis-à-vis both Taiwan and the United States will be a far more important indicator of China's willingness to employ force than the sort of absolute capabilities projected above.

Overall, the above analysis indicates that China is in the process of acquiring new military capabilities and undertaking new force deployments that will fundamentally alter security perceptions in the region and stimulate a more widespread military response among the major powers. Although this dynamic is not fated to produce conflict—even in the case of Taiwan—it will likely increase the chances of regional tension and instability, thus requiring more deliberate and coordinated political, diplomatic, and military efforts. The United States will, by necessity, play the most decisive role in this effort.

NOTES

1. The Chinese principle of "strategic frontier" is intended to encompass the full range of competitive areas or boundaries implied by the notion of comprehensive national strength, including land, maritime, and outer space frontiers, as well as more abstract strategic realms related to China's economic and technological development. The principle of "strategic deterrence" was formulated to emphasize the nonviolent use of military power to deter war or achieve political or diplomatic ends, in contrast to the traditional Chinese emphasis on the use of military forces in actual combat. An increased emphasis on gaining the initiative by striking first (rather than waiting for the enemy to strike) reflects the need to act quickly and decisively to pre-

empt an attack, restore lost territories, protect economic resources, or resolve a conflict before it escalates. For further details on these and other principles basic to China's post–Cold War defense doctrine, see David Shambaugh, *Modernizing China's Military: Progress, Problems, and Prospects* (Berkeley: University of California Press, 2002), especially chapter 3. Also see Paul H. B. Godwin, "Changing Concepts of Doctrine, Strategy, and Operations in the People's Liberation Army 1978–87," *China Quarterly* 112 (December 1987): 573–90.

2. See Dennis Blasko, "PLA Ground Forces after the 16th Party Congress," paper presented at the CAPS-RAND conference, "Whither the PLA after the 16th Party Congress?" Taipei, Taiwan, November 2002. Also see Blasko, "Statement before the U.S.-China Security Review Commission, December 7, 2001," in *Compilation of Hearings Held Before the U.S.-China Security Review Commission, Fiscal Years 2001 and 2002* (*Washington, DC: U.S. Government Printing Office, 2002*), 897–909, for a detailed discussion of the ground force component of China's rapid reaction forces.

3. Bernard D. Cole, *The Great Wall at Sea: China's Navy Enters the Twenty-First Century* (Annapolis, MD: Naval Institute Press, 2001); and Christopher D. Yung, *People's War at Sea: Chinese Naval Power in the Twenty-first Century* (Alexandria, VA: Center for Naval Analysis, 1996).

4. Kenneth W. Allen, Glenn Krumel, and Jonathan D. Pollack, *China's Air Force Enters the 21st Century* (Santa Monica, CA: Rand Corporation, 1995).

5. Mark Stokes, *China's Strategic Modernization: Implications for the United States* (Carlisle, PA: U.S. Army War College Strategic Studies Institute, 1999).

6. China's long-standing "minimum deterrence" doctrine generally assumes that China would absorb an initial nuclear attack rather than undertake a launch-under-attack (LUA) or a launch-on-warning (LOW). Perhaps most important, the effectiveness of this deterrence hinges on the inability of an adversary to destroy all of China's WMD capabilities, especially its strategic missile force, in a first strike.

7. The number of Asia-oriented missiles that China deploys over the next ten to fifteen years will undoubtedly depend significantly not only on the state of tensions within the region (and especially regarding Taiwan), but also on whether the United States and key Asian nations such as Japan and India deploy an effective missile defense system in the region.

8. For a detailed assessment of the doctrine and force structure objectives of the PLA, see Shambaugh, *Modernizing China's Military,* especially chapters 3 and 4; and Harold Brown et al., *Chinese Military Power,* report of the Independent Task Force (New York: Council on Foreign Relations, 2003), especially 37–62. Also see Michael D. Swaine, "The Modernization of the People's Liberation Army: Prospects and Implications for Northeast Asia," *NBR Analysis* 5, no. 3 (Seattle, WA: National Bureau of Asian Research, 1994); and David Shambaugh and Richard H. Yang, eds., *China's Military in Transition* (Oxford: Clarendon Press, 1997).

9. The preceding estimates are my own, derived from more than a decade of studying the PLA. For a recent assessment of PLA capabilities that tends to reinforce these judgments, see Brown et al., *Chinese Military Power,* 24–62. Also see Paul Godwin, "From Continent to Periphery: PLA Doctrine, Strategy, and Capabilities Towards 2000," in *China's Military in Transition.*

10. Brown et al., *Chinese Military Power,* 37–62; and Shambaugh, *Modernizing China's Military.*

11. Brown et al., *Chinese Military Power*, and Shambaugh, *Modernizing China's Military*.

12. The word "limited" here denotes the ability to carry out sea denial activities primarily against a small number of surface and subsurface assets in selected, limited areas over short periods of time.

13. Such targets would theoretically include all major metropolitan areas in Japan, Korea, Taiwan, the Philippines, Southeast Asia, and India, and most major U.S. military installations in Asia.

14. Again, these estimates are my own. See Michael D. Swaine and Ashley J. Tellis, *Interpreting China's Grand Strategy: Past, Present, and Future* (Santa Monica, CA: RAND Corporation, 2000), 164–65.

15. According to Bates Gill, regional military buildups and deployments were driven by external security concerns such as piracy, the protection of offshore resources and territorial claims, and the maintenance of open and safe shipping lanes; a growing need among many Asian countries to address the deepening obsolescence of their military forces; and a desire to counter emerging vulnerabilities associated with the enhanced influence of major regional powers or of local rivalries, such as those between North and South Korea, India and Pakistan, Japan and North Korea, and among some Southeast Asian states. These latter concerns were magnified by the fear in some quarters that America's long-standing role in the region as a security balancer or broker might diminish in response to the collapse of the Soviet security threat. See Bates Gill, "Chinese Military Modernization and Arms Proliferation in the Asia-Pacific," in *In China's Shadow: Regional Perspectives on Chinese Foreign Policy and Military Development*, ed. Jonathan D. Pollack and Richard H. Yang (Santa Monica, CA: RAND Corporation, 1998), 10–36.

16. Jonathan D. Pollack, "Asian-Pacific Responses to a Rising China," in *In China's Shadow*, 2–3.

17. Russia and Central Asia are not included in this more detailed assessment of regional reactions to China's military posture because these areas have thus far displayed little in the way of a significant reaction to Beijing's military modernization effort. Of course, Russia has always been concerned, to varying degrees, with the potential security threat posed by China's military, given its long border with China, its recent history of armed conflict with Beijing over disputed boundaries, and the much longer history of Sino-Russian tension and distrust. Moreover, an arguably growing number of Russian observers express concern about China's current military buildup. But such views do not constitute the mainstream in Russian leadership circles. To the contrary, Sino-Russian relations have improved enormously since the late 1980s, and Moscow's economic problems have resulted in China's emergence as a major purchaser of Russian weapons and military assistance. In addition, the low level of threat from China sensed by most Russian leaders, combined with the major overall decline of the Russian armed forces, have obviated Russia's need or ability to strengthen significantly military deployments relevant to China.

18. Eric Heginbotham and Richard J. Samuels, "Japan," in *Strategic Asia 2002–03: Asian Aftershocks*, ed. Richard J. Ellings and Aaron L. Friedberg with Michael Wills (Seattle, WA: National Bureau of Asian Research, 2002), 96–97.

19. Ibid., 96.

20. For an assessment of Japan's ballistic missile defense program and its relation to China, see Michael D. Swaine, Rachel Swanger, and Takashi Kawakami, *Japan and Ballistic Missile Defense* (Santa Monica, CA: Rand Corporation, 2001).

21. Tsuneo Watanabe, "Changing Japanese Views of China: A New Generation Moves Toward Realism and Nationalism," in *The Rise of China in Asia: Security Implications,* ed. Carolyn W. Pumphrey (Carlisle, PA: U.S. Army War College Strategic Studies Institute, 2002), 176–83; and Gill, "Chinese Military Modernization and Arms Proliferation in the Asia-Pacific," 29–30.

22. Heginbotham and Samuels, "Japan," 112.

23. Taeho Kim, "Korean Perspectives on PLA Modernization and the Future East Asian Security Environment," in *In China's Shadow,* 54.

24. In fact, as some analysts have observed, China's leader and the Chinese military evince little enthusiasm for intervening militarily in a future conflict on the Korean peninsula. See, for example, Eric McVadon, "Chinese Military Strategy for the Korean Peninsula," in *China's Military Faces the Future,* ed. James R. Lilley and David Shambaugh (Armonk, NY: M. E. Sharpe, 1999), 283–84.

25. Since at least 2000 South Korea's defense doctrine has been the subject of serious reconsideration, marked by heated debates over whether or not to drop the "main enemy" designation for DPRK forces. See Nicholas Eberstadt, "Korea," in *Strategic Asia 2002–03,* 162.

26. Ibid., 163.

27. Gill, "Chinese Military Modernization and Arms Proliferation in the Asia-Pacific," 30–31. As Eberstadt states, at the start of the new century, "ROK defense allocations were being increasingly invested in systems only tangentially related to potential DPRK aggression, but integral to the development of a regional 'force projection' capability" ("Korea," 162).

28. Eberstadt, "Korea," 162–63. Also see Kim, "Korean Perspectives on PLA Modernization and the Future East Asian Security Environment," 50–67.

29. Those areas of Chinese weapons development and military deployments of greatest relevance to Taiwan include the increased production and deployment of short- and medium-range ballistic missiles, as well as improvements in missile accuracy and payload packages (including MIRVs and countermeasures); efforts to deploy land-attack cruise missiles on naval and air platforms; efforts to deploy improved antiship cruise missiles; increased deployments of AA-12 or similar air-to-air (AAMRAM)-type missiles; improvements in submunitions capable of severely disrupting air bases and C⁴ISR facilities; improvements in electronic warfare capabilities, including anti–electronic intelligence (ELINT), anti-satellite (ASAT), and anti–global positioning system (GPS) capabilities; the acquisition of intelligence, surveillance, and reconnaissance (ISR) to detect and track U.S. carrier battle groups; improvements in data/intelligence fusion and dissemination for battle management and C⁴ISR; the ability to mount sustained air sorties and to avoid friendly shoot-downs; the deployment of—or intent to deploy—large numbers of fourth-generation and third-generation fighters (Su-30s, Su-27s, J-8IIs, JH-7s, and J-10s); the development of an ability by aviation forces to support ground and naval operations; improvements in combined submarine-and-surface naval operations; efforts to increase the number of more sophisticated diesel- and nuclear-powered submarines, and to produce new types of such submarines (Kilo-class, Types 093,

094); and significant increases in the number of troops (airborne, SOF, and marines) considered deployable and supportable across the Taiwan Strait.

30. For a detailed discussion of the problems and successes of Taiwan's defense reform and modernization program, see Michael D. Swaine, "Taiwan's Defense Reforms and Military Modernization Program: Objectives, Achievements, and Obstacles," in *No Way Out? New Thoughts on the U.S.-Taiwan-China Crisis,* ed. Nancy B. Tucker (New York: Columbia University Press, 2005). The following paragraph on the likely future course of that response was also largely drawn from this study.

31. These could include the ability to strike Taiwan with a significant number of highly accurate, short-range ballistic and cruise missiles, to severely damage Taiwan's offshore defenses with a larger number of more capable submarines and surface combatants, to severely disrupt Taiwan's communication capabilities with new space-based and information warfare systems, and perhaps even to seize strategic locations on Taiwan with a significant number of special operation forces.

32. Pollack, "Asian-Pacific Responses to a Rising China," 3.

33. Swaine and Tellis, *Interpreting China's Grand Strategy,* 166.

34. Ibid., 166–67. Also see Derek Da Cunha, "Southeast Asian Perceptions of China's Future Security Role In Its 'Backyard,'" in *In China's Shadow,* 119. Da Cunha states that none of the ASEAN states has the military capability alone to successfully oppose a determined military advance by China into the South China Sea, and that they are unlikely to acquire such a capability in the foreseeable future.

35. Gill, "Chinese Military Modernization and Arms Proliferation in the Asia-Pacific," 29.

36. Although the claim is unconfirmed, some analysts believe that Indonesia concluded a defense cooperation pact with Australia in late 1995 and purchased British Hawk fighter/ground attack aircraft—and possibly advanced combat aircraft from Russia—because of concerns about China. See ibid., 31.

37. Da Cunha, "Southeast Asian Perceptions of China's Future Security Role In Its 'Backyard,'" 117–18.

38. Gill, "Chinese Military Modernization and Arms Proliferation in the Asia-Pacific," 31.

39. Sujit Dutta, "China's Emerging Power and Military Role: Implications for South Asia," in *In China's Shadow,* 104–5.

40. Ashley J. Tellis, "Appendix D: The Changing Political-Military Environment: South Asia," in *The United States and Asia: Toward a New U.S. Strategy and Force Posture,* ed. Zalmay Khalilzad et al. (Santa Monica, CA: RAND Corporation, 2001), 206–15.

41. Dutta, "China's Emerging Power and Military Role," 105.

42. Ibid., 100.

43. Ibid.

44. Michael D. Swaine with Loren H. Runyon, "Ballistic Missiles and Missile Defense in Asia," *NBR Analysis* 13, no. 3 (Seattle, WA: National Bureau of Asian Research, 2002).

45. At that time, Lee Teng-hui stated that Taiwan and China had a special "state-to-state" relationship across the Taiwan Strait. For many Chinese, this amounted to a de facto declaration of Taiwan's separateness and independence from the mainland and thus, when coupled with the 1995–96 crisis, led to a decision to acquire genuine military capabilities to deter Taiwan.

PART FIVE

Implications for the United States

13

China's Regional Strategy and Why It May Not Be Good for America

Robert Sutter

Chinese foreign policy has long focused on Asia, and the Chinese leadership has been developing a relatively pragmatic approach to China's Asian neighbors for more than twenty years.[1] While China's security concerns have long centered on Asia, its military power has not extended much into the region. China's political and cultural influence has been strongest in Asia, and the largest proportion of its foreign trade has been conducted with Asian neighbors. In the post-Mao period, even though China grew into a global political and economic actor, its foreign policy was still concerned predominantly with Asia.

In the 1980s, Chinese leaders tended to talk a lot about the global international order, but actual Chinese interests were concerned with issues closer to home. Heading the list was ensuring that hostile powers—particularly the United States and the Soviet Union, but also Japan and India—did not establish dominance around China's periphery. When Chinese leaders discussed these issues, however, they insisted on doing so in a global context, with China positioned as a world leader. Thus, China's conflict with Vietnam in the late 1970s and 1980s was seen as part of the global struggle against Soviet expansionism, and Chinese opposition to U.S. policies in Taiwan and South Korea was part of worldwide opposition to American imperialism. Such tension between China's regional interests and its global ambitions complicated Western assessments of China's "Asian" policy, as China at the time was seen as "a regional power without a regional policy."[2]

JIANG ZEMIN AND CHINA'S NEW REGIONAL STRATEGY

Coincident with the decline and death of Deng Xiaoping, China's president and Communist Party leader Jiang Zemin led Chinese officials in pursuing a more active foreign policy that has focused important attention on grad-ually improving China's influence throughout its periphery. The year 1997 saw the transition of Hong Kong to Chinese rule, the reconfiguration of Chinese leadership and policy at the Fifteenth CCP Congress, and a Sino-American presidential summit.[3]

The top policy priority was an ambitious multiyear effort to transform tens of thousands of China's money-losing state-owned enterprises (SOEs). Beijing also embarked on programs to promote economic and administra-tive efficiency and protect China's potentially vulnerable financial systems from the 1997–98 Asian economic crisis and subsequent uncertainties.[4] Foreign affairs generally remained an area of less urgent policy priority. Broad international trends, notably somewhat improved relations with the United States, supported the efforts by the Chinese authorities to pursue policies intended to minimize disruptions and to assist domestic reform endeavors.[5]

Giving priority to domestic economic development, political stability, and the attempt to avoid major confrontation or controversy in foreign affairs, China's leaders also shifted to a more active posture in Asia. In 1997 China unveiled its "new security concept." According to the principles of this concept, relations among nations should be based on the Five Princi-ples of Peaceful Coexistence and countries should avoid interference in others' internal affairs; the promotion of mutually beneficial economic con-tacts creates a stable security and economic environment; and greater dia-logue promotes trust and allows disputes to be settled peacefully. Though the concept opposed using improved Chinese relations against a third party, it took repeated and often strident aim at the "Cold War mentality" seen in U.S. efforts to strengthen alliances with NATO and Japan.[6]

The emphasis on the new security concept operated in tandem with Chi-nese leaders' efforts beginning in 1996 to establish "partnerships" or "stra-tegic partnerships" with most of the powers along China's periphery (e.g., Russia, ASEAN, Japan, and South Korea) as well as other world powers. These partnerships and other high-level Chinese interaction emphasized putting aside differences and seeking common ground. Beijing also stressed the importance of the United Nations and other multilateral organizations in safeguarding world norms supported by China and as a check against hegemonism and power politics.[7]

Other features of Chinese policy included a very active schedule of Chi-nese political and military leaders meeting visitors from Asia and traveling throughout the region. Regarding regional organizations, Chinese officials were instrumental in the establishment in 2001 of the Shanghai Coopera-tion Organization, which included Russia, Kazakhstan, Kyrgyzstan, Tajik-istan, and Uzbekistan, and they worked assiduously to improve China's rela-tions with ASEAN, proposing an ASEAN-China Free Trade Agreement and

Chinese security arrangements with ASEAN and the ASEAN Regional Forum (ARF) that appeared at odds with U.S.-backed security efforts in Southeast Asia. China also worked closely with Japan and South Korea as well as ASEAN in the so-called ASEAN Plus Three dialogue that emerged around the time of the Asian economic crisis.[8]

A review of Chinese relations with neighboring states and recent in-depth consultations with Chinese foreign policy planners and specialists show that Chinese leaders seem more confident of China's power and influence than in the past, but they are also keenly aware of the continued predominance of the United States in China's environment and elsewhere—a dominance that will probably continue for the foreseeable future.[9] They acknowledge that China is now constrained to deal with U.S. power and influence by using less confrontational tactics than those they were able to use up until 2001, finding their earlier approach on balance counterproductive. Currently China endeavors to deal with U.S. power and influence by, among other methods, employing multilateral and cooperative approaches designed to steer U.S. policy and actions in directions not adverse to core Chinese interests. They also seem anxious to find ways that China's rising influence in Asia and world affairs can be seen as no challenge to U.S. power and influence, for challenging the United States would not be in China's interest because of the great difference in the power and influence of the two countries.[10]

China's relations with all its neighbors, with the exception of Taiwan and possibly Japan, have improved in recent years. It is hard to measure exactly how much influence this allows Beijing to exert in Asia, however, especially because China's current strategy emphasizes seeking common ground with neighbors, and China generally does not ask other countries to do things they are not already inclined to do. There is no question, however, that the perception that China's influence is increasing has been important, particularly in Southeast Asia and Korea, where Chinese relations have improved markedly. The Chinese government is also playing the key mediating role in dealing with the North Korean nuclear crisis of 2002–2004.[11]

In sum, China's clearer focus on Asia and its more active stance in the region reflect multifaceted and long-term objectives:[12]

- They help to secure China's foreign policy environment at a time when the PRC government is focused on sustaining economic development and political stability.
- They promote economic exchange that assists China's internal economic development.
- They support PRC efforts to isolate Taiwan internationally and to secure the flow of advanced arms and military technology to China despite a continuing Western embargo on such transfers.

- They calm regional fears and reassure Asian neighbors about how China will use its rising power and influence.
- They also work against U.S.-led or other regional efforts seen as contrary to China's interests.

THE U.S. ROLE IN CHINA'S REGIONAL POLICY

American analysts and other outside observers seem to disagree little about the above Chinese objectives, except for the last. In regard to the latter, some specialists say China's primary long-term regional goal is to push the United States out of Asia and assert regional dominance. Their analysis assigns U.S. policy a primary role in determining Chinese policy in the region. It forecasts a generally negative outlook for the United States and the region, and it predicts more friction as China's rise forces it into competition with the United States for influence in Asia.[13]

Other specialists expect a more confident approach to Asia from the Chinese leadership. Over time Chinese leaders have embraced economic interdependence and globalization as providing great benefits to them as rulers of China. They also have come to appreciate some of the benefits of U.S. primacy in world affairs. These specialists forecast a generally positive outlook for the region and U.S. interests in Asia, as Chinese leaders see their interests best served by a cooperative stance that will over time add significantly to Chinese wealth and power.[14]

A third group of specialists, including this observer, sees continued anti-U.S. tendencies in Chinese policy that are currently held in check by circumstances, especially the predominance of U.S. power and influence in Asia. According to these specialists, China's strategy in Asia is contingent, and U.S. power and policies play a large role in determining Chinese policy in the region. They acknowledge that there has been a change in the Chinese leaders' attitudes toward economic interdependence and their willingness to work with U.S. primacy in many areas of the post–Cold War world, and that China's influence has spread incrementally throughout the region. But these analysts are heavily influenced by an assessment of factors that appear to make China's recent stance tentative and tactical. Chinese leaders seem wary of pressures and events that could compel them to shift to different and perhaps more hard-line positions in Asian affairs. As the acknowledged dominant power in the region, the United States looms large in the calculations of the Chinese leadership.[15]

THE UNITED STATES AND CHINA'S CONTINGENT APPROACH TO ASIA

Contingent policies based on pragmatic cost-benefit analyses developed during the post-Mao period as a central feature of Chinese leaders' decision making about foreign policy, especially regarding important issues along China's periphery in Asia.[16] A review of the record shows that for two decades, from the late 1960s to the mid-1980s, the strategic focus of Chinese leaders was guarding and maneuvering against expanding and threatening Soviet power, especially military power, around China's periphery.[17]

The end of the Cold War and the collapse of the USSR improved China's security situation. However, U.S.-led Western reaction to the 1989 Tiananmen crackdown, stronger emphasis on nationalistic themes by Chinese leaders, and perceived separatist trends in Taiwan backed by the United States headed the list of reasons why Chinese leaders came to see the United States as the new hegemon, striving to pressure and intimidate China and hold back its rise in Asia. Deng Xiaoping advised Chinese leaders to try to avoid confrontation, to "bide time," to work to take advantage of developing international opportunities in order to build up China's "comprehensive national power" and secure a more advantageous world leadership position over the longer term. Chinese leaders continue to reaffirm their commitment to Deng's maxims.[18]

Throughout the 1990s, and arguably up to the present, according to Beijing, the main obstacle to China's rise has been the regional dominance of the United States and its allies and associates, notably Japan, but also India, NATO, and other international organizations and groups in which the United States plays a leadership role. U.S. opposition and "containment" have been clearly evident to Chinese leaders in the complex security, economic, political, and other arenas. Chinese grievances have focused on U.S. resolve to continue its support for Taiwan, to remain the leading power in Asian and world affairs, and to promote change in China's political system.[19]

China's negative views of the United States are based on deeply rooted suspicions of the United States on the part of Chinese elites and even Chinese academic and government specialists on U.S. affairs. These suspicions are reinforced by a national education system and media network that have conditioned the broader Chinese public to think of China as a long-suffering target of depredations and pressures from outside powers, with the United States as the leading oppressor in the recent period. Following the Tiananmen crackdown and the collapse of international communism, Chinese leaders gave greater salience to such nationalistic conditioning, which had an impact on the sharp deterioration of popular opinions about the United States.[20]

The George W. Bush administration has done a better job than many previous U.S. administrations in employing incentives and disincentives from a position of overall strength to persuade Chinese leaders to pursue cooperative and moderate policies toward the United States and its allies and associates. U.S.-China relations are seen as better today than at any time since the Tiananmen incident and the end of the Cold War, despite the

Bush administration's expanded support for Taiwan, construction of missile defenses, enhancing security ties with Japan, NATO expansion, sanctions on Chinese weapons proliferation, the U.S. invasion and occupation of Iraq, and other measures long sensitive to, and until recently sharply criticized by, China.[21]

CHINA'S MODERATION TOWARD THE UNITED STATES IN ASIA—TACTICAL OR STRATEGIC?

Among the various Chinese moves in recent years toward greater moderation and accommodation in Asian and world affairs, perhaps the most striking has been the abrupt falloff in mid-2001 of the wide-ranging and often very harsh public Chinese criticism of U.S. policy that prevailed throughout the previous decade. For years, and with varying degrees of intensity, the U.S. was portrayed by Chinese polemicists and officials as the "hegemon" and the object of a worldwide struggle. Asia was the primary intended audience for these Chinese criticisms.[22]

The Chinese decision to stop this public campaign contributed markedly to the recent improvement in U.S.-China relations. This decision also raises an important question, debated by U.S. and other analysts, as to whether this shift represents a basic change in China's approach to the United States in Asian and world affairs. Those who see a more confident Chinese leadership tend to believe that there has indeed been a fundamental shift toward "new thinking" in Beijing.[23] Chinese leaders are seen as markedly less prone to react sharply and negatively to U.S. policies and practices that in the recent past would have triggered strident Chinese invective and other assertive actions. Considered a newly "responsible" international player, China is assumed by some to have put aside its efforts—until recently very strong—to work against U.S. influence and power in Asia.

In contrast there are those, including this observer, who find this argument unconvincing for several reasons. First, they see U.S. policies and behavior under the Bush administration as markedly *more* hegemonic and offensive to long-standing Chinese sensitivities in such areas as Taiwan, missile defense, U.S. defense ties with Japan, U.S. sanctions against China, and the U.S. military posture in Iraq, Central Asia, and Southeast Asia. They find it hard to believe that the Chinese elite's long-standing and deeply rooted suspicion of U.S. policy could change so quickly. Under these circumstances, they consider it more likely that the Chinese government decided to mute anti-U.S. rhetoric and assertiveness for tactical reasons involving China's need to maintain a cooperative relationship with the United States, rather than because of any fundamental change in China's opposition to many aspects of U.S. policy in Asia and elsewhere.[24]

Indeed, the Bush administration officials privately warned Chinese counterparts in early 2001 against continuing strident anti-U.S. rhetoric.[25] As the United States seemed to be determined to confront its enemies and likely to remain the dominant power for some time, other power centers, even Russia, were reluctant to confront or seriously challenge U.S. leadership. Under these circumstances, Chinese officials recognized that China was in no position to challenge the United States and attempt to balance U.S. power, even in Asia. This effort would attract few allies and would endanger core Chinese interests in maintaining stability and promoting economic development.[26]

Second, reflecting clear limits on China's accommodation with the United States in Asia, Chinese policy continues to work over the longer term to weaken the predominance of the United States around China's periphery. In the lead-up to the Iraq war, China straddled the fence, privately pledging not to block U.S. military action but siding publicly with France and others in calling for protracted inspections. Beijing's advances in working to resolve the crisis over North Korea's nuclear program still falls short of U.S. expectations that China place more concrete pressure on the government in Pyongyang. A more forceful U.S. stance on North Korea would alarm China, which would very likely take strong measures to block the U.S. pressure.[27] The day-to-day interface of U.S. and Chinese military forces along China's periphery has not been without significant incident, even as the two powers endeavored to resume more normal ties after the April 2001 EP-3 episode. Perhaps of most importance, the PLA buildup targeted at Taiwan and at U.S. forces that might help Taiwan, and U.S. military preparations to deal with Taiwan contingencies, continue unabated. These events suggest that a major breakthrough toward strategic cooperation has not occurred and is unlikely.[28]

Third, constructivist theories regarding learning and change in international relations suggest that Chinese leaders, deeply influenced by nationalistic feelings and anti-American conditioning, will have great difficulty "learning" a more broadly cooperative approach to the United States in Asia.[29] The leaders may also have difficulty refraining from the long-standing tendency to exaggerate the perceived threats posed by the United States or others. Imbued with such a suspicious mindset regarding the United States, Chinese leaders are unlikely to change their minds unless some major event causes them to do so. It is difficult to see such an event in recent Chinese foreign policy.[30]

Fourth, there remains plenty of evidence that Chinese leaders continue to oppose U.S. policy in many areas, notably in U.S. support for Taiwan and U.S. strategic leadership on a number of sensitive issues in Asian and world affairs. Although this opposition has been much less public since mid-2001, it can be seen in a variety of circumstances. A recent book based on files documenting the deliberations of the Chinese leadership shows repeatedly that opposition to U.S. policy in Asia remains a driving force in Chinese policy. Typical of the negative views of U.S. intentions expressed privately by Chinese leaders was the following statement attributed to Hu Jintao:

> [The United States has] strengthened its military deployments in the Asia-Pacific region, strengthened the US-Japan military alliance, strengthened strategic cooperation with India, improved relations with Vietnam, inveigled Pakistan, established a pro-American government in Afghanistan, increased arms sales to Taiwan, and so on. They have extended outposts and placed pressure points on us from the east, south, and west. This makes a great change in our geopolitical environment.[31]

To deal with these adverse trends while simultaneously avoiding confrontation with the United States, Chinese leaders have settled on a long-term approach that attempts to balance real or potential adverse U.S. power and influence in nonconfrontational ways, implemented so subtly so as not to draw the attention of or irritate U.S. policy makers and Asian leaders, and thereby avoiding adverse consequences for Chinese interests. The competitive and antagonistic aspects of China's stance toward the United States in Asia are more evident in some areas of Asia than others.

Taiwan, as might be expected, is in a class by itself. Official Chinese complaints, though much muted after 2001, repeatedly lay down public markers against U.S. policy and behavior.[32]

Chinese rhetoric against Japan is more restrained than it was in the late 1990s, despite Prime Minister Koizumi's repeated visits to the Yakasuni shrine against explicit warnings from top Chinese officials, and much greater Japanese military activism in Asian and world affairs. Nevertheless there are frequent sharp complaints in the Chinese media against Japanese military activism, which is seen as fostered by U.S. policy as a means to enhance U.S. dominance in Asia.[33]

Chinese leaders have been notably restrained in dealing with anti-U.S. themes in Korea.[34] They have generally avoided explicit comment on the anti-American sentiment sweeping South Korea since 2002 and the often-sharp U.S.–South Korean differences on relations with North Korea. Presumably they judge that such Chinese rhetoric, which appeared at times in the 1990s, would work against immediate Chinese concerns to avoid military conflict and encourage engagement among the powers concerned with the volatile situation on the peninsula.[35]

In Southeast Asia, Chinese policy and behavior often only thinly veil competition or opposition to U.S. or other powers.[36] Chinese officials initially inaugurated their "new security concept" (NSC) at an ASEAN meeting.[37] The moderating effect of the new security concept was offset by the strident

Chinese opposition to American power, influence, and policies. The moderation in Chinese policy toward the United States during 2001 was evident when China revised and relaunched its new security concept in meetings in Southeast Asia in 2002, as the NSC was no longer sandwiched between strong anti-U.S. rhetoric.[38]

Nonetheless, Chinese policy and behavior have continued to work, albeit much more subtly, to increase Chinese influence at the expense of the United States and other powers in Southeast Asia. Although the "Shangri-la Dialogue," a high-level security forum convened annually in Singapore by the U.K.-based International Institute for Strategic Studies (IISS), attracted regional defense ministers, China sent only low-level functionaries, instead devoting high-level attention to promoting a new Asia-centered security dialogue (the ARF Security Policy Conference) that marginalized the United States. Greater Chinese flexibility and a willingness to engage in negotiations with the various claimants to South China Sea territories also saw Chinese officials endeavor to use the discussions as a means to restrict U.S. naval exercises in the area. During the multilateral U.S. "Cobra Gold" military exercise in 2001, China conducted its own military exercise in apparent competition. In 2003, lower-level Chinese officials occasionally resorted to strident anti-U.S. rhetoric decrying the occupation of Iraq, which played well in Southeast Asian countries. China also maneuvered in its Free Trade Agreement initiative with ASEAN to shore up China's position relative to the United States, as well as to compete with Japan, South Korea, and India. In 2003 China became the first nation to agree to sign ASEAN's 1976 Treaty of Amity and Cooperation, prompting Russia, India, and Japan to pledge to do the same and placing the United States in a less flattering light.[39]

ASEAN also has been the main arena for Chinese multilateral initiatives that have excluded or tried to marginalize the United States. While cooperating with Japan, South Korea, and other Asian powers in promoting Asia-only groups that explicitly exclude the United States, China at the same time also competes with them for leadership in Asian forums.

The ASEAN Plus Three mechanism emerged in the late 1990s as the most important of the regional groupings designed to promote Asian economic cooperation that excluded the United States and other outside powers, and Chinese leaders took a leading role in the group's various initiatives to promote intraregional cooperation and economic safeguards. China opposed Japan's initiative to establish an Asian monetary fund at the height of the Asian economic crisis in 1997, but it came to support a more recent Asian Monetary Fund initiative sponsored by ASEAN Plus Three, which did not directly redound to Japan's leadership role in regional affairs. With Chinese entry into the WTO seen as a driver of Asian growth, Chinese officials and media since 2000 have highlighted China's free trade initiatives with

ASEAN, including the "early harvest" concessions dealing with agricultural trade, which have served to undercut concurrent Japanese and South Korean trade initiatives toward Southeast Asia that do not include liberalized agricultural trade. Chinese leaders over the past year supported efforts to broaden the ASEAN Plus Three dialogue to include salient political and security as well as economic issues.[40]

Beijing also initiated important regional multilateral mechanisms. The Boao Forum for Asia (BFA), which meets annually on Hainan Island, was presented by China as the "first annual session" of an Asian version of the Davos World Economic Forum. The Boao Forum's goal was to provide a platform for Asian countries to conduct a high-level dialogue about addressing economic and social challenges and promoting economic cooperation in Asia. Working with the Chinese sponsors of the forum, Thailand's prime minister proposed the Asian Cooperation Dialogue (ACD) of foreign ministers as an official counterpart to the BFA. Its first meeting was held in Thailand in June 2002. The foreign ministers of most ASEAN Plus Three members attended and agreed to further meetings.[41]

Elsewhere around China's periphery, the tendency of Chinese leaders to work explicitly against U.S. interests has been muted. In Russia, President Putin has been less willing in recent years to forge a united front with China against U.S. policy, though occasional references to multipolarity and opposition to hegemonism and unilateralism are seen in Russian-Chinese pronouncements. Russia remains willing to supply China with sophisticated weapons for use in a possible Taiwan contingency that could involve the United States, and Russian-Chinese trade is growing from a low level.[42] Chinese commentators in the 1990s envisaged the Shanghai Cooperation Organization (SCO) as excluding the United States from Central Asia. They also often commented negatively on the rapid upswing of the U.S. military presence and U.S. influence in Central and South Asia in 2001, but China adjusted without marshaling a major opposition. China has been in the lead in keeping the SCO moving forward, providing funding and participating in small joint and multilateral military exercises with SCO members— unprecedented steps for the PLA. Beijing has also stressed broadening SCO interests to include economic interchange—steps that may enhance China's leadership role based on the overall strength of the Chinese economy. The United States and other interested powers (e.g., India) are kept out of the SCO deliberations. China has also sought and received Mongolia's pledge not to allow foreign troops in Mongolia.

In South Asia, Chinese leaders have cooperated with the United States, even though their leading position in Pakistan has changed as a result of the strong assertion of U.S. leadership there in 2001.[43] Incremental Chinese efforts to improve relations with India had in the recent past focused on some Sino-Indian common ground against U.S. foreign policy, but this was largely put aside as New Delhi rapidly improved relations—especially military relations—with the United States, even before September 11, 2001. Sino-Indian relations continue to improve, even though they are hampered by key differences, notably the differing stances of the two countries toward Pakistan. India and China have generally eschewed criticism of the United States in their recent interaction.[44]

CONCLUSION

The post–Cold War Chinese leadership, more focused on domestic issues than on expanding foreign power, have established a strategy that emphasizes conventional nation building and gradually strengthening China's influence. That strategy reflects greater Chinese confidence, which has resulted in a more moderate posture on territorial issues and more initiatives involving bilateral ties and multilateral arrangements.

Because China's approach is to emphasize common ground with neighbors, there is little concrete evidence of how much China's influence has actually increased in Asia—something that would be clearer were China to get neighboring countries to follow policies that China favors and they do not. Meanwhile, Chinese officials appear to remain highly sensitive to the policies and power of the United States and U.S.-backed allies and associates, especially Taiwan and Japan. North Korea represents another source of uncertainty. The overall rise of U.S. power and assertiveness in post–Cold War Asian and world affairs has many drawbacks for long-standing Chinese interests in Asia. China has viewed negatively or with suspicion greater U.S. support for Taiwan and Japanese military activism, U.S. ballistic missile defense, strengthened U.S. military deployments and closer military cooperation in Central, South, and Southeast Asia, and closer U.S. military and foreign policy cooperation with India and Russia.

Chinese leaders have learned, after considerable debate over the last twenty-five years, that economic globalization is in China's interests, and they have come to embrace it. On political and security issues, however, China's prevailing pattern is to deal with these questions on a case-by-case basis, taking into account in each instance the costs and benefits for China. In this regard, China is less a "responsible" power, fully embracing international norms in security and political affairs, and more a "responsive" power, carefully maneuvering to preserve long-standing interests despite changing circumstances.

In particular, Chinese leaders have concluded that public opposition to U.S. policies and trends has become counterproductive, especially given the Bush administration's power and firmness against adversaries and the strong opposition of Asian governments to great power contention in the region. Nonetheless, Chinese officials continue to oppose U.S. dominance in Asia and world affairs, and to work against adverse trends involving the United States in subtle and indirect ways. At the same time, they seem to believe that the overall growth of Chinese power and influence in Asia will secure Chinese interests over the long term, despite the contrary actions and interests of the United States.

Looking forward, Taiwan and North Korea have the ability to take provocative actions that could change the course of China's moderate and cooperative approach in Asia. Of more long-term importance are U.S. power, policy, and behavior, which are likely to remain key determinants in China's regional stance. A more hard-line U.S. posture with respect to sensitive issues like support for Taiwan, military deployments, or closer strategic cooperation with Japan could prompt a reassessment of China's regional stance and a harsh reaction affecting its overall Asian strategy. A weakening of U.S. power through failure in Iraq or U.S. economic decline could prompt more Chinese pressure against U.S. interests, Beijing's probing to roll back recent advances in U.S. support for Taiwan or other recent U.S. initiatives that have worked against Chinese interests.

To hold in check long-standing Chinese tendencies to assertively challenge U.S. interests and developments in Asia that are perceived to be adverse, the United States should carefully manage the U.S.-China relationship from an overall position of U.S. confidence and strength. Alternatively, the United States may over time move away from its insistence on maintaining the dominant strategic position in Asian and world affairs. This could set the stage for a different kind of Sino-American accommodation, with the United States pulling back strategically from Asia as China rises to regional leadership.

NOTES

1. Suisheng Zhao, *China's Periphery Policy* (Taipei: Cross Strait Interflow Prospect Foundation, 2001), available at www.future-china.org.

2. Steven Levine, "China in Asia," in *China's Foreign Relations in the 1980s,* ed. Harry Harding (New Haven, CT: Yale University Press, 1984), 109–14.

3. Robert Sutter, *Chinese Policy Priorities* (Lanham MD: Rowman and Littlefield, 2000), 18

4. Barry Naughton, "China's Economy: Buffeted from Within and Without," *Current History* (September 1998): 273–78; Joseph Fewsmith, "China in 1998," *Asian Survey* 39, no. 1: 99–113.

5. The government remained wary and often sharply critical of the real or potential challenges posed by a possible renewed economic crisis, by Taiwan, by efforts of Japan and the United States to increase their international influence in ways seen as contrary to Beijing's interests, by India's great power aspirations and nuclear capability, and by other concerns. For a time, the PRC voiced special concern about the implications for China's interests of U.S. plans to develop and deploy ballistic mis-

sile defense systems in East Asia, and a national missile defense for the United States. Chinese officials also voiced concern about the downturn in U.S.-China relations at the outset of the George W. Bush administration, but they appeared determined to cooperate with the U.S.-led antiterrorism campaign begun in September 2001. See Michael Swaine, *Reverse Course? The Fragile Turnaround in US-China Relations* (Washington, DC: Carnegie Endowment for International Peace, Policy Brief 22, 2003); Kerry Dumbaugh, "China-US Relations: Current Issues for the 108th Congress," Library of Congress, Congressional Research Service, Report RL31815, updated September 15, 2003.

6. David Finkelstein, *China's New Security Concept* (Alexandria VA: CNA Corporation, April 1999).

7. Reviewed in Sutter, *Chinese Policy Priorities,* 193–96.

8. Robert Marquand, "Central Asian Group to Counterweigh US," *Christian Science Monitor,* June 15, 2001; Ho Khai Leong, "China and ASEAN in the Coming Decades," *Journal of Contemporary China* 10, no. 29: 683–94.

9. G. John Ikenberry, "Strategic Reactions to American Preeminence," U.S. National Intelligence Council Conference Report, July 28, 2003, available at http://www.odci.gov/nic/confreports_stratreact.html. These claims are also based on consultations with twenty Chinese foreign policy planners and specialists in November–December 2003.

10. Yoichi Funabashi, "China's 'Peaceful Ascendancy,'" *YaleGlobal Online,* December 19, 2003, available at http://www.taiwansecurity.org/News/2003/YG191203.htm (accessed December 20, 2003).

11. Elsewhere in the region, the results for Chinese interests were more mixed. The Sino-Russian strategic partnership has served the interests of both sides, despite obvious limitations. Chinese efforts to use improved ties with Russia as a counterweight to the United States were set back by Russian president Vladimir Putin's forthcoming approach to Washington prior to and following the September 11, 2001, attack on the United States. For an excellent review of how Putin came to terms with the Bush administration *prior* to September 11, 2001, see William Wohlforth, "Russia," in *Strategic Asia 2002–2003,* ed. Richard Ellings and Aaron Friedberg (Seattle, WA: National Bureau of Asian Research, 2002), 183–222. The U.S.-led war against terrorism in Afghanistan markedly increased the U.S. military presence and influence throughout Central Asia and South Asia, and upset Chinese efforts to use the SCO and other means to check the spread of U.S. influence along China's western flank. The antiterrorism campaign also lowered the priority China and India placed upon their slow but steady efforts to improve relations in recent years. Nonetheless, China's relations with Russia, the SCO, and India registered steady gains. To keep track of developments in China's relations with neighboring states, see the quarterly reviews provided in *Comparative Connections,* available at http://www.csis.org/pacfor.

12. Robert Sutter, "China's Recent Approach to Asia: Seeking Long-term Gains," *NBR Analysis* 13, no. 1 (March 2002): 20–21; Alastair Iain Johnston, "China's International Relations: Political and Security Dimensions," in *The International Relations of Northeast Asia,* ed. Samuel S. Kim (Lanham MD: Rowman and Littlefield, 2004), 65–100. Asia Pacific Center for Security Studies, "Asia's China Debate," December 2003, available at http://www.apcss.org/Publications/APSSS/ChinaDebate/Asias

%20China%20Debate%20complete.pdf (accessed December 30, 2003); Alastair Iain Johnston and Robert Ross, eds., *Engaging China* (London: Routledge, 1999); Kenneth Allen, "China's Foreign Military Relations with Asia-Pacific," *Journal of Contemporary China* 10, no. 29: 645–62; Herbert Yee and Ian Storey, *The China Threat: Perceptions, Myths, and Realities* (London: Routledge, 2002).

13. Michael McDevitt, "The China Factor in US Defense Planning," in *Strategic Surprise?* ed. Jonathan Pollack (Newport, RI: Naval War College Press, 2004); Richard Sokolsky, Angel Rabasa, and C. R. Neu, *The Role of Southeast Asia in US Policy Toward China* (Santa Monica, CA: Rand Corporation, 2000); John Pomfret, "In Its Own Neighborhood, China Emerges as a Leader," *Washington Post,* October 18, 2001; Jane Perlez, "China Races to Replace U.S. as Economic Power in Asia," *New York Times,* June 28, 2002; U.S.-China Security Review Commission, Report to Congress, July 2002, available at http://www.uscc.gov/anrp02.htm; Eric Eckholm and Joseph Kahn, "Asia Worries about Growth of China's Economic Power," *New York Times,* November 24, 2002; Thomas Woodrow, "The New Great Game," *China Brief,* February 11, 2003.

14. For variations on this perspective, see the chapter by David M. Lampton in this volume; David Shambaugh, "China Engages Asia: Reshaping the Regional Order," *International Security* 29, no. 3 (Winter 2004/2005): 64–99; Michael Yahuda, "China's Win-Win Globalization," *YaleGlobal Online,* February 19, 2003, available at http://www.yaleglobal.yale.edu; Joseph Kahn, "Hands across the Pacific," *New York Times,* November 11, 2002; and Evan Medeiros and M. Taylor Fravel, "China's New Diplomacy," *Foreign Affairs* (November–December 2003). Proponents of this perspective note that China benefits from the free flow of oil from Middle East suppliers via sea lines of communications secured to a large extent by the U.S. Navy.

15. Robert Sutter, "China Remains Wary of US-led World Order," *YaleGlobal Online,* June 8, 2003, available at http://www.yaleglobal.yale.edu; consultations with twenty Chinese foreign policy planners and specialists, November–December 2003.

16. David M. Lampton, *The Making of Chinese Foreign and Security Policy* (Stanford, CA: Stanford University Press, 2001), 1–36.

17. This involved changing degrees of Chinese cooperation with the United States and its allies and associates, depending on variables that included changing Chinese perceptions of the Soviet threat, the extent of U.S. resolve, and the assessed utility of alignment with the United States to counter the USSR. See John W. Garver, *Foreign Relations of the People's Republic of China* (Englewood Cliffs, NJ: Prentice Hall, 1993), 70–110; Michael Yahuda, *Towards the End of Isolation* (New York: St. Martins Press, 1983); Robert Sutter, *Chinese Foreign Policy: Developments after Mao* (New York: Praeger, 1986), 10–13.

18. Tony Saich, *Governance and Politics of China* (London: Palgrave, 2001), 274; Yong Deng, "Hegemon on the Offensive," *Political Science Quarterly* 116, no. 3 (2001): 359; Nailene Chou West, "Low Profile on Foreign Affairs Set to Continue," *South China Morning Post,* December 24, 2003 (online version, accessed December 27, 2003).

19. Dumbaugh, "China-US Relations."

20. Joseph Fewsmith, *China Since Tiananmen* (Cambridge: Cambridge University Press, 2001), 132–58; Rosalie Chen, "China Perceives America," *Journal of Contemporary China* 12, no. 35: 239–64.

21. Michael Swaine, *Reverse Course?*; Robert Sutter, "Bush Policy toward Beijing and Taipei," *Journal of Contemporary China* 12, no. 36 (August 2003): 477–92.

22. These criticisms centered on alleged U.S. efforts to contain China's rise, attempts to weaken the country through interference in Chinese internal affairs, support for Taiwan and Tibetan separatists, and strategic alignments and deployments around China's periphery involving Japan, NATO's Partnership for Peace program in Central Asia, India, and Southeast Asian states. Official Chinese rhetoric reached several high points of invective, notably when *People's Daily* "Observer" articles equated the U.S. military campaign against Yugoslavia in 1999 with the Nazi advances in World War II and compared President Clinton with Adolph Hitler. *People's Daily*, May 27, 1999; *People's Daily*, June 22, 1999.

23. For variations on this perspective, see the chapter by David M. Lampton in this volume; Michael Yahuda, "China's Win-Win Globalization"; Joseph Kahn, "Hands across the Pacific"; Medeiros and Fravel, "China's New Diplomacy."

24. As noted earlier, Chinese officials reevaluated China's strategy against the United States in 2000–2001 and concluded that China did not want to be in a position of confronting alone the U.S. superpower. U.S. military and other strengths, backed by the Bush administration's clear willingness to use them against opponents, are additional factors that contribute to the serious costs that China will incur if it continues a confrontational approach toward the United States. These circumstances favor muting differences for now and following Deng's strategy to bide time and await opportunities while continuing to develop greater national wealth and power. For a comprehensive assessment of recent China-U.S. relations, see David Shambaugh, "New Stability in U.S.-China Relations: Causes and Consequences," in *Strategic Surprise?*, ed. Jonathan Pollack, op cit.

25. Consultations with Bush administration Asian affairs policy makers, Washington, D.C., March 2001.

26. Consultations with Chinese foreign policy officials and specialists, 2001–2002; Li Zhongjie, "Background Report on the 16th CCP Congress: How to Deal with the Current International Strategic Situation," *Liaowang* (Beijing), June 3, 2002, 3–9; Li Shaojun, "Where Do Opportunities Lie?—Viewing Future Great Power Relations," *Shijie Zhishi* (Beijing), January 1, 2003, 8–10; Gu Dexin, "The US-Iraq War and China's National Security," *Xiandai Guoji Guanxi* 4 (Beijing), April 20, 2003, 20–22.

27. David Shambaugh, "China and the Korean Peninsula: Playing for the Long Term," *Washington Quarterly* (Spring 2003): 43–56. Chinese officials told U.S. media of their impatience with U.S. demands for support on Iraq and North Korea that were not accompanied by a change in U.S. policy where it matters most to China, i.e., Taiwan. Sutter, "China Remains Wary of US-led World Order."

28. Robert Sutter, "China's Rise in Asia," *PACNET*, March 7, 2003, available at http://www.csis.org/pacfor.

29. Robert Jervis, *Perception and Misperception in International Politics* (Princeton, NJ: Princeton University Press, 1976), 217; Dan Reiter, "Learning, Realism and Alliances," *World Politics* 46, no. 2 (July 1994): 493.

30. Some Chinese foreign policy specialists privately acknowledged to me in late 2003 that both Chinese and U.S. leaders will probably have great difficulty in changing long-standing mutual suspicions.

31. Andrew Nathan and Bruce Gilley, *China's New Rulers: The Secret Files* (New York: New York Review Books, 2002), 207–9.

32. See quarterly reviews by David Brown and Bonnie Glaser in *Comparative Connections*, available at http://www.csis.org/pacfor.

33. "Japan Building up Its Arsenal," *China Daily*, July 5, 2003, 4; Li Heng, "Is Japan Advancing toward a 'Normal Country,'" *People's Daily*, July 3, 2003; Chen Zhi-jiang, "Japan Accelerates Construction of Missile Defense System," *Guangming Ribao*, June 24, 2003; "Japan Has an Ax to Grind," *People's Daily* (online edition), August 7, 2003; Zhi Qiu, "Maritime Interception Exercise Conducted by Member States of the 'Proliferation Security Initiative,'" *Zhongguo Guofang Bao*, September 23, 2003, 2.

34. See Scott Snyder's quarterly reviews of China-Korea relations in *Comparative Connections;* David Shambaugh, "China and the Korean Peninsula," 43–56; You Ji, "China and North Korea," *Journal of Contemporary China* 10, no. 28: 387–98; and Victor Cha, "Engaging China: The View from Korea," in *Engaging China*, ed. Alaistair Iain Johnston and Robert Ross, 32–56.

35. While Chinese officials work with the United States and other powers in dealing with the North Korean nuclear crisis, the Chinese media has sided with South Korea in occasionally criticizing U.S. pressure tactics against North Korea. The Chinese media has also taken the South Korean side in criticizing Japan about its alleged inadequate sensitivity to its colonial past, but, presumably on account of the South Korean president Kim Dae Jung's moderation toward Japan in the late 1990s, there has been no repetition of Jiang Zemin's joint statement with the previous South Korean president in 1995 explicitly criticizing Japan. "The New Korea," *Asiaweek*, December 1, 1995, available at http://www.asiaweek.com/asiaweek/95/1201/ed.html.

36. For quarterly reviews of developments in China–Southeast Asian relations, see *Comparative Connections Honolulu,* CSIS, Pacific Forum, available at http://www.csis.org/pacfor. Other sources for this section include Rosemary Foot, "China and the ASEAN Regional Forum," *Asian Survey* 38, no. 5: 425–40; Ho Khai Leong, "Rituals, Risks and Rivalries: China and ASEAN in the Coming Decades," *Journal of Contemporary China* 10, no. 29: 683–94; John Pomfret, "In Its Own Neighborhood, China Emerges as a Leader," 1; Kenneth Allen, "China's Foreign Military Relations with Asia-Pacific," 645–62; Michael Richardson, "Seeking Allies in Terror War, US Woos Southeast Asia," *International Herald Tribune*, November 29, 2001; Lee Lai To "The Lion and the Dragon," *Journal of Contemporary China* 10, no. 28: 415–26; and the articles by Michael Leifer, Yuen Foong Khong, and Amitav Acharya in *Engaging China*, ed. Alistair Iain Johnston and Robert Ross.

37. By this time, Chinese leaders were showing more flexibility in dealing with territorial issues with many neighbors, and they were more willing to participate in multilateral forums that focused on these and other regional concerns. Chinese leaders from that time forward were also very active in diplomatic, economic, and military contacts to persuade Southeast Asian neighbors and others that the perception of a "China threat" was an illusion.

38. Lyall Breckon, "Beijing Pushes 'Asia for Asians,'" *Comparative Connections*, October 2002. Subsequently, Chinese officials were said to devote less attention to the NSC, preferring to be more flexible in responding constructively to security arrangements proposed by ASEAN and other neighbors, and to avoid calling atten-

tion to China as a "leader" in Asia. Consultations with Chinese foreign policy specialists, December 2003.

39. These events are noted in the quarterly reviews of Lyall Breckon in *Comparative Connections*.

40. See coverage of Chinese activities during various ASEAN-related meetings in October 2003, available at http://www.aseansec.org.

41. Lyall Breckon, "Former Tigers under Dragon's Spell," *Comparative Connections*, July 2002.

42. Sherman Garnett, ed., *Rapprochement or Rivalry? Russia-China Relations in a Changing Asia* (Washington, DC: Carnegie Endowment for International Peace, 2000); Alexander Lukin, "Russian Perceptions of the China Threat," in *The China Threat*, 86–114; Gang Lin, "Sino-Russian Strategic Partnership: A Threat to American Interests?" (Washington, D.C.: Woodrow Wilson International Center for Scholars, Asia Program special report, September 2001); Rajan Menon, "Russia," in *Strategic Asia: Power and Purpose 2001–2002*, ed. Richard Ellings and Aaron Friedberg (Seattle WA: National Bureau of Asian Research, 2001), 200–206; Lowell Dittmer, "The Sino-Russian Partnership," *Journal of Contemporary China* 10, no. 28: 399–414. See also Yu Bin's quarterly reviews of Russia-China relations in *Comparative Connections*. Energy projects are central to future Russian-Chinese trade, though Russia barters with Japan in seeking a better deal for its limited Far Eastern oil exports.

43. C. V. Ranganathan, "The Chinese Threat: A View from India," and Pervaiz Iqbal Cheema, "The China Threat: A View from Pakistan," both in *The China Threat*, 288–301 and 302–11; John W. Garver, *Protracted Contest: Sino-Indian Rivalry in the 20th Century* (Seattle: University of Washington, 2002); Mohan Malik, "High Hopes: India's Response to US Security Policies," in *Asia-Pacific Responses to US Security Policies* (Honolulu: Asia Pacific Center for Security Studies, 2003) (online version), available at http://www.apcss.org/Publications/APSSS/ChinaDebate/Asias%20China%20Debate%20complete.pdf.

44. China also saw that its interests were better served by focusing on improved relations with the United States than by seeking common ground with India against U.S. interests. Mohan Malik, "Eyeing the Dragon: India's China Debate," in *Asia's China Debate* (Honolulu: Asia Pacific Center for Security Studies, December 2003), available at http://www.apcss.org/Publications/APSSS/ChinaDebate/Asias%20China%20Debate%20complete.pdf.

14

China's Rise in Asia Need Not Be at America's Expense

David M. Lampton

As oil is to the Saudi economy, labor is to the Chinese economy. They set the floor price.
Chan Heng Chee, Ambassador to the United States from Singapore, Fall 2003

Farewell to verities about China's foreign policy behavior in Asia and beyond. As China's power has increased there have been, and will continue to be, important changes in how Beijing defines its interests, the kinds and mixes of power it employs to achieve its ends, the effectiveness of its policies, and the structure of the East Asian regional system. These changes require alterations in U.S. policy and behavior at the same time that China is developing a stake in a stable yet dynamic status quo in East Asia and beyond. East Asia is not becoming Sinocentric, but it is becoming a place in which Chinese interests and influence cannot be disregarded.

Among the verities receding from view is the notion that China is a nation extensively shaped by a "victim mentality," prickly to deal with because of its attempts to compensate for a hundred-plus years of humiliation. Instead, Chinese leaders now refer to China and the United States as "two influential countries," both of which have "responsibilities," though Beijing still eschews the word "leadership." Also living on borrowed time is the platitude that China is only a "regional power." Indeed, the "region" in which China is active has expanded considerably, now embracing Central Asia, South Asia, and Southeast Asia, with ever more activity in the Middle East and beyond (for more on this, see John Garver's contribution to this volume). China's reach into U.S. financial markets has grown gradually, and it has now achieved significant proportions.[1] Though this chapter focuses on Asia, there are fewer and fewer issues or places in which China has neither interest nor influence.

The reasons these verities are receding are to be found in four variables, one of which is changes in the international system, particularly the pre-eminence of the United States in the post–Cold War and post–9/11 eras, and China's felt need to cooperate with others to constrain Washington. China is gaining a certain normative appeal in East Asia and beyond simply by defining a foreign policy paradigm that many nations feel contrasts favorably with that of the Bush Administration in the post–9/11 period. The second factor is China's impressive and sustained economic success, which has provided Beijing with tools and options it never before had, while the third variable is closely connected to the second—interdependence. A new economic order is taking shape in East Asia in which the PRC is becoming a major purchaser of what its neighbors have to sell and a growing investor in their economies. This situation provides the PRC leverage. Cooperation is currently seen in Beijing as a more feasible way to protect economic interests and interdependencies than a ruinous drive for military power that Beijing's leaders believe brought the Soviet Union down. And the final set of factors is the changed leadership in China, that leadership's placement of foreign policy in the context of domestic economic development, and that leadership's greater comfort level with China being an influential country with both responsibilities and grievances.

The net effect of these variables has been to progressively and fundamentally alter the style and substance of Chinese foreign policy, with the Asian financial crisis of 1997–98 having been a watershed. No single decision was more important than Beijing's policy of holding stable the value of the renminbi (RMB) and contributing to the stabilization funds for Thailand and Indonesia through the International Monetary Fund (IMF). The regional and global praise China's leadership received for these moves was important, notwithstanding the fact Beijing made those decisions out of consideration of its own interests.[2] Reinforcing this positive experience has been the largely favorable outcome of China's accession to the World Trade Organization (WTO) and the accelerated growth and development that has followed. Once the international business community was assured that Beijing was irrevocably committed to joining the global trading system, foreign direct investment (FDI) has surged into the PRC even as investments going to Asia and the rest of the world have declined.

The core of China's contemporary foreign policy is reassurance of neighbors, peacefully securing China's economic lifelines (strategic resources), and building relationships that can constrain the unbridled exercise of U.S. power at the same time that Beijing's influence grows and it continues to draw on the resources of the global system, most importantly the United States. Against this background, this chapter deals with the implications for the United States of China's rise and its evolving foreign policy. Two broad sets of questions animate this chapter: To start, how should we conceive of China's power? What kinds of power are we talking about? For Beijing, what is the preferred mix of power types, now and in the future? And, how are

China's neighbors responding to this shifting power mix? Second, what policy issues and challenges do the foregoing developments present to the United States, now and for the foreseeable future?

My conclusion differs somewhat from Robert Sutter's in his contribution to this volume: I argue below that although China's rising power will certainly present the United States, as well as the PRC's neighbors, with challenges, Beijing's increased capabilities are also becoming a powerful engine for regional and global economic growth and essential to meeting current and future transnational challenges. How the outside world responds to China's rise in the short and medium term will importantly influence how China's power is exercised in the long term, notwithstanding the fact that the most important determinant of China's future international behavior will be its people and the domestic system they create. Although suitable hedges against the risks of China's modernization are appropriate, the emphasis of U.S. policy should be placed upon positive integration.

THE CHANGING MIX OF CHINESE POWER: THE DOMINANCE OF REMUNERATIVE POWER

In his classic study entitled *A Comparative Analysis of Complex Organizations*,[3] Amitai Etzioni disaggregated the concept of "power" into three categories: coercive, normative, and remunerative, or, crudely put, the power of guns, ideas, and money. The "open and reform policy" of China *(kaifang, gaige zhengce)* substantially has been about the increase of the PRC's remunerative power. Though China's military power has grown modestly to date (and certainly will grow significantly in the future),[4] and though the attractiveness of China's foreign policy pursuit of multipolarity has contributed to a modest rise in the "normative" dimension of Chinese power (especially as many around the world have become concerned about U.S. dominance), it is in the realm of remunerative power growth that China's ascent has been most marked.

The expansion of its remunerative power has given China options and avenues for influence that it has not previously enjoyed in the modern era. Beijing's remunerative power is both manifest and latent. China is gaining power as a rapidly growing purchaser of what others throughout Asia have to sell, and the PRC has also become a key part of the global supply chain, producing goods destined for North America, Japan, and Europe. China increasingly is investing throughout Asia while U.S. investment, both monetary and political, has declined.[5] The rapid expansion of China's middle class and its domestic purchasing power gives Beijing leverage as the gatekeeper to that middle-class market. So, for example, the business page of the *New York Times* recently noted that the prospects for growth in Japan were brightening because "Shipments of cars, electronics and other goods to China and the United States helped offset slower sales at home."[6]

An Emerging New Economic Order in East, Northeast, and Southeast Asia

Globalization has put every economy in the world on a treadmill on which the search for a society's comparative advantages is never ending and accelerating. Americans have unhappily discovered this with the nearly three-decade-long decline in manufacturing employment, with the textiles, clothing, leather goods, and footwear industries hit particularly hard. More recently higher-value-added manufacturing, white collar employment, and even jobs higher "up the skills ladder to include workers like aeronautical engineers, software designers and stock analysts" have been hit "as China, Russia and India, with big stocks of educated workers, merge rapidly into the global labor market."[7] The PRC, by virtue of its high savings rate (35 percent to 40 percent of GDP), its large and comparatively educated labor force (China's schools turn out hundreds of thousands of engineers annually), and the torrent of export-oriented FDI into the country, is making China a broad-based and formidable manufacturing competitor. Moreover, just as Taiwan, South Korea, Hong Kong, and Japan in the past gained labor-intensive jobs at "America's expense," so China is now gaining those jobs from the earlier beneficiaries of the migrations of manufacturing. As the World Bank put it, "Most of the drop in U.S. manufacturing jobs occurred before Chinese exports penetrated the U.S. market."[8] It also is worth noting that given global gains in productivity, many economies are losing manufacturing jobs in the aggregate, with China having lost far more than the United States.[9] As in the past, when the switch from agriculture to industry led to a declining percentage of the U.S. population in agriculture, globalization is now forcing a restructuring of the U.S. occupational profile away from manufacturing toward services and knowledge/analytic jobs. Each such social transformation is painful, of course, and the affected social sectors and industries, particularly in democratic polities, have considerable ability to defend the old order.

Added to this dynamic is the fact that China's middle class is growing rapidly (real GDP per capita rose from $183 to $920 in the 1979–2001 period),[10] and therefore its consumption is also expanding quickly (net urban income has grown dramatically over the last decade),[11] making the PRC the hottest long-term prospect for domestically fueled growth. Markets in Japan and Europe are more mature, and therefore consumption there is not growing so rapidly. Therefore, China's remunerative power derives not only from being a purchaser from suppliers, but also from its expanding domestic market. This is reflected in the fact that U.S. exports to the PRC in 2003 grew more than 30 percent, while U.S. exports to the European Community and Japan combined grew at about one-tenth that rate, albeit from a much larger base. Growth rates will vary over time, of course, but Lehman Brothers reports that, "China is already emerging as an important growth pole, not just for the Asian region, but also for the world."[12] In their contribution to this volume, Zhang and Tang elevate this innate attraction to the plane of Chinese strategy, claiming, "By opening up its own market and letting regional states enjoy the growth opportunity with China, China hopes that regional states will be more receptive to China's economic growth and consider it a greater opportunity than a threat."

Because of the preceding developments, a new economic configuration is emerging in Asia. China increasingly is becoming a principal export destination for nations and economies in East, Northeast, and Southeast Asia, with significant increases in the export percentages going to China occurring since the mid-1990s. For example, in 2000 China was the recipient of about 9.2 percent of Australia's exports (up from 6 percent in 1994); in 2001 it received about 13.2 percent of Singapore's exports (up from about 2.5 percent in 1993) and about 18.5 percent of ROK exports (up from about 6 percent in 1993). As well, there have been more recent significant increases in the percentage of Philippine, Indonesian, and Thai exports going to the PRC. These exports to China from East and Southeast Asia are primarily either raw materials or intermediate goods that are transformed into finished products in the PRC and then shipped to the United States and Europe, or consumed in China itself. As the economist Pieter Bottelier notes, "China's [share of] exports [of East Asia, minus Japan] to NAFTA and the EU increased dramatically from 25 percent to 45 percent [from 1985 to 2001]."[13] This phenomenon is also seen in the fact that China's share of total U.S. merchandise imports rose to about 11 percent in 2002, from about 3 percent in 1990. At the same time, the rest of Asia's share of total U.S. merchandise imports fell from about 17 percent in 1990 to about 13 percent in 2002.[14]

Much of Asia is orienting itself around the PRC in a very complex division of economic labor. This is forcing every economy in the region, including the United States', to find its niche and participate in this division of labor, as well as to reform its own educational system and economy so that it can move up the value-added chain. In the aggregate, according to the World Bank's Ng and Yeats, "China's emergence has had a major positive impact on the trade of other East Asian countries."[15]

Because China is becoming a very important customer for so many countries and economies in the region (as Robert Ash's contribution to this volume demonstrates in great detail), the PRC's power and influence among its suppliers is growing. Beijing, having already in 2002 closed one deal with Australia for natural gas worth about $US 17.5 billion, in October 2003 signed a framework agreement for another natural gas deal in the range of $17 billion to $21 billion during President Hu Jintao's visit.[16] These trans-actions, the biggest Australia ever had agreed to at that time, in part account for the fact that Hu Jintao received a warmer welcome in Australia than did President George W. Bush when both visited there in fall 2003. At about the same time that Hu Jintao was exercising dollar diplomacy in Canberra, Pre-mier Wen Jiabao was in Indonesia telling ASEAN business leaders that in two years China's trade with ASEAN would near or overtake the ten-nation organization's trade with the United States.[17] Adding to China's economic clout has been the fact that Chinese tourists have emerged as a major pres-ence in Asia, with the total number of Chinese tourists to all destinations worldwide reaching 11.8 million in the first eight months of 2003, 15 per-cent greater than during the corresponding period of the prior year.[18]

With China's high rate of sustained economic expansion in a world of generally flaccid growth, Chinese imports have "brought a windfall to coun-tries across Asia, with their exports cranking up to feed China's growth." As one economist put it, "The faster and farther China grows, the better for many countries in [the] region. . . . They are the suppliers."[19] For example, India's exports to China grew 96 percent in 2002–2003, while New Delhi's exports to the EU grew only 15 percent in the same period.[20]

China's rapidly growing links to South, Southeast, and Northeast Asian economies not only reflect the attractiveness of China's market, the PRC's role in the global supply chain,[21] and the PRC's role as an investor in the region (China's FDI there is growing at about 20 percent a year,[22] with 60 percent of its total worldwide FDI going to Asia,[23] and Chinese investment in ASEAN countries growing 60 percent in 2002),[24] but they also represent Beijing's strategy of diversifying its sources of raw materials (energy and other strategic minerals) for its rapidly growing economy. As Hideo Ohashi says in his contribution to this volume, "China is among the largest exporters of capital to developing countries."[25] By late 2003, China's over-all imports of materials such as cotton, copper, iron, and timber were rising at double- and triple-digit annual rates in terms of value.[26] With respect to oil, China imports about one-third of its domestic annual oil consumption, and by around 2020 it will import about 60 percent, an absolute volume and dependence ratio equal to that of the United States.[27] In short, if you are a nation seeking investment, seeking buyers for your intermediate parts, or looking to export commodities, the PRC is a country with which you wish to do business. This is remunerative power.

Manifestations of Remunerative Power

The importance of China's growing remunerative power can not only be deduced from trade and investment flows, but it is also manifest in a variety of tangible policies that Beijing has initiated and the responses these initiatives have elicited in the region. Beyond the aforementioned role China played in regional economic stabilization during the Asian financial crisis, among the most significant developments have been Premier Zhu Rongji's proposal in Singapore in November 2000[28] to set up an ASEAN-China Free Trade Zone, and the agreement in late 2002 with ASEAN in Phnom Penh to establish a free trade bloc by 2010,[29] an agreement that Jiang Zemin's and Zhu's successors have not only reaffirmed but also accelerated. During his October 2003 trip to Southeast Asia, Premier Wen Jiabao gave considerable emphasis to the "early harvest" initiative, or China's willingness to drop its barriers on the agricultural exports of some Southeast Asian countries ahead of schedule (Thailand and China, for example, signed an agreement to end tariffs on 188 types of fruits and vegetables in June 2003).[30]

While it is true that many Southeast Asian nations fear China as a competitor, it also is true that the economic integration of Asia is proving attractive throughout the region, in part because of the stalled global trade liberalization process under the WTO (the Doha Round). Thailand's prime minister, Thaksin Shinawatra, said in October 2003 at the ASEAN summit in Bali, Indonesia, "For all of us in ASEAN, there is no time for complacency, no time to waste and no time to delay. With the failure at Cancun [of the WTO talks] and the delay of the Doha Round, ASEAN should quickly shift gears into offensive mode for economic integration."[31]

Not only is Beijing seizing the opportunities afforded by economic integration to its south, but it also is looking to a similar development in Northeast Asia. In October 2003, at the Bali ASEAN summit, Premier Wen Jiabao proposed the establishment of a "Tripartite Committee" of China, South Korea, and Japan to study a Free Trade Area among the three and cooperation between that group and ASEAN,[32] following up on an earlier proposal by former premier Zhu Rongji in November 2002.[33] While this proposal will take time to come to fruition, if it ever does, a recent survey in the three countries indicated that the concept had wide appeal among enterprises in each society.[34] Moreover, not only is Beijing seeking to build free trade agreements with the United States' allies in Northeast Asia (Japan and the ROK), it has also proposed a free trade agreement with Australia, a longtime U.S. ally in the South Pacific. When President Hu Jintao was in Australia in October 2003, the two nations signed a framework agreement to study the feasibility of such a deal.

At the same time that Beijing is promoting free trade arrangements throughout the region, the region's economies are taking advantage of the growth of the Chinese domestic market and a change in Chinese strategy toward placing greater emphasis on imports (and domestic demand-driven growth). China's neighbors have been motivated to reach that expanding consumer market, and therefore a Free Trade Area is potentially attractive.

South Korea's Trade-Investment Promotion Agency (KOTARA) spokesman put it this way: "China, the largest market for about 100 items like steel, cement and cell phone[s], will have to increase import[s] as its market is ever growing. Expansion of import[s] will have the effect of reducing trade friction and easing the pressure to revalue the *yuan* alike."[35]

Turning to its own Hong Kong Special Administrative Region (SAR), Beijing has moved to jump-start the city's anemic economy by responding to Hong Kong chief executive Tung Chee-hwa's 2001 proposal for a Free Trade Area with the mainland.[36] The pact (the Closer Economic Partnership Agreement, or CEPA), which went into effect in June 2003, gives the SAR's companies preferred access to the mainland for eighteen different services, as well as reduces tariffs on 273 categories of goods.[37]

China is also building economic linkages with Central Asia, although these currently seem to be taking the form of pipeline and transportation routes and the acquisition of rights for mineral exploration and development. For their part, energy-rich states such as Kazakhstan are seeking to secure their own futures by building export routes and tapping markets that reduce their dependence on Russia.[38] In his contribution to this volume, John Garver makes the central point that, "while China's trade importance relative to all the Central Asian countries has increased . . . [t]he broad picture is that as Central Asia moves out of Russia's economic orbit, it is moving into the Western economic sphere, and not China's."

Nonetheless, the PRC has not relied upon remunerative inducements as the only instrument of its influence. The use of coercive and normative instruments is evident as well. Beginning in the second half of the 1990s, along with its ongoing conventional and nuclear force modernization and evolving military doctrines, Beijing also began to appropriate aspects of Western liberal "internationalism" into its foreign policy repertoire—ideas of cooperative security, multilateral forums, and confidence-building measures. These instruments, to which we now turn, contribute to China's still modest stock of normative influence.

DECLINING EMPHASIS ON EXPANDING COERCIVE POWER

Along with the rise of China's remunerative power has come the PRC's capacity to convert money into coercive strength. Indeed, it is the fungibility of resources that underlies the concern, expressed both by statesmen such as Singapore's Goh Chok Tong[39] and international relations theorists such as John Mearsheimer, that a growing China will convert its increasing resources to the coercive means to unilaterally assure its own security and other interests in a predatory world.[40]

Beijing has been increasing its military capabilities by professionalizing its armed forces; introducing elements of the revolution in military affairs into its command, control, intelligence, and combat structures; modernizing its deterrent nuclear systems; acquiring force projection capabilities (including rapid reaction forces); and focusing its force modernization efforts on a Taiwan Strait conflict scenario, in which the apparent goal would be the ability to disrupt and deny access to U.S. forces.[41] If we project out to 2020, as Michael Swaine has done in his chapter, we see that these developments could have important perceptual effects on the United States' allies and China's neighbors, "increase the costs and risks involved in deploying U.S. forces in East Asia," affect Taiwan's security dramatically, and probably overwhelm any antimissile system the United States might build.

These modernization efforts have required budgetary increases: official (reported) defense expenditures rose at a double-digit pace for fourteen years straight (1989–2002) before falling into the high single-digit range for budget year 2003.[42] Although there is an important debate over the true size and allocation of Chinese defense expenditures, and discussion about which indicators are most revealing (e.g., absolute amounts, percent of government budget, or percent of national income), most observers would agree that China's actual defense expenditures are somewhere near the size of Japan's and that, as David Shambaugh has written, military expenditures have represented a generally declining and small share of national income during the reform era, having been 6.35 percent from 1950 to 1980, 2.3 percent in the 1980s, and 1.4 percent during the 1990s.[43] In the budget year 2003, China's National People's Congress announced that the increase in official defense spending would be about 9.6 percent, the lowest rate of increase in many years, though by no means a trivial rise.[44] An important bellwether will be the rate of budgetary increase in future years and whether or not the PLA's military budget becomes more transparent.

Focusing on the resource end of China's security policy, however, obscures how broadly China's regional security behavior has been changing since the formation of the Shanghai Five organization in 1996 and Foreign Minister Qian Qichen's articulation of the "new security concept" in early 1997.[45] The new approach could be summarized as *reassurance* based upon *cooperative security,* dialogue, and mutual economic benefit. Though one has to keep the hard capacities of China's security (coercive) forces in mind, China's emphasis has been in other areas. The overall success of Chinese policy in the region has been considerable, though regional anxieties remain.

Beijing has employed several instruments to advance its new-look foreign policy: increasing joint military exercises with neighbors; employing confidence-building measures; shelving, downplaying, or resolving contentious maritime and/or territorial disputes with India, South China Sea claimants, Vietnam, Russia, Tajikistan, and Kazakhstan;[46] pursuing active crisis management (for example, in North Korea); taking a lead role in building multilateral organizations (such as the Shanghai Cooperation

Organization, or SCO);[47] emphasizing that Beijing does not seek to drive the United States from East Asia militarily,[48] even as the PRC aims to ensure that major security-related actions incompatible with its interests may not be taken in the region; and beginning to think about alternative, multilateral security structures, such as gradually morphing the "Six-Party Talks" into a security organization for Northeast Asia.

More specifically, in Central Asia, the Shanghai Five organization, consisting of China, Russia, Kazakhstan, Kyrgyzstan, and Tajikistan, was founded in April 1996. From Beijing's perspective, the twin goals of the organization are to act as a restraint on U.S. military entry into (or domination of) the region and to constitute a regional security agreement to reduce armed forces along the shared borders of these nations. "In June 2001, the group adopted a new name, the Shanghai Cooperation Organization; a new charter, which obligated states to coordinate efforts to combat the three 'isms' of Islamic extremism, terrorism, and separatism; and a new member, Uzbekistan."[49] In October 2002 China undertook a joint military exercise with Kyrgyzstan aimed at combating terrorist groups—China's first-ever joint military exercise—followed the next year in August by a six-day joint military exercise (conducted in both Xinjiang and Kazakhstan with four SCO members, excluding Uzbekistan) rehearsing a strike on terrorist training camps.[50] Prior to these activities, the People's Liberation Army did not undertake joint exercises with foreign militaries. This departure presumably enhances the confidence with which participating neighbors regard China, but, the main point is, as John Garver notes in his chapter, "the expansion of Chinese influence [in Central Asia] has also paled beside the expansion of Western influence."

Turning to the Korean peninsula and the nuclear crisis involving North Korea (DPRK), Beijing has been engaged in active crisis management[51] since April 2003, when it convened the Three-Party Talks (involving the United States, China, and North Korea) after having applied both diplomatic and economic pressure on Pyongyang. Subsequently, Beijing applied more pressure (on both Washington and Pyongyang) to convene the Six-Party Talks (involving China, the United States, Russia, North Korea, South Korea, and Japan) in August 2003 and again in late February 2004. Equally as striking, Chinese security experts now often initiate discussions with Americans and others about the possibility of gradually converting the Six-Party Talks into a more coherent and enduring collective security structure.[52] Were this to occur, it might have significant consequences for U.S. alliances with both Japan and South Korea.

Moving southward to Southeast Asia and ASEAN, in early October 2003, China became the first nation outside ASEAN to sign the 1976 Treaty of Amity and Cooperation in Southeast Asia, whose key security-related provision stipulates that "in case disputes on matters directly affecting them should arise, especially disputes likely to disturb regional peace and harmony, they [the contracting parties] shall refrain from the threat or use of force and shall at all times settle such disputes among themselves through friendly negotiations."[53] Given China's (as well as others') use of force in the South China Sea from time to time (most notably at Mischief Reef in 1995), Beijing's willingness to sign the treaty is notable. Moreover, at the same time it signed the treaty, Beijing agreed to continue discussing the Protocol to the Treaty on the Southeast Asia Nuclear Weapon Free Zone.[54]

Moving west from Southeast Asia, China has been improving relations with both India and Pakistan. Its economic and diplomatic relationships with India have been growing and improving; Prime Minister Vajpayee's June 2003 visit to Beijing was an important signpost. Moreover, there have been numerous quiet consultations of the joint working group on the Sino-Indian boundary, and in mid-November 2003 a search-and-rescue mission was jointly conducted by the two navies.[55] With respect to Pakistan, while Beijing played a crucial and constructive role in Islamabad's decision in late 2001 to cooperate with Washington to prosecute the war in Afghanistan against Al Qaeda and the Taliban regime in Kabul, Beijing and Pakistan have further solidified their own security relationship,[56] and in late 2003 they conducted joint search-and-rescue exercises. With respect to the mid-2002 Indo-Pakistani crisis over Kashmir that had the potential to explode into nuclear conflict, China urged both sides to avoid dangerous escalation. One can see, therefore, that as Beijing has gradually acquired more coercive capacity, it has implemented parallel efforts to reassure, build confidence, actively manage crises, and express greater interest in formal security organizations in both Southeast and Northeast Asia.

The one exception to this generally constructive posture has been China's activity in the Taiwan Strait, where there has been a steady buildup of short-range missiles (perhaps numbering six hundred by the end of 2004) and the acquisition of military forces (air and naval) designed for a conflict scenario. Here, the Chinese strategy is to emphasize their desire for a "peaceful resolution," while not excluding the possible use of force if Taiwan were to move too far toward de jure independence. China has simultaneously made it clear that PRC forces have been increased in order to deter what Beijing would consider the worst outcome (a move toward independence that could not be ignored), not to achieve the "best" outcome (reunification).

Beijing's leaders know that using force against Taiwan, no matter what the cause, would not only alienate Taiwan's citizenry but would also tear asunder the fabric of the security policies described above and rekindle distrust of China throughout Asia—not to mention having grave consequences for Sino-American ties. Nonetheless, the mixture of identity politics, micronationalism, and partisan electoral struggle on Taiwan, combined with nationalism on the mainland, poses the gravest danger to the PRC's effort to rely on economic power and to reassure the region about its coercive capacities, even as those capacities expand.

CHINA'S GRADUALLY GROWING NORMATIVE POWER

To many Americans it might seem wrong to assert that China's "normative power" is growing, given ongoing human rights problems in the PRC and Beijing's "deterrence" posture with respect to Taiwan independence. And yet, three developments are contributing to just this result.

The first is the overall direction of Chinese policy and behavior described above, which is generally reassuring to China's neighbors. Second, as repeatedly evidenced in international public opinion polls,[57] there is growing resentment both regionally and globally of America's use of power in the post–9/11 world. In the eyes of many around the world, Beijing's policies contrast favorably with Washington's. And, finally, with the north-south economic gap widening and the Doha Round of the WTO talks seemingly stalled, Beijing is seeking to play a constructive role in creating a bridge between the developed economies and poorer nations. Moreover, the apparent success of China's development path of combining economic liberalization with political authoritarianism has at least some members of the U.S. Congress concerned, with one saying in early 2004 that the United States needs to "be concerned about what kind of example it [the PRC] will become. So we need to be concerned about achieving these changes [e.g., in practices of torture, incommunicado detention, etc.]. If we don't address this, the risk is China will develop a different model for the rest of the world."[58]

Economic engagement, security assurances, opposing superpower domination, championing a level trade playing field for developing countries, and being economically successful constitute a posture that resonates with many in Asia: this is normative power. That posture was most clearly explicated by outgoing Chinese president Jiang Zemin in his November 2002 report to the Sixteenth Party Congress when he said, "We oppose all forms of *hegemonism and power politics.* . . . We stand for *maintaining the diversity of the world* and are in favor of *promoting democracy in international relations* and *diversifying development models.* Ours is a colorful world. Countries having different civilizations and social systems and taking different roads to development should respect one another" (emphases added).[59] In short, China emphasizes democracy *in the world system* and *between* nations, while the United States emphasizes democracy *within* nations. Some Chinese scholars of independent bent are beginning to equate past Soviet behavior with current American foreign policy. Says one such scholar, "the behavior of the

United States reminds me of the former Soviet Union. That is, the Soviet theory that the interests of the USSR were in the highest interest of the world. So, others should subordinate [themselves]."[60]

The September 2002 *National Security Strategy of the United States of America*, which emphasizes U.S. willingness to "act preemptively," utilizing ad hoc coalitions rather than relying on established multilateral organizations; recommends actively promoting democratic and market transitions; and states the intent of the United States to "dissuade potential adversaries from pursuing a military build-up in hopes of surpassing, or equaling, the power of the United States," has contributed to an anxiety about America's role in the world, which in turn creates a receptivity to Chinese policy and rhetoric. These general anxieties were given specific content by the U.S. invasion of Iraq in 2003 and all that has followed. Speaking in New York City in November 2003, one Chinese scholar spoke of Professor Joe Nye's use of the concept of "soft power"[61] and drew parallels to Beijing's current approach. "Joe Nye talked about soft power, and in traditional [Chinese] culture emphasized by Confucius and Lao-tzu, if you are powerful it is better to follow the kingly way *[wang dao]* than the way of the hegemon *[ba dao]*. So China in Asia is trying to use soft power. . . . China . . . [has] cultural power; there are many Overseas Chinese in Malaysia, Singapore, [and] Indonesia, and China's culture is important in the region."

In recent decades it has been Americans who have enjoyed soft power in abundance. Today, however, serious Chinese also are thinking systematically about their assets in this regard, and they are not being entirely unsuccessful in using it. China has a long history of traditional foreign policy practice in the region upon which to draw. One Chinese professor put it, "The idea of soft power . . . is seen at Peking University, where 800 of the 3000 foreign students are from South Korea and one-fourth of my [own] students are South Korean. This is our soft power. This new relationship with our neighboring countries reminds us to think of our history."[62]

And, finally, discussions about the role of the International Monetary Fund (IMF) in Asia, particularly during the Asian financial crisis and its aftermath, and more recently with respect to painfully slow free trade discussions in the WTO (the Doha Round), have given China the opportunity to occupy the moral high ground in Asia and beyond. With respect to the IMF's call for uncompromising austerity policies to restore order to Asian economies in 1997 and 1998 (and the relatively passive role the United States played compared to Washington's activism when Mexico had problems in 1995), China's combination of financial assistance and moderate policy attracted considerable support in Asia. As Alice Ba put it,

> Specifically, the crisis provided China with opportunities to demonstrate its political and economic value as a partner, even a regional leader. China was

especially able to take advantage of ASEAN's disappointment with the international response to the economic crisis. ASEAN found International Monetary Fund (IMF) conditions intrusive, inappropriate, and insensitive to specific economic and political conditions in affected countries; however, its greatest unhappiness lay with the US, which was not only associated with the problematic IMF conditions but also was viewed as benefiting from Southeast Asia's financial problems.[63]

More recently, with respect to WTO negotiations, the combination of U.S. election–driven protectionism on steel and textiles and developed countries' reticence to widely open their domestic markets to the agricultural exports of the world's poor countries (here the United States is by no means the worst offender) has given Beijing an opportunity to speak on behalf of developing country exports, and thereby to some extent to win gratitude.

> The collapse of the World Trade Organization talks in Mexico was applauded yesterday as a victory against the powerful rich nations that cemented China's role as a leader of the developing world. The meeting in Cancun ended yesterday after a coalition of 21 developing nations—led by China, Brazil, and India—refused to continue the talks, having failed to force western economic powers to agree to cut agricultural subsidies.[64]

Beyond the moral high ground, however, Beijing also gains more tangible benefits. According to the *Wall Street Journal,* "the head of the World Trade Organization has asked for China's help getting the current round of global-trade negotiations back on track, in another sign of how Beijing is gaining clout by straddling the camps of both developed and developing countries."[65]

The PRC, then, is not only exerting increasing economic power and converting that economic power into coercive capability, but it is also transforming economic strength into moral suasion.

IMPLICATIONS FOR THE UNITED STATES

The claim that Asia has become Sinocentric is supported neither by this chapter nor by the others that comprise this volume. The economic and military power of the United States remains a central geopolitical and economic fact for every nation on the PRC's periphery. Moreover, China is not yet a balanced comprehensive power; its coercive and normative power remain weak compared to its growing economic muscle. Also, China's influence remains uneven around its circumference: it is strongest on the Korean peninsula, weakest (but growing) in Central Asia, and growing briskly throughout East and Southeast Asia. Moreover, it is fashionable to ignore Japan's current power and future potential because of its protracted national malaise, but it is also mistaken. And finally, at the same time that the PRC's neighbors seek to gain from enhanced Chinese capabilities, they also seek more distant balancers to hedge against Beijing's power. Simply put, although neither the United States nor others ought to overreact to the trends described above, they have implications for U.S. policy.

The most important of these implications is that the principal directions in which Chinese policy has moved (toward the use of remunerative and normative instruments, and away from coercive power) are consistent with fundamental U.S. interests. Washington ought not deflect China from its basic heading. Nonetheless, rising Chinese power requires some adjustments, and perhaps profound changes, both in U.S. policies of long standing and those of more recent vintage. China's rise has implications for regional alliance and security structures, the kinds and mixes of power the United States exerts in the region, and Washington's ability to use sanctions and other instruments of policy.

A key point made in many chapters in this volume is that Washington's post–9/11 mix of power has been lopsided: it overemphasizes military strength and takes insufficient advantage of the United States' economic and potential normative muscle. Normatively, the United States is now less attractive throughout Asia than it has been in decades. Washington has become too distracted, and Americans need to do more listening throughout the region. Finally, Washington needs to place more emphasis on multilateral security and economic relationships.

With respect to the realm of coercive power, perhaps the most dramatic consequence of China's rise has been the weakening of the U.S.–South Korea alliance and the longer-term effects that China's growing strength may have on Washington's other regional alliances. While growing Chinese military power may strengthen the perceived need in Japan, the Philippines, and perhaps Australia for some form of protection provided by the United States, the PRC's growing economic attraction and its currently benign foreign policy may simultaneously lessen the perceived need for the traditional alliances. Which of these contending forces prevails (the China threat or China's attractiveness) will depend greatly on how both Beijing and Washington play their cards in the future. Thus far, Beijing has played them skillfully.

In the case of South Korea, the strains in the U.S.-ROK alliance are already apparent everywhere. Beijing's economic attraction to Seoul, China's greater leverage over North Korea than any other outside power, and a U.S. policy toward Pyongyang that worries South Koreans cumulatively have put China in the catbird seat.[66] Although it is far too early to pronounce the death of the alliance, restoring its vitality is going to require changes. In the more distant future, Washington may have to consider whether a new security framework (perhaps involving the six parties in Northeast Asia) is needed to replace or supplement the traditional bilateral alliances in the region.

The Taiwan Strait is the one issue that, if mismanaged (whether by Taipei, Beijing, or Washington), could produce a dramatic increase in the acquisition and use of Chinese coercive power. Micronationalism on Taiwan creates dangerous pressure on the island to assert autonomy. Washington's policy of deterrence has helped restrain Beijing from either overreacting to Taipei's actions or being proactively coercive. But Washington should be no less vigilant with respect to provocations from Taipei. The issues on which Washington should focus are stability and growth in the region as a whole and encouraging Beijing to remain on the policy trajectory described above. This likely will require U.S. administrations and the U.S. Congress to be as firm with Taipei as they are with Beijing. President George W. Bush's December 9, 2003, statement in front of visiting Chinese premier Wen Jiabao ("The comments and actions made by the leader of Taiwan indicate that he may be willing to make decisions unilaterally to change the status quo, which we oppose")[67] is an example of what may be required.

Even more fundamentally, as more and more U.S. allies and friends in the region develop positive stakes with the PRC, how supportive are they likely to be of a U.S. intervention in the Taiwan Strait? When Deputy Secretary of State Armitage went to Australia in early 2002 and suggested that Washington expected Canberra to be at its side in a Taiwan contingency, former Australian prime minister Malcolm Fraser said, "[The Australia–New Zealand–United States Defense Treaty] designed to achieve Australian security is now being distorted potentially to embroil us in a conflict of America's choosing with another super power [China]."[68]

The PRC's rise also has important implications for the remunerative realm of U.S. policy. Most fundamentally, as the PRC increasingly becomes an engine for regional and global growth, the strategic importance of stable ties between Washington and Beijing will grow beyond narrowly defined security interests.

The fact that China is deeply embedded within key global supply chains and increasingly has become the final assembly point for products that incorporate the value-added components made by many of the United States' friends throughout the region means that Washington increasingly will discover that to economically retaliate against China is to economically strike allies and friends of the United States. Put crudely, if for a given item produced for export to the United States China's value added is 15 cents per dollar, one dollar of U.S. retaliation directed at this product will inflict 85 cents of pain on Washington's friends. Using such policy instruments too frequently is not simply bad economics; it is bad international politics. Interdependence is not something the United States does to others; rather, it is a relationship that simultaneously constrains the United States in the application of its own power as it constrains others.

U.S. multinational firms that have invested in the PRC *both* as an export platform *and* as a base from which to penetrate China's domestic market increasingly will resist unilateral, punitive impulses in Washington. Moreover, the degree to which China recycles dollars earned in this globalized trade into the United States (in the form of U.S. Treasury notes and other debt instruments) means that Washington will find it increasingly difficult to punish Beijing without punishing itself.

Further, as more and more countries become significant suppliers to China, they may well find that their economic interests often parallel those of the PRC. For example, when in late 2003 and 2004 many in Washington called for Beijing to revalue or float its currency, few in Asia supported the U.S. position. As Taiwan's *China Post* put it, "So the notion of getting Beijing to relax its currency controls—an American economic priority—is hardly a top goal in this part of the planet."[69] In short, domestically driven demands or pleas in the United States may fall on increasingly deaf ears in Asia as China's centrality grows.

Turning to the realm of normative power, the United States not only needs to pursue the war on terror and associated activities, but it must also devote much more economic and diplomatic effort to remaining a nation that attracts through the power of positive example. If the only songs Washington sings in Asia are about the war on terror and human rights problems, its music may well have declining appeal. Writing in the *Asia Times* Keith Bettinger hit the point: "In contrast to the apparent U.S. view of developing nations as pawns in a geopolitical chess match, China's approach has economic benefits that a shaky government can take to its people."[70]

If it is to replenish its stock of soft power, the United States must begin, as several of the chapters in this volume suggest, by following the example of the Europeans, who have placed great emphasis, both rhetorical and financial, on economic, social, and political development through institution building, talking more about development as a process than simply as an end state in which there is democracy and human rights. In addition, it does no good to U.S. credibility as the standard bearer for free trade and economic reciprocity when Washington adopts protectionist policies itself.

The developments described in this chapter point to something fundamental. China is becoming a more adept player in the emerging regional and global orders, and the United States must adapt its economy and its policies to the logic of the system it has played a central role in creating. China's rise could be profoundly positive for the United States and for the world system, or it could lead to friction and even conflict between the United States and the PRC. If positive outcomes are to occur, it will be because both countries responded constructively to the opportunities for cooperation that interdependence creates. In short, the story of China's rise is still to be written in the present and the future. The story is not foreordained to end badly.

NOTES

The author would like to thank Mr. Kong Bo and Ms. Ji Zhaojin for their research assistance.

1. David M. Lampton, "The Stealth Normalization of U.S.-China Relations," *National Interest* (Fall 2003): 42.

2. Thomas G. Moore and Dixia Yang, "Empowered and Restrained: Chinese Foreign Policy in the Age of Economic Interdependence," in *The Making of Chinese Foreign and Security Policy in the Era of Reform,* ed. David M. Lampton (Stanford, CA: Stanford University Press, 2001), 191–229.

3. Amitai Etzioni, *A Comparative Analysis of Complex Organizations,* revised ed. (New York: The Free Press, 1975).

4. David Shambaugh, *Modernizing China's Military: Progress, Problems, and Prospects* (Berkeley: University of California Press, 2002), writes, "Although the PLA has embarked on a systematic and extensive modernization program, entailing reforms in all sectors and services, and although there is a comprehensive vision for pursuing that program, a combination of domestic handicaps and foreign constraints severely limits both the pace and the scope of China's military progress" (10).

5. Jane Perlez, "Southeast Asian Nations Meet to Tighten Economic Bonds," *New York Times,* October 6, 2003, A4.

6. Ken Belson, "Japan's Economy Grows at 3.9% Pace," *New York Times,* September 11, 2003, W1.

7. Louis Uchitelle, "A Statistic That's Missing: Jobs That Moved Overseas," *New York Times,* October 5, 2003, 20.

8. World Bank, *China Engaged* (Washington, DC: World Bank, 1997), 33.

9. Jon E. Hilsenrath and Rebecca Buckman, "Factory Employment Is Falling World-Wide," *Wall Street Journal,* October 20, 2003, A2.

10. Lawrence J. Lau, "China's Economy and Implications for U.S. Policy," in *U.S.-China Relations,* ed. Dick Clark (Washington, DC: Aspen Institute Congressional Program, 2002), 17.

11. Lehman Brothers, "The Growing China," Global Economics Series, June 9, 2003, 14.

12. Ibid., 1.

13. Pieter Bottelier, "Comments," Atlantic Council Meeting on WTO Compliance Across the Strait, October 2, 2003, Washington, D.C.

14. Lehman Brothers, "The Growing China," 12.

15. Phillip Day, "China's Trade Lifts Neighbors," *Wall Street Journal,* August 18, 2003.

16. See Economist Intelligence Unit, "China: Business: News Analysis—CNOC to Take Large Equity Stake in Gorgon Project," *EIU riskwire,* November 11, 2003, available at http://riskwire.eiu.com/index.asp?layout=display_print&doc_id=301283;

"China Briefing," *Far Eastern Economic Review,* November 6, 2003; and Robert Marquand, "China Gains on Japan in Age-old Rivalry for Asia Influence," *Christian Science Monitor,* October 29, 2003.

17. Jane Perlez, "China Promises More Investment in Southeast Asia," *New York Times,* October 8, 2003.

18. Economist Intelligence Unit, *EIU riskwire,* October 28, 2003, available at http://riskwire.eiu.com/index.asp?layout = display_print&doc_id = 298333.

19. Thomas Crampton, "Big Chinese Rebound Pumps Growth to 9.1%," *International Herald Tribune,* October 18–19, 2003.

20. Xinhua General News Service, April 29, 2003. For more on growing Indian-Chinese economic ties, see Sidhartha Cancun, "Closer India-China Ties Seen," *Business Standard,* September 12, 2003, available at http://global.factiva.com/en/arch/print_results.asp.

21. Tung Chen-yuan and Yao Symin, *Taipei Times,* November 18, 2003, 8. "The global market share of Chinese non–resource oriented low-tech products increased from 4.5 percent in 1985 to 18.7 percent in 2000," mid-tech from .4 percent to 3.6 percent, and high-tech from .4 percent to 6 percent.

22. Perlez, "China Promises More Investment in Southeast Asia."

23. "A Rise in Trade," *Beijing Review,* October 20, 2003, available at http://asia.proquestreference.info/pqrasia.

24. "China Backs Mekong Project," *China Daily,* August 20, 2003, available at http://www.eastday.com.cn.

25. See Hideo Ohashi's chapter in this volume.

26. Peter Wonacott, "China Saps Commodity Supplies," *Wall Street Journal,* October 24, 2003.

27. David M. Lampton and Richard Daniel Ewing, *The U.S.-China Relationship Facing International Security Crises* (Washington, DC: The Nixon Center, 2003), 27.

28. *The Economist,* December 2, 2000, 42; John Wong and Sarah Chan, "China-ASEAN Free Trade Agreement," *Asian Survey* 43, no. 3 (May–June 2003): 507–26; Zhu Rongji, "Zai di wutse dong meng yu zhongguo lingdaoren huiyishang fabiao zhongyao jianghua," available at http://www.people.com.cn/GB/shizheng/16/20011107/599525.html.

29. "East Asia Trade Bloc to Emerge within 20 Years," available at http://english.peopledaily.com.cn/200212/01/eng20021201_107737.shtml.

30. "China Backs Mekong Project." See also Michael Vatikiotis and Murray Hiebert, "China Pushes Economic Ties with Southeast Asia," *Wall Street Journal,* July 16, 2003.

31. John McBeth, "Taking the Helm," *Far Eastern Economic Review,* October 16, 2003, available at http://www.feer.com/cgi-bin/prog/printeasy?id = 60341.60411777567.

32. "Chinese, Japanese, South Korean Leaders Discuss Creating 'Tripartite Committee,'" *Xinhua* (Beijing), in English, October 7, 2003, FBIS-CHI-2003–1007.

33. "Chinese, Japanese, ROK Leaders Call for Greater Asian Cooperation," available at http://english.peopledaily.com.cn/200211/04/eng20021104_106247.shtml.

34. "Survey Conducted in China, Japan, ROK Finds Most Firms Support Free Trade Area," *Xinhua* (Beijing), in English, November 18, 2003, FBIS-CHI-2003–1118.

35. "ROK's Yonhap: China Seen to Shift Trade Policy Emphasis," Yonhap (Seoul), in English, October 23, 2003, FBIS-CHI-2003–1023.

36. Howard Winn, "Foreign Firms in Trade Pact Fears," *Hong Kong IMAIL*, March 14, 2002.

37. "Hong Kong Pact Clears Route to China," *Far Eastern Economic Review*, October 9, 2003.

38. Hugh Pope, "Balancing Act Gives China a Key Role," *Wall Street Journal*, November 21, 2003.

39. Jane Perlez, "Chinese Are Eroding Influence of the U.S.," *International Herald Tribune*, October 18, 2003.

40. John Mearsheimer, *The Tragedy of Great Power Politics* (New York: W. W. Norton, 2001).

41. Shambaugh, *Modernizing China's Military;* see also Michael Swaine's contribution to this volume.

42. For budget figures for 1989–2001, see Shambaugh, *Modernizing China's Military*, 188–89.

43. Ibid., 191.

44. "China's Defense Spending up 9.6 Percent This Year," *People's Daily*, available at http://english.peopledaily.com.cn/200303/06/eng20030306_112802.shtml.

45. Shambaugh, *Modernizing China's Military*, 292–93.

46. Allen Carlson, "Constructing the Dragon's Scales: China's Approach to Territorial Sovereignty and Border Relations in the 1980s and 1990s," *Journal of Contemporary China* 12, no. 37 (November 2003): 677–98.

47. For more on the Shanghai Cooperation Organization, its history, and its current operation, see Lampton and Ewing, *The U.S.-China Relationship Facing International Security Crises*, 6–7.

48. Pang Zhongying, "Some Points on Understanding China's International Environment," *In the National Interest*, October 16, 2002, available at www.inthenationalinterest.org.

49. Lampton and Ewing, *The U.S.-China Relationship Facing International Security Crises*, 7; see also "Far East: China," *Komersant*, June 15, 2001, 2, carried by *Current Digest of the Post-Soviet Press* 53, no. 24 (2001): 15–16.

50. Lampton and Ewing, *The U.S.-China Relationship Facing International Security Crises*, 6.

51. Ibid., 67–69.

52. See, for example, Jaewoo Choo, "China Plans for a Regional Security Forum," *Asia Times*, available at http://www.atimes.com/atimes/printN.html.

53. Isagani de Castro, "China Snuggles up to Southeast Asia," *Asia Times*, October 7, 2003; Zhang Xizhen, "Treaty Develops Relations with ASEAN," *China Daily*, September 8, 2003.

54. "China and ASEAN Sign Partnership Pact," *Xinhua* (Beijing), in English, October 8, 2003, carried by Economist Intelligence Unit, *WIU viewswire*, available at http://www.viewswire.com/index.asp?layout = display_print&doc_id = 294409.

55. See the editorial "Naval Exercises Indicate Sea Change in Relations," *South China Morning Post*, November 15, 2003, 12. See also James J. Przystup, "China's Great Power Diplomacy: Implications for the United States," carried in *The Nelson Report*, October 10, 2003.

56. "Joint Declaration Describes Pakistan, China Cooperation as Indispensable for Asia," *The News* (Islamabad), November 6, 2003, FBIS-CHI-2003–1106.

57. Peter G. Peterson et al., *Finding America's Voice: A Strategy for Reinvigorating U.S. Public Diplomacy* (New York: Council on Foreign Relations, 2003).

58. David M. Lampton, "Meeting Notes," Aspen Institute Conference on "U.S.-China Relations and China's Integration with the World," January 8, 2004, Honolulu, Hawaii, 6–7.

59. Jiang Zemin, "'Report' to the Sixteenth Party Congress," Section IX, "The International Situation and Our External Work," available at http://english.people.com.cn/features/16thpartyreport/16thpartyreport9 . . . .

60. David M. Lampton, notes on public remarks by Chinese academic in Washington, D.C., November 2003.

61. Joseph S. Nye Jr., *Bound to Lead: The Changing Nature of American Power* (New York: Basic Books, 1990).

62. David M. Lampton, notes of panel presentation at the Annual Meeting of the National Committee on U.S.-China Relations, New York City, November 12, 2003.

63. Alice D. Ba, "China and ASEAN: Renavigating Relations for a 21st-Century Asia," *Asian Survey* 43, no. 4 (July–August 2003): 635.

64. Allen T. Cheng, "China Has Success at Failed WTO Talks," *South China Morning Post,* September 16, 2003.

65. Rebecca Buckman, "The Economy: WTO Director Seeks China's Help to Get Trade Talks Back on Track," *Wall Street Journal,* November 11, 2003, A2.

66. David M. Lampton, "U.S.-China Security Relations and America's Pacific Alliances in the Post-9/11 Era," in *The Future of America's Alliances in Northeast Asia,* ed. Michael Armacost and Daniel Okimoto (Stanford, CA: Asia-Pacific Research Center, Stanford University, 2004), 221–36.

67. David E. Sanger, "Bush Lauds China Leader as 'Partner' in Diplomacy," *New York Times,* December 10, 2003.

68. "Clashes Mar Clinton China Conference in Sydney," *Agence France-Presse,* February 23, 2002.

69. Elaine Kurtenback, "China's Neighbors Value Its Currency Checks," *China Post,* October 16, 2003, 12.

70. Keith Andrew Bettinger, "US Edged Out as China Woos Indonesia," *Asia Times,* available at http://www.atimes.com/atimes/printN.html (accessed November 15, 2003).

PART SIX

Implications for the Asian Region

15

The Transformation of the Asian Security Order

Assessing China's Impact

Jonathan D. Pollack

A major transition in Asian security is underway in the early twenty-first century, with China at the epicenter of this process. Depending on future
events and policy developments, regional security could undergo change
that is more profound than at any time since the early years of the Cold War.
American global primacy and the Bush administration's redesign of U.S.
national security strategy; regional responses to U.S. predominance; the
economic, technological, and military emergence of major regional powers, especially China and India; and a political and institutional maturation
across Asia are the principal manifestations of such change. The possibility
of an acute political-military crisis in East Asia or in South Asia also hovers
over this transition process. China and other states remain closely attuned
to American power and its potential effects on their strategic interests. Each
seeks to combine enhanced military capabilities, restraint in the coercive
use of military power, and pursuit of collective norms and policies to facilitate larger strategic goals. The European balance-of-power system and the
Cold War offer only limited insight into the security identities and historical circumstances shaping these possibilities.[1]

China's ascendance, in conjunction with enhanced national power elsewhere in the region, seems likely to dilute the singularity of American military predominance and alliance relationships evident in Asia during the
Cold War. Though the U.S. military role remains decisive and American military primacy is still unchallenged, an unmistakable recalibration of power
and influence is underway. Increased regional confidence and competence
portend a more indigenously shaped security order in which American leadership will be less pronounced. But these looming shifts raise additional
questions. As long-standing security arrangements diminish in relevance,
what structures, institutions, and processes will supplant the earlier order? Is

it possible to reconcile the lack of a larger security structure with the growth of more autonomous military capabilities in China and in other states? What if new security policies and relationships prove unable to prevent a major regional crisis or heightened strategic competition? How will China's increased power and enhanced international role redefine regional security as a whole? These issues constitute the subtext of the region's strategic future.

At present, three broad objectives shape Chinese security strategy and Beijing's enhanced commitment to security collaboration. First, China is attempting to limit its exposure in America's strategic headlights, thus deflecting a direct U.S. focus on China's political-military capabilities and strategies. Second, China hopes to prevent any countervailing strategy that could limit the country's future military options and strategic reach. Third, China seeks to forestall or discourage coordinated regional responses to its enhanced economic power, military capabilities, and political influence. All three objectives help define China's regional security strategy and its bilateral and multilateral security alternatives.

CHINA AND THE REGION

China is the only regional power with meaningful security involvement in the four principal subregions of Asia and the Pacific (Northeast Asia, Southeast Asia, South Asia, and Central Asia). The latent potential for a military conflict in the Taiwan Strait, combined with the lack of durable Sino-American political and strategic understandings, reinforces China's centrality in regional security. The country's sustained high growth rate and its ever more prominent position in global trade, energy flows, and natural resource requirements have resulted in regional interdependence unimaginable during decades of domestic upheaval and economic autarky. Sustained double-digit increases in China's defense budget are also contributing to the development of a more capable, externally relevant military force. In a word, China has arrived as a regional power. However, its size, strategic weight, and past hegemonic influence generate ample wariness within the region about the longer-term implications of Beijing's economic, political, and military ascendance.

Numerous international relations theorists and national security specialists first expressed concern about the enhancement of Chinese national power during the 1990s. Many viewed China's rise primarily through the framework of nineteenth-century European balance-of-power politics, with scholars positing that China was the quintessential rising power and that the region was "ripe for rivalry."[2] China's burgeoning economic and military capabilities, its presumed geopolitical ambitions, its characterization as an aggrieved power, and its intense wariness of American strategic intentions all contributed to the potential for instability, crisis, and realignment. Strategists foresaw a struggle for domination among Asia's leading states; the denigration of multilateral institutions as peripheral if not irrelevant to international stability; and China's supposed intention to displace American power within the region. A parallel Chinese debate provided a mirror image of these judgments, characterizing China's rise in more benign terms and deeming the United States the primary but diminishing force in long-term Asian security.[3]

However, the warnings contained in many Western and Chinese strategic writings have not materialized. The United States has experienced a strategic resurgence that few anticipated, prompting most Chinese scholars to retreat from earlier claims that multipolarization would constrain the exercise of U.S. power. At the same time, most of Asia (especially East Asia) has proven far more stable and resilient than predicted by international relations theorists. Despite intermittent political crises, the region has not experienced war across national borders since the Vietnamese invasion of Cambodia in 1978 and the Chinese thrust into Vietnam in 1979. Equally important, a nascent Sino-American strategic competition has been supplanted by a growing and largely unanticipated accommodation between Beijing and Washington.[4] To some observers, these patterns suggest a regional preference for indirection and informal security norms, a preference that eschews explicit balance-of-power strategies. Others contend that developmental goals provide shared incentives to avoid (or at least obscure) the latent elements of heightened security competition. Some interpret the present calm as prefiguring regional accommodation to Chinese primacy. Still others believe that China's current political-military restraint is intended to defer a longer-term strategic reckoning with the United States until Beijing is better prepared to confront the U.S. political-military challenge.

However, generalizing about Asia as a whole is problematic. Given the region's political, linguistic, cultural, historical, and geographic complexity, any characterization of Asia as a unitary or integrated security system is highly misleading. Regional states include lightly armed, landlocked entities; major maritime powers; peninsular and archipelagic states; close U.S. allies; autonomous major powers with large military establishments; and states confronting profound challenges to their internal viability. Levels of development within and across national boundaries are also widely divergent. Asia is a shorthand designation for an area that extends to Afghanistan in the west, to Russia and various Central Asian successor states in the north, to Australia in the south, and to Japan and various Pacific island microstates and territories in the east, all without an inclusive security structure. The United States also remains deeply involved in security planning across the entire Asian landmass and the surrounding maritime environment. Any characterization of an "Asian security order" (or, even less, a presumptive Sinocentric order) is a major oversimplification.

Among the various subregions of Asia, Northeast Asia (the primary focus of U.S. regional strategy during the Cold War) most closely corresponds to a balance-of-power system. It was the primary if not exclusive pivot of great power rivalry in Asia during the late nineteenth century and twentieth centuries. With the partial exception of the Indo-Pak rivalry, the concentration of military power in this area far surpasses that found anywhere else in the Asia-Pacific region. In addition, the political divisions between the two Koreas and between China and Taiwan continue to define the primary fault lines of the region's strategic geography. But economic, societal, and political interactions across Northeast Asia are at historic highs; only North Korea remains largely apart from a burgeoning process of regional integration.

However, expectations of a cooperative security order seem equally premature. The enhanced military capabilities of various regional powers, including declared or de facto nuclear weapons states in India, Pakistan, and North Korea, loom large in this caution. Wars of territorial conquest may well be an artifact of the past, but major changes in defense technology and military doctrine are redefining national security strategies, especially for states seeking to protect modern industrial and commercial assets that increasingly determine their well-being. Major improvements in the reach, accuracy, and lethality of modern air and naval power and vastly enhanced information and missile capabilities have compressed the warning time available to military planners. These developments have placed major urban and industrial centers across Asia at potential risk of devastating long-range attack, possibly explaining China's recent attention to civil defense and domestic defense mobilization measures.

The prominence of preemption and prevention in the strategic commentaries and defense policies of the United States, Japan, China, and Taiwan also reflect these concerns. Any armed conflict that extends to national homelands would hugely disrupt internal and regional stability and would severely impinge on global transactions in commerce, high technology, and energy. There is an inescapable paradox of vastly heightened interdependence, and the parallel vulnerability of these societies to attack. Some observers highlight the increased salience of terrorist threats, especially in societies with pronounced ethnic and religious cleavages. However, terrorist activities in Asia derive almost exclusively from threats posed by various groups and networks, as opposed to a regional state being complicit with activities intended to destabilize other societies.[5]

To date, there has been no regional crisis entailing a major military attack by one state against the capital or industrial and commercial infrastructure of another. Few venture definitive predictions on whether this pattern will hold in the future. Some (including China) are investing heavily in more advanced capabilities for deterrence, defense, assertion of sovereign prerogatives, and the use of force. The autonomous, unregulated growth of such capabilities underscores two conclusions: there is no assurance of lasting security in Asia, and China remains pivotal in all regional security futures.

CHINA'S STRATEGIC ALTERNATIVES

What assumptions govern Beijing's expectations of a future security order? What military requirements underlie its defense modernization goals? Have China's leaders defined a strategy to ensure the country's posited vital interests without stimulating major political-military rivalries or renewed armed conflict? None of these questions admits to easy answers, and they are not for China alone to address. Rather than identify a single logic underlying China's regional role, it is necessary to analyze a more differentiated set of national policies. China's policy machinery increasingly draws on specialized expertise, entailing far more coordination and bargaining across complex bureaucracies. But these changes reveal more about the "how" of Chinese policy making, not the underlying premises and assumptions on which such behavior is based.[6]

As noted throughout this volume, there is a broad policy consensus in Beijing on the primacy of China's developmental goals and the parallel need for accommodation with neighboring states. Senior Chinese officials repeatedly express (despite an abiding wariness about U.S. policies toward China) their hopes to avoid a political-military confrontation with the United States.[7] Beijing's increased stakeholder role in international politics is another essential component in this process. It simultaneously vests China in collaborative relations and diminishes any prospect of China's marginalization or exclusion from regional institutions.[8] During the 1990s, Beijing normalized or greatly improved relations with all neighboring states, including Russia and other former Soviet successor states, the Republic of Korea, Indonesia, Singapore, and Vietnam. Relations with India are also on a more solid footing. China has achieved near-total resolution of long-standing border disputes with its continental neighbors, as well as more exploratory understandings with rival maritime claimants in Southeast Asia. These actions reflect a conscious decision by policy makers, with which military leaders have concurred and to which they have contributed.[9] Finally, Beijing is now a full participant in (and a primary sponsor of) various bilateral and multilateral security processes, reviewed at length in the chapters in this volume by David Shambaugh, Bates Gill, and Robert Sutter.

These actions underscore China's growing involvement in regional security arrangements, in particular along China's inner Asian frontiers. To optimistic observers, these activities suggest China's assent to cooperative security norms, confidence-building measures, enhanced transparency, and preventive diplomacy to constrain power rivalries and potential crises. However, these activities reflect opportunities for security collaboration that do not impose significant restraints on Beijing's pursuit of larger security goals. One leading Chinese scholar has voiced skepticism that China is yet prepared to play a true regional leadership role, as opposed to taking prudent, low-key actions designed to limit any potential risks to Chinese interests.[10] Changing realities also have clear significance for U.S. strategic options with respect to China. With Beijing committed to enhanced political-security relations with its continental neighbors, any presumptive containment strategy directed against China is now virtually impossible to execute from the Asian mainland. This does not preclude the mobilization and deployment of military power in an acute crisis, but it imposes significant political and operational constraints on any such actions.

Sustained military modernization is simultaneously underway. As reviewed at length by Michael Swaine in this volume, China is in the gestational stages of military development that will ultimately elevate it to the front ranks of the world's military powers. (A parallel and equally far reaching transformation is occurring in India.) The People's Liberation Army (PLA) is building capabilities geared to the postulated requirements of deterrence and armed conflict in the twenty-first century. These changes are evident in the continental and maritime dimensions of Chinese military power, and in nuclear weapons, ballistic missiles, intelligence, and space assets.[11] The primary near to mid-term focus is on capabilities deemed necessary to coerce Taiwan through decisive military action, thereby diminishing the possibility of a U.S. military intervention. Chinese military doctrine is increasingly focused on the rapid, unfettered use of force to rapidly overwhelm inferior adversaries.[12] Such modernization goals are constrained principally by budgetary and technological considerations and by calculations of political self-interest. They are also part of the leadership consensus underlying Chinese national security strategy.

With or without a major crisis over Taiwan, China will become a far more militarily consequential power in the coming decades. The largest uncertainties concern China's future maritime role. Robert Ross, for example, argues that the divide in Asian geopolitics between China's natural dominance of continental Asia and America's natural dominance of maritime Asia ensures stable bipolarity in the region, which he contends will likely be maintained over the next quarter century.[13] Although he makes a provocative case, Ross does not fully weigh how the national security policies and power trajectories of both countries could intersect in future years. Given China's burgeoning energy dependence and the disproportionate role of foreign trade in Chinese economic development, maritime capabilities constitute an increasing priority for PLA modernization plans. Even more important, Taiwan is inescapably a maritime theater of operations, with China's military options against the island predicated on control of the surrounding sea and air space. Conversely, America's long-run military advantage is based heavily on its power projection capabilities and its information and strategic assets (including sea-based missile defense), which Chinese military planners view as a growing challenge to Beijing's less formidable capabilities.

In contrast to the negotiated agreements with continental Asia and Beijing's accession to the Treaty of Amity and Cooperation with the Association of Southeast Asian Nations (ASEAN) and the South China Sea Code of Conduct, China and its principal eastern rivals have not constrained the prospective use of maritime or missile capabilities. No measures have been undertaken to reduce the risks of a maritime conflict in the west Pacific, or to fully disclose data on the burgeoning capabilities and activities of China and its putative maritime adversaries (Taiwan, the United States, and Japan). This does not make future conflict inevitable, but it injects major uncertainties into regional defense planning, very possibly compounding the risks in a major crisis.

China's national security continues to rest on its autonomous military capabilities. Beijing seeks to enhance its aggregate national power, deter perceived threats to its vital interests short of armed conflict, and reserve the right to employ force as a last resort. This pertains most immediately to Taiwan, which Beijing deems a matter of territorial integrity and undisputed sovereignty. But it could extend to other locales where territorial delimitations are still under contention. China's assent to the South China Sea Code of Conduct commits Beijing to the nonuse of force in resolving disputes with the other signatories. However, this pledge does not preclude military activities in various contested waters, even as Beijing has substantial incentives to maintain political-military restraint. China's enhanced military capabilities and the increased power of various neighboring states (much of it increasingly relevant to the exercise of power beyond land borders) remain unaddressed in all regional security forums.

THE CHINESE DEBATE OVER U.S. POWER AND INTENTIONS

Chinese assessments of U.S. power and strategic intentions are closely linked to its regional security policies. Although China has vigorously and successfully pursued an "Asia-based" security strategy, U.S. military power is far too potent and pervasive for any serious Chinese strategic thinker to neglect. Chinese specialist writings on the United States are not a new phenomenon,[14] but their prevailing purposes have broadened, enabling important insights into Chinese national security strategy as a whole. Many participants in these debates are specialists on international relations and national security policy, not experts on the United States per se. Some focus more narrowly on operational and doctrinal concerns related to future military planning, especially the application of advanced technologies to warfare.

This pattern parallels the U.S. security debate. To U.S. scholars and strategists, China is a principal vehicle in longer-term national security deliberations, much as the United States is a primary vehicle for comparable deliberations in China. U.S. and Chinese assessments reverberate within and between both systems. Our purpose here is to illustrate how Chinese evaluations of U.S. power and strategic goals are shaping Chinese views of the future regional security system and Beijing's place in it.

Chinese analysts acknowledge many unsettled questions about the new regional order, with the longer-term U.S. strategy with regard to China being uppermost among these uncertainties.[15] Judgments range between innovative approaches to the security dilemma to wary optimism about extant trends and possibilities to deep pessimism over longer-term U.S. intentions. Some analysts favor more cooperative security strategies that avoid explicit characterizations of a U.S. threat to China. They argue that a more threat-based approach will only trigger equivalent actions by the United States that would diminish China's security and compel Beijing to allocate additional resources to defense modernization.[16] Others contend that the inexorable growth of Chinese economic power will ultimately trump any presumed U.S. effort to constrain China's larger political and security goals, as well as facilitate regional cooperation as a whole.[17]

A more mainstream assessment seems largely aligned with official policy. It argues for deeper, more diversified relations across the region, pursuit of political-diplomatic collaboration with the United States where feasible (but without excessive expectations of such ties), and the enhanced augmentation of Chinese military power. These mainstream views also highlight U.S. preoccupations in the greater Middle East and the Persian Gulf and the United States' intense focus on international terrorism. U.S. strategic attention is now largely directed away from China; indeed, the Bush administration actively solicits Chinese support for (or acquiescence to) U.S. policy objectives. For China's pragmatic nationalists, current U.S. policy diminishes pressure on China and provides Beijing enhanced freedom of maneuver in its regional activities.[18] A fourth viewpoint is far more worrisome, with proponents advocating accelerated weapons development and more assertive protection of Chinese national security interests. In the view of these analysts, U.S. intentions toward China remain fundamentally malign. Heightened regional collaboration can help deflect U.S. pressure, but it cannot fully turn back a larger U.S. strategic challenge.[19] Taiwan looms very large in these assessments, with more pessimistic analysts describing the implications of Taiwan's increased assertiveness (and defiance of Beijing) in very stark terms.[20]

It is not possible to determine whether various specialists are shaping or following the views of senior officials, or the extent of influence wielded by various thinkers. However, divergent viewpoints could not be disseminated without official sanction. The range of views likely reflects tacit leadership support for airing diverse policy options: if policy "red lines" were being breached, analysts would either demur from publishing them, or they would be unable to air them in authoritative media. But the parameters of debate are now far more permissive, and some writers continue to probe and test these limits. Even allowing for the congenital caution among national security specialists (a phenomenon hardly limited to Chinese analysts), opinions in the Chinese security debate still err on the side of prudence, if not abject pessimism. Beneath the confident veneer about China's economic success and its enhanced international standing, a more contingent forecast predominates.

Chinese strategy with respect to Japan furnishes an apt example of the limits on Chinese debate. In early 2003, a leading Chinese scholar, Shi Yinhong of People's University, urged that China adopt a more innovative and flexible policy toward Japan, based on "the fundamental principle of coordination and cooperation [in East Asia] between great powers instead of a power struggle between them."[21] Shi argued that a more flexible Chinese strategy would deflate the growing strength of right nationalist forces in Japan, who advocate a more confrontational strategy with regard to China and far closer ties with Taiwan. He also contended that such changes in Chinese policy would encourage Japan to depart from its asymmetrical security ties with the United States while becoming a more "normal power," without triggering renewed militarization. Shi and another Chinese commentator, Ma Licheng, were widely criticized for their call for "new thinking" on policy towards Japan.[22] In the aftermath of these harsh criticisms, discussion of this issue has been largely quashed in Chinese media, perhaps for emotional as well as strategic reasons. Thus, unlike the major departures in Chinese policy toward another long-standing U.S. ally, the Republic of Korea (ROK), a new strategy with respect to Japan still represents a bridge too far.

IDENTIFYING THE LONGER-TERM SECURITY ALTERNATIVES

How is China contemplating its future regional security options? Four alternative strategic futures seem possible, all linked to longer-term Sino-American ties: (1) a convergent, more diversified security order largely acceptable to the United States and to China; (2) a mixed security order simultaneously entailing elements of Sino-American competition and collaboration; (3) an overt Sino-American political-military competition; and (4) a Sino-American regional security condominium.

The critical uncertainties are fourfold. First, will the United States maintain security commitments and military capabilities similar to those of the past? Second, will Washington and Beijing agree on "rules of engagement" in zones of potential conflict? Third, will China achieve durable security understandings in all contiguous subregions as its military power continues to grow? Fourth, will the region as a whole avoid a strategic breakdown or major crisis that destabilizes Asia's future? Each warrants separate discussion.

How Will American Regional Defense Strategy Shape Regional Security Perceptions?

Despite the desire of nearly all regional states (including China) to realize more autonomous security strategies, U.S. military power retains singular importance in the long-range defense thinking of all regional actors. American military power is in the gestational stages of major change, as posited threats, shifting regional attitudes toward the presence of U.S. forces, and major changes in defense capabilities redefine U.S. strategy options. The predominant thrust of U.S. planning is increasingly contingency- and crisis-driven, with less emphasis on the open-ended presence of U.S. forces long deemed a bedrock of regional security. Should the United States again employ major forces in a regional conflict, the primary emphasis would be on achieving declared objectives as decisively and as rapidly as possible, exploiting U.S. technological advantages and denying any presumptive opponent the opportunity to interfere with the conduct of U.S. military operations. Though there are parallels in how other military establishments prepare for war, no other state comes remotely close to the U.S. pursuit of "full-spectrum dominance." U.S. defense strategy therefore presents a potential U.S. adversary with two basic options: (1) to acquire military capabilities that would amply raise the costs, risks, and complications of any major U.S. use of force; or (2) to reconfigure regional security arrangements so as to negate the factors that would lead the United States to use force. China is doing both.

These looming changes in U.S. defense strategy leave unspecified the precise contingencies where the United States might intervene, though crises in Korea or in the Taiwan Strait top the prospective list. U.S. forces would be drawn substantially from those deployed within the region, but also from forces introduced over greater distance. These circumstances reflect the increasing expectation of senior U.S. policy makers that American military commanders be able to rapidly deploy power projection capabilities to very distant theaters, often with minimal warning. The open-ended deployment of major U.S. forces in specific locations (most notably in Korea) is almost certain to change over the next decade.[23] It seems increasingly unlikely that the United States will maintain the 100,000-manpower levels in East Asia long deemed a requirement for regional stability. This does not preclude the

U.S. capability to deploy massive forces in a crisis. The question is whether a more "over-the-horizon" capability will reshape regional perceptions of U.S. power. To the extent that the United States decides that its military might will only be used *in extremis*, this affects the incentives of regional states to rely on American power. Large-scale crisis interventions are always a rare event. The looming issue is how the United States persuasively maintains its declared commitment to regional security at lower force levels, without regional actors pursuing alternative approaches to security that diminish the relevance of U.S. power.

Such circumstances could provide opportunities for a more creative Chinese security strategy. China's advocacy of a "new security concept," though widely dismissed as formulaic and even propagandistic, has growing significance in this context. China's stated (if now somewhat muted) opposition to U.S. bilateral alliances as a residue of the Cold War would seem less challenging to American interests if the United States were already redefining the basis of its alliance ties. For example, should Washington proceed, of its own volition, to more of an "offshore" strategy in Korea, then Beijing would likely prove a beneficiary of such a decision, inasmuch as it would reinforce China's predominance on the East Asian mainland. But a more fundamental question persists for both Beijing and Washington: what do these shifts in U.S. strategy imply for a Taiwan crisis?

Will China and the United States Avoid a Major Crisis?

Chinese military planning for a Taiwan crisis constitutes the definitive exception to Beijing's emphasis on a collaborative Asia-Pacific security order. It is the singular example of China's continued pursuit of threat-based military planning. Irrespective of how China would justify a decision to use force against Taiwan (and irrespective of the outcome of such a crisis), the implications of such a decision would be profound. China is acquiring military capabilities that it believes will ultimately enable a short-warning, high-intensity attack against Taiwan. These include a growing inventory of short-range ballistic missiles, advanced conventionally powered submarines and other naval platforms, longer-range aircraft, and a host of related capabilities.[24] There is a wide range of scenarios for employing such capabilities. China is also seeking to preempt U.S. involvement in such a conflict, presumably expecting that the crisis could be brought to a speedy and minimally destructive conclusion before Washington could intervene. But China is also building capabilities that would put U.S. military assets at risk and also impart to Japan the potential dangers of contributing to U.S. actions. The risks and consequences inherent in any expanded conflict could hardly be greater.

Are there realistic possibilities for the parties to forestall such a crisis, or (in the event of deterrence failure) to limit its scope? The indications are not encouraging. Policy makers in Taipei, Beijing, and Washington all premise their planning calculations on assumptions that can only be tested fully in armed conflict. Many of these assumptions seem highly questionable, and some are directly contradictory to one another, especially divergent judgments in Beijing and Taipei on the likelihood and scale of a U.S. military intervention. The respective policy trajectories in all three capitals thus seem largely independent of one another, underscoring the risks of horrific miscalculation.

Though most regional actors would prefer to stand apart from the fray, major hostilities in the Taiwan Strait—even if a military conflict were concluded speedily—would trigger significant reverberations across the region. China would seek to characterize its actions as defending its territorial sovereignty and national unity, but its willingness to use force would constitute a lasting precedent in Asian security. The likeliest long-term effects would be on various maritime states, especially where territorial demarcations with China are still contested. It remains conjectural whether China's continental neighbors would reassess their prevailing policy assumptions toward Beijing. Much would depend on the extent of political, economic, and security investment extant between China and its neighbors at the time of such a conflict.

Will China Build Lasting Subregional Security Cooperation?

China's active pursuit of security collaboration with neighboring states has reinforced a larger process of accommodation between Beijing and the region. The ultimate scope of such collaboration depends on whether China is prepared to move toward meaningful security interdependence with neighboring states, and whether others pursue such ties with equal vigor. Excepting Taiwan, China is pursuing a more positional approach to regional security, as distinct from the war-fighting emphasis in U.S. defense planning. Beijing hopes to exploit its geographic contiguity and increased economic and political interdependence with neighbors to shape outcomes less driven by the potential for major crisis. In each regional setting, China has sought a "voice" in policy consultations, while hoping to preclude any third-party involvement that would impinge on China's political and security equities. The primary contexts for multilateral collaboration are threefold: with ASEAN, with the Shanghai Cooperation Organization (SCO), and on the Korean peninsula. Each constitutes a very different case.

Increased collaboration with ASEAN would entail further accommodation to the "ASEAN Way," reflecting the group's predilection for consultation, agreement by consensus, and symbolic deference to fellow members, all with a minimum of operational security content. It is possible that ASEAN might ultimately move toward more substantial collaboration (for example, on sea lane security and on counterterrorism), but the obstacles to collective security goals remain daunting. Beijing and ASEAN have nevertheless achieved a measure of mutual assurance. This has facilitated bilateral economic and political cooperation, with China assenting to noncoercive approaches to territorial and resource disputes. But it is unlikely that China will attempt to "outpace" ASEAN on the goals and modalities of future cooperation, since it would likely trigger heightened unease within the association about an overly fulsome embrace of Beijing. Indeed, ASEAN membership in no way precludes alliance and access agreements with the United States, most notably with the Philippines, Thailand, and Singapore. In Southeast Asia, China will continue to follow, not lead.

China's collaboration under the SCO process is quite different. As a founding member of the organization named for the city in which the original understandings were reached, Beijing is both a stakeholder and a pivotal participant. The SCO process comes closer to cooperative security norms, in that it has operational content and obligations to which all signatories are accountable. It has also helped secure Russia's consent for a more active and visible Chinese role where Moscow has substantial strategic interests. Chinese officials also recognize that the United States has reached basing and access agreements with several SCO member states (e.g., Kyrgyzstan and Uzbekistan). Despite the concerns of some Chinese strategists about the geopolitical implications of an American military presence in Central Asia, this is not inhibiting China's pursuit of larger strategic goals, especially related to energy development. Some U.S. and Chinese security interests in the subregion seem complementary (e.g., counterterrorism and border security); this seems likely to preclude major strategic divergence between Washington and Beijing in the area. But the larger tests are yet to come, especially if Pakistan and Afghanistan become open-ended security priorities for the United States, which seems likely. A more encumbering U.S. strategic relationship with different regional states might then affect Chinese interests, especially if the SCO process does not fulfill the expectations of its member states.

China's security collaboration in Northeast Asia entails far larger risks. A failure to prevent unambiguous nuclear weapons development in North Korea would directly undermine China's vital security interests. One leading Chinese international relations specialist, Wang Jisi of the Institute of American Studies of the Chinese Academy of Social Sciences, has noted, "No other country would be strategically more concerned than China about nuclear threats, as China now borders on three powers with nuclear arsenals . . . and must also deal with the United States that used to threaten China with its nuclear arsenal. An additional nuclear power so close to the very center of China's territory not only would provide a lasting problem for China's national security, but could also provide the rationale and pretense for other regional players to develop nuclear arms, notably Japan and Taiwan."[25] China has undertaken unprecedented efforts to forestall a larger crisis, notably through leadership of the Six-Party Talks and its intermediary role between Washington and Beijing. As Wang further observes, "This is the first time in China's diplomatic history that it is serving as a major mediator between two important rival powers."[26]

Beijing has repeatedly emphasized three priorities in these discussions: (1) the maintenance of peace and stability on the Korean peninsula; (2) ensuring the nonnuclear status of the peninsula; and (3) addressing Pyongyang's legitimate security needs. Despite Beijing's clear frustrations with North Korean obduracy, Chinese officials insist that a successful outcome in the six-party process will depend as much on American actions as on North Korean restraint. If the six-party process does not achieve its stated goals, it would be a dual setback for China. It would highlight the inability of China and others to forestall North Korean nuclear weapons development by diplomatic means alone, and it would constitute a major failed test case of Sino-American security collaboration.

However, the close congruence between Chinese and South Korean policies bears careful notice. As Jae Ho Chung notes in this volume, Beijing has sought to exploit the sea change in South Korean domestic attitudes, which are simultaneously more nationalistic and favorably disposed toward much closer ties with China. A U.S. and North Korean commitment to peaceful coexistence (ultimately extending to normal political and diplomatic relations) would open the door to alternative security arrangements on the Korean peninsula, quite possibly including major reductions or the outright withdrawal of U.S. forces. A negation of the core assumptions underlying the U.S.-ROK alliance, amidst growing political and economic interdependence between China and the ROK, would constitute a major reconfiguration in Northeast Asian security. The nuclear crisis thus confers ample opportunities as well as significant risks for Beijing. Should Pyongyang claim avowed status as a nuclear weapons state, it would pose an acute challenge to Chinese security interests. Indeed, the United States would then very likely reinforce a U.S.-led regional maritime coalition geared toward missile defense, counterproliferation, and more coercive military options, all of which would work against pivotal Chinese security priorities. A busier, more "crowded" security environment, especially one involving unprecedented military activities near Chinese territory in which China is not vested, would be decidedly unfavorable to Beijing's interests.

Will Asia Experience a Strategic Breakdown?

In the final analysis, future regional strategic patterns will be driven by events. A collapse in the nonproliferation regime in East Asia, a major conflict over Taiwan, or a breakdown in U.S. regional alliance relations (especially in Korea) constitute the principal nightmare scenarios. Any would likely trigger a longer-term U.S.-Chinese strategic competition, if not outright bipolarity in the region. The parallels with the events of June 1950, which largely established the strategic geography of East Asia for the entirety of the Cold War, are self-evident. As Shi Yinhong has also observed, "China was a winner [in the Korean War], but winning was very painful, and the long-term cost was considerable. . . . China and the United States were locked in a fierce Cold War confrontation for as long as 20 years, and this indeed played quite a serious negative role in China's international environment and even its internal development. . . . [T]remendous difficulties were [also] created for resolving the Taiwan problem, and there was 'an alliance too tangled to unravel' with the DPRK."[27] Such memories hover over current crises, all of which occupy the very same strategic space as those of a half-century ago.

Alternatively, the ability of China, the United States, and other regional powers to achieve noncoercive outcomes to these potential crises would attest to a longer-term strategic convergence between Washington and Beijing. This would likely enable creation of a hybrid security order that constrained major rivalry amidst predominantly convergent security goals. Given the absolute magnitude of China and America's economic, political, and military weight, and the increasing congruence of U.S. and Chinese interests in nonproliferation, energy security, and unrestricted maritime commerce, both countries might ultimately decide to share responsibilities for long-term regional security. But there is a "to-be-determined" flavor to such possibilities. Even amidst ever-growing regional interdependence, there is nothing foreordained in the region's strategic future, or in the U.S.-Chinese strategic pattern that could underlie it.

NOTES

1. Muthiah Alagappa, ed., *Asian Security Practice: Material and Ideational Influences* (Stanford, CA: Stanford University Press, 1998); and Muthiah Alagappa, ed., *Asian Security Order: Instrumental and Normative Features* (Stanford, CA: Stanford University Press, 2003).

2. For illustrative examples, see Aaron Friedberg, "Ripe for Rivalry: Prospects for Peace in a Multipolar Asia," *International Security* 18, no. 3 (Winter 1993/1994): 5–33; and Aaron Friedberg, "Will Europe's Past Be Asia's Future?" *Survival* 42, no. 3 (Autumn 2000): 147–60.

3. This phenomenon is closely related to the increased prominence of a public intellectual class in China associated with various universities, research institutes, and journals. For an overview, see Michael Pillsbury, *China Debates the Future Security Environment* (Washington, DC: National Defense University Press, 2000).

4. Jonathan D. Pollack, ed., *Strategic Surprise? U.S.-China Relations in the Early Twenty-first Century* (Newport, RI: Naval War College Press, 2003).

5. Pakistan's supposed harboring of terrorist groups and its pre–September 11 support for the Taliban-led government in Afghanistan as well as its support for Islamic militants in Kashmir constitute the major exceptions to this conclusion.

6. See, in particular, Lu Ning, "The Central Leadership, Supraministry Coordinating Bodies, State Council Ministries, and Party Departments," in *The Making of Chinese Foreign and Security Policy in the Era of Reform, 1978–2000*, ed. David M. Lampton (Stanford, CA: Stanford University Press, 2001), 39–60.

7. Qian Qichen, "The International Situation and Sino-U.S. Relations Since the 11 September Incident," *Beijing Waijiao Xueyuan Xuebao* no. 3, September 25, 2002, 1–6. See also the senior leadership comments cited in Andrew J. Nathan, "The Succession and Sino-American Relations," in *Strategic Surprise?*, especially 117–22.

8. For a comprehensive review, consult Alastair Iain Johnston, "Is China a Status Quo Power?" *International Security* 27, no. 4 (Spring 2003): 5–56.

9. Evan Medeiros and M. Taylor Fravel, "China's New Diplomacy," *Foreign Affairs* 82, no. 6 (November–December 2003): 22–35; and Kenneth W. Allen and Eric A. McVadon, *China's Foreign Military Relations* (Washington, DC: Henry L. Stimson Center, Report no. 32, October 1999).

10. Wang Jisi, *China's Changing Role in Asia* (Washington, DC: Atlantic Council of the United States, Asia Programs Occasional Paper, January 2004), 5, 9.

11. See, in particular, David Shambaugh, *Modernizing China's Military: Progress, Problems, Prospects* (Berkeley: University of California Press, 2002); *Annual Report on the Military Power of the People's Republic of China* (Washington, DC: U.S. Department of Defense, Report to Congress Pursuant to the FY 2000 National Defense Authorization Act, July 28, 2003); and *Chinese Military Power* (New York: Council on Foreign Relations, 2003).

12. Nan Li, "The PLA's Evolving Campaign Doctrine and Strategies," in *The People's Liberation Army in the Information Age*, ed. James C. Mulvenon and Richard Yang (Santa Monica, CA: RAND, 1999), 146–74.

13. Robert S. Ross, "The Geography of the Peace: East Asia in the Twenty-first Century," *International Security* 23, no. 4 (Spring 1999): 81–118.

14. See especially David L. Shambaugh, *Beautiful Imperialist: China Perceives America, 1972–1990* (Princeton, NJ: Princeton University Press, 1991); and David M. Lampton, *Same Bed Different Dreams: Managing U.S.-China Relations, 1989–2000* (Berkeley: University of California Press, 2001).

15. For further discussion, see Yong Deng, "Hegemon on the Offensive: Chinese Perspectives on U.S. Global Strategy," *Political Science Quarterly* 116, no. 3 (Fall 2001): 343–65; Jonathan D. Pollack, "Chinese Security in the Post–11 September World," *Asia-Pacific Review* 9, no. 2 (November 2002): 12–30; and Johnston, "Is China a Status Quo Power?"

16. Ye Zicheng and Feng Yin, "Eight Key Characteristics of Current Sino-U.S. Relations," *Guangzhou Nanfang Zhoumo* (online version), February 21, 2002; Guo Zhenyuan, "A Word of Advice to the New Government: Maintain Peaceful and Stable Environment, Seize International Strategic Opportunity," *Hong Kong Zhongguo Pinglun* no. 63 (March 1, 2003): 15–18.

17. Wu Xinbo, "Globalization and the Restructuring of the Strategic Foundation of Sino-U.S. Relations On Sino-U.S. Economic and Trade Cooperation in the

World," *Shijie Jingji yu Zhengzhi,* September 14, 2002, 55–60; Zhao Nianchi, "The 16th CCP National Congress and Cross-Strait Relations," *Hong Kong Zhongguo Pinglun* no. 60, December 1, 2002, 6–8; Zhang Yunling, "The Process of East Asian Cooperation and Its Prospects," *Qiushi* no. 24, December 16, 2002 (online version); and Yu Xintai, "East Asian Cooperation in the Early 21st Century," *Dangdai Yatai* no. 10, October 15, 2003, 3–9.

18. Chu Shulong, "Bilateral and Regional Strategic and Security Relationship between China and the United States after the Cold War," *Xiandai Guoji Guanxi* 5, May 20, 2000, 7–14; Wang Jisi, "Several Points of Analysis on Sino-U.S. Relations," in ibid., no. 6, June 20, 2001, 7–10; Li Zhongjie, "Understanding and Promoting the Process of World Multipolarization: Part 3 of 'How to Understand and Deal with the Current International Strategic Situation,'" *Liaowang* no. 23, June 3, 2002, 3–9; Tang Shiping, "China's Peripheral Security Environment in 2010–2015: Decisive Factors, Trends, and Prospects," *Zhanlue yu Guanli* no. 5, October 1, 2002, 34–45; Wang Jisi, "Main Characteristics of the New Situation and China's Diplomacy," *Xiandai Guoji Guanxi* 4, April 20, 2003, 1–3; Shi Yinhong, "China's External Difficulties and Challenges Faced by the New Leadership: International Politics, Foreign Policy, and the Taiwan Issue," *Zhanlue yu Guanli* 3, May 1, 2003, 34–39; and Shi Yinhong, "Major Strategic Issues of Chinese Foreign Policy in the Short Run and Basic Strategic Opportunities in the Long Run," in ibid., no. 6, November 1, 2003, 21–25; and Xu Shiquan, "Examining the Bush Administration's Taiwan Policy," *Guoji Wenti Yanjiu* 6, November 13, 2003, 1–6.

19. Yan Xuetong, "Post–Cold War Continuity—Major Post–Cold War International Political Contradictions," *Zhanlue yu Guanli,* June 1, 2000, 58–66; Yang Yunzhong, "Some Strategic Reflections on the Main Threats to China's Security in the Early 21st Century," *Dangdai Yatai* no. 10, October 15, 2002, 3–12; and Lin Limin, "New Trend of International Pattern in This Year," *Liaowang* no. 45, November 11, 2002, 62–64.

20. See the comments of Major General Peng Guangqian and Senior Colonel Luo Yuan of the Academy of Military Sciences, as reported in Huang Hai and Yang Liu, "Military Experts on War to Counter 'Taiwan Independence': Six Prices; War Criminals Cannot Escape Punishment," *Renmin Wang* (online version, in Chinese), December 3, 2003; and Yan Xuetong, "Separatism Poses Grave National Threat," *China Daily* (online version), March 2, 2004.

21. Shi Yinhong, "Sino-Japanese Rapprochement and 'Diplomatic Revolution,'" *Zhanlue yu Guanli* 2, March 1, 2003, 71–75.

22. For relevant examples, see Sun Yafei, "Is 'New Thinking' Needed about Japan?" *Guangzhou Nanfang Zhoumo* (online version, in Chinese), June 12, 2003; Liu Xiaobiao, "Where Are Sino-Japanese Relations Heading: A Commentary on Observations by Scholars and Concerns Among the People," *Renmin Wang* (online version, in Chinese), August 13, 2003; and Lin Zhibo, "Further Questioning of the 'New Thinking' on Relations with Japan," in ibid.

23. "American Forces in South Korea: The End of an Era?" International Institute for Strategic Studies, *Strategic Comments* 9, no. 5 (July 2003).

24. For a detailed review, consult *Annual Report on the Military Power of the People's Republic of China,* especially 43–49.

25. Wang, *China's Changing Role in Asia*, 10.

26. Ibid., 11.

27. "Shi Yinhong: The Korean War Could Have Been Avoided; The Soviet Union Was the Biggest Loser," *Beijing Qianlong Wang* (online version, in Chinese), July 28, 2003, 8.

16

The Evolving Asian Order
The Accommodation of Rising Chinese Power

Michael Yahuda

China has entered the twenty-first century as the rising power in Asia. As it rises, China becomes increasingly integrated into the region not only in terms of economics, but also in terms of politics. The rise of the Chinese economy and the deepening of its significance as a key driver of the East Asian economy and the impact of China's growing military power on regional security are treated elsewhere in this volume. China's political integration in the region is perhaps less well known and appreciated, and shall be considered in this concluding chapter.

Historically, rising powers have been regarded as challengers to the existing order and have often precipitated major wars. China's rise has also evoked concern from its neighbors and from other major powers, including the United States. However, China and its neighbors have found ways of mitigating many of these concerns, principally through a process of integrating China into the region through its participation in a number of multilateral institutions based on the principles of cooperation and consensus. To be sure, such institutions do not, in and of themselves, meet all the standard security needs of member states,[1] but they are well suited to improving relations between states that are neither adversaries nor allies. Such institutions facilitate interactions between governments and societies, and they provide the means for leaders to better understand the interests and security concerns of others. Given China's previous relative isolation and its inexperience in institutionalized cooperation, these institutions have provided mechanisms for China and its neighbors to work together and to mitigate incipient conflicts.

These cooperative multilateral institutions have developed alongside the established series of bilateral alliances long established by the United States with key states along the littoral of the western Pacific. Although China's leaders have long regarded these alliances as designed at least in part against their country, China's neighbors have seen them and other defense arrangements with the United States as a means of hedging against potential Chinese power. Since the end of the Cold War they have regarded them as a constraint upon China that facilitated their accommodation or engagement with China on terms that were neither those of appeasement nor bandwagoning. At the turn of the century Chinese commentators and officials stopped openly challenging the American security alliances, thereby tacitly accepting that they contributed to regional order, at least for the time being.[2] That of course eased the task of East Asian neighbors, in particular as they accommodated China's growing significance.

Since the end of the Cold War the regional powers have been repositioning themselves. The removal of the bipolar or tripolar order has permitted regional powers various forms of maneuver relative to each other as each has focused primarily on its domestic agenda. Once it was recognized by the mid-1990s that, far from declining, the sole surviving superpower was gathering in strength, the regional great powers accepted that they had more to gain by engaging than by opposing the United States. Some had envisioned that it might be possible to constrain the United States' preeminence by encouraging the emergence of a multipolar world, but as the hopes for that too faded in practice, the regional powers entered the new century both cooperating and competing with each other under the aegis of a not wholly uncontested American hegemony.

Thus the Asian order at the beginning of the twenty-first century may be conceived as a pattern of overlapping forms of security. In addition to the long-standing traditional alliance system of the United States, there has emerged a regionally generated system of multilateral institutions based on cooperative security and an incipient complex balance of power involving the regional major states. The U.S.-led alliance system is reasonably well known and understood. Since many of the challenges and problems it encounters as a result of China's newfound power are addressed elsewhere in this volume, this chapter will focus on those dimensions of regional security that have been instrumental in integrating China into the region.

REGIONAL INSTITUTIONS WITH ASIAN CHARACTERISTICS

During the last decade Asia has experienced an unprecedented growth of regional institutions, with China playing the role of a central and increasingly active member. The new multilateral institutions presage the emergence of a new diplomatic order in the region. It is, however, one that reflects the special characteristics of Asian states. The European experience of pooling sovereignty with the aim of establishing an ever-closer political union through a process of rule-based integration is not appropriate for Asia, and it is misleading to regard the European Union as the model for regionalism. The diplomatic order that is emerging in Asia is based on consultative and consensual processes that are designed to uphold sovereignty and consolidate statehood rather than to submerge it in the search for integration. These processes do not involve legally binding rules or institutions capable of compelling compliance. Thus the American attempt in 1993 to convert the Asia Pacific Economic Cooperation (APEC) forum into a community with binding commitments to establish free trade by certain dates failed within two years, when APEC agreed that the commitment to meet the targeted dates was entirely voluntary. In so doing, APEC in effect relinquished its potential to promote free trade among its members, as few governments would voluntarily pay the often heavy political price at home for opening their country to more foreign goods and competition.[3] However, the Asian approach, known as the "ASEAN Way," is well suited to the fragility and the sense of flux and transition that characterizes most Asian states.

In considering regionalism and security in Asia, it behooves us to recognize that an overwhelming number of the states in China's neighborhood must be regarded as fragile, or relatively fragile, especially in comparison with their Western counterparts. Most have gained their independence within the last fifty years and still bear the marks of a colonial legacy, both domestically and externally. Arguably, it is that legacy that is largely responsible for their long-standing disputes over their respective territorial bounds. Few have established political systems that can be expected to endure in their current form. Many may still be regarded as in the process of consolidating their national identities. Most are undergoing rapid economic development and are experiencing concomitant social change. Many states incorporate within their territories divergent ethnic and religious groups that have required careful management to prevent violence from erupting between them. This potential for violence has been exacerbated by the fact that the post-colonial borders paid little regard to ethnic or religious homogeneity. Not surprisingly, most of these states are conscious of their vulnerabilities, and hence they have tended to be strong upholders of their sovereignty and have been alert to the problems of external intervention.[4]

ASEAN emerged in 1967 out of the ashes of Sukarno's *confrontasi* with Malaysia. Just as the European Union was founded on the accommodation of the long-standing Franco-German conflict, ASEAN emerged under similar circumstances, although there were significant differences. Malaysia and Indonesia were entirely new states, creations of their colonial legacies, which sought to solidify their newfound respect for each other's statehood by confirming their sovereignty in a multilateral regional agreement. Recognizing that the domestic stability they sought was linked with regional harmony—or at least the avoidance of open conflict between regional states—Indonesia and Malaysia helped found an association to meet those needs. Hence the norms of ASEAN from the beginning emphasized noninterference in each other's internal affairs, consultation, consensus, and conflict avoidance. These norms, known as the "ASEAN Way," helped to mask intramural political differences and significant divergences in strategic outlooks. The salience of these differences may be gauged from the fact that, despite the fact that ASEAN was founded in 1967, it was not until 1976, when the member countries faced the common danger posed by the Communist victories in Vietnam and Cambodia, that the political leaders of ASEAN met in conclave for the first time, at which point they drew up the Treaty of Amity and Cooperation, which set out in treaty form the code of conduct among regional states that had been implicit in the ASEAN Way. Back in 1967, the founding documents had primarily expressed economic and social goals, avoiding making commitments to common political goals.[5]

European regionalism, unlike Asian regionalism, used the language of economic integration for political purposes, but a major difference between the two was that unlike the Asian undertakings, in Europe economic integration was real and the intended political spillover was intended—hence the fierce arguments between the Eurofederalists and the Eurosceptics. Thus the bulk of European trade is intramural, whereas the intramural trade of ASEAN has never accounted for more than 20 percent of the trade of member states. Even the language of economic integration in ASEAN is largely rhetorical.

Finally, it should be noted that the order that Southeast Asia has enjoyed at the behest of ASEAN has not been achieved as an alternative to the bilateral alliances and other security arrangements led by the United States, but as a corollary to them. This is true of the period since the end of the Cold War, as it was for most of the period of bipolarity. Although the United States has been careful not to commit itself to the defense of its allies' territorial claims in the South China Sea, and in that sense it is not involved in obstructing China's claims as it is on the Taiwan issue, the United States has repeatedly declared its intention to ensure that the vital sea lanes of communication (SLOCs) running through the South China Sea are kept open.

The end of the Cold War provided the occasion for the significant development of multilateral institutions of the consultative kind in Asia. Many of these were conceived with the goal of both drawing in China and discouraging the Americans from leaving the region. This was true especially of the ASEAN Regional Forum (ARF) and, as we have already seen, APEC. China responded positively to these overtures, and its responses are best considered by looking at the subregions adjacent to China.

CHINA'S CONTRIBUTION TO REGIONAL ORDER

Central Asia

During the Cold War China did not formally address issues of regional order. China's leaders typically tended to direct themselves to universal rather than regional themes. Insofar as China's leaders focused on relations with their neighbors, they did so either in terms of strict bilateral matters, or as a function of Chinese strategic concerns with the two superpowers.[6] This began to change, however, as the Cold War came to an end, partly through China's development of new relations with the USSR and its successor states, and partly through China's reaching out to its neighbors to overcome the diplomatic isolation arising from the Western sanctions after the Tiananmen incident. In the process, the Chinese began to gain more experience in the development of confidence-building measures (CBMs) and in multilateral diplomacy. The latter had begun as a consequence of Chinese attempts to cultivate the more tranquil international environment that was necessary for its new economic policies. Thus China joined the consultative Track II Pacific Economic Cooperation Council (PECC) in the early 1980s, which enabled officials from the foreign affairs and trade ministries as well as associated academics to gain experience in Asian multilateralism. This was a significant advantage when China was invited to join APEC in 1990.[7]

More pertinent, perhaps, was the Chinese experience in developing CBMs with the USSR and its successor states that bordered China. Beginning in the late 1980s, as both the Chinese and Soviet leaders sought to reduce tension and withdraw forces from the borders, they first took separate initiatives and waited for the other to reciprocate. This gradually created sufficient trust for the two sides to cooperate in forming border patrols and to offer mutual assistance when addressing accidents and local incidents. They were then able to coordinate troop withdrawals, military exercises, and other activities. Enhanced confidence led to better demarcation of borders, and even to a settling of past border disputes.

This cooperation soon resumed after the dissolution of the Soviet Union, but this time it operated on a multilateral level, involving the three new Central Asian republics of Kazakhstan, Kyrgyzstan, and Tajikistan. The transition from bilateral to multilateral diplomacy in this case was relatively smooth. Border and security issues were treated multilaterally. The longstanding Soviet-Chinese militarized divide was no more.[8]

New questions arose about the viability and stability of the newly established Central Asian states and what their relations with Russia, as members of the Commonwealth of Independent States (CIS), would be.[9] Afghanistan, with its militant Taliban regime, was potentially subversive of the new regimes. For its part, China had its own reasons for seeking stability in what had suddenly become a highly volatile regime whose instabilities could instigate trouble in adjoining Xinjiang. China's leaders developed policies that sought to assuage Moscow's fears that they were seeking to undermine Russian influence. At the same time, they attempted to assure the new governments of Central Asia that China endorsed their territorial integrity (in light of unstated fears that Russia might seek to redraw their borders) and that China wanted to help their governments to become more effective domestically, so as to gain their cooperation in stopping the movement of militant Uyghurs across the porous borders. China also hoped to gain access to Central Asian oil and natural gas while encouraging cross-border trade in the hope of tying the new states into China's western region in forms of mutually beneficial economic interdependency (albeit on a small scale).[10]

By 1996 China's leaders and diplomats and branches of the Chinese military had gained experience in multilateralism through participation in a number of regional institutions, notably APEC and the ARF. They felt sufficiently confident to develop a multilateral institution of their own to bolster their interests and address their concerns in Central Asia. The Shanghai Five, soon to be expanded and renamed the Shanghai Cooperation Organization (SCO) when Uzbekistan was added to the original five members, was overtly political in its goal of upholding the existing territorial and political order by opposing the "three evils" of extremist Islam, terrorism, and "splitism." The creation of the SCO was buttressed by the newly announced strategic partnership between Beijing and Moscow. At that point the new regional institution had the additional attraction of its membership being limited strictly to locally resident states, which meant that both the United States and Japan were excluded.

The last situation did not last long, as the events of September 11, 2001, suddenly brought an extensive American military presence to Central Asia. At first these events seemed so overwhelming as to make the SCO impotent. Nevertheless within eighteen months of the deployment of American bases in Central Asia, the Chinese had revitalized the organization by establishing a permanent secretariat in Shanghai, by establishing an antiterrorism center in Bishkek, and by conducting a number of antiterrorism exercises with Kyrgyzstan in October 2002 and with Kazakhstan a year later.[11] Chinese activism here must be assessed alongside the much greater regional military presence of Russia, which has forces deployed in Kyrgyzstan, where it exercises the main responsibility for defense of the country. Russia is also the principal arms supplier to the Central Asian countries. In addition to the CIS, Russia also heads a regional military alliance called the Collective Security Treaty Organization (CSTO), with a NATO-like provision for a joint response to an attack on any of its members. NATO, too, has links with the region through its Partnership for Peace program, and its secretary general has visited Kazakhstan and Kyrgyzstan to enhance practical cooperation in countering terrorism and the smuggling of drugs and radioactive materials.

Interestingly, China, too, has expressed an interest in opening a dialogue with NATO.[12] This development, like several others mentioned above, is unprecedented and contrary to previous Chinese practice. The significance of these new developments will be explored in greater detail later, but at this point it is sufficient to note that they correspond to practical Chinese interests in addressing genuine security concerns affecting Xinjiang and in cultivating goodwill for commercial advantage, as China is the only successful economy in the region capable of satisfying the demand for consumer goods.

South Asia

As part of China's policy of diffusing border conflicts and of improving their relationship with major powers *(daguo)*, the Chinese began to cultivate better relations with India in the mid-1990s. As along the border with Russia, here, too, local CBMs were instituted, including mutual troop withdrawals from positions close to the lines of actual control, the organization of some joint patrols, and the establishment of provisions to handle accidental crossings, prior notification of military exercises, and other matters. The *daguo* diplomacy was related to the Chinese expectation of the emergence of a more multipolar world, able to counter the United States as the sole surviving superpower. Both India and China shared reservations about the new Anglo-American doctrine of humanitarian intervention. But even as these joint sentiments were expressed, there was evidence that the United States and India were expressing a renewed interest in each other as fellow democracies, now that the Cold War animosities were over.

The long history of Sino-Indian discord and mutual suspicion could not be easily overcome. This unease arose on the Chinese side from the hospitality the Indian government offered to the Dalai Lama and his government in exile, which was seen as indicative of possible residual Indian interest in Tibet, and on the Indian side from Chinese support for Pakistan and the fear that China would continually seek to marginalize India.[13] Indian suspicions were seemingly confirmed when Jiang Zemin joined with Bill Clinton in jointly condemning the Indian nuclear tests in 1998, especially as these were immediately followed by tests by Pakistan, which was only able to accomplish such a test because of long-standing Chinese assistance. Yet the high point of Sino-American summitry soon passed, and both China and the United States put their opposition to the tests aside as each sought an accommodation with India. Their respective interests in cultivating India were enhanced by the consequences of 9/11, as India was seen by the United States as a stable counter to terrorism, whereas China, which recognized the significance of the long-term growth of the Indian economy, did not want India to become

˙part of a great power coalition aimed at constraining China. Interestingly, neither the United States nor China sought to cultivate India at the expense of Pakistan, and therefore they both had an interest in lowering the temperature of the Kashmir problem, which meant being less sympathetic to the Pakistani case.[14]

China's interest was intensified as at long last the two economies began to find opportunities to develop long moribund economic relations (the value of mutual trade leapt from less than $1 billion in 1999 to more than $8 billion in 2002). The Indian economy had experienced sustained growth rates of more than 5 percent for more than ten years, and India had a comparative advantage in computer software that the Chinese were keen to exploit. In short, far from seeing India as an adversary, the Chinese were beginning to see India as having an important role to play in the continual development of the Chinese economy.[15]

A significant high point in the confidence and trust developed between the two sides was reached in November 2003, when the two navies conducted joint exercises in the East China Sea.[16] The two regional great powers are seeking to show that they can work together, and that whatever rivalries may remain are to be contained. Even though it may not have been possible to reach agreement over the much-disputed border, the two countries have addressed each other's concerns about Tibet and Sikkim, respectively, and they have also signaled that they will not allow differences over Pakistan to prevent them from establishing workable cooperative relations. As will be suggested later, their new relationship derives from their common acceptance of U.S. strategic predominance, and their recognition that a multipolar structure capable of constraining the United States is unlikely to emerge in the foreseeable future.

Southeast Asia

As already noted, the two key economic and security organizations of the region, APEC and the ARF, are consultative bodies whose nonbinding decisions are reached by consensus. These organizations have suited the Chinese, while at the same time inducting them into the multilateral practices and norms associated with the ASEAN Way. Thus the Chinese have been persuaded of the virtues of pursuing collective CBMs, and they have agreed that South China Sea issues can be addressed collectively by the resident states, even as they continue to insist that the resolution of territorial disputes can only be done on a bilateral basis. It could be argued that an implicit bargain has been struck between China and the Southeast Asian states in particular, whereby China, as a great power, has to accept the disadvantage of dealing with the lesser states together, while they in turn have to accept limits set by the Chinese about the degree and pace of progress possible in the evolution of the ARF. In 1995 the ARF envisioned a three-stage progression toward the establishment of comprehensive security that would start with CBMs, proceed to preventive diplomacy, and end up with the "elaboration of approaches to conflict" (the Chinese insisted upon this wording, as they objected to the use of the term "conflict resolution.") In any event, the ARF has been stalled somewhere between the first two stages, mainly because of Chinese foot-dragging.[17]

However, it would be invidious to hold China exclusively responsible for the delays in the evolution of the ARF. There are other divisions between members, and ASEAN is no longer well placed to be the driving force behind the ARF, partly because of the problems derived from its own enlargement in 1997 and also because of impact of the Asian financial crisis that exposed inherent weaknesses in ASEAN and some of its key members.[18] Moreover, because of a structural weakness in the ARF, leadership over sensitive issues is expected to be provided by lesser powers on key security issues. This stems from the fact that there are fundamental security differences between the great powers themselves. One of the strengths of the ARF has always been its capacity to include among its members the United States, China, India, Japan, and Russia, as well as eighteen other states. However, that capacity is also one of its principal weaknesses.

Many have argued that the ARF has nevertheless made important contributions, notably by simply providing a framework for inducting China into the processes of multilateralism in Asia. According to this view, China has been socialized into accepting a number of obligations that it might not otherwise have accepted. These obligations include a readiness to discuss South China Sea issues with the ASEAN countries and a willingness to agree to a code of conduct that calls on signatories not to alter by unilateral measures the status quo regarding disputed maritime claims. The ARF has also prompted China to carry out a variety of CBMs such as the publication of defense white papers, the exchange of military personnel, allowing observers from other member states to observe major military exercises, and so on. It is further argued that the trust and experience that China built up through participation in the ARF has encouraged the Chinese to reach agreements with separate states addressing problems such as sea rescues, smuggling, piracy, money laundering, and energy security. In other words, the ARF process has been a learning experience for the Chinese that has contributed to improving its conduct in the neighborhood and to deepening its integration into the international community.[19]

While the ARF may be one of the important building blocks of the new order, in Southeast Asia especially, it would be a mistake to place more weight upon it than it can bear. Although it may be effective in facilitating dialogue, eliminating misunderstandings, and promoting common action in CBMs where little previously existed, it is doubtful whether it can do more. It cannot overcome great power differences, although it can help to diffuse them. Thus for a long time the United States and China had different expectations of the ARF. The United States tended to see the organization as an instrument for constraining China, but also as a possible threat to its own treaty-based security arrangements in East Asia. Until recently, the Chinese openly saw the ARF as a means for restricting U.S. "hegemony" and for weakening American ties in East Asia.

The "new security concept" that the Chinese began to articulate in 1996–97, ostensibly designed to promote cooperative and coordinated security in the region, had an anti-American edge until very recently. Visiting Chinese leaders often presented the new concept, as it applied to Southeast Asia, as an alternative to what was depicted as the outdated (U.S.) security alliances that were products of the Cold War and that still supposedly exhibited a "Cold War mentality."[20] If the idea was to plant a wedge between the United States and states in Southeast Asia, the new security concept had the opposite effect, as most sought to enhance their security links with the United States. The anti-American dimension of the new security concept was quietly dropped once the Chinese accepted that U.S. predominance was not going to be challenged any time soon, and that the much-anticipated multipolar system was not going to emerge in the foreseeable future. This new view was enforced by the consequences of 9/11.

Thus the diplomatic order in Southeast Asia manifests a large number of meetings of multilateral forums and organizations whose immediate impact on the actual political and security arrangements of the region is somewhat limited. But there is also considerable activity by the great powers in consolidating and refining bilateral relationships. At the same time, new associations that exclude Western states have been formed, perhaps the most notable of which is the ASEAN + 3 (the ten ASEAN member states, plus China, Japan, and South Korea).[21] This has facilitated a great deal of Chinese activism. Perhaps the most significant was the announcement that a free trade agreement between China and the ASEAN ten would be settled by the year 2010. Not only did that give expression to China's newfound economic importance, but it also helped to diffuse concerns about the so-called Chinese economic threat to its southern neighbors. It also induced Japanese attempts to respond in a series of bilateral free trade agreements, and indeed it strengthened that tendency by others in the region at the expense of weakening the multilateralism of the 1990s.

Although there remain residual concerns as to how the maritime territorial disputes in the South China Sea are to be resolved, the main threats to the stability of the subregion stem from the domestic fragilities of resident states and transnational problems. The latter include the links between local Islamic extremist groups and international terror groups, as well as a host of issues associated with the new softer kind of security such as environmental degradation, smuggling, piracy, money laundering, international criminal networks, and so on.

Northeast Asia

Not withstanding the high degree of activity, including various meetings, conferences, and innovative contributions by Track II institutions, there is no overarching body that brings together the key actors in Northeast Asia on a regular basis. Such multilateralism that does exist in this subregion is too weak and limited in scope to be the basis for order. The one regional meeting that brings together the key actors is an ad hoc grouping designed to address the North Korean nuclear issue in a way that is satisfactory to the United States. At the core of the grouping is the U.S. insistence that the North Korean problem should not be seen as a matter to be treated bilaterally between the United States and the North—even though most of the other members of the group would prefer that it were dealt with that way. The fact that there is little multilateralism in evidence in this subregion where the interests of the major powers intersect and where the two most intractable conflicts of Asia are located attests to the absence of a true regional order.

Notwithstanding the rise of China, the order that does exist depends heavily on the United States. It is the U.S. alliance with Japan that is central to the Northeast Asian order, and it still lies at the heart of the U.S. security commitment to the region. It is this alliance that has largely underwritten the larger strategic framework that has served nearly all the East Asian states so well in providing the safety net that has facilitated their economic growth and stability in interstate relations. Since the end of the Cold War, as the international security and diplomatic environment has changed, it has been the continuing security arrangements centering on the United States that have enabled the new multilateral cooperative institutions to emerge and flourish alongside the security architecture provided by the United States. This is as true of the ASEAN Plus Three (APT) mechanism, from which the United States is excluded, as it is of the more broadly based APEC and ARF. These regional institutions place a premium on process through consultation and nonbinding agreements reached by consensus at the expense of hard and fast rules, binding commitments, and attempts to address conflicts.

The APT, for example, has sought to establish a currency swap arrangement to mitigate potential financial crises such as the one that devastated the region in 1997–98, but few expect there to be either sufficient capital or the mechanisms to monitor the domestic financial management of member governments, such as those available to the IMF. Meanwhile the APT seems to be little more than an executive "talking shop" for the promotion of CBMs. As ever in regional organizations of this kind, the key is the symbolic significance of who is in and who is out. The fact that this is an all–East Asian affair from which the United States is excluded may mean a great deal in identity politics, but it is difficult to see what substantive contribution the APT can make to diplomatic order when its members appear to put more effort into establishing separate free trade agreements with each other than into measures to develop free trade and economic cooperation collectively. Moreover, it is the security and public goods provided by the United States that establish the framework within which the Chinese and Japanese have been able to establish highly successful economic relations without having to come to terms with the deep-seated problems that they would both have to confront if they had to manage their political and security relations by themselves.

Similarly, it is the role of the United States that has so far been the key to the maintenance of the status quo across the Taiwan Strait. The domestic politics of all three parties to the Taiwan problem pose a major threat to the continuation of this seemingly fragile status quo that has lasted so long and that has arguably served both Taiwan and the PRC well, even though neither side will admit that this is so. China's rising power and growing international economic influence have not in themselves changed the core dynamics of the incipient conflict. The growing economic integration across the Taiwan Strait also has not had a significant effect on the political dimensions of the problem. As long as the United States continues to be ready to help Taiwan defend itself and, if necessary, to prevent the PRC from imposing unification by force, there is little reason to believe that the PRC will risk overt military conflict. It may, however, do so if it were to believe that the island were irrevocably moving toward independence, or if political leaders in Taiwan were to provoke China into believing that they were foreclosing the path to eventual unification. Only these scenarios might make leaders in Beijing risk a confrontation with the United States and risk creating instability within the region that could even threaten China's foreign economic relations, on which the regime ultimately depends for the economic growth that keeps it in power. Thus the main diplomacy of the conflict consists of attempts by the two protagonists to gain support within the United States at the expense of the other. Yet China has clearly taken an unprecedented initiative in lending its good offices to effecting a settlement in a context fraught with dangers. Yet here, too, it is the American role that is critical. Any agreement (provisional or otherwise) and the means of arriving at one will in reality be between North Korea and the United States. Others may have roles to play both in facilitating the process and in contributing to its implementation, but it is the United States that will call the shots.

CONCLUSION

There is no overarching diplomatic order that embraces all parts of China's region. The diplomatic order in Central Asia involves multilateral security organizations that organize common military activity and broker precise security commitments between states. Southeast Asia demonstrates considerable diplomatic activity, both bilateral and multilateral, that addresses cooperative security questions. Although this activity has improved the security atmosphere in Southeast Asia and has made military conflicts less likely, it is nevertheless quietly underpinned by American security commitments of varying quality. South Asia has benefited from an accommodation between China and India, their traditional rivalry mitigated by a readiness to work together. But this improved relationship is just beginning, and it is too early to assume that the earlier distrust has been eliminated. Moreover, the Sino-Indian relationship is still dependent on activities by third parties, notably Pakistan. The intractable conflicts of Northeast Asia depend very much on the role played by the United States, rather than on any discernible diplomatic order. However, Chinese new diplomatic activism may foreshadow new approaches and a possible new political architecture.

Alongside the U.S.-dominated security arrangements have emerged several new multilateral institutions that initially served the purpose of integrating China into the region, and that have since enabled China to play an increasingly active role. Much of China's integration stems from its more prominent economic role, which has enhanced its self-confidence and prompted it to demonstrate to neighbors that the rising Chinese economy, far from being a threat, offers them great opportunities. Although Chinese investments and the quality of China's economic relations do not yet match those of Japan by a large margin, the rapidity of China's emergence as a regional economic powerhouse has suddenly changed the pattern of economic relations in the region. Given the expectation that the impact of the Chinese economy will continue to grow and deepen, the perception of Chinese power has changed accordingly.

The United States, however, remains predominant, and the current order in the region will change in a fundamental way only when China and Japan find a way to reconcile their deep differences that have so far prevented them from even acknowledging the national security concerns of the other. As there are no signs of such a reconciliation occurring in the near future, it seems likely that the United States will continue to be the principal guarantor of order in East Asia for the foreseeable future.

NOTES

1. See Michael Leifer's analysis of the principal regional security organization, *The ASEAN Regional Forum*, Adelphi Paper 301 (Oxford: Oxford University Press for the International Institute of Strategic Studies, July 1996).

2. Evan S. Medeiros and M. Taylor Fravel, "China's New Diplomacy," *Foreign Affairs* 82, no. 6 (November–December 2003): 22–35.

3. For a penetrating analysis of this weakness of APEC, see John Ravenhill, *APEC and the Construction of Pacific Rim Regionalism* (Cambridge: Cambridge University Press, 2001). See especially the chapter "APEC Adrift," 186–222.

4. For accounts of these problems and how they impinge on security and foreign policy, see, among the vast literature, Muthiah Alagappa, ed., *Asian Security Practice* (Stanford, CA: Stanford University Press, 1998); and Michael Leifer, *ASEAN and the Security of Southeast Asia* (London: Routledge, 1988).

5. For a careful account of the "ASEAN Way," see Jurgen Haacke, *ASEAN's Diplomatic and Security Culture: Origins, Development and Prospects* (London: Routledge, 2003).

6. Steven I. Levine, "China in Asia: The PRC as a Regional Power," in *China's Foreign Relations in the 1980s*, ed. Harry Harding (New Haven, CT: Yale University Press, 1984), 107–45.

7. Lawrence T. Woods, *Asia-Pacific Diplomacy: Nongovernmental Organizations and International Relations* (Vancouver: University of British Columbia Press, 1993); and Stuart Harris, "Policy Networks and Economic Cooperation: Policy Coordination in the Asia-Pacific Region," *Pacific Review* 4, no. 4 (1994): 381–95.

8. For further elaboration, see Chikahito Harada, *Russia and Northeast Asia*, Adelphi Paper 310 (Oxford: Oxford University Press for the International Institute of Strategic Studies, July 1997); and Jennifer Anderson, *The Limits of Sino-Russian Strategic Partnership*, Adelphi Paper 315 (Oxford: Oxford University Press for the International Institute of Strategic Studies, December 1997).

9. Karen Dawisha and Bruce Parrott, *Russia and the New States of Eurasia* (Cambridge: Cambridge University Press, 1994).

10. Ross H. Munro, "Central Asia and China," in *Central Asia and the World*, ed. Michael Mandelbaum (New York: Council on Foreign Affairs Press, 1994), 225–38.

11. For analysis see Sean L. Yom, "The Future of the Shanghai Cooperation Organization," *Harvard Asia Quarterly* (Autumn 2002), available at http://www.fas.harvard.edu/~asiactr/haq/200204/0204a003.htm (accessed on January 28, 2004).

12. See *Strategic Survey 2002/2003* (Oxford: Oxford University Press for the International Institute of Strategic Studies, 2003).

13. For extended authoritative analysis, see John Garver, *Protracted Conflict: Sino-Indian Rivalry in the Twentieth Century* (Seattle: University of Washington Press, 2001).

14. See Mohan Malik, "Eyeing the Dragon: India's China Debate," in *Asia's China Debate* (Honolulu: Asia-Pacific Center for Security Studies, December 2003), available at http://www.apccs.org (accessed January 28, 2004).

15. Ibid.

16. The exercises were conducted near Shanghai on November 14, 2003. See http://www.china.org.cn/english2003/Nov/79318.htm (accessed January 28, 2004).

17. Rosemary Foot, "China in the ASEAN Regional Forum: Organizational Processes and Domestic Modes of Thought," *Asian Survey* 38, no. 5 (May 1998): 425–40.

18. Jeannie Henderson, *Reassessing ASEAN*, Adelphi Paper 328 (Oxford: Oxford University Press for the International Institute of Strategic Studies, May 1999).

19. Foot, "China in the ASEAN Regional Forum."

20. See, for example, the summary of the speech by the then Chinese defense minister, Chi Haotian, in Singapore, in *International Herald Tribune,* November 28, 1998. For a revised version of the cooperative approach to security, see General Xiong Guangkai, "The New Security Concept Initiated by China," *International Strategic Studies* 65, no. 3 (July 2002).

21. For an account see Carlyle A. Thayer, "ASEAN Ten Plus Three: An Evolving East Asian Community" (Honolulu: Pacific Forum CSIS, 2002), available at http://www.csis.org/pacfor/cc0004Qchina_asean.html (accessed January 28, 2004).

Index

Abdullah bin Haji Ahmad Badawi, Datuk, 203n35
ABM Treaty, 243n21, 304n36
Acharya, Amitav, 15, 64n41
Afghanistan: cross-border trade with, 127n28; Pakistani support for Taliban in, 344n5; PRC aid to, 37; Russia-Central Asian relations and, 351–52; Soviet invasion of, 214, 218; Soviet withdrawal from, as precondition for relations, 242n8
Afghanistan War (2001–): India-PRC relations and, 301n11; Japan-PRC relations and, 145; PRC regional security strategy and, 258, 341; U.S.-Central Asia relations and, 212; U.S. hegemonism and, 225; U.S.-PRC relations and, 57, 301n11, 316
Africa, FDI in, 88
Afro-Asian People's Solidarity Organization (AAPSO), 6. See also Bandung Conference
Akamatsu, Kaname, 92n4
Akihito (Japanese emperor), 136
Aktyubinsk-Urumqi pipeline, 208, 209
Alagappa, Muthiah, 15
Albright, Madeleine, 233–34
Almaty (Kazakhstan), 206, 208
Andijan (Uzbekistan), 209
Angarsk-Daqing oil pipeline, 238–40
Angarsk-Nakhoda oil pipeline, 238, 241
anti-Americanism, 296
anti-Chinese sentiments, 219–20

anticommunism, 158, 167n46, 188, 197
anti-Japanese sentiments, 137
APEC: Asian characteristics of, 349, 350, 354, 357; Japan-Taiwan relations and, 147; PRC engagement with, 30; PRC regional security strategy and, 251, 259; regional diplomatic order and, 352; regional influence and, 25; trade liberalization and, 90
Arabian Sea, 217
Arab League-PRC relations, 252
ARF. See ASEAN Regional Forum
Armitage, Richard, 321
arms buildups, 280
arms control, 249
arms embargo, 291
arms sales/transfers: PRC, 278, 279; PRC, sanctions on, 294; Russian, 240, 244n44, 285n36
Asahi Shimbun (Japanese newspaper), 138
ASEAN: Asian characteristics of, 349–50; Asian systems and, 17, 23–24; China policy of, 67n69; counter-dominance strategy of, 64n41; economic integration in, 350; establishment of, 196, 349; FDI in, 88–89; military capabilities of, 285n34; Myanmar-PRC relations and, 192, 220; new security concept and, 304–5n38; as normative community, 15–16; ODI from, 107, 108–10, 122–24; PRC engagement with, 31–33; PRC influence in, 25; PRC perception of, 26–27; PRC regional

363

Text: 10/12 Baskerville
Display: Baskerville
Compositor, printer, and binder: Sheridan Books, Inc.